The Meaning of Christ

FAITH MEETS FAITH

An Orbis Series in Interreligious Dialogue

Paul F. Knitter, General Editor

In our contemporary world, the many religions and spiritualities stand in need of greater intercommunication and cooperation. More than ever before, they must speak to, learn from, and work with each other, in order to maintain their own identity and vitality and so to contribute to fashioning a better world.

FAITH MEETS FAITH seeks to promote interreligious dialogue by providing an open forum for the exchanges between and among followers of different religious paths. While the series wants to encourage creative and bold responses to the new questions of pluralism confronting religious persons today, it also recognizes the present plurality of perspectives concerning the methods and content of interreligious dialogue.

This series, therefore, does not want to endorse any one school of thought. By making available to both the scholarly community and the general public works that represent a variety of religious and methodological viewpoints, FAITH MEETS FAITH hopes to foster and focus the emerging encounter among the religions of the world.

Already published:

Toward a Universal Theology of Religion, Leonard Swidler, Editor
The Myth of Christian Uniqueness, John Hick and Paul F. Knitter, Editors
An Asian Theology of Liberation, Aloysius Pieris, S.J.
The Dialogical Imperative, David Lochhead
Love Meets Wisdom, Aloysius Pieris, S.J.
Many Paths, Eugene Hillman
The Silence of God, Raimundo Panikkar
The Challenge of the Scriptures, Groupe de Recherches
    Islamo-Chrétien
Hindu-Christian Dialogue, Harold Coward, Editor

FAITH MEETS FAITH SERIES

The Meaning of Christ

A Mahāyāna Theology

John P. Keenan

ORBIS BOOKS

Maryknoll, New York 10545

The Catholic Foreign Mission Society of America (Maryknoll) recruits and trains people for overseas missionary service. Through Orbis Books Maryknoll aims to foster the international dialogue that is essential to mission. The books published, however, reflect the opinions of their authors and are not meant to represent the official position of the society.

Biblical quotes, unless otherwise indicated, were taken from *The Jerusalem Bible,* copyright © 1966 by Darton, Longman & Todd, Ltd. and Doubleday & Company, Inc. Reprinted by permission of the publisher.

Library of Congress Cataloging-in-Publication Data

Keenan, John P.
    The meaning of Christ: a Mahāyāna theology/John P. Keenan.
       p.   cm.—(Faith meets faith series)
    Includes bibliographical references.
    ISBN 0-88344-641-3.—ISBN 0-88344-640-5 (pbk.)
    1. Jesus Christ—Person and offices. 2. Jesus Christ—Buddhist interpretations. 3. Faith. 4. Enlightenment (Buddhism)
5. Mysticism. 6. Christianity and other religions—Mahāyāna Buddhism. 7. Mahāyāna Buddhism—Relations—Christianity.
I. Title. ii. Series: Faith meets faith.
BT205.K43   1989
232—dc20
                                                     89-37873
                                                       CIP

For
MINORU KIYOTA
who teaches Buddhist texts
and
JOHN J. O'ROURKE
who teaches Christian texts

In a Mahāyāna understanding of dependent co-arising,
however unwittingly, they also are responsible.

Contents

II
MĀHĀYANA THOUGHT AS THEOLOGIAE ANCILLA

Introduction

The apostle Paul, apparently quoting an early Christian hymn of baptismal awakening, encourages the Ephesians to

> Wake up from your sleep,
> rise from the dead,
> and Christ will enlighten you [Eph. 4:14].

This book is about awakening to that Christ meaning. It attempts to present in clear language the meaning of being enlightened by Christ, the meaning of Christian awakening and rising from the dead. It is directed to an understanding of the core Christian doctrines of Incarnation and Trinity, for these are the traditional thematizations of the meaning of Christ.

It is not, however, a traditional attempt that considers the meaning of those doctrines by analyzing their terms and explicating their significance, although it does involve some of that. Rather, it aims at objectifying the genesis and nature of being awakened in Christ. It is an attempt to bring to speech the interior experience of Christian enlightenment.

The Christ meaning is born from and moves within a mystic realm of meaning in which meaning is constituted not by thinking and judging, but by the immediacy of contact, of being touched. Indeed, this base experience is the source from which all theologizing springs. The question is not what the doctrines of Incarnation and Trinity mean in themselves, but what they mean in the lived experience of Christians. This book is then also an invitation to appropriate Christian interiority, to identify its contours, to put on the mind of Christ. Its approach is not to sketch the objective meaning of Jesus as a statement of Christian belief to which all must assent in order to retain their union cards as believers. Rather, the Christ meaning is considered and recommended from an understanding of the faith consciousness from which it is generated.

However, that understanding of faith is not itself derived from the Christian tradition. Rather, it comes from pondering the scriptures and commentaries of the Buddhist Mahāyāna tradition. This exposition of the Christ meaning is the result of an ongoing intrareligious dialogue,[1] a dialogue between an affirmed Christian faith in Christ and a Mahāyāna understanding of faith awakening.

The structure of this endeavor is divided into two parts. The first part is a sketchy consideration of the Christ meaning as it was developed in the early church. It attempts both to outline the developing pattern of orthodoxy and to highlight the early understanding of Christ as wisdom, for this latter theme anticipates the development of a Christology that would understand Christ through the patterns of Buddhist wisdom. It is based on the cumulative research, interpretation, and historical understanding of a broad host of Christian scholars. The account begins with a consideration of wisdom in the Old Testament, for these notions informed the wisdom theology of Paul and the early church. It then attempts to outline the lines of New Testament affirmation of faith in Christ, the subsequent development of Patristic theology toward theoretical conciseness, and the constant, if peripheral, witness of the mystic writers to the ineffability of that faith meaning. It is argued here that, to date, the Christian West has been unable organically to relate its own mystic thinkers to its doctrinal, theoretical thinking. The reason for this inability was not simply, as Adolph von Harnack thought, the adoption and superimposition of Greek patterns of ontology upon the gospel. Rather, it is an inability to differentiate that realm of Greek, logos-centered theory from the more primal realm of mystic awareness, an inability to understand the mind of faith in its polyvalent realms of meaning. The first part, then, traces Christian thinking about Christ with a view to highlighting this unresolved tension between a theological understanding of Christ and the primal experience of being in Christ.

Chapter 6, the first chapter of the second part, outlines the main lines of Indian Buddhist thinking, from the early *Nikāyas* to the Abhidharma theorists, on to the reversal and rejection of theory in the Prajñāpāramitā and Mādhyamika, and beyond to the development of critical theory in Yogācāra. The developments of Buddhist theory and mystic thinking, represented respectively by the Abhidharma enterprise and the Prajñāpāramitā literature, parallel the Christian West in bifurcating mystic from theoretical modes of thought, although in Buddhist India prize of place goes to the mystic strain. Tension was created between those who focused single-mindedly upon the direct realization of awakening, and those, of a more discursive disposition, who simply could not stop themselves from thinking about things. But, unlike the Christian case, in Buddhist India the early Yogācārins, Maitreya, Asaṅga, and Vasubandhu, evolved a critical understanding of understanding that would enable them both to affirm the primacy of mystic meaning and to maintain a limited, but valid role for theoretical discourse.[2] The evolution of this critical realm, this turn toward religious interiority, took place some thousand years before Immanuel Kant, but it developed in a specific religious context and was aimed directly at balancing different kinds of conscious activities within the same Buddhist mind. Without such an organic balancing of theory and mystic insight, doctrinal discourse is fated either to usurp the place of primal mystic insight or to be dismissed out of hand as an unwanted intruder upon the scene of devotion and practice. It is here that Mādhyamika and Yogācāra recommend themselves to Christian thinkers, concerned today with questions of theological deconstruction and phenomenological validity. Without a critical understanding of the mind of religious understanding, of the relationships between theory and mystic insight, doctrinal discourse is doomed forever to chase its intellectual tail, unless it succeeds in biting it off. The seventh and eighth chapters present the Yogācāra understanding of consciousness as (1) constructive of meaning (*vijñaptimātratā*) under the themes of the mind as dependently co-arisen (*pratītyasamutpāda*) in its structure, as (2) functioning in three patterns (*trisvabhāva*), and as (3) issuing in a hermeneutic that, while granting primacy to mystic awakening, grounds doctrinal discourse. These Mahāyāna themes are meant to introduce a philosophic model for the expression of Christian faith in Christ.

Chapter 9 attempts to answer some of the obvious objections to the adoption of Mahāyāna philosophy in Christian theology, while the remaining two chapters do apply that approach to the base doctrines of Incarnation and Trinity and attempt to think on these doctrines not from a Greek ontological standpoint, but from the Mahāyāna themes of emptiness, dependent co-arising, the three bodies of awakening (*buddha-trikāya*) and the two truths (*satya-dvaya*). Such a consideration can perhaps embody the Christ meaning in terms that cast a stronger focus upon the humanness of the Christ experience of suffering and dying as a mirror of the resurrection, of being enlightened by Christ.

PART I

Western Understandings
of the Meaning of Christ

1

The Scope of Wisdom
in the Old Testament

The New Testament understanding of Christ as the wisdom of the Father presupposes notions of wisdom, *ḥokmah*, derived from the Tanach/Old Testament tradition. A brief overview of that earlier tradition is thus necessary.

The wisdom tradition in Israel is quite ancient, dating from a period even before the time of the monarchy (ca. 1000 B.C.E.).[1] Here, in examining the scope and role of wisdom, our attention will focus only upon the principal texts identified clearly as wisdom compositions.[2] Wisdom texts include three canonical texts, Job, Proverbs, and Qoheleth (Ecclesiastes), as well as two apocryphal texts, Sirach (Ecclesiasticus) and the Wisdom of Solomon. Job was probably composed in the sixth century B.C.E.[3] Proverbs is a collection of various wisdom sayings and appears to be the most primitive record of Israelite wisdom. Qoheleth is to be dated from the late third or early second century.[4] In the main these texts presuppose the existence of a fairly well-defined faith understanding, articulated in the Hexateuch[5] and codified in Deuteronomy.

Since the notion of wisdom developed within the context of an already established Yahwistic faith understanding, it is necessary first to look at the salient points of that traditional faith understanding.

FAITH IN YAHWEH AND THE WORD OF YAHWEH

In Israel's understanding of its faith, the Israelites were the chosen people, the portion of Yahweh selected from the nations and brought out of Egypt by the mighty acts of Yahweh. The foundational experience of that faith was the delivery from bondage in Egypt, in which Yahweh consistently showed his favor toward the chosen people and his wrath against their oppressors.[6] Yahweh himself inflicted harsh plagues upon the Egyptians, led his people from bondage, watched over them through their wanderings in the wilderness, and fought at their side to occupy the promised land.

The pattern is one of frequent intervention by Yahweh in the history and lives of the people, and his mighty deeds are recorded in the books of the Hexateuch.

But in time the reality of Israel's splendid past began to slip from the minds of the people, and in about 622 B.C.E. the book of Deuteronomy was composed to reaffirm and revive traditional faith in Yahweh within the changing context of Israel's historical and social development.[7] Deuteronomy codified the faith and concretized the implications of the covenant between the chosen people and Yahweh in the form of laws and injunctions that could apply to the Jews of its day. This book then embodied the Yahwistic faith and served as a criterion for later faith understandings.

Some accounts of Yahweh's dealings with the chosen people depict him as conversing directly with the patriarchs. He stands over against his chosen people and demands their faith and allegiance. He comes and converses with the patriarchs and prophets. He speaks directly with Abraham and promises to make him a great nation (Gen. 12:1). The description of his speaking with Abraham parallels his walking with Adam and Eve in the garden and a note of familiarity is clearly evident. Abraham discourses with Yahweh as one might talk with a powerful friend or benefactor.

But the experience of such direct conversation with Yahweh is not the norm. The most common scenario has revelatory experience coming through the word of Yahweh, not from his actual presence: "It happened some time later that the word of Yahweh was spoken to Abram in a vision, 'Have not fear, Abram, I am your shield; your reward will be great' " (Gen. 15:1).[8]

Here the presence of Yahweh has become more distant and is now mediated by his word. In the Exodus account of Yahweh's dealings with Moses, there is a consistent emphasis upon the hiddenness and transcendence of Yahweh. Revelatory experiences become numinous and clothed in mystery. When Moses first encounters the burning bush and goes up to see "this strange thing," he is bidden to "come no nearer" (Ex. 3:2). When he requests that Yahweh identify himself by name, he is given the cryptic reply, "I am what I am" (*ehyeh asher ehyeh*; Ex. 3:13), which seems to imply that Yahweh cannot be named or defined in any manner whatsoever. When Moses asks to see the glory of Yahweh, he is told that he cannot see Yahweh's face. Rather, placed in the cleft of a rock for protection, he is allowed to catch only a glimpse of Yahweh's back side, for no one can look upon Yahweh directly or see his face (Ex. 33:18–23). So, although Yahweh does speak to Moses, he remains hidden in unapproachable mystery.

It was perhaps due to such an awareness of the hiddenness and transcendence of Yahweh that the function of the word of Yahweh came to play such a principal role in revelatory experiences. The word (*dabar*) of Yahweh becomes the hinge upon which biblical history turns, for it manifests Yahweh's intentions for his people. From Yahweh's first creative word whereby the world is brought about, the word of Yahweh is active in revealing and effecting the purposes of Yahweh in the history of Israel.[9] As C. H. Dodd explains, the whole idea of revelation in the Old Testament "is determined by the analogy of the word spoken and heard, as distinct from the idea of revelation as vision."[10]

Vision experiences do indeed occur and are frequently described in the Old Testament,[11] but by themselves they remain numinous and mysterious. They remain unintelligible until they are interpreted by the word of Yahweh. Micaiah ben Imlah's vision of the defeat of Israel (1 Ki. 22:17), Isaiah's temple vision (Is. 6:1ff.), Ezekiel's vision of the chariot (Ezek. 1:1–2:8), Amos' vision of the plumb line (Am. 7:7–9), his vision of the basket of fruit (Am. 8:1–3), and Jeremiah's vision of the almond tree (Jer. 1:11–12) are all immediately followed by the explanatory "words of Yahweh," which serve to make the vision intelligible.[12]

Vision experiences cannot penetrate the hiddenness of Yahweh, but the word renders the numinous intelligible and clothes in understandable terms the naked experience of the unapproachable Yahweh. This theme of a verbal rendering of ineffable experiences forms a persistent motif and explains how Yahweh, whose name could not even be pronounced, could nevertheless become known to the verbal consciousness of people and be understood. It is the means by which the numinous is embodied in human categories of thought and experience.

However, the word of Yahweh is more than simply a means for communicating meaning. It is also described as having an effective and dynamic existence of its own. Coming from Yahweh, it shares his power. The Hebrew term for "word," *dabar*, is understood by most philologists to derive from the root *dbr*, to drive, to get behind and push.[13] This dynamism is particularly evident in accounts of prophetic experience. In his analysis of prophetic experience, Oskar Grether shows that in 225 of 241 occurrences, this term "designates the word of Yahweh received or declared by a prophet."[14] The term *dabar* thus becomes a technical term for prophetic experience. The prophets do not simply listen to or hear that word. They are grasped and driven by it.

Jeremiah says that the word was put into his mouth and that, when he tried to keep silent, it became unbearable. Fearing to suffer the derision common to those who announced the word of Yahweh, he vainly tried to put it out of his mind. But it burned within him and he was constrained to declare it (Jer. 20:9). The prophet cannot maintain his silence because the word has a dynamic revelatory force. It pushes him to speak and has the power to bring about what is uttered, for the word of Yahweh does not return to him empty, but carries out his will and succeeds in what it was sent out to do (Is. 55:10–11).

The medium whereby the intentions of the hidden Yahweh were manifested is the word of Yahweh spoken to the patriarchs and prophets. The content of that word was the faithfulness of Yahweh in watching over his people and the consequent need for the chosen people to remain faithful to Yahweh. As the prophets constantly reiterate, Yahweh will guard and protect Israel and make his chosen people secure among the nations, as long as they remain faithful to Yahweh alone (Deut. 8:1). But if Israel forgets the covenant and fails to keep the commandments of Yahweh, his protection will be removed and Israel will perish (Deut. 8:19–20).

Just as Israel will be cared for by Yahweh and rewarded with life only if the Israelites guard the commandments, so in the life of each individual, prosperity and security come only if one follows the path Yahweh has laid out. From an early date the prophets and sages affirmed a doctrine of exact retribution for all human actions. The good will live long and prosper, but the wicked will be cut off and suffer sundry disasters from the wrath of Yahweh (Deut. 9:1).

Thus faith in Yahweh centered upon the covenant relationship and was mediated through the word of Yahweh, who demanded from his people commitment to that covenant. It was codified in the Deuteronomic laws and became the religious criterion for the people. Its content was a firm belief that Yahweh rewarded the upright person with life and prosperity, while punishing the wicked with death and suffering.

THE RISE OF SKEPTICISM AND DOUBT

The maintenance of Israel's faith in Yahweh was, however, a continually precarious enterprise, for Yahweh's stated purposes were in fact frequently not carried out. Although his word was held to be dynamic and effective, Israel's geopolitical history was determined by the ebb and flow of power politics between the two superpowers, Egypt and Assyria.

As James Crenshaw explains:

> ... both corporate and individual existence achieved significance in the course of history, upon which the divine word worked with matchless success. Israel's enemies fled when the Lord lifted his mighty arm, and God's people marched joyously from bondage into liberty. Valiant soldiers wasted away when the death angel spread its wings and flew into the midst of God's enemies. So ran the embellished account of Israel's history, a story so far from the truth that it sowed seeds of skepticism at every telling. The disparity between present reality and grandiose confessions of God's mighty deeds in the past demanded an adequate explanation, lest wholesale abandonment of the Lord take place.[15]

The authors of Deuteronomy seem to have been directly concerned with meeting this need, and their efforts were directed to applying Israel's traditional faith to changing circumstances. "They were concerned to make the old cultic and legal traditions relevant for their time. The urgent tone of these sermons conveys the feeling that the people to whom they were addressed had almost outgrown those old ordinances of Israel."[16] Deuteronomy insisted upon the need for individuals to maintain faith in Yahweh. Laws were evolved to correspond to the changing social and historical situation and stress was laid upon avoiding unfaithfulness to those laws. The doctrine of exact retribution became the authoritative explanation for both prosperity and suffering. Disasters experienced either by Israel as a whole or by individual Israelites were the direct result of the wrath of Yahweh incurred by unfaithfulness to him. If Yahweh's mighty deeds were absent, it was because of the failure of the chosen people to remain faithful.

Yet doubt and unbelief continued. Two factors seem particularly to have fostered the growth of skepticism. The first is the disparity, stated above, between the traditional faith in Yahweh as active on behalf of his chosen people and the actual course of events. The second is the identification of the word of Yahweh with the codified tradition and the legal corpus. Both these concerns are evident in the prophetic literature.

Factors Leading to Skepticism

It is the disparity between faith and actual experience that underlies the prophets' constant lament that Israel has forsaken the covenant, runs after false gods, and is unmindful of Yahweh. Isaiah summarizes the refrain:

> Listen, you heavens; earth, attend
> for Yahweh is speaking,
> "I reared sons, I brought them up,
> but they have rebelled against me.
> The ox knows its owner
> and the ass its master's crib,
> Israel knows nothing,
> my people understands nothing" [Is. 1:2–3].

The prophets constantly voice such laments to the point where they themselves seem to have "stimulated a sense of moral defeatism by repeated denunciations of the people as a *massa damnationis*."[17] Their preaching led not only to the reaffirmation of faith, but also to the growth of skepticism. Since the proclamation of the efficacy of good deeds in attaining life and prosperity ran counter to actual experience, no matter how much was promised by the prophets in Yahweh's name, the never-fulfilled hopes for corporate and individual prosperity evinced a general trend toward doubt and lack of faith.[18]

The second factor that seems to have led to such skepticism was the identification of the word of Yahweh with the codified traditions and the legal corpus. As noted above, the word of Yahweh became identified with prophetic experience, that is, it was experienced only by prophets. It was embodied for the ordinary people in the canons of belief and law and presented to them secondhand by the sometimes strident cries of those prophets. Without in any way experiencing that word themselves, the people were asked to affirm laws and prophetic oracles that ran counter to their own experience of the almost universal nature of suffering and injustice. The prophet Isaiah curses those who dare to say:

> Quick! Let him hurry his work
> so that we can see it;
> these plans of the Holy One of Israel,
> let them happen and come true
> so that we can know what they are [Is. 5:19].

The embellished account of the mighty plans of Yahweh strains the belief of the chosen people. But such a strain was not confined merely to the ordinary people, for the prophets also wondered how long the Lord would tarry. The following passage seems to concede that Yahweh has not yet established his presence and that experiential verification lies in the promised future:

> I will establish my integrity speedily,
> my salvation shall come like the light,
> my arm shall judge the peoples [Is. 51:5].

Again we read the cry of a believer that his hopes might be fulfilled:

> Awake, awake! Clothe yourself in strength,
> arm of Yahweh.
> Awake, as in the past,
> in times of generations long ago [Is. 51:9].

The author of this verse experienced the same feeling that was cursed in Isaiah 5:19 above, for to him Yahweh was asleep.

Such sentiments must have been widespread. The prophet Zephaniah accuses his contemporaries of thinking that God "will not do good, nor will he do ill" (Zeph. 1:12). According to this idea God simply does nothing at all. "When tested in the crucible of experience, the people's miserable circumstances hardly accord with the religious contentions that God actively worked to sustain Israel," Crenshaw writes. And in Judges 6:13 we read: "Pray, sir, if the Lord is with us, why has all this befallen us? And where are his wonderful deeds which our fathers recounted to us?"[19] Yahweh's transcendence and hiddenness at times came to be considered as his aloofness and indifference, to be simply his absence. And Israel's penchant for infidelity and lack of understanding sprang from the felt inability to know Yahweh at all. If not the inevitable result, skepticism and doubt are at least a reasonable response to such a situation.

Furthermore, the traditional teaching, especially as embodied in Deuteronomy, affirmed that not only did Yahweh watch over the affairs of Israel and punish its enemies, but that he performed the same functions for each and every individual. He would make the good prosper and have a long and fruitful life, while the wicked would be cut off and destroyed. The complete inability to verify such a teaching in actual life was what led to the dilemma so dramatically recorded in the book of Job. If everyday living convinces one that suffering and pain bear no relationship to the traditional teaching of exact retribution, then what is one to think about Yahweh? Can he see human affairs? Is he asleep? Is he indeed more powerful than other gods?

Job is usually regarded as a wisdom text and it shares an experiential focus with the other wisdom texts. But it deals specifically with the believability of the teaching of exact retribution, and, behind that question, the believability of Yahweh as the protector of the righteous.[20] Bildad, one of Job's antagonists, affirms the traditional teaching of the Yahwistic faith. He invites Job, despite his own experience of undeserved suffering, to affirm the experience of former generations. But Job cannot square that tradition with his own experience:

> It is all one, and this I dare to say:
> innocent and guilty, he destroys all alike.
> When a sudden deadly scourge descends,
> he laughs at the plight of the innocent.
> When a country falls into a tyrant's hand,
> it is he who blindfolds the judges.
> Or if not he, who else? [Job 9:22–24].

Job dares to question the truth of Yahweh's intervention on behalf of the innocent. In response to Zophar's defense of the traditional teaching, Job sarcastically declares:

> Doubtless, you are the voice of the people,
> and when you die, wisdom will die with you!
> I can reflect as deeply as ever you can,
> I am no way inferior to you.
> And who, for that matter, has not observed as much?
> A man becomes a laughing-stock to his friends
> if he cries to God and expects an answer [Job 12:1–3].

Job regards the teaching on exact retribution as small comfort indeed:

> How often have I heard all this before!
> What sorry comforters you are!
> Is there never to be an end of airy words! [Job 16:1–2].

The central belief of Israel's faith in the faithfulness and efficacy of Yahweh is here referred to as airy words. God is aloof and Job cannot find him to take him to account. Even at the conclusion to the verse section of Job, when God speaks out of the tempest, he offers no answer to Job's dilemma. Rather, he overwhelms Job with the awareness of his might in creation and nature. The designs of Yahweh remain unknown and Job simply admits that he cannot understand:

> I know that you are all-powerful:
> what you conceive, you can perform.
> I am the man who obscured your designs
> with my empty-headed words.
> I have been holding forth on matters I cannot understand,
> on marvels beyond me and my knowledge [Job 42:1–3].

Although Job repents his foolishness, no answer is forthcoming that might explain and vindicate Yahweh in his dealings with humans. Rather, "the divine speeches remind Job of fixed limits which have been imposed upon human knowledge and power."[21]

THE RESPONSE OF THE WISDOM LITERATURE

In the face of such doubt and skepticism, new understandings of faith had to be worked out, new understandings that would relate that faith meaning to felt experience. Such had been the intent of the author of Deuteronomy; such also was the central concern of the wisdom writers.

The book of Proverbs, drawing upon ancient clan, court, and theological traditions,[22] did not thematize a sacral understanding of the mighty acts of Yahweh in Israel's history but based itself, rather, upon the immediate concerns of practical living. In this book the revelatory and dynamic functions of the word of Yahweh are taken over by wisdom, which conveys an understanding of the meaning of human existence in terms intelligible to anyone engaged in the living of life. In Proverbs there is no mention of Israel as a covenant people.[23] It aims, rather, to outline a commonsense path that anyone might follow to attain a long and prosperous life.

But the doctrinal background of Proverbs on the teaching of exact retribution differs little from the traditional Yahwistic faith. Strict retribution is affirmed: "Commend what you do to Yahweh, and your plans will find achievement. Yahweh made everything for his own purpose, yes, even the wicked for the day of destruction. The arrogant heart is abhorrent to Yahweh, be sure it will not go unpunished" (Prov. 16:3–5).

Yet this wisdom approach does offer an alternative to the Yahwistic affirmation of faith. Walther Zimmerli writes:

> The sages offered an alternate mode of interpreting reality to the Yahwehistic one in which God was actively involved in guiding history

toward a worthy goal. The claim that God chose a particular people, fought on their behalf, called prophets, issued legal codes, sent angels to maintain contact with humans, enlisted foreign powers to discipline the chosen race, and promised to bestow a new covenant upon inveterate sinners for the sake of God's honor represents a way of looking at the human situation that is wholly alien to the sapiential one.[24]

The wisdom writers understood God's relationship with the world quite differently. On their understanding, truth was planted within the universe and humans could search and find it by using their intelligence.[25] The sapiential understanding of reality rested upon a universal base: Everyone could make contact with the transcendent reality, regardless of historical position or situation.[26]

With such a focus upon concrete experience, the main emphasis of the wisdom literature tended to be placed upon practical concerns of living an upright and cultured life. The themes treated in the collections of wisdom sayings that comprise the book of Proverbs deal with sundry topics of moral conduct and good manners. Discovery of and meditation upon such wisdom sayings would lead to the attainment of the good life, a prosperous and long life. In Proverbs there is little space allotted to consideration of doctrinal concerns about the exodus, covenant, and conquest, and no word of Yahweh announces his intentions. Rather, wisdom becomes the means whereby one might, by understanding the truth implicit in human affairs, attain to the promises of the good life. Attention is directed toward human understanding. This appears to be more important than any sacred affirmation of faith in the divine trustworthiness of Yahweh, although that faith is not denied.

Just as the word of Yahweh was described as having a dynamic force, so wisdom is here depicted as having existed from the beginning and as being itself creative:

> Yahweh created me when his purpose first unfolded,
> before the oldest of his works.
> From everlasting I was firmly set,
> from the beginning, before earth came into being.
> The deep was not, when I was born,
> there were no springs to gush with water.
> Before the mountains were settled,
> before the hills, I came to birth;
> before he made the earth, the countryside,
> or the first grains of the world's dust.
> When he fixed the heavens firm, I was there,
> when he drew a ring on the surface of the deep,
> when he thickened the clouds above,

> when he fixed fast the springs of the deep,
> when he assigned the sea its boundaries
> ... when he laid down the foundations of the earth,
> I was by his side, a master craftsman,
> delighting him day after day,
> ever at play in his presence,
> at play everywhere in his world,
> delighting to be with the sons of men [Prov. 8:22–31].

The main point of this passage is more than simply to sing the praises of wisdom. Wisdom here parallels the word of Yahweh in being granted a semi-independent existence. It moves beyond the practical morality of everyday life and takes on the numinous quality of Yahweh's presence. But, unlike that word which after creation had to be constantly sent through the prophets and patriarchs, wisdom is already present from the beginning and available to all who seek to understand. The discovery of wisdom and truth is not merely the receiving of sound practical advice on human conduct, but, as wisdom is from the beginning with Yahweh, it has an ultimate meaning and value ascertainable by all. Wisdom makes her cry: "O men! I am calling to you; my cry goes out to the sons of men" (Prov. 8:4). Wisdom is the connecting link between human understanding and transcendent truth. Being associated with Yahweh in creation, it is always present in the world. It needs the mediation of no prophet, but is capable of being experienced by each person who seeks to understand.[27]

In this theme of wisdom as revealer, Proverbs does indeed extend to all the possibility of experiencing and discerning the purposes of Yahweh. And yet, in its affirmation of exact retribution, it still runs counter to actual experiences of unmerited suffering among the just and undeserved prosperity among the wicked. It thus offers no adequate response to the skepticism and doubt that had been engendered by prophetic insistence on the teaching of exact retribution.

The Unbelief of Agur

The Saying of Agur (Prov. 30:1–9) seems to record an instance of such skepticism.[28] The initial verse presents a declaration of unbelief: "The words of Agur ben Yaqeh, of Massa, the portentous saying of a man who has no God; 'I have no God, but I can [face this or survive].' "

Verses 2–3 embody an ironical and sarcastic self-deprecation, belittling the value of wisdom: "Surely I must be more brute than man, and devoid of human understanding! I have not learned 'wisdom,' nor have I knowledge of [any] holy being." Agur here negates wisdom as the link between humans and truth, even doubting the very existence of a transcendent Yahweh.

Verse 4 presents a string of rhetorical questions challenging the validity of the wisdom tradition: "Who has ascended the sky and assumed dominion? Who has gathered up the wind in his cupped hands? Who has wrapped the waters in his robe? Who has fixed the limits of the world? What is his name, and what is his son's name?—as if you knew!" Agur sarcastically negates the claims of wisdom to reveal Yahweh. In fact, although wisdom may take over the functions of the word, the bulk of its teachings are directed to practical affairs and do seem to be able to stand on purely humanistic grounds, without an appeal to any "holy being." Perhaps the thrust of Agur's challenge is directed toward the attempt to use the rather commonsense wisdom tradition of ancient Israel to bolster the flagging faith in Yahweh.

But Agur does not go unanswered. Verses 5–6 represent a believer's reply: "All that God says has stood the test; he is a shield to those who take refuge with him. Do not add to his words, lest he correct you and you be exposed as a liar." Just as Yahweh was a shield for Abraham in leading him from his Father's house, so he is a shield for all who take refuge in him. This seems to be a rather straightforward statement of faith in Yahweh. His word has stood the test, as evidenced by the history of Israel. The believer's response is simply a reaffirmation of the Yahwistic faith.

Qoheleth's Tedium in the Face of Dying

But it is precisely that affirmation that causes the most doubt. Such a belief, that Yahweh is a shield to the faithful, finds no echo in Qoheleth (Ecclesiastes), the most skeptical book of the scriptures. Its initial refrain, "Vanity of vanities. All is vanity! For all his toil . . . under the sun, what does man gain by it?" (Qo. 1:2–3) sums up the content of this text. Qoheleth's single-minded focus is upon coping with the tedium of everyday living. No numinous experiences await anyone, and even if they did, all purpose is wiped out by dying. "There is no happiness for man but to eat and drink and to be content with his work" (Qo. 2:24).

The wisdom seeker, typified as Solomon, is described as concluding that all his achievements had been meaningless. "I then reflected on all that my hands had achieved and on all the effort that I had put into the achieving. What vanity it all is, and chasing of the wind! There is nothing to be gained under the sun" (Qo. 2:11). Both dreams and words are devoid of meaning. There are no numinous visions and no mediating words.

> For every dream, a vanity to match;
> too many words, a chasing of the wind [Qo. 5:6].

But Qoheleth directs his skepticism not to the Yahwistic faith of the prophets, but to the claims of wise men actually to understand something. The presence of such a text in the canon witnesses to the existence of a wisdom tradition that was attempting to offer an alternative to the Yahwistic faith. But, in Qoheleth's judgment, that attempt failed to offer a viable alternative. Even wisdom, once acquired, reveals no ultimate meaning. Solomon is depicted as lamenting:

> I have acquired a greater stock of wisdom than any of my predecessors in Jerusalem. I have great experience of wisdom and learning. Wisdom has been my careful study; stupidity, too, and folly. And now I have come to recognise that even this is chasing of the wind.
>> Much wisdom, much grief,
>> the more knowledge, the more sorrow [Qo. 1:16–18].

Wisdom brings grief and sorrow because all efforts are doomed to come to an end at death.

> More is to be had from wisdom than from folly, as from light than from darkness; this, of course, I know.
>> The wise man sees ahead,
>> the fool walks in the dark.
> No doubt! But I know, too, that one fate awaits them both, "The fool's fate," I thought to myself, "will be my fate too. Of what use my wisdom, then? This too," I thought, "is vanity." Since there is no lasting memory for wise man or for fool, and in the days to come both will be forgotten; wise man, alas, no less than fool must die. Life I have come to hate, for what is done under the sun disgusts me, since all is vanity and chasing of the wind [Qo. 2:13–18].

In the face of the inevitability of dying, Qoheleth finds no solace either in Yahwistic faith or in the attainment of wisdom. He has given up on the good life. But his skepticism is specifically directed against the pretensions of wisdom. All meaning floats away like a mist before one's face.

Although wisdom might supplant the word of Yahweh, it is still a poor substitute, for all it attains is a more certain knowledge of the suffering and miseries of living and dying. No amount of good advice on how to behave correctly alleviates the basic questions of meaning in the face of death. The good life is achievable only by insulating oneself from the awareness of death, and thus wisdom, which breaks through that insulation, scarcely leads to the prosperity of the good life. Without some awareness of transcendent meaning, worldly wisdom is next to worthless.

Perhaps wisdom can go beyond to grasp the meaning of deeper realities, but Qoheleth has no experience of it: "I have put all this to the test by wisdom, claiming to be wise; but wisdom has been beyond my reach. Reality lies beyond my grasp; and deep, so deep, who can discover it?" (Qo. 7:24–25).

There is no personification of wisdom in this text, for wisdom reveals little of ultimate value. It is not associated with Yahweh but, rather, consists in the meager insights gained by humans in the few brief days they have before forever passing away.

For Job, the Yahwistic faith seemed irrelevant because Yahweh's hiddenness appeared to be simply indifference, if not actual cruelty. The claim of transcendent value for the teaching of exact retribution was simply discordant with his actual experience. For Qoheleth the more experiential attainment of wisdom revealed no deep meaning; no doctrine of retribution from Yahweh caused him pain; and all effort was a worthless mist floating away to nothingness. While both authors evince deep skepticism, Job starts from the position of faith in Yahweh's faithfulness and tries to square that with experience. By contrast, Qoheleth begins with his own experience of wisdom, which he finds opens up onto nothing at all.

The basic dilemma appears from a comparison of Job with Qoheleth. If one insists upon the hiddenness and transcendence of Yahweh, then there is the ever-present danger of rendering such faith awareness irrelevant to the actual experience of living. But, on the other hand, if one focuses upon the human ability to discern meaning in experience, then there is the danger that the resultant understanding might be disappointing indeed.

FURTHER RESPONSES OF THE WISDOM LITERATURE

The alternative offered to the Yahwistic faith by the wisdom literature itself engendered further doubts and dilemmas. Two subsequent deutero-canonical wisdom texts attempted to answer those doubts. The first is the book of Sirach (Ecclesiasticus), written by one Jesus Eleasar ben Sirach sometime around 180 B.C.E. in Jerusalem.[29]

The Amalgamation of Wisdom and Faith in Sirach

It seems that the intention of Sirach was to respond to persons who tended to reject Jewish faith because of their inability to accept the doctrines of divine justice in the face of human experience. Thus Sirach tries to amalgamate experiential wisdom with traditional Yahwistic faith. Besides offering wisdom insights, Sirach quotes the scriptural histories that recount Yahweh's favors to Israel in the past. The text begins with a description of wisdom that clearly identifies its source as Yahweh.

> All wisdom is from the Lord,
> and it is his own for ever. . . .
> Before all other things wisdom was created,
> shrewd understanding is everlasting [Si. 1:1,4].

This passage echoes Proverbs 8:22 and describes wisdom as being present at creation, and therefore present in the universe. Wisdom is the means whereby Yahweh communicates with human beings. The verse that follows in the Hebrew text states: "Wisdom's source is the word of God in the heavens; her ways are the eternal laws."[30] Thus Sirach joins together the notion of wisdom with that of the word of Yahweh and sees the following of the path of wisdom as identical with keeping the laws of Yahweh.

The functions of wisdom, however, are broader than those of the word, for wisdom is available to all and it is the means whereby Yahweh nurtures and cares for all the righteous.

> Wisdom brings up her own sons,
> and cares for those who seek her.
> Whoever loves her loves life,
> those who wait on her early will be filled with happiness.
> Whoever holds her close will inherit honour,
> and wherever he walks the Lord will bless him.
>   [Si. 4:11–13 (12–14)]

But, although from the Lord, wisdom is not aloof, for it must be verbally expressed.

> Do not refrain from speech at an opportune time,
> and do not hide your wisdom;
> for wisdom shall be recognized in speech,
> and instruction by what the tongue utters.
>   [Si. 4:23–24 (27–28)]

Wisdom is thus the clothing of the numinous in human language. It is a gift from Yahweh whereby he discloses his intentions.

> Reflect on the injunctions of the Lord,
> busy yourself at all times with his commandments.
> He will strengthen your mind,
> and the wisdom you desire will be granted you [Si. 6:37].

The content of wisdom then becomes faith in Yahweh and is identified with the Torāh.

> Whoever fears the Lord will act like this,
> and whoever grasps the Law will obtain wisdom [Si. 15:1].

Wisdom consists entirely in fearing the Lord and wisdom is entirely constituted by fulfilling the Law.

To emphasize the identification of wisdom with the Yahwistic faith, Sirach ends his treatise by recounting the mighty deeds of Yahweh on behalf of the patriarchs, prophets, and sages of Israel. He attempts to synthesize wisdom themes within the Yahwistic faith. He tries to avoid the charge that

Yahweh is aloof by stressing that the gift of wisdom enables one to gain understanding of Yahweh's purposes. He tries to avoid the skepticism of Job, Agur, and Qoheleth by basing wisdom not merely upon human experience, but also upon the word of Yahweh as manifested in Israel's history.

But the inability to verify that history in experience was precisely what led Job, Agur, and Qoheleth to their doubt and skepticism. It would seem that Sirach was quite aware of such thinking, for in a number of passages he refutes such ideas (see Si. 2:17). The presence of adversity does not mean that Yahweh is necessarily punishing sins. Even in the prologue and epilogue of Job, which are apparently later additions to the text,[31] such suffering is seen as in some sense purgative. Yahweh is merciful (Si. 2:18 [23]) and, despite suffering, he will indeed bring happiness.

But again this interpretation goes little beyond the traditional teaching of exact retribution. Indeed one can cling to the hope that experienced suffering is but a test, but how can that be verified? It was just such explanations that Job had rejected. Why does it appear that Yahweh sleeps? What need is there for such contrived trials? Why do the unjust prosper? Job deconstructed the traditional answers in favor of a direct encounter with Yahweh in the whirlwind. Sirach offers no direct answer, sees such questioning as presumptuous, and recommends that it not be pursued: "You must not say, 'What is this? Why is that?' " [Si. 39:21 (26)].

Job's questioning was overcome by the might of Yahweh in the tempest. Sirach similarly advises that one place faith in Yahweh without inappropriate questioning.

A further section on death seems aimed at Qoheleth himself, who so worried about everything. The first two stanzas echo Qoheleth's dread of dying.

> O death, how bitter it is to remember you
> for a man at peace among his goods,
> to a man without worries, who prospers in everything,
> and still has the strength to feed himself [Si. 41:1–2].

But Sirach advises:

> Do not dread death's sentence;
> remember those who came before you and those who will
> come after.
> This is the sentence passed on all living creatures by the
> Lord,
> so why object to what seems good to the Most High?
> [Si. 41:3–4 (5–6)]

Here the sentence of death is not seen as just a fact of universal experience, but also as directly coming from Yahweh in Genesis 3:19. Sirach's answer is thus a faith response based on scripture, for Yahweh and his

wisdom go before and structure human existence before any doubts or
questions can occur. He is not concerned with questions that he cannot
answer.

> Do not try to understand things that are too difficult for you,
> or try to discover what is beyond your powers.
> Concentrate on what has been assigned to you,
> you have no need to worry over mysteries.
> Do not meddle with matters that are beyond you;
> what you have been taught already exceeds the scope of
>   the human mind.
> For many have been misled by their own presumptions,
> and wrong-headed opinions have warped their ideas.
>   [Si. 3:21–22 (22–26)]

In the face of skepticism and abandonment of faith in Yahweh, Sirach
stresses the gift of wisdom as surpassing opinions, as embodying an awareness of Yahweh in encounter, despite our inability to make sense out of
the experienced world. The content of such wisdom is circumscribed in the
Torāh and any questioning that leads away from Torāh is deemed unnecessary and dangerous. But such questions of ultimate meaning are raised
and clamor for answers. They can hardly be forbidden, for tempestlike
encounters with Yahweh are not everyday happenings.

Solomon's Philosophic Answer

The Wisdom of Solomon is another text that attempts to respond to
these difficulties. But rather than taking its stand upon a phenomenological
experience of Yahweh that is beyond questioning, it tries to present a
coherent understanding of wisdom and Yahweh. This text differs signifi-
cantly from the earlier wisdom literature. While all the former were written
in Hebrew, this one was written in Greek by a Hellenized Jew in the first
century B.C.E. and aimed at the Jewish community in Alexandria. It does
not embrace the skepticism of Job, Agur, or Qoheleth, but presents itself
as a philosophic essay on wisdom and seeks "to expound and defend . . .
faith on reasonable grounds, in order to preserve it from erosion in an alien
country."[32]
Two significant insights are added to the development of the notion of
wisdom. The first is the treatment and explanation of the nature of wisdom.
The second regards the content of wisdom.

THE NATURE OF WISDOM
The nature of wisdom is treated in chapter 7, which is addressed to
Gentiles and recommends Israel's wisdom tradition for their consideration.
Here wisdom is described as being a gift from God that enables humans

to speak as God would wish (Wi. 7:15). But the range of that wisdom extends not only over faith themes, but encompasses all understanding, all that is knowable.

> We are indeed in his hand, we ourselves and our words,
> with all our understanding, too,
> and technical knowledge.
> It was he who gave me true knowledge of all that is [Wi. 7:16].

Here follows a listing of the basic curriculum of a Greek school: philosophy, physics, history, astronomy, zoology, religion, botany, and medicine.[33] The scope of wisdom is enlarged to include all that is (*tōn ontōn gnōsin apseudē*), including even the technical knowledge of the Greeks. The author of this text, trained in Greek philosophy, attributes to wisdom not only the functions of the word of Yahweh, but the entirety of Greek culture. All understanding is due to this gift. Wisdom takes over some of the characteristics (Wi. 7:22–24) previously attributed only to Yahweh, for it is steadfast, dependable, and almighty. There is none of Qoheleth's pessimism here, for wisdom bridges the gap between humans and God. In the account of wisdom and God's intervention in the history of Israel, starting from 11:4, the subject active in that history shifts from wisdom to God, as if these two terms were simply synonymous. In the same way that Yahweh fills the universe, just so wisdom "pervades . . . all things" (Wi. 7:24).

The author further offers a series of metaphors describing the relationship of wisdom to God:

> She is a breath of the power of God,
> pure emanation of the glory of the Almighty;
> hence nothing impure can find a way into her.
> She is a reflection of the eternal light,
> untarnished mirror of God's active power,
> image of his goodness [Wi. 7:25–26].

This passage parallels Proverbs 8:22–31, but "here wisdom goes beyond personification to hypothesis; she becomes a manifestation of God to human beings."[34] Wisdom is conceived not as an understanding of God by humans, but as a Platonic essence existing prior to human existence. Such wisdom is associated with Yahweh because she is his presence or manifestation.

In place of the doubt or skepticism of a Job or a Qoheleth, this text offers a philosophic notion of wisdom as a direct link to the divine. The first metaphor in the passage above, "She is a breath of the power of God" (*atmis gar esti tēs tou theou dunameōs*), as it stands is a mixed metaphor, for breath is not usually associated with power. The term *atmis* means breath, mist, or vapor such as arises from water. It signifies the transitoriness and vanishing traces left behind when a thing disappears.[35] As such it seems cognate to the Septuagint's rendering of Qoheleth's Hebrew term *hebel*,[36] the basic meaning of which is also mist, vapor, or breath, and which refers to something fleeting or transitory, as *mataiotēs*, vanity. But whereas *hebel* for Qoheleth represented his pessimistic mood in the face of the constant passing away of all things (himself included) and is thus often translated as "vanity," to the author of Wisdom the term *atmis* denotes the perceptible traces left behind after the passing of God. Thus this first metaphor seems intended to respond to Qoheleth and sees wisdom as the identifiable sign of God's power rather than as meaningless vanity.

The other metaphors in the passage stress the role of wisdom as manifesting God. It is a pure emanation, a reflection or radiance, an untarnished mirror, an image of the ultimate in his action in the world. Wisdom is the mediation of ultimate meaning.

> Although alone, she can do all;
> herself unchanging, she makes all things new.
> In each generation she passes into holy souls,
> she makes them friends of God and prophets [Wi. 7:27].

The words "herself unchanging" (*menousa en autē*) literally mean "remaining in herself" and suggest the Greek idea of divinity as characterized by immutability, which has a Platonic origin,[37] as does the subsequent use of the dichotomy between soul and body.[38] One can detect the dominant influence of Greek categories of thinking common in Alexandria when this text was composed and which were adopted to express the author's understanding of the nature of wisdom as a preexistent reality that, in virtue of its dynamic power, manifests to the changing world the immutable God.[39] Its dynamism makes one a friend of God, for it comes as a friend from God.

> Wisdom is a spirit, a friend to man. . . .
> The spirit of the Lord, indeed, fills the whole world,
> and that which holds all things together knows every word
>   that is said [Wi. 1:6–7].

The words "that which holds all things together" (*to sunechon ta panta*) appear to be derived from Stoic philosophy, where they referred to the concept of nature as holding all the parts of the universe in balanced hierarchy.[40] Again the author borrows Greek philosophic ideas to interpret the action of God's wisdom.

But wisdom does not stand opposite human beings and confront them, as does the word of Yahweh delivered through a prophet. Rather, permeating the world as she does, all is already included within her sphere, as all is in the hand of God. Emphasis is here upon becoming aware of wisdom already present and preceding either faith or questioning.

> Quick to anticipate those who desire her, she makes
>   herself known to them.
> Watch for her early and you will have no trouble;
> you will find her sitting at your gates.
> Even to think about her is understanding full grown.
>   [Wi. 6:13–16 (15–17)]

Wisdom is anticipatory (*prognōsthēnai*) because it is present before one might begin to desire it. One finds wisdom not by long journeys and searching, but by taking note that it is already present sitting at the gates of one's own house. And even to think about wisdom is wisdom fully grown, or, in another translation, the perfection of wisdom (*phronēseōs teleiotēs*),[41] since that thought awakens one to the already present spirit of wisdom. Otherwise a mere thought about a far distant objective could hardly be the full maturity of wisdom. It lies, then, at the base of human consciousness, and religious meaning is not an apprehension of external objects, no matter how supreme. Rather, it is a deepening awareness of the presence of God manifest from the beginning. The Greek ideal of the philosopher (*philosophos*) signifies that the person who loves wisdom is to seek after her until finding her. But the nature of wisdom is reversed here to mean that it is wisdom who is the lover of humans (*philanthrōpon*), for wisdom has the initiative.

Wisdom does not for this author mediate the gap between two separately established beings, God and humans. Rather, humans are established only in the hand of God, and wisdom is present even before the search begins. As the mirror of God's power, wisdom encompasses all that is. Humans then do not need to establish a link with a hidden God, for wisdom surrounds all as the manifesting spirit of God, loving all human beings.

The explanation of the nature of wisdom has been expanded and developed by the author of Wisdom. Based upon the doctrine of Proverbs and Sirach, that author enlarges its scope through the adoption of Greek philosophic thinking in hypostasizing wisdom as the dynamic spirit of God acting on behalf of human beings.

THE CONTENT OF SOLOMON'S WISDOM: IMMORTALITY

But, as is clear from the previous discussion, the constant source of doubt in the earlier wisdom literature was the experience of innocent suffering and the silence of Yahweh in the face of death and abandonment. The book of Wisdom attempts a response to these dilemmas by affirming the immortality of the righteous.

In a long passage the author of Wisdom describes the thinking of the godless as if to point to Qoheleth.

For they say to themselves, with their misguided reasoning:
"Our life is short and dreary,
nor is there any relief when man's end comes,
nor is anyone known who can give release from Hades.
By chance we came to birth,
and after this life we shall be as if we had never been.
The breath in our nostrils is a puff of smoke,
reason a spark from the beating of our hearts;
put this out and our body turns to ashes,
and the spirit melts away like idle air.
In time, our name will be forgotten,
nobody will remember what we have done;
our life will pass away like wisps of clouds,
dissolve like the mist
that the sun's rays drive away
and the heat of it overwhelms.
Yes, our days are like the passing of a shadow,
from our death there is no turning back,
the seal is set: no one returns.
Come then, let us enjoy what good things there are. . . .
[Wi. 2:1–6]

This passage seems to be a fair summary of Qoheleth's thinking, for he bemoans the sad fate of all people (Qo. 2:15); he discourses on the chance occurrence of events (Qo. 9:11–20); he complains that one's memory will soon be forgotten (Qo. 2:16). His constant refrain that all is transitory mist passing away before our eyes seems to be echoed in the foregoing passage in the words "a puff of smoke" (*kapnos ē pnoē*), "idle air" (*chaunos aēr*), "wisps of cloud" (*ichnē nephelēs*), "mist" (*homichlē*), and the "passing of a shadow" (*skias gar parodos*). Qoheleth's image of sultry tedium under the burning sun in the words "There is nothing new under the sun" finds an echo in the use of the image of the sun's rays burning away and overwhelming the morning mist.

But the author of Wisdom is not rendered despondent by such dire forebodings, for the content of wisdom has shifted from the promise of prosperity and long life, a promise always circumscribed by the inevitability of dying, to the possibility of attaining immortality. The verification of the teaching of exact retribution is postponed from the empirical world to the afterlife. A good life, then, does bring its reward.

They do not know the hidden things of God,
they have no hope that holiness will be rewarded,
they can see no reward for blameless souls.
Yet God did make man imperishable,
he made him in the image of his own nature;

it was the devil's envy that brought death into the world,
as those who are his partners will discover [Wi. 2:22–24].

Here the author of Wisdom has adopted the Greek notion of the natural immortality of the soul, which he then combines with the Genesis account that Yahweh created humans in his image (Gen. 1:27) and that death entered the world through the devil's enticement of Adam and Eve (Gen. 3:19). He introduces these Platonic ideas of the soul and immortality specifically to answer Qoheleth's skepticism and despondency. He can thus maintain that, despite suffering and the apparent silence of God,

> . . . the souls of the virtuous are in the hands of God,
> no torment shall ever touch them.
> In the eyes of the universe, they did appear to die,
> their going looked like a disaster,
> their leaving us, like annihilation;
> but they are in peace.
> If they experienced punishment as men see it,
> their hope was rich with immortality;
> slight was their affliction, great will their blessings be.
> [Wi. 3:1–4]

With this new Greek doctrine, the book of Wisdom attempts to reinterpret faith in Yahweh. From chapters 10 to 19 the author recounts the actions of wisdom and/or God in Israel's history in order to reaffirm faith in Yahweh. By its very nature wisdom goes before and encompasses all humans. Its content is the promise of immortality for the virtuous, those who have been made friends of God through wisdom.

And yet promises of eternal life are not experientially obvious and it remains unclear just how this wisdom mediates God. Its nature is akin to philosophical wisdom conceived by the Greek thinkers. Indeed it would seem that in order to answer the deep questioning and doubt of Job, Agur, and Qoheleth, the book of Wisdom has lost all existential grounding. The meaning of wisdom is found only upon the affirmation of a sacral faith that sees all suffering and pain *sub specie aeternitatis*, namely, *sub specie sapientiae*. In the light of promised immortality, all Israel's adversities, Job's suffering, Agur's nihilism, and Qoheleth's moroseness are deemed to be illusions. The argument of the book of Wisdom is persuasive only to those who already have faith in God, only to those who already affirm the Platonic notion of the immortality of the soul. One wonders what Qoheleth's reaction to it would have been, for he experienced no ultimate insight through wisdom. How indeed can one verify whether wisdom does lead to an awareness of immortality? How can one ascertain that by wisdom one has been made a friend of God?

CONCLUSION

This brief outline of Israel's wisdom tradition has attempted to focus upon the doctrinal problematic that arises from these texts. That problematic is embodied in two stated concerns: How does one find faith and meaning in the face of apparently meaningless suffering and death? How is one to interpret and relate the hidden, transcendent God, who seems assiduously to maintain silence despite such suffering, to concrete human experience? That is, how can one understand God as transcendent and yet relevant to human existence?

The book of Proverbs emphasizes experiential wisdom and offers a broader base for insight into religious meaning in that wisdom, available to all who seek her, takes over the functions of the word of Yahweh. But the insistence in Proverbs on the teaching of exact retribution invited the skepticism of Job, Agur, and Qoheleth. In Agur and Qoheleth one finds a radical doubt that the Yahweh-word complex offers any solution or comfort. But one also finds that, having departed from the numinous awareness of Yahweh embodied in the Yahwistic tradition, the wisdom alternative itself becomes bankrupt. By contrast, Job deconstructs the doctrine of exact retribution in favor of a phenomenological encounter with God, an encounter that, though not itself understood, eradicates the need for questioning. Yet the questions still come, for the encounter is not common property. The book of Wisdom, borrowing Greek ideas and adapting them to its purposes, constructs a faith understanding by taking wisdom as the spirit of Yahweh dwelling in humans and assuring the friends of God that their reward will be immortality. But this also presupposes that one has understood and accepted those ideas.

These questions point to a more general question, the nature and validity of doctrinal statements about God. Proverbs constructs doctrine, while Job deconstructs. The book of Wisdom reconstructs. Qoheleth, claiming to have understood all those constructs, finds them sadly inadequate.

In broad outline these themes and questions form the background in which wisdom was understood in the Old Testament. When Christian thinkers employ wisdom as a doctrinal theme to understand the meaning of Christ, it will be with these same questions that they deal, for they will understand Christ as the embodiment of the wisdom of God who concretizes the divine presence among us.

2

The New Testament Confession of Christ as Wisdom

The wisdom themes of the Old Testament provided the New Testament writers with a number of patterns for interpreting the Christ meaning. Their Christological understanding reflects the concerns of the authors of Proverbs, Sirach, Qoheleth, Job, and Wisdom. They came to identify Christ with wisdom and saw in the pattern of his life, death, and resurrection an answer to the dilemmas about human suffering, death, and the silence of God.

But wisdom as described in the New Testament is distinct from empirical knowing, and New Testament writers stress the need for a conversion of consciousness in order to gain mystic insight into Christ as wisdom. Christ wisdom is to be sought, they teach, in the face of God's silence and human suffering.

THE IDENTIFICATION OF CHRIST WITH WISDOM

As with all doctrinal development, a growth process can be detected in the understanding of Christ as wisdom. The final result of that development in the New Testament, the full identification of Christ as God's wisdom and power, did not spring forth immediately and without precedent.

Matthew's Reworking of the Q Source

This developmental process can be seen in the progression from the understanding of Christ in the Q text to that in the Gospel of Matthew. The Q (*Quelle*, source) text is identified by exegetes as the no longer extant source for the passages that appear in Matthew and Luke, but which have no Marcan parallel.

James M. Robinson has convincingly argued that the *gattung* (the genre of the overall literary composition) of Q is that of "the sayings of the sages" (*logoi sophōn*), a *gattung* that finds its fuller development and expression in the aprocryphal Gospel of Thomas.[1] M. Jack Suggs has analyzed the Q passages,[2] and shown that they understand Christ as the final prophet of wisdom.[3] The Christian community that produced this Q text saw Jesus as the last in the succession of wisdom's envoys, such as described in the Wisdom of Solomon.[4] In the strict sense, then, Q had no Christology but, rather, expressed a sophiology, a doctrine of wisdom in which Christ plays a significant but subordinate role to wisdom herself.[5] It is still wisdom, then, that serves here — as in the Old Testament — as the manifestation of God and the means for rendering God's presence understandable.

But the author of the Gospel of Matthew alters and amends the Q source so that Jesus is no longer merely an envoy of wisdom, but the embodiment of wisdom itself. This progression is evident in Matthew's alteration of wisdom's oracle of doom (Mt. 23:34–36; parallel Lk. 11:49–51) so that the wisdom saying is predicated of Christ (*ego apostellō*), rather than referred to personified wisdom (*kai ē sophia tou theou eipen. apostelō*).[6] This same identification of wisdom with Jesus is apparent in the passage on wisdom's children and the children in the market place (Mt. 11:2–19; parallel Lk. 7:18–35). The Lucan expression "Wisdom is justified by [all] her children" seems closer to the Q text, which saw Jesus and John as "children of wisdom."[7] But Matthew's substitution of "wisdom is justified by her deeds" refers back to the deeds of Christ (*ta erga tou Christou*), which John had heard about in prison (Mt. 11:1), implying that Matthew "has consciously modified the saying about 'Wisdom's children' into one about 'Wisdom's deeds' in order to identify wisdom with Jesus. In this way, Jesus is no longer the last and greatest of Wisdom's children; in him are the deeds of Wisdom to be uniquely seen. . . . It would not greatly overstate the case to say that for Matthew Wisdom 'has become flesh and dwelled among us.' "[8]

The identification of the *gattung* of Q as "sayings of the wise," rather than as gospel, and its doctrinal focus upon wisdom explain the rather anomalous fact that Q apparently has no passion or resurrection account. The focus was upon the content of wisdom dispensed by Jesus and not upon the meaning of his death and resurrection.[9] Matthew, however, understanding Christ as wisdom itself, "brings the [Q] tradition within the framework of the passion-dominated gospel form."[10]

Paul's Affirmation of Christ as Wisdom

This same process of identifying Jesus with wisdom is found in the Pauline corpus. From his analysis of a number of passages from 1 Corinthians, 2 Corinthians, and Romans, Hans Conzelmann argues that there existed a wisdom school of Paul located at Ephesus, which wove wisdom themes into its Christological understanding.[11] Thus 1 Corinthians 1:24 describes Christ as "the power and wisdom of God" (*theou dunamin kai theou sophian*), and in Colossians 1:15–16 Christ is again described in wisdom terms: "He is the image of the unseen God and the first-born of all creatures, for in him were created all things in heaven and earth: everything visible and invisible." Christ here is conceived as personified, embodied wisdom after the pattern of the Old Testament wisdom texts. He takes over the functions of Old Testament wisdom in imaging forth the unseen Yahweh in creation.

The statement of the Epistle to the Hebrews continues the theme in terms reminiscent of the book of Wisdom 7:25–26: "He is the radiant light of God's glory and the perfect copy of his nature" (Heb. 1:3). Christ is the lighting up (*apaugasma*) and revelation of God's glory because Christ is the perfect copy (*charaktēr tēs upostaseōs autou*) of what God is.

John's Understanding of Jesus

The Logos hymn of the prologue to the Gospel of John echoes the same theme. As Dodd explains, the concept of wisdom in the wisdom literature of the Old Testament represents the thought of God, immanent in the world. It takes over the functions of "the word of Yahweh." Thus, "in composing the Prologue [to John], the author's mind was moving along lines similar to those followed by Jewish wisdom writers of the 'Wisdom' school. . . . The Logos is . . . a concept similar to that of wisdom."[12] The description of the word being "in the beginning with God" parallels wisdom in Proverbs 8 and in Sirach 1:1. It also shares the cosmological role of wisdom, for "through him all things came into being" (Jn. 1:2). Furthermore, the prologue's use of the masculine term *logos*, rather than the feminine *sophia*, makes subsequent identification with Jesus more appropriate. Just as wisdom draws near in the sages and prophets and is not recognized, so the word remains hidden and unaccepted. Those who do accept it, however, become children of God, just as those holy souls in the book of Wisdom, who have accepted wisdom, become friends of God.

Verse 13 of the Logos hymn[13] of the prologue begins to identify the word with Christ, for all before this verse refers to wisdom, that is, the preincarnate logos.[14] "And the word became flesh and made his dwelling among us. And we have seen his glory, the glory of an only son coming from the father, filled with enduring love. . . . " Here the notion of personified wisdom working through her children is left behind in favor of the identification of wisdom and word with Jesus, for Jesus is the incarnate word, the embodiment of wisdom.[15]

What does such an identification mean? One might describe a person as being wise, but what could it mean to say that Christ was wisdom itself? One must not think here of the theological expositions on the divine persons of later trinitarian thinking, for at this stage of Christian thought, such questions had not yet been put into focus.

This question is not easily answered, for it presupposes an understanding not only of the meaning of Christ, but also of the meaning of wisdom as understood in the New Testament. Therefore, before wrestling with the meaning of Christ as wisdom, we shall treat the nature of wisdom consciousness in the New Testament.

WISDOM CONSCIOUSNESS IN THE NEW TESTAMENT

Wisdom in the New Testament, as in some parts of the Old Testament wisdom tradition such as the book of Job, moves in a context of mystic meaning in which immediate, direct experience overwhelms the expressive ability of language.[16] Such wisdom experience is not amenable to verbal understanding or logic and does not issue in answers to questions, even the most existentially pressing questions. This notion is present throughout the New Testament.

Matthew's Notion of Wisdom

Matthew 11:25–27 (parallel Lk. 10:21–22) presents a passage that some think influenced Paul's discourse on wisdom in 1 Corinthians.[17]

At that time Jesus exclaimed, "I bless you, Father, Lord of heaven and of earth, for hiding these things from the wise and intelligent and revealing them to mere children. Yes, Father, for that is what it pleased you to do. Everything has been entrusted to me by my Father, and no one knows the son except the Father, just as no one knows the Father except the son and those to whom the son chooses to grant a revelation.[18]

Here wisdom revelation is given not to the worldly wise and intelligent (*apo sophōn kai sunetōn*), but to mere children (*nēpiois*), childlike persons who have not been spoiled by learning.[19] It is such childlike consciousness that can participate in wisdom insight, for it experiences God directly and is yet unencumbered by verbal reasonings. Thus this passage seems to suggest two levels of consciousness. The one is verbally educated and mediates understanding through images and language symbols, while the other is an awareness that is immediately experienced.

Paul's Notion of Wisdom

This same understanding of two levels of consciousness is presented also in the most developed treatment of wisdom in the New Testament, Paul's sermon on wisdom in 1 Corinthians, chapters 1 to 3.[20] The sermon is addressed to the existence of factionalism within the Corinthian community and seems to refute those who claimed to possess an elitist wisdom whereby they boasted that they were "already satiated (*ēde kekoresmenoi este*), already fulfilled (*ēde eploutēsate*), already entered into the kingdom (*ebasi-*

leusate)" (1 Cor. 4:8). They seem to have applied "the exalted state of Christ to themselves."[21]

However, Paul does not direct his sermon against the positions of any of these Corinthian factions, even those who equated their positions with that of the exalted Christ.[22] Rather, in a two-tiered sermon on the nature of wisdom consciousness, he thematizes the mind of wisdom in contrast to the mind-set that generates partisan standpoints and clings to them as truth. The first tier refutes the consciousness that cannot understand the wisdom of God, while the second tier, from 2:6, thematizes the true nature of wisdom consciousness. The question for Paul is not one "of doctrinal statements, but of the believing understanding."[23]

The first tier of the sermon focuses upon the Old Testament theme of wisdom hidden from those who do not seek her and parallels the Matthean passage about hiding wisdom from the wise and the intelligent. Paul thus presents a negation of the value of intellectual wisdom, claiming that he preaches, "not with the wisdom of words, lest the cross of Christ be emptied of meaning. For the word of the cross is to those who are lost foolishness, but to those who are saved, the power of God" (1 Cor. 1:17–18).

It is the verbal wisdom (*sophia tou logou*) of the worldly debater (*suzētētēs*) that constitutes boasting (*kauchēsis*), Paul's word for the basic self-centered consciousness whereby humans live only for themselves. Such self-boasting consciousness is elsewhere described by Paul as understanding according to the flesh (2 Cor. 5:16—*oidamen kata sarka*), whereby humans "boast in appearances and not in [what they understand] in their hearts" (2 Cor. 5:12—*tous en prosōpō kauchōmenous kai mē en kardia*).

The basic defect with the Corinthian factions was not that they had adopted incorrect doctrinal standpoints, and Paul does not seem to be concerned with correcting the presentation of such verbal understandings. Rather, he seems concerned with the fact that they had transformed "the understanding of faith into the support of a standpoint, [which] leads automatically to a multiplicity of standpoints, and hence to division. Over against this Paul defines his position first of all in negative terms, as a non-standpoint."[24] He is not concerned with "the propagating of [any] *Weltanschauung*, but [with] the destruction of every attempt to regard a *Weltanschauung* as the way of salvation."[25]

The second tier of the sermon begins from 1 Corinthians 2:6. Having stated that, in contrast to the persuasive words of human (some texts read *anthrōpinēs*) wisdom, his preaching consists in a demonstration (*en apodeizei*) of the spirit and of power, he then proceeds to declare: "We speak the wisdom of God in mystery." The contrast here is again between human wisdom, which issues in standpoints, and God's wisdom, which is spoken only in mystery. Then in verses 7–10 the theme of hidden wisdom is changed into one of revealed wisdom, for it has been made manifest by God through the spirit. This shift is not from a rebuttal of human wisdom to a statement of divine wisdom, as if these were parallel options in the same realm of meaning. Rather, the shift implies a change of consciousness from one that imagines that it captures wisdom and boasts of its attainments to one that is able to abide in mystery, in verbal unknowing. It is a rejection of Qoheleth's Solomon who boasted that he had attained the summit of wisdom. In 1 Corinthians 2:10–13, this converted (i.e., turned around) consciousness (*metanoia*) is described as the receiving of the spirit of God:

> For to us God has revealed . . . through the spirit, including even the depths of God. For who among men knows what a man is but the man's own spirit within him? In the same way no one has recognized what God is, except by the spirit of God. We, however, have received not the spirit of the world, but the spirit that comes from God, so that we may know what has been bestowed upon us by God. And it is also of this that we speak, not in words taught by human wisdom, but in words taught by the spirit, interpreting spiritual things in spiritual terms.[26]

The double-tiered structure of this sermon is grounded in Paul's understanding of human understanding and human speech, an understanding in which the main thrust is not toward the content understood (for all factions claimed to understand the depths of God, *ta bathē tou theou*), but the spirit in which that content is understood. The understanding that appears to be wise in this world (1 Cor. 1:8), that boasts in what is merely appearance (the *en prosōpō kauchōmenos* of 2 Cor. 5:12) is incapable of understanding the wisdom of God, because it would demand that the depths of God be conformed to its own language-formed self-consciousness. Such is the understanding that interprets spiritual things in an unspiritual manner (*psuchikos*) and which sees the wisdom of God as foolishness (*mōria*).

James' Notion of Wisdom

The difference between human, verbal understanding and the wisdom of God can also be seen in the Epistle of James, itself written in a wisdom *gattung*. But here the salient characteristic of human consciousness is not described as boasting or self-centeredness, but as wavering and doubt:

> If there is any one of you who needs wisdom, he must ask God, who gives freely and ungrudgingly, and it will be given to him. But he must ask in faith, and without wavering, because a person who wavers is like waves in the sea moved and tossed about by the wind. That sort of person, being in two minds, buffeted between going two ways, must not expect that the Lord will give him anything [Jm. 1:5–8] (Author's trans.).

The term here translated as "wavering" is *diakrinomenos* from the verb *diakrinō*, the basic meaning of which is to make distinctions, to differentiate, to judge, to hesitate between options, and thus to waver between alternatives. Just as Paul contrasts the wisdom of God with the mind that generates standpoints, so James recommends that, in order to be open to the gift of wisdom, one must not engage in discriminative thinking, weighing this standpoint against that, as if a correct standpoint could lead to salvation. It is not that thinking and questioning are of no value whatsoever, but that they block the immediacy of mystic meaning. As long as one "wavers in two minds," all meaning is confined to judgments on the validity of mediated concepts. Such a balancing of standpoints precludes the possibility of wisdom, because it itself arises from a need to ascertain and grasp truth for and by oneself. James' description is in harmony with Paul's description of worldly wisdom as boasting and self-centeredness. As will be thematized afterward, it is further in full parallel with the Mahāyāna Buddhist rejection of discrimination (*vikalpa*) as the principal obstacle to the mind of wisdom. James' metaphor about being buffeted about as waves in the sea tossed by the wind is a frequent description of the mind of discrimination in the Buddhist texts.

While Paul presents worldly wisdom as characterized by the reprehensible qualities of boasting and self-centeredness, James describes it simply in terms of the everyday activities of judging and weighing evidence. We place obstacles to the attainment of wisdom not just by the commission of some sinful action, but because of the empirical structure of our consciousness as grasping at truth, wavering in doubt, self-centered, and boasting. This criticism of empirical consciousness does not, however, signify the rejection of human thinking, but rather, its ineptness in understanding within a mystic realm of meaning. That consciousness is nurtured and developed by controlling meanings in language symbols and is ill equipped to embody a meaning not so mediated. "Natural" human thinking, being centered upon the self and regarding death as the ultimate calamity, finds it difficult to approach any area over which it has no control.

John's Treatment of Signs

The Gospel of John presents a parallel understanding of human consciousness, which can perhaps best be extracted from the treatment of Jesus' signs (*sēmeia*), in the passage that is bounded by the accounts of the changing of the water into wine at Cana (2:1–12) and the cure of the nobleman's son (4:46–54).

It would appear from the analysis of modern exegetes[27] that the evangelist is here using an earlier miracle source text (*sēmeia Quelle*) as the basis for his account of Jesus' signs, but, being not quite satisfied with its interpretation, breaks its narrative at 2:13 and picks it up again only at 4:46. John 4:43–46 forms a further interpretation of the evangelist that serves to patch together the broken thread of the narrative of Jesus' signs. Thus the material bounded by these two miracle stories should offer insight into the evangelist's understanding of signs. In 1 Corinthians 2:2 such signs were seen as objects sought by the consciousness of worldly wisdom, that is, as objects of a boasting and self-centered consciousness.

In John 2:12 it is reported of the first of Jesus' signs that "he let his glory be seen, and his disciples believed in him." This positive evaluation of signs is characteristic of the miracle source, the *sēmeia Quelle*, and should not be taken uncritically as expressing the intention of the evangelist, for the Gospel of John not only appropriates its miracle source, but there is an "equally pervasive Johannine criticism of that [miracle] tradition, the constant tendency to interpret the miracles transparently, as a sign or pointer toward Jesus himself, to oppose the crude faith in miracle, and to chastise the persistent earthbound lack of understanding characteristic of unbelief. . . ."[28] This judgment accords with the overall theme of John that the disciples, despite their presence at numerous "miracles," did not actually come to have faith in Jesus until after his death and resurrection, and that thus the belief of the disciples in 2:12 is a poor and meager faith indeed.

In the miracle source used by the author of the Gospel of John, "Jesus' miracles proved directly and visibly for everyone Jesus' divine status."[29] But the evangelist accepts no such direct and visible proof as leading to faith. His attitude is summed up in the ironic insertion in the second miracle story in John 4:48: "So you will not believe unless you see signs and wonders, eh!"[30] If such a criticism of signs and wonders does in fact reflect a central intention of the evangelist, then the material that intervenes between the Cana sign and the cure of the nobleman's son should highlight the evangelist's understanding.

And indeed, it does appear to do just that. John 2:13–22 recounts the cleansing of the temple. But John adds a key difference to the account as it appears in Matthew 21:12–13 or in Mark 11:15–17, for in John, after Jesus has driven the merchants out of the temple, the Jews intervene and ask: "What sign (*ti sēmeion*) can you show us to justify what you have done?" (2:18). Jesus answers not by performing any sign at all but, rather, by uttering an enigmatic saying about raising up the destroyed temple. The point to notice is not just the meaning of the saying,[31] but the refusal on Jesus' part to grant the request of the Jews for a sign.

John 2:23–25 seems to support this interpretation of the Johannine understanding of the meaning of signs:

> While he was in Jerusalem during the Passover festival, many believed in his name, for they could see the signs he was performing. For his part, Jesus would not trust himself to them because he knew them all. He needed no one to testify about human nature, for he was aware of what was in man's heart (Trans. Raymond E. Brown, *The Gospel According to John*, p. 126.).

This negative judgment about those who believed because they see signs (*theōrountes authou ta sēmeia ha epoiei*) is then to be extended back to 2:11–12, where the disciples believe in Jesus because of his first sign at Cana. Human nature has a constant tendency to erect heroes to overcome its fears and negate its creatureliness. But Jesus, knowing what was in the hearts of men and women, refuses to acquiesce in such role expectations.

John 3:1–21 presents the story of Nicodemus. Again the key to understanding the passage turns upon the relationship between signs and faith, for, moving in a meaning realm in which signs do lead to understanding, Nicodemus addresses Jesus: "Rabbi, we know you are a teacher who comes from God, for, unless God is with him, no one can perform the signs you perform." If the evangelist actually did think that signs lead to faith, it is extremely difficult to understand the bewildering response that Jesus offers: "I solemnly assure you, no one can enter the kingdom of God without being born from above." In response to Nicodemus' confusion,[32] Jesus performs no sign, but emphasizes that there are two levels of understanding and that sign-grasping consciousness cannot understand the things of the spirit. The words "flesh begets flesh" (3:6) parallel Paul's "knowing according to the flesh," while the words "spirit begets spirit" are Paul's "wisdom of God in mystery."

John 3:22–36 presents John the Baptist's final witness concerning Jesus, in which he affirms that Jesus is "he who comes from above" (3:31), he who "speaks God's own words" (3:34), which is contrasted with the statement that "he who is born of the earth is earthly himself and speaks in an earthly way" (3:31). This passage is joined in theme to the Nicodemus account and emphasizes the passage:

> If you do not believe me
> when I speak about things in this world,
> how are you going to believe me
> when I speak to you about heavenly things?
> No one has gone up to heaven,
> except the one who came down from heaven [Jn. 3:12–13].

The point is not that Jesus validates his words in the empirical pattern of self-centered thinking, but that a new, converted consciousness is needed to understand and believe.

John 4:1–41 again focuses upon faith consciousness. The Samaritan woman comes to believe "because he told me all I have ever done" (4:40), that is, through a wondrous sign. She immediately raises the question of the proper place in which to worship. Jesus, like Paul in 1 Corinthians, takes no position on the question, but refers her back to a consideration of the consciousness that generates true worship, wherever that may be located. The woman recruits people from town to come and "see a man who has told me everything I ever did" (4:29). They came and, seeing that he was a wonder worker, "believed in him on the strength of the woman's testimony." But the account does not end here, for these Samaritans, though simply speaking with Jesus, came to a deeper level of belief, not because of the sign granted to the woman, but because they themselves had heard the words of Jesus, the words of God's wisdom spoken in mystery, that is, through faith insight.

Thus, in these various passages, the evangelist expresses his negative attitude toward sign-grasping faith, and then once again takes up his miracle source text in the account of the cure of the nobleman's son. Without specifically thematizing wisdom, the same double-tiered understanding of consciousness and belief as present in Paul and James permeates the Fourth Gospel. Verbal human understanding that grasps at signs and abides in appearances does not lead to wisdom or faith insight.

What then is the content of this wisdom and faith insight? If signs do not lead to faith, if weighing options precludes the gift of wisdom, if verbal wisdom forms an obstacle to the wisdom of God, then just what do Christian faith and wisdom mean?

The point of the foregoing analysis was to highlight two levels of consciousness precisely because faith wisdom moves in a mystic realm of meaning. One must not then expect any clear, well-defined formula to express faith content in a demonstrable manner, for faith becomes meaningful only in direct, immediate contact with God. It cannot be mediated by the worldly words that interpose self-centered concern, even about one's own ultimate fate, between consciousness and the action of God. Neither can it be circumscribed within any ideological or theological position.

THE CONTENT OF WISDOM

Yet the New Testament writers do not fail to describe the content of the wisdom of God. Quite the contrary, it is often and variously presented. Ephesians 3:10 speaks of "the many-sided wisdom of God (*hē polupoikilos sophia tou theou*)," for, transcending verbal definition, that wisdom consciousness has been and must be expressed in a myriad of language structures and thematic patterns. In 2 Timothy 3:15 the scriptures as the bearers of wisdom is emphasized:

> You must keep to what you have been taught and know to be true; remember who your teachers were and how, ever since you were a child, you have known the holy scriptures — from these you can learn the wisdom that leads to salvation through faith in Christ Jesus.

This does not mean that mystic insight into the meaning of Christ can be extracted from the pages of scripture by logical analysis or by looking for signs; rather, as Ephesians 3:4 says: "If you are able to read [my words], you will understand my insight into the mystery of Christ." The words of scripture serve, as do the signs of Jesus, as pointers to lead beyond worldly consciousness to an awareness of the saving mystery of Christ. Scripture does not present itself as a Christian standpoint but, rather, records the experiences of those early Christians who entered into wisdom through faith, thus inviting others to do likewise.

But the content of wisdom, even though mystic, is described. Here we will focus upon principal themes of Christian wisdom: the experience of God as Abba, Paul's theology of the cross, and the resurrection.

God as Abba

Following the lead of Joachim Jeremias,[33] it is now generally admitted by scholars[34] that Jesus' persistent habit of referring to God as "my Father," as "Abba," is unique; perhaps so unique to Jesus that it enables us to get behind the Christian kerygma to the very words (*ipsissima vox*) of the historical Jesus.[35] Even if such a usage reflects, rather, the faith of the later church, it is at least clear that the progressive[36] use of the term "Abba" by Jesus in the Gospels reflects a growing awareness that the experience thus implied was indeed central to the early understanding of the meaning of Christ.

In all the prayers of Jesus, except the prayer from the cross (Mk. 15:34; Mt. 27:46), which is itself a quotation from Psalm 22:1, it is reported that he used the term "my father."[37] The implication of this is not only that Jesus experienced a direct, immediate awareness of God as his own father, but also that he has received wisdom and revelation based upon that experience, inasmuch as the experience itself was wisdom and revelation. The theme of sons receiving instruction from their fathers is often found in the wisdom literature of the Old Testament (Prov. 1:8; 2:12; 3:1; 4:1; 5:1; 6:20; 7:1; 10:1).[38] Such a father-son motif is employed as "an illustration of how revelation is transmitted."[39] This wisdom-revelation pattern should be kept in mind when reading the Q passage quoted above, where the son's knowing of the father issues in the giving of revelations.[40] Thus the Abba experience denotes not only an immediate, direct experience of Jesus with God as his Father, but also the ensuing wisdom revelation that the Son, Jesus, receives from that experience. Such a direct experience of God as Abba is not meant to be limited to Jesus solely, for when requested to teach the disciples how to pray, Jesus instructs them in the "Our Father."

Paul sees the experience of God as Abba as being moved by the spirit, and thus as constituting the understanding of the wisdom of God. In Romans 8:14–15 we read: "Everyone moved by the spirit is a son of God. The spirit you received is not the spirit of slaves bringing fear into your lives again; it is the spirit of sons, and it makes us cry out, Abba, father." Galatians 4:6 adds: "The proof that you are sons is that God has sent the spirit of his son into our hearts: the spirit that cries, "Abba, father. . . ."

To be moved by such a spirit is to share the mind of Christ (1 Cor. 2:16) and to gain insight into the wisdom of God. The content of such wisdom is, then, that direct, immediate experience of God as Abba. Such a direct, immediate awareness of God as Abba constitutes a Christian understanding of the mystery of Yahweh's silence. Yahweh is silent to the mind of worldly wisdom, but directly present to the mind formed after the image of Christ. But it is far from perfectly clear just how that experience of God as Abba can alleviate the ever-present reality of suffering and dying. For this we turn to Paul's theology of the cross.

The Theology of the Cross

With the first tier of his wisdom sermon in 1 Corinthians, Paul contrasts verbal wisdom (*sophia logou*), not with the wisdom of God (*sophia tou theou*), but with the word of the cross (*ho logos tou staurou*; 1:18). He does not describe in any detail the meaning of "the word of the cross," and even in the second tier of his sermon from 2:6 he discourses on the wisdom of God without offering any exposition of the cross. For the meaning of Christ crucified is "not taught in learned words of human wisdom, but in the teaching of the spirit" (1 Cor. 2:13).

It would seem then that the impact of Paul's contrast between the word of the cross and worldly wisdom lies in the plain fact of the cross, namely, in the death of Christ. In the face of the Corinthian factions, who each boasted of having the correct standpoint, Paul counterposes as paradigmatic the death of Christ, for all boasting consciousness and clinging to standpoints dissolve with the final dissolution of self-consciousness at death. As long as human consciousness operates in boasting reliance on its supposed ability to validate a final standpoint, that is, a way of salvation, Paul perforce must express the wisdom of God as the negation of such consciousness, namely, as the word of the cross. It is thus that this word of the cross is an obstacle (*skandalon*) and madness (*mōria*), for the death of Christ is "the destruction of every attempt to regard a Weltanschauung as the way of salvation,"[41] to regard worldly consciousness as grasping salvation. Awareness of life as life unto death leaves no room for boasting or pride. The consciousness of Jesus as reported in the Gospels is not one that boasts in the Abba experience, but one that anticipates none too readily the experience of suffering and dying.

The Gethsemane experience of Jesus highlights both the persistence of the Abba experience and the distress at the imminent prospect of dying:

> And a sudden fear came over him, and great distress. And he said to them, "My soul is sorrowful to the point of death. Wait here and keep awake." And going on a little further he threw himself on the ground and prayed that, if it were possible, this hour might pass him by. "Abba!" he said, "Everything is possible for you. Take this cup away

from me. But let it be as you, not I, would have it. . . . The spirit is willing, but the flesh is weak" [Mk. 14:34–39].

The great sorrow and distress occasioned by the awareness of imminent dying is not transposed to some supernatural plane, for Jesus, just as Qoheleth before him, tasted the fear and apprehension of anyone in the face of death. It is hard to find any other interpretation of his prayer that "this cup" might pass him by. He prays that if it be possible, he might be saved from dying. Such is the desire of the weak flesh, the flesh that is always concerned with its own self-preservation. But even in the midst of such distress and fear, Jesus still prays to God as Abba. His experience of God as his father remains even in the face of the certain coming of suffering and dying. Jesus' response, "let it be as you, not I, would have it," means that in Jesus, as the Gospel writers remember him, self-centered, fleshly consciousness is overcome by awareness of God's wisdom in mystery, by self-sacrificing consciousness. God is not to be expected to save one from suffering and dying, for God is not at the service of self-preservation. Wisdom consciousness does not answer the question of Qoheleth and Job by alleviating or delivering one from dying. Rather, by shifting consciousness into a realm of self-negating love, it enables one to leave off the clinging to the flesh, the boasting of life, the self-centeredness of pride.

That this consciousness of Jesus is paradigmatic is shown by 2 Corinthians 5:12ff. Paul here presents himself to the Corinthians so that they "will have an answer ready for the people who boast in appearances and not in [what they understand] in their hearts." Again the contrast is between worldly wisdom that grasps what merely seems to be so and the faith understanding that takes to heart the death of Christ. The reason for this death is explained:

> The love of Christ overwhelms us when we reflect if one has died for all, then all are dead. And he died for all so that living men should no longer live for themselves, but for him who died and was raised to life for them [2 Cor 5:14–16].

If Christ died for all, then the Christian should realize that death is indeed organic to Christian life and not to be regarded as the end of all meaning. The words "then all are dead" (*pantes apethanon*) mean that all have died to self-centered, boasting consciousness and no longer live for themselves (*heautois zōsin*). Thus to have the mind of Christ (1 Cor. 2:16) means not to expect that God will be the support for the flesh, for the worldly, bodily existence that lies at the center of human concerns. It means not to expect that God would rescue one from adversity, suffering, and anguish. Such is simply not the wisdom understanding of God; it is, rather, an imagined projection from human anguish that refuses to be converted away from self. It is the genesis of religious illusion. Despite the intimate awareness of God as Abba, no legion of angels did in fact arrive to deliver Jesus from the cross. The outcome of wisdom is, then, not the attainment of a long and prosperous life, as Job and his friends thought. After the abandonment of Christ on the cross, one could hardly expect any mighty acts of God to intervene in the sufferings of the living. It is the abandoning of such fleshly expectations and a shifting to a mystic realm of understanding that Paul demands, a realm in which anguished questioning and worry over the fate of the self is gradually transformed into a living for others in commitment to the practice of the rule of God in the world, namely, into "living for Christ who died and was raised for us."

Resurrection

It is in this context that the resurrection of Jesus is to be understood. The raising of Jesus is not "God's correction of the scandal of the cross."[42] The fundamental reality to which Christians gave expression when they proclaimed that Jesus had risen from the dead was that his Abba experience was not severed by dying.[43] Dying does not sever the immediacy and directness that characterize that awareness. The content of "the Christian resurrection vision (the Easter appearances) is a conversion to Jesus as the Christ, who now comes as the light of the world."[44] Only such a wisdom understanding can see the risen Jesus as transparent, as mirroring forth the Father, for he is the true light that enlightens all persons (Jn. 1:8). Jesus is not then a hero figure that has "come back into our world."[45] Nor does the fatherhood of God mean that Christ will protect us from all adversity. Such ideas spring not from faith, but from grasping signs in a self-centered manner.

Consequently, this wisdom understanding of the death and resurrection of Jesus provides little comfort to the self-justifying plea of a Job or to the self-centered depression of a Qoheleth. Neither is it a reaffirmation of the philosophic promise of Greek immortality, such as appeared in the book of Wisdom. Rather, it is an invitation to shift the context in which life unto death is understood and lived. It necessitates an awareness and acceptance of human finitude.

> The fact that Jesus became reconciled to this radical finitude, that in death he became reconciled with himself, with God, makes it clear to us that within the limits of our history redemption can never be achieved by some heroic transcending of our finitude, but only on a readiness to refuse within our own limits, that which can never be fulfilled in history.[46]

It is, I think, with some such understanding that Paul writes in 2 Corinthians 5:16–17: "From now onwards, therefore, we do not understand according to the flesh. Even if we knew Christ in the flesh, that is not how we know him now. And for anyone who is in Christ, there is a new creation; the old creation is gone, and now the new one is here." Understanding according to the flesh (*oidamen kata sarka*) is the worldly wisdom that would see Christ as a hero figure, as the empirical victor over the cross. To be in Christ (*en christō*) means that, not knowing him according to the flesh, Christ becomes the mirroring of Abba wisdom.[47]

CONCLUSION

The basic Christian experience and understanding of the meaning of Christ revolves upon the conversion from boasting consciousness to a mystic, direct, immediate experience of God as Abba, which, while not avoiding death but accepting radical finitude and the entire flow of changing conditions from birth to death, is not severed or rendered meaningless by that river of changes or by its consummation in dying. Ignatius of Antioch said that Christ is the word of God from silence.[48] But to verbal, worldly understanding, that silence remains, for all expectations of an intervening father-god who might take away human finitude and thus save us from suffering and dying are illusions.

It is this reversal of self-clinging consciousness that allowed God as Abba to be mirrored forth in Jesus and that elicited the New Testament identification of him with wisdom, the untarnished mirror of God's active power.

In this chapter we have focused upon the mystic understanding of the meaning of Christ as presented in a number of passages in the New Testament. However, the need to conceive and objectify that meaning precisely and express it clearly was indeed felt from the early times. Despite the fact that only in the mystic realm of understanding might one gain insight into Christ as the wisdom of God, human understanding is not limited to this realm alone. In the subsequent development of Christian thinking, questions for concise, theoretical understanding came more and more into focus and answers had to be more clearly formulated. The early Christian thinkers soon (one might say, almost immediately) began to construct theologies and started to express their understanding of faith in terms of available thought patterns. It is these patterns—with their implicit assumptions and explicit tenets—that prove troublesome in contemporary attempts to enunciate the meaning of Christ in the context of our world. In the second movement of this present endeavor, Buddhist thought will be enlisted precisely as an alternative to Greek philosophical theology and presented as better adapted to enunciate a mystic understanding of Christ: Abba, the cross, and the resurrection. But to suggest that the Greek forms of traditional Christian faith understanding are inadequate is not to reject them wholesale. It is, rather, to see theology itself as always embedded in its historical context and limited to its language base. One must then be familiar with the historically first developments of christology. Thus the next chapter will turn to a brief consideration of the beginning of that development and the consequent shift in the pattern of consciousness that it entailed.

3

Theoretical Insight
into the Meaning of Christ

The preceding chapter outlined the base experience of the early Christians as the direct, immediate experience of God as Abba, an experience that, modeled upon the pattern of Jesus, is not negated by dying and that transcends self-centered clinging to life. Such an experience moves in a mystic realm of meaning, wherein the meaning of Christ is appropriated and realized without necessarily being expressed in clear, logically consistent terms.

However, this does not imply that those early Christians were critically conscious of the meaning realm in which they functioned. Rather, like most people, they did not bother to distinguish one realm of meaning from another.[1] They passed their lives for the most part in an undifferentiated state of consciousness in which one does not distinguish practical, everyday commonsense meanings from theoretical meanings, nor either of these two from mystic meanings. Most Christians were neither professional religious nor educated philosophers and they felt no pressing need for a clear delineation of the meaning of what it means directly to experience God as Abba from theoretical attempts to unfold the meaning of that experience in language.

But as the early Christian thinkers found themselves more and more engaged in the Greek cultural milieu of reasoned argument and practiced rhetoric, the need for explicit theoretical development of their faith grew more pressing. Not only is it true that the Christians of the first few centuries had to defend themselves against both Jewish and pagan critics, but it is also true that, as the new religion became a more respectable option of cultured Gentiles, a number of Christians were themselves conversant with and nurtured by Greek philosophical thinking.[2] In order for them to understand and verbalize their Christian faith, they had to express it within the pattern of their philosophical mind-set.

THE ADOPTION OF GREEK THINKING AND ITS ENSUING PROBLEMATIC

This philosophic understanding of faith is aptly illustrated by the famed account of the conversion of Justin Martyr, who was converted before the year 132. In the stylized narrative of his conversion, Justin states that he had sought religious understanding from among the contending philosophies. Having found the Stoic, Peripatetic, and Pythagorean options lacking in meaning, he embraced Platonic thinking and found that "the perception of immaterial things quite overpowered me and the contemplation of ideas furnished my mind with wings."[3] But then he met a Christian old man who exposed the inadequacies of such Platonic thinking and converted him to faith in Christ. Justin describes the process:

> Straightway a flame was kindled in my soul, and a love of the prophets and of those men who are friends of Christ possessed me, and while revolving his (i.e., the old man's) words in my mind, I found this philosophy [of Christian faith] alone to be safe and profitable. Thus for this reason am I a philosopher.[4]

The development of philosophical, theoretical understanding of Christian faith was not, then, an alien element imposed from outside, but the organic search for understanding of philosophically minded Christians.

Such a theoretical endeavor focuses on how the various separate faith insights are related one to another and it attempts to express them in a logical, consistent fashion.[5] In order to do this, one must make use of a logical and consistent set of terms, namely, of a technical language. The only such language available was the language of Greek philosophy, for the biblical writers had evolved no consistent, technical set of terms for the theoretical expression of faith. It was thus that the Christian thinkers adopted, and where needed adapted, Greek patterns of thinking to understand and express their faith insight.[6] There were models to follow, for not only had the great Jewish theologian Philo of Alexandria reworked Greek patterns to express his deep faith awareness,[7] but even the author of the Epistle to the Colossians takes over and reinterprets themes derived from middle Platonic and Stoic sources.[8]

But this bifurcation of Christian understanding of theoretical meaning from the practical and mystic understanding of the gospel was not easily and smoothly achieved. It did create problems and tensions within Christian communities that are felt even today. In Christian theory, the focus shifts from the realization of grace and salvation in one's life to the clear enunciation of Christian insight in a logical and consistent fashion. But although such a bifurcation in the understanding of meaning was indeed taking place, there were apparently few, if any, who developed a critical understanding of meaning such as would facilitate the growth of faith in both mystic and theoretical realms of meaning. There were few who could identify the shift between the mystic, commonsense, and theoretical realms without unconscious bias. To thinkers like Tertullian (ca. 160–ca. 220), who, although himself a keen theoretical mind, yet saw no value in Greek philosophical inquiry, theoretical formulations were unnecessary and dangerous, for they transferred attention away from the living of the rule of faith to useless speculations.[9] Even as late as the Council of Chalcedon in 451 some Christian thinkers were still offering the rather anachronistic advice that words not found in the scriptures should not be used in formulating the faith.[10]

But because there was a shift in consciousness from the undifferentiated realm of mystic meaning embodied in the practice of the rule of God to that of the realm of theory, the criteria for Christian meaning began to differ. To the theoretician meaning consists in understanding the inner coherence of religious teachings one to another, whether that meaning is realized by anyone or not, while for the mystic thinker meaning occurs only in its realization and embodiment in practice. Eusebius of Caesarea (ca. 260–339) in his *Ecclesiastical History* reports a controversy between Apelles, who was not engaged in searching out theoretical meanings, and Rhodon, who regarded theorizing as essential to the role of a Christian teacher:

> [Apelles] was often refuted for his errors, which indeed made him say that we ought not to inquire too closely into doctrine, but that as everyone had believed so he should remain. For he declared that those who set their hopes on the Crucified One would be saved, if only they were found in good works. But the most uncertain thing of all that he said was what he said about God. He held no doubt that there was One Principle, just as we do too; but when I said to him, "Tell us how you demonstrate that, on what grounds you are able to assert that there is One Principle," . . . he said that he did not know, but that that was his conviction. When I thereupon abjured him to tell the truth, he said that he was telling the truth, that he did not know how there is one unbegotten God, but that, nevertheless, so he believed. Then I laughed at him and denounced him, for that, giving himself out to be a teacher, he did not know how to prove what he taught.[11]

In the theoretical realm of Rhodon, Apelles' focus upon practice and his neglect of argumentation simply fails to be respectable. Rhodon saw meaning attainable only within the theoretical realm of reasoned argument, for he suffered under a theoretical bias against other realms of meaning.

Clement of Alexandria (fl. 200), one of the Christian thinkers most open to Greek theoretical patterns of thought, ran up against the reluctance of less theoretical Christians and their commonsense bias against adopting

Greek philosophy and theorizing upon the meaning of faith.[12] He complains:

> I am not unaware of what is dinned into our ears by the ignorant timidity of those who tell us that we ought to occupy ourselves with the most necessary matters, those in which the faith consists, and that we should pass by the superfluous matters that lie outside them, which vex and detain us over points that contribute nothing to the end in view. There are others who think that philosophy will prove to have been introduced from an evil source at the hands of a mischievous inventor, for the ruin of men.[13]

The objection here recorded by Clement is that, since philosophic theory does not conduce to the end of salvation, but detains one from attaining that end, it is better abandoned. In a practical, commonsense realm of meaning, theory is simply beside the point of practice. In a mystic understanding of meaning, theory distracts the mind from direct, immediate insight. The failure of Clement's critics was their lack of understanding of just what theory is all about, for if the task of theoretical thinking on faith is to evolve and enunciate a logical and consistent understanding of faith, then it is not germane to reject it because it does not lead to salvation. These dilemmas were caused by the fact that both the critics and the theoreticians were not themselves aware of the different realms in which they understood meaning and were thus unable to distinguish clearly the exigency for theoretical understanding of the philosopher from the mystic exigency of the saint or the need for practical implementation of the commonsense believer.

Theoretical development of Christian thinking is not, then, a total abandonment of the gospel, as claimed by some,[14] not a unilinear growth from the gospel, as claimed by others.[15] It is, rather, an organic growth from the basically mystic gospel experience, shifted into the developing content of Christian theory. Its continuity comes from that base experience, which is the source and the center from which Christian thinkers thought. Its difference is a shifting of realms, and the consequent shifting in the understanding of just what constitutes meaning.

These theoretical attempts to understand the meaning of Christ focus upon the meaning of Christ as both God and human, and the parallel meaning of God as somehow including both Christ and the Spirit. The ensuing christology and trinitarian thought constitute the traditional pattern of Western theology and serve as a counterfoil for the Mahāyāna theology to be presented in part II of this volume. Thus we turn briefly to a sketch of the main lines of the development of the doctrines of Incarnation and Trinity. But one must first understand the conceptual and terminological background of that development.

THE CONCEPTUAL FORM OF THE DEVELOPING
ARGUMENTATION

The development of the doctrine of Christ as both divine and human was structured by the conceptual understanding of just what is meant by God and what is meant by human, for both poles have to be understood in such a fashion that they could be simultaneously applied to the same Christ.

The early Christians were heirs of the scriptural traditions and were at home with an awareness of God as Yahweh, revealed as Abba in the life and death of Christ. They were conversant with the association of wisdom with Yahweh and knew the identification of Christ as the wisdom of God. But those notions were not easily transferred into the emerging theoretical enunciation of doctrine, for they focused not on what God is, but rather, on how God acts in relationship to humans. However, a well-developed pagan Greek theology of God had already been evolved and was ready at hand for Christian use. It was easy and apparently unobjectionable for Christians to adopt the Greek notion of God as unoriginated and impassible being, such as expressed by Plutarch (b. ca. 45 C.E.) or Maximus of Tyre (ca. 180 C.E.),[16] and this idea of God became the starting point for understanding the theoretical meaning of the divine. Such ideas, themselves the results of a long philosophic process of demythologizing the ancient Greek myths, were attractive to Christian thinkers, for they did represent well-developed theory free from anthropomorphic imaginings. Thus in the evolution of Christian doctrine it was quite natural that those ideas of God came to serve as one pole for understanding Christ as both God and human. If Christ be God, then Christ is to be identified with unoriginated, impassible being.

As impassible and unoriginated,[17] Christ must be somehow free from and beyond the change and suffering of the created world. The problem, of course, is that Christ did indeed act like a human being with all the constant change and suffering that that implies, that Christ did actually suffer and die, as recorded in the New Testament scriptures.

The other pole of Christology was the question of just what constitutes a human being. But, while the Greek philosophical theology on God as unoriginated and impassible being permeated the Mediterranean basin, there was no parallel anthropological consensus. Gnostic sects, basing themselves on middle Platonic themes, understood the human as possessing an incorruptible soul that had fallen into matter, but which still united the person with the higher realms, and thus salvation consisted in awakening to this "true" self and regaining those higher realms.[18] Such anthropological patterns were adopted and adapted by some Christians, who then tended to see Christ as the first emanation from God in the descent of matter from the One. It was perhaps because of the influence of such anthropological ideas of the soul that early Christian thinkers were hesitant to emphasize, or even admit, that Christ had a human soul, lest that be taken to mean that Christ was an emanation in some Gnostic sense. They also tended to deny that the human soul was immortal. Rather, immortality was conferred upon the soul by God as a result of a life of faith.[19]

The principal alternate understanding of what constituted the human being was that offered by Aristotle, who attempted to define all things by identifying their genus and species. A human being, he taught, was a rational animal,[20] and the soul was the rational form that determined what he or she was. In this understanding, the soul is not a link to the higher realms, but the principle of human activity. It was this notion that eventually came to be dominant in the Christological discussion, and Christ was understood as a human being with both body and soul.

While it is true that the doctrine of the Trinity developed in tandem with that of the Incarnation, there was no parallel conceptual philosophic framework that could be adapted for use in expressing this faith awareness. In treating the question of the divine and the human in Christ, the church fathers had at their disposal fairly well-defined ideas about God and about the human being. But the evolution of the doctrine of God as three in one found no such conceptual or linguistic underpinnings, for indeed the Greek philosophers had developed their idea of the unoriginated, unmitigated essence of God specifically to transcend any idea of divine multiplicity.

In their understanding of God as three in one, the fathers had to work up a new conceptual and terminological apparatus, and the history of that process is often a history of refining the meaning of the terms used and excluding unwanted connotations.

Most of the principal terms used did not have any extended history in Greek philosophy. Neither *hupostasis* nor *prosōpon* were well-defined philosophical terms. Although the term *ousia* was a common one in Greek thinking in the sense of "being" or "essence," its application to the essence of God as one rather than three had to be worked out by the Christians.

However, this lack of philosophic conceptual and linguistic underpinnings for the expression of the Christian doctrine of the Trinity does not mean that the Greek Christian thinkers proceeded in a cultural vacuum. It was not the awareness of God as Abba, but the idea of the unmitigated, unoriginated essence of God that formed the unquestioned standard against which the enunciation of the distinctness of the three had to be measured. And the ontological thrust of Greek thinking that attempted to identify the real, objective content of each idea and each term was very much at play, as is apparent in the course of that evolution.

THE CONTENT OF CHRISTOLOGY

The development of Christological thinking in the first centuries of the church does indeed reflect the faith of believing Christians. Even in offering a Mahāyāna alternative to this theology, one should not denigrate it or fail to appreciate its appropriateness within its particular linguistic and cultural context. If it is to be left behind, that is because the context has shifted. And if new theologies are to be developed, they must understand its import and rethink its basic themes in new languages. No one can develop a Christology without being familiar with the early traditions, however much one might try to go beyond them.

The insistence that Christ must somehow be understood as both God and human echoes the base experience of Jesus as opening up God to humans. If Jesus were not in some sense divine, then how could such a revelation be possible? And if he were not human, then how could such an experience be relevant to human beings? The ebb and flow of the argumentation in its excluding of options that negated either pole makes sense only when seen in the light of this base experience of Christian faith, the awareness of Abba through Jesus. How could one express the content of that experience in clear, consistent, logical language?

The basic theme is presented in the antithetical, two-membered formula of Ignatius of Antioch (d. ca. 107). In his Epistle to the Ephesians, he describes "Jesus Christ, our Lord" as:

both fleshy	and spiritual
begotten	and unbegotten
having come into flesh	and God
[experiencing] death	and true life
both from Mary	and from God
the first to suffer	and yet impassible.[21]

Such an antithetical description echoes the descriptions of Jesus in scripture and tradition, which attribute both divine and human qualities to Jesus. And yet, such an explanation was clearly open to the criticism that it was simply contradictory.[22] Such a criticism was leveled at the Christians by Celsus, who argued that "either God really changes himself, as they say, into a mortal body, . . . or he is not changed, but makes those who see him think that he is so changed. But in that case he is a deceiver and a liar."[23] The attempts of Christians to respond to such criticism formed a kind of acrobatic balancing act in which constant readjustments were performed to avoid leaning too far to one side or the other.

One such leaning was in the direction of emphasizing the humanness of Christ to such a point that the divinity was negated. Paul of Samosata (d. after 268) is the most extreme example of such a tendency, for he solved the dilemma by stating that Christ was a "mere man." But such a solution found no resonance within the consciousness of most Christians, accustomed to regarding Jesus as in some sense embodying divine wisdom and power.

Other explanations that seemed to do more justice to the basic tenet of

Christian experience that Christ was more than human, did safeguard monotheism, but diminished Christ's transcendence in regard to the Father. Justin's *logos*, while divine, was not quite as divine as the Father.[24] Some thinkers, such as Origen,[25] were inclined toward various middle Platonic theories of a descending order of emanations from the One Ultimate, for that provided a background pattern that could and was employed as a framework for interpreting Christ as somehow divine and yet not as fully divine as the Father.

This teaching, which subordinated the Logos, namely, Christ, to the Father, was taken to its final development by Arius (d. ca. 336), a priest from Alexandria. Athanasius reports the Arian position as follows: "If he (the Logos) was very God, how could he become man? . . . How dare you say that the Logos shares in the Father's existence, if he had a body so as to experience all this!"[26] At the base of such an objection is a clear grasp of the philosophical notion of God as unoriginated and unborn. Only God is the "one and only, is without beginning and utterly one," but God became "two" with the creation of the Logos. As Pelikan explains, "God in his transcendent being had to be kept aloof from any involvement with the world of becoming. His 'unoriginated and unmitigated essence' transcended the realm of created and changeable things so totally that there was not and ontologically could not be, a direct point of contact between them."[27] Thus the Son had to be a creature (*ktisma*), although created before the constitution of the world. Identifying the Logos with God's wisdom, Proverbs 8:22–31 is cited as the proof text, for it says that Yahweh created wisdom before the ages. Yet although apparently in harmony with the wisdom tradition, this Arian teaching was excluded at the Council of Nicea in 325 by its creedal definition of the Son as *homoousios*, that is, "of the same substance" with the Father.[28]

It was not sufficient to regard Christ as the first among creatures, and the council fathers adopted the language of Greek philosophy in order to negate this option. As Maurice Wiles explains, Athanasius (d. 373), in his argumentation with the Arians, insists "that the root of the Arian error lies in the replacement of the scriptural idea of God as Father with the philosophical idea of God as unoriginated being (essence)."[29] It is the Arians, therefore, Wiles argues, "who made necessary the Church's use of the nonscriptural term *homoousios*. . . ."[30] It seems unfair to single out Arius for this use of nonscriptural terminology, since many more orthodox thinkers were engaged in like pursuits, yet it does appear that in bringing the base idea of God as unoriginated, unchangeable essence to its logical conclusion, Arius did force the fathers of Nicea to both adopt and adapt Greek terminology in their formulation of the *homoousios*. Furthermore, by bolstering their argumentation with appeals to the wisdom themes of the Old Testament, the Arians placed those themes further from the sphere of orthodox discussion and coerced Christian thinkers to reinterpret its content in terms of the essential categories of Greek philosophy.

Thus the contrasting tendency leaned to the side of stressing the divinity of Christ to the point where one approached Celsus' notion that God only *seemed* to become human. As Pelikan notes, "the existence of docetism [that God only seemed to become man] is also a testimony to the tenacity that Christ has to be God, even at the cost of his humanity."[31]

This line of Christology tended to negate the presence of human consciousness in Christ. The divine "descended into the flesh of the Lord," in the words of Clement of Alexandria.[32] It is the divine Logos that is the dynamic center (*hēgemonikon*) of Christ's thinking and acting, and little room is left for human feeling or activity. Being divine, Christ is thus impassible. The picture of Christ that emerges is rather ethereal, for the Logos so transformed the body of Christ that no true digestion or elimination of food took place.[33] Such docetizing tendencies could indeed lead to Celsus' conclusion that, if God actually did become human, God only seemed to do so — and thus God is a deceiver.

Aloys Grillmeier explains that, in contrast to the Arians and the followers of Paul of Samosata, Christian thinkers began to focus all the more on a Logos-sarx theme, the main feature of which was to bring the divine Logos into direct, immediate contact with the flesh (*sarx*) of Christ, thus downplaying the need or importance of a human soul or human consciousness in Christ.[34] After Nicea this trend, already present in such thinkers as Clement of Alexandria, mentioned above, came more and more to the forefront. In contrast to the subordinatist and Arian errors, thinkers such as Eusebius of Caesarea (d. ca. 340) held that the Logos, who has neither body nor soul, takes on the flesh of Christ as an instrument and vehicle of the indwelling Logos.[35]

The intent of such thinkers was to protect the notion of divine impassibility against Arius who thought that the Logos, being a creature, could experience change and suffering. To do this they had to downplay the human consciousness of Christ, especially the experience of suffering, and emphasize the divine subject who assumed human flesh.

The *Pseudo-Ignatian Epistles* point out the options clearly.[36] One must choose either the option that "Christ is the true union of Logos and sarx," without a human soul, or that "he is a mere man," in whom God dwells. In the philosophic context focused on the definition of essences, no other option seemed possible. The greatest orthodox exponent of this Logos-sarx theory was probably Athanasius (d. 373). As Grillmeier explains, "the soul of Christ plays no part in his explanation . . . and is not a factor in the inner life of Christ."[37] Athanasius sees the Logos as the life-giving force of the entire cosmos. Thus there is no problem for the Logos to give life to the body of Christ, which is, after all, a part of the cosmos. When forced to explain the scriptural passages that treat of Christ's sufferings or of his human experiences, Athanasius essays to explain them away. Christ's anguish was "feigned," Christ's ignorance was not actually ignorance. The

Logos merely uses the body as an instrument (*organon*),[38] and there is no active center of human experience in Christ.

Just as Arius took the previous subordinatist ideas to their logical conclusion that the Logos was a creature, so Apollinaris (d. ca. 390), bishop of Laodicea, took this Logos-sarx pattern of thinking to its logical conclusion that in Christ there was only one nature (*mia phusis*), namely, the one self-determining divine being who in a vitalistic dynamism uses the body merely as its instrument.[39] With Apollinaris, the Logos-sarx pattern runs its course. It did maintain the unity of the person of Jesus by making the divine Logos the subject of all the actions and experiences of Jesus. But, in this explanation, rather than becoming a person, the Logos is understood to have taken up a body. The humanness of Christ is driven back and ignored. Consequently, this understanding of Christ failed to win approval by Christian theologians.

Thus Apollinaris stands at the end of a Christological tradition.[40] After him, Christian thinkers had to consider not only the danger of the Arian notion that Christ was a creature, but also Apollinaris' idea that Christ was simply the divine Logos in a body. These two opposing concepts formed the parameters within which the fathers had to evolve an understanding of Christ as *homoousios* with the divine Father and as *homoousios* with human beings.

With the eclipse of Apollinaris' teaching it became the general trend to recognize that Christ was a fully human being with a human soul.[41] Having focused on the reality of both the divine and the human in Christ, the question moved to a consideration of the manner in which that might be understood. The Logos-sarx framework, which tended to overlook or omit human consciousness in Christ, gave way to a Logos-anthropos (man) framework in which Christ is affirmed to be fully God and fully human. But again the voice of Celsus can be heard, for how can the impassible divine nature become human?

The problem was especially difficult because the conceptual framework defined the terms "divine" and "human" in opposition to each other. The essence of divinity was that which is unoriginated and unchangeable, while the essence of humanity denoted that which is subject to change and has an origin. The attempts to understand just how Christ can be both unchangeable and impassible God and human, with body and soul, subject to both change and suffering, engaged an array of thinkers. In broad, oversimplified outline, those associated with the Alexandrian center tended to emphasize the unity of Christ, the divine subject in all his actions, while the Antiochene thinkers focused on the distinctive humanness of those actions. The ensuing theological argumentation functioned within the parameters established by the condemnation of both Arian and Apollinarian thinking, but at times it all but burst those limits to follow the logic of one side or the other. Often, thinkers were criticized not for what they had actually said, but for where their ideas were perceived logically to lead.

The principal Antiochene thinker, Theodore of Mopsuesta (d. 428), in attempting to treat the question, evolved a "theology of the indwelling Logos." As Pelikan explains, "the theology of the indwelling Logos may be defined as an interpretation of the relation between the divine and the human in Jesus Christ that sought to preserve the distinction between their union as the indwelling of the Logos in a man whom he has assumed."[42] Theodore himself describes his thinking as follows: "This one (i.e., Christ) we understand to be one Lord who is of the divine nature of God the Father, who for our salvation put on a man in whom he dwelt and through whom he appeared and became known to mankind."[43] Theodore rejects the notion that the dynamic center (*hēgemon*) of Christ is the Logos and asserts that Christ had assumed a complete human, body and soul. As Grillmeier aptly states, "the human nature of Christ regains its real physical human inner life and its capacity for action."[44]

But although Theodore stresses the distinction between the divine and the human in Christ and focuses on Christ's human experience, yet Theodore had at his disposal no adequate tools, either linguistic or conceptual, to deal with the unity of the person of Christ. His teaching could be and indeed was interpreted to mean that the Logos has assumed an already self-sufficient man. Such a judgment equates Theodore's ideas with adoptionism, the theory that the Logos had not really become incarnate, but simply adopted an already existing man.

In contrast, Cyril of Alexandria (d. 444) stressed the unity of the divine subject. He did accept some of the formulations of Apollinarianism, but corrected them by insisting on the centrality of the soul of Christ. In the main, Cyril, and the Alexandrian theology in general, focused upon the divinity of Christ, while making various attempts to maintain an adequate explanation of Christ's humanity. As Grillmeier explains, "God did not come into a man (as the theology of the indwelling Logos implied), but he truly became man, while remaining God."[45] However, as Cyril adheres to the "one nature" (*mia phusis*) formula of Apollinaris, he did have problems in explaining the distinction between the divine and the human in Christ. With Cyril, Christ maintains this unity, but tends to be seen as rather more than human and aloof.

Nestorius (d. 451), bishop of Constantinople and proponent of the Antiochene line of thought, enters the scene when, seeking to play a peacekeeping role over the dispute on the propriety of the use of the term *theotokos* (God-bearing), as applied to the Virgin Mary, he questioned not only the correctness of this phrase, but also of the term "suffering God" that was being applied to Christ.[46] He further criticized the theology of Cyril and his followers, called it Apollinarianism, and attacked the Alexandrian notion of the sharing of qualities (*communicatio idiomatum*), which was used by Cyril to explain how the attributes of both divinity and humanity could be applied to the one Christ, and which served as the underlying principle for the use of the terms "God-bearing" and "suffering God."

But again Nestorius could not explain just how the human is united with the divine in Christ so as to be one subject and avoid a kind of schizoid picture of the Lord.

With the *Tome to Flavian* of Pope Leo (d. 461), bishop of Rome, the central insight that led to the Chalcedonian resolution of these questions was finally reached. Previously the terms of the argumentation—*prosōpon, hupostatis,* and *phusis*—had been used quite interchangeably to refer to the essence or nature of Christ. But Leo assigned them more exact meanings and differentiated nature from person in Christ. The distinction of the divine and the human in Christ was explained as taking place on the level of the two natures, while the unity of subject was found on the level of person. Leo interprets the word *prosōpon*, which had meant "countenance" or "manifestation,"[47] and the word *hupostatis*, which had meant "substance," to refer to the person of Christ, while reserving the word *phusis* to refer to the two natures. Thus unity is not sought in the sphere of nature, while diversity is not sought in the sphere of person. The divine and the human can then be distinguished in terms of nature, while the unity of subject can be found in the sameness of the person.

The Council of Chalcedon in 451 united Cyril's insistence on unity in Christ with Leo's insight and terminology to define the "being" of Christ as one person in two natures: *hen prosōpon, mia hupostasis en duo phusesin.*[48] Chalcedon did not further define the terms it used, but remained content with stating that the Logos is one and the same (*eis kai ho autos*) in both natures. The end result is a summation statement of the foregoing theology, a somewhat precarious balancing act in both doctrine and language, which set the pattern for subsequent christology.

The influence of the conceptual form of the argumentation was immense in the outcome of this theologizing. Grillmeier writes that the driving force of pagan philosophy "has important consequences for christology: the economy of salvation was impregnated more and more with a static-ontological awareness of the reality of Christ as God and man."[49] And Pelikan, much to the same point, writes:

> As the Son and Logos of God, Christ was the revelation of the nature of God; in the formula of Irenaeus, "the Father is that which is invisible about the Son, the Son is that which is visible about the Father." If, in a phrase that Ireneaus quoted from an even earlier source, "the Son is the measure of the Father," one would expect that the Christian definition of the deity of God would be regulated by the content of the divine as revealed in Christ. In fact, however, the early Christian picture of God was controlled by the self-evident axiom, accepted by all, of the absoluteness and impassibility of the divine nature. Nowhere in all of Christian doctrine was that axiom more influential than in christology, with the result that the content

of the divine as revealed in Christ was itself regulated by the axiomatically given definition of the deity of God.[50]

However, it is not surprising that the early Christian thinkers did not use the biblical notion of God as Abba, as revealed by Jesus, for that notion moved in a mystic realm and it was not clear just how such a mystic meaning could be put into service in the development of theoretical theology. One should not wonder then that the argumentation on christology seems more like a philosophical disquisition than a gospel statement. Indeed, that is just what it was!

THE THEORETICAL UNDERSTANDING OF THE TRINITY

Having recognized the divinity of Christ, Christians were faced with an apparent denial of the oneness of God. If God is one, then how could their experience of Jesus as Lord, as ultimate, be understood? The attempts to interpret the Logos-Christ as subordinate to the Father or as a creature were motivated by an intense awareness that there simply could not be two Gods. Thus the problematic for a Christian understanding of God was evoked precisely from the recognition of Christ as divine, as *homoousios* with the Father.

The explicit recognition of the divinity of the Spirit lagged far behind that of the Son,[51] although in the nontheoretical life of the church that divinity was surely accepted. But as late as 380, Gregory of Nanzianzus records a wide variety of theories on the status of the Spirit.[52] Some think that the Spirit is a force, some that it is a creature, and some that it is God.[53] The full theoretical recognition of the Spirit as divine seems to have become explicit with Athanasius' refutation of the notion of the Spirit as creature, a tenet propounded by a group of Egyptian exegetes, the Tropici.[54] In his *Epistle to Seraphion* (ca. 360) he argues that we must affirm

the Spirit's divinity from the fact that He makes us all partakers of God. If the Holy Spirit were a creature, we should have no participation in God through him; we should be united to a creature and alien from the divine nature. . . . If he does make men divine, His nature must undoubtedly be that of God.[55]

The consubstantiality of the Spirit came to be explicitly affirmed at the Council of Constantinople in the year 381.[56] But the problematic of a diversity in God did not await this explicit formulation of the divine nature of the Spirit. As Canon Prestige explains: . . .

if the godhead was not unitary, it was as simple to conceive of three Persons as of two; hence the deity of Christ carried the weight of Trinitarian controversies without any necessity for extending the range of dispute, and as a matter of history, the settlement of the problem connected with the Father and the Son was found to lead to an immediate solution of the whole Trinitarian difficulty.[57]

In developing their thinking, the fathers had to avoid two extremes. Any explanation that there were three Gods was recognized as absurd and in principle rejected by all. Any explanation that denied that in some sense God was really three ran counter to the Christian experience that Jesus and the Spirit were indeed ultimate. Within the parameters of these two poles evolved the orthodox understanding of God as One in Three.

No one explicitly affirmed the first alternative that there were actually three Gods. Charges of tritheism were leveled at this or that thinker not because of explicit statements, but rather because his teaching was understood logically to imply tritheism. Thus the history of the evolution of Trinitarian thought is occupied for the most part with the rejection of theories that tended to negate the threeness of God.

The early pre-Nicene fathers, focusing on the affirmation of monotheism, thought of the Trinity on the analogy of a single Father, who is one God, together with his rationality, the Logos, and his wisdom, the Spirit.[58] They gave much attention to the divine plane or dispensation (i.e., the divine economy, *oikonomia*)[59] whereby the Father, Son, and Spirit became manifest in the world, and thus their thinking is termed "economic Trinitarianism."[60] But this kind of economic trinitarian thought subordinated the Son and Spirit to functions of the Father, much as a man's rationality and wisdom are functions of the man. Furthermore, even the presentation of such distinct manifestations of Father, Son, and Spirit in the dispensation (economy) of salvation led to the fear among some that the oneness of God was being threatened. Thus there arose the current of thought known as monarchianism, which stressed the one divine principle (*monarchia*).[61] "Son" and "Spirit" were merely names for the One Father principle manifested differently in the economy.[62]

This teaching came to its most developed form in Sabellius (ca. 217) who is reported to have termed the Godhead "Sonfather" (*huiopatōr*), that is, the one God is either Son or Father depending upon the mode of presentation.[63] The one God is simply manifested in three different manners.

It was in contrast to such teaching that the orthodox understanding of Trinity was evolved. The principal need for the enunciation of the orthodox faith was the development of concepts and terms that allowed for an affirmation of God as three, while yet adhering to the oneness of God. Although there are a number of instances where the term *ousia* was used by the fathers to refer to the three, its semantic range was gradually restricted to denote the oneness of God. The main task was then to find conceptual terms for the three. Two terms were evolved, *hupostasis* and *prosōpon*.

In its nontrinitarian usage, *hupostasis* is sometimes synonymous with *ousia*, and means simply the nature or the essence of a thing (as in the christological definition at Chalcedon). But this is not its meaning in the trinitarian evolution. The term derived from the verb *huphistēmi*, which means "that which underlies," or "that which gives support."[64] In its non-theological use, it means the basic foundation or the underlying substance of something and thus is often equivalent to *ousia* as meaning simply the "being" of a thing. But the meaning of *hupostasis* in this debate does differ from *ousia*. As Canon Prestige explains:

> ... there was, however, another and a much more frequent use of *hupostasis*, in which the emphasis was different. It is important to remember that this second is the normal usage. *Ousia* means a single object of which the individuality is disclosed by means of an internal analysis, an object abstractly or philosophically a unit. But in the sense of *hupostasis* to which we shall now turn, the emphasis lay not on content, but on external concrete independence: objectivity, that is to say, in relation to other objects. Thus, when the doctrine of the Trinity finally came to be formulated as one *ousia* in three *hupostaseis*, it implied that God, regarded from the point of view of internal analysis, is one object; but that regarded from the point of view of external presentation, He is three objects; His unity being safeguarded by the doctrine that these three objects of presentation are ... identically one.[65]

Thus such thinkers as Tertullian and Hippolytus (d. ca. 236) understood God, as existing in eternal being, to be a unity, and saw the Father, Son, and Spirit as one in *ousia*. But as God is revealed in the "economy" or the unfolding plan of the saving Incarnation, there are the distinct *hupostaseis* of Father, Son, and Spirit.[66]

Prestige continues, "both *hupostasis* and *ousia* describe positive, substantial existence, that which is, that which subsists; *to on, to huphestēkos*. But *ousia* tends to regard internal characteristics and relations, or metaphysical reality; while *hupostasis* regularly emphasizes the external concrete character, or empirical objectivity."[67] And so God, one in *ousia*, is presented as a triple objective reality. Being one in *ousia*, Son and Spirit are not functions or modes of the Father, for all are equally the same divine *ousia*, and thus modalism is excluded. But, in line with the Christian experience of ultimacy in Jesus and the Spirit, they are termed *hupostaseis* to emphasize the reality of their objective givenness.

The term *prosōpon* was used with much the same meaning. Originally meaning "face" or "external expression," it came to express "the external being or individual as presented to the onlooker," and it comes to mean simply the concrete individuality of presentation.[68] In trinitarian thinking it thus means "the permanent and objective forms or Persons in which the godhead is presented to human vision."[69] It is this meaning of *prosōpon* that is intended in the Latin term *persona*. This word must not be taken to mean a person in the modern notion of a self-conscious individual. While it is true that in the Latin West, the threeness of God was understood as subjective rather than as objective presentation, yet this does not mean that such subjects are each possessed of self-consciousness. For the Greek Fathers, divine consciousness is always to be found in the *ousia*, in the unitary being of God.[70] As J. N. D. Kelly clearly explains, the Greek notion of *prosōpon* has no connotation of "the idea of self-consciousness nowadays associated with 'person' and 'personal.' "[71]

The key to understanding this doctrine of one *ousia* in three *hupostaseis*, aptly expressed by Kelly in his discussion of Hippolytus and Tertullian, "is to approach it simultaneously from two opposite directions, considering God (a) as He exists in His eternal being and (b) as He reveals Himself in the process of creation and redemption."[72] In God's eternal being, the Father, Son, and Spirit are one in *ousia*. But, as revealed in the economy, there are the distinct objective presentations of Father, Son, and Spirit expressed by the term *hupostaseis* or *prosōpon*.[73]

The classical formulation of trinitarian thinking was achieved by the Cappadocians in the East and Augustine (d. 430) in the West. The base notion is that the one God exists in three objective presentations. These three objective presentations are understood by Basil to be paternity, sonship, and sanctification.[74]

The term used by Basil to express the individual characteristics of the three objective presentations of the one God was "identifying particularities, *gnōristikai idiotētes*."[75] The identifying particularity for the Father is being unbegotten, for the Son is being begotten, and for the Spirit is procession, for the Spirit comes forth from the Father through the Son. These are modes of being, whereby the Three possess the same one *ousia*. Later theology called them *idiotētes hupostatikai*, hypostatic particularities.[76] Pseudo-Cyril in his *De Sacrosancta Trinitate*, says that "in these hypostatic particularities [of being unbegotten, being begotten, and proceeding] alone do the three *hupostaseis* differ from one another."[77] Inasmuch as these particularities represent modes whereby the *hupostaseis* exist as the one *ousia*, they are also termed "modes of existence," *tropos huparzeōs*. The Father's mode of existence is the distinctly objective presentation of the one divine essence as unbegotten. The Son's mode of existence is the distinctly objective presentation of that same one divine *ousia* as begotten. And the Spirit's mode of existence is the distinctly objective presentation of the same one divine essence as processing from the Father through the Son.

Pseudo-Cyril takes this development a step further in his formulation of the notion of the co-inherence (*perichōrēsis*) of the divine *hupostaseis* in one another. The term *perichōreo* implies "an interchange produced by the revolution of cycles."[78] Its application to the divine *hupostaseis* means that Father, Son, and Spirit co-inhere in one another and are coterminous and coextensive in the one divine *ousia*, thus emphasizing again the Christian doctrine of the Trinity as one God presented in three distinct but mutually coextensive embodiments.

This same emphasis is seen in the thought of Augustine in the Latin West. In contrast to the Greek Eastern fathers, who began their treatment of the Trinity with the Father, he starts his presentation of the Trinity with the divine, immutable essence of the Godhead. He then attempts to explain the three in terms of the particular manner in which they possess that essence. The distinction between the persons is found in their mutual relationships within the Godhead. As Kelly explains:

> ... the question then arises what in fact the three are. Augustine recognizes that they are traditionally designated Persons, but is clearly unhappy about the term; probably it conveyed the suggestion of separate individuals to him. If in the end he consents to adopt the current usage, it is because of the necessity of affirming the distinctions of the Three against Modalistic Monarchanism, and with a deep sense of the inadequacy of human language. His own position was the original and, for the history of Western Trinitarianism, highly important one that the Three are real or subsistent relations.[79]

This is expressed later by Anselm, bishop of Canterbury (d. 1109), by stating that in the Trinity everything is one, except where there is relative opposition.[80] This speculative theology in the West reached its apogee in Thomas Aquinas (d. 1274), from whom the main lines of trinitarian thought were inherited by later Western theologians.[81]

THE QUESTION OF HELLENIZATION

These brief sketches of the development of christological and trinitarian thinking, culled in the main from modern scholars, principally Jaroslav Pelikan, J. N. D. Kelly, Aloys Grillmeier, and G. L. Prestige, highlight the theoretical nature of Christian theoretical understanding of the meaning of Christ and they are presented here to furnish some idea of the historical background from which a few tentative conclusions may be drawn.

The first of these conclusions, although obvious, is that these developments do indeed occur in the content of theoretical meaning. They constitute, in the words of Canon Prestige, "an inspired Christian rationalism."[82] The objective was to present a clear, logical, consistent enunciation of the basic tenets of Christian faith. It is then simply beside the point to fault this development for being theoretical or "metaphysical," for that was its aim. It is culturally biased to decry such theorizing as a "Hellenization" of the gospel, for how else would the gospel be received and interpreted by cultured Greeks? The only other option would be to forbid people in non-biblical cultural contexts from thinking upon faith in terms of their culture.

However, this does not mean that the pattern of Greek thinking evinced in these developments is the only pattern capable of expressing Christian faith theoretically, and in the following attempt to develop a Mahāyāna theology this entire conceptual pattern will be abandoned. Greek philosophy, for all its glory, remains but one particular philosophic tradition in a world full of traditions. It can claim no exclusive privilege for interpreting Christian faith, or for that matter, anything else. The concepts of nature, substance, essence, and person that determined the structure of this thinking are not present in all cultural contexts and when they are, they are often negated as philosophical errors. A naïve claim for the universal validity of such philosophical notions ill serves either clear thinking or theological understanding.

The specific concepts that influenced the evolution above are open to further questioning and alternate understanding. The notion of God as impassible, unmitigated essence is indeed a well-developed and precise theoretical notion of divinity. The notion of a human being as body and soul represents the culmination of long reflection. But both notions come from within the ontological thrust of Greek thinking, from an understanding of meaning that seeks to identify clearly the content of each act of understanding with the essence of the being of something. As Wiles explains, the Greek framework "suggests an approach to theology in which its affirmations are regarded as descriptive accounts (albeit very imperfect accounts) of ultimate realities in the spiritual world. The fact that Patristic theology grew up against such a background gave to it an ontological urge and an ontological confidence which are both its glory and its weakness."[83] It is, he continues, this "tendency to objectification" that "can be seen as the source of a number of problems and difficulties we face today about early doctrinal formulation."[84] Such an understanding of meaning, implicit in most of Greek thought, obviously can make no claim to being either specifically Christian or particularly adapted to the enunciation of Christian teaching.

But, despite the fact that it is inappropriate to negate this philosophic evolution of Christian understanding for being theoretical, for being a "Hellenization," it does remain true that the mystic content of the Abba experience and the awareness of the Son and Spirit of the first Christians can scarcely be seen here at all. The examples quoted above from Eusebius and Clement show that the Christian theoreticians not uncommonly labored under their own theoretical bias. One not so inclined was unworthy to be called a teacher, as in the case of Apelles, or was to be dismissed as being superfluous or mischievous, as in the case of Clement's critics.

With such a bias, it is no surprise that the Christian theoreticians were unable and uninterested in evolving an understanding of understanding that could both understand and relate to one another the various realms of meaning in which faith is in fact lived and practiced. Karl Rahner has complained that, with a few exceptions, the doctrine of the Trinity has remained isolated from the living of the Christian faith.[85] Moreover, it is for similar reasons that Paul Tillich concludes that while

> originally its [i.e., the doctrine of the Trinity] function was to express in three central symbols the self-manifestation of God to man, opening up the depths of the divine abyss and giving answers to the question of the meaning of existence, it later became an impenetrable mystery, put on the altar to be adored. And the mystery ceased to be the mystery of the ground of being; it became instead the riddle of an unsolved theological problem. . . . In this form it became a powerful weapon for ecclesiastical authoritarianism, and the suppression of the searching mind.[86]

G. W. H. Lampe, who argues in favor of reclaiming a christology of Spirit possession, asserts that the notion of Christ as a divine person, even with a human soul,

> in the last resort almost inevitably suggests that Christ's manhood is no more than an outward form, like a suit of clothes in which God the Son has dressed up like a man—the king disguised as a beggar. The classical affirmation that the Word became man, but not a man, indicates that once Christian thought had identified the person of Jesus with the Logos/Son, and had transferred the image of "Son of God" from the historical figure of Jesus to the pre-existent Logos as the Second Person of the Godhead, it was set on a course which was bound to lead to a reductionist doctrine of Christ's manhood and a weakening of the force of those insights which had found expression in the belief that Christ is the new Adam and "the eldest among a large family of brothers."[87]

As a reflection of its prayer and confession, the Christian tradition did indeed also develop a rich mystic tradition, but that trend of thinking was never fully related to its theoretical thinking. Precisely because of its refusal to identify the objective essences of things divine, it was regarded as philosophically suspect and theologically underdeveloped. And so this mystical thought, especially in the Latin West, has remained peripheral, the sphere of monks and nuns perhaps, but hardly to be adopted by serious theologians or shared by the commonality of Christian peoples.

A clearly desirable goal is, then, an understanding of Christian understanding that can function not only in theory, but also in mystic realm of meaning, that can keep both realms of meaning in healthy, dynamic tension. It is such an understanding that is the objective of this book. But before we begin to sketch such a pattern of religious understanding in the Buddhist philosophical perspective, we must devote attention to the Christian mystic tradition, which ran parallel to, frequently intersected, and at times opposed the theoretical insights of the main doctrinal tradition, for the overall argument of this book is that Buddhist thinking can both help in reclaiming as central the Christian mystical tradition of darkness and assist in deepening Christian insight into the Christ meaning.

4

The Initial Patristic
Mysticism of Light

Chapter 3 outlined the main themes of the theoretical understanding of Christ as it developed in the faith, teaching, and confession of the early church.[1] But, in addition to that theoretical realm of meaning, there is also a mystic realm in which meaning is appropriated and constituted only in direct contact. As the aim of this book is to offer a Buddhist philosophic interpretation of religious consciousness that might, by organically relating both theory and mystic insight, reclaim the centrality of the Christian mystic tradition, the following two chapters will attempt to examine the same meaning of Christ as it was embodied in the mystic thinking of the early Christian mystics and fathers of the church.

In the understanding of mystic meaning the point is not logical, consistent thinking about truth but, rather, the direct, immediate appropriation of that truth in conscious experience. The goal is not to know the theoretical meaning of Christ and how that may be correctly understood but, rather, to make that meaning one's own. In the words of Gregory of Nyssa, "it is not the knowing of something about God that the Lord declared blessed, but the having of God in oneself."[2] The focus of mystic understanding is not to know that God is immutable, unchanging essence, but somehow to participate in that immutability. It is not enough simply to understand the doctrine of the Trinity; one must pass over to a conscious experience of the Trinity.[3] To paraphrase the *Imitation of Christ*, one would rather feel the presence of Christ than know how to define Christ's relationship to the Father.

The early Christian mystics reiterate that such mystic consciousness transcends conceptual enunciation and thus also the language in which that enunciation is formed. And herein lies the stumbling block for those who would write upon the nature of mysticism. As Thomas Merton notes, "one of the chief problems of mystical theology is to account for a loving, unitive and supernatural love of God that is beyond concepts, and to do so in a language that does not in one way or the other become completely misleading. The mystical theologian faces the problem of saying what cannot really be said."[4]

It cannot really be said because the mystic experience of Christ is a state of consciousness that does not necessarily and always elicit enunciable meaning. As Bernard Lonergan explains, dynamic states of consciousness are not always enunciable in acts of insight, understanding, and judgment. Rather, they are base experiences upon which verbalized meanings are constructed. It is precisely because such mystic states are conscious without being known that they constitute an experience of mystic meaning.[5]

Nevertheless, since this most intimate of immediate experiences is perceived as being the central experience of faith, Christians have seldom been content with maintaining those experiences as their own private property, but seem to have been driven, prophetlike, to express them openly and publicly. The fathers have thus evolved a mystic theology that attempts to thematize and embody that mystic understanding.

The initial development of such mystic thinking by the fathers followed closely the pattern of doctrinal thinking, for it was expressed in the same Neoplatonic framework that served for Christian theory. If this pattern — aptly described as a mysticism of light — had gone completely unchallenged, no dichotomy would have occurred in Christian thought. But the cost would have been an ever-increasing irrelevance to Christian experience in favor of theological consistency.

THE PLATONIC FORM OF THE MYSTIC TRADITION

The New Testament did indeed describe mystic experiences of the meaning of Christ,[6] but, just as it offered no theoretical language for the development of Christian theory, so it did not present any well-articulated framework for the explanation of Christian mystic thinking. In the process of moving from faith to teaching to confession, the gospel writers spoke of life in Christ and the experience of God as Abba in the context of faith, that is, in the realm of mystic meaning itself, but they did not develop a consistent mystic theological doctrine that could be used by later thinkers.

Thus, just as with theory, so here a language of mystic ascent had to be developed. Again the Christian mystic thinkers adopted and adapted Greek patterns of thinking, for most of them were, of course, themselves Greek. The preoccupation of the Christian mystics with participation in the divine, if it were to be expressed in an explanatory fashion, needed a conceptual framework in which to locate the enunciation of that experience. It implied "a metaphysics, an anthropology, a theory of the world; and neo-Platonism offered a ready-made system of thought that, by its contemplative character, its scorn for the tangible, its theocentrism, seemed marvelously adapted to the particular insights of the [mystic] monastic movement."[7] It should be no surprise that Christian mystic thought should have found a conceptual framework in the same place as Christian theoretical understanding, for, at times, the Christian mystics were the same thinkers who were responsible for the theoretical development of the doctrinal understanding of the Incarnation and the Trinity. Thus, instead of trying to evolve a conceptual framework directly from the New Testament writings, they grafted their explanations of Christian mystic meaning onto the trunk of an already existing Greek, Platonic mystical doctrine. As A. J. Festugière states, "The movement that issued from Jesus has given a new life to a preexistent organism, the structure of which leads back to Plato. When the Fathers 'think' their mysticism, they Platonize."[8] It would then be well here to mention the broad lines of the content of that Platonic modeling of mystic thought, especially as subsequent chapters of the present endeavor will offer an alternative Buddhist doctrinal framework for the enunciation of mystic experience.

In considering the thought of Plato it is necessary to be aware that, for Plato, knowledge (*epistēmē*) is not a detached theoretical knowledge about something, but rather, a participation in what is to be known.[9] The entire thrust of Plato is itself mystic, both in that it strives for a participation in the truth known and in that its starting point seems to have been just such a mystic experience. As Festugière explains, the awareness of the reality of the realm of the immutable, ideal forms "resulted from an experience. It is known because it has been seen. It is a truth of intuition, of an intuition borne not upon reason, but upon a fact of psychological experience that I do not know how better to define than to term it mystical."[10] Thus, Festugière continues, "knowing transcends language and intellection. The object seen is beyond *ousia* (being). It is ineffable. It cannot be circumscribed in any definition."[11]

The fact that such knowledge does indeed occur implied that there was a natural similitude and kinship between the mind that knows the ideal forms, that is, the *nous*, and those immutable ideal forms that are known, the *noēta*, and which alone rendered true knowing possible. In the *Phaedo* Plato explains that "the soul resembles the divine and the body the mortal, for the soul is the very likeness of the divine and immortal."[12] The soul has a natural affinity (*suggeneia*) with the divine, and the philosophers must stir up their "connatural desire for truth."[13]

However, such a natural affinity and similitude cannot derive from human life in the sensible, visible world, for that world is one of constant change, unending flux, and illusory confusion. Indeed, a deep appreciation of Heraclitus' insight that "all things flow" (*panta rei*)[14] seems to have been the springboard that launched Plato's notion of the existence of the immutable, ideal forms. If everything, including the philosopher, is changing, dying, and passing away, then true stable knowledge can be possible only if there exists another world, stable and unchanging, with which the soul has some affinity.[15] Plato concludes that the soul has such a kinship because it has actually seen those immutable, ideal forms in a previous, nonempirical existence. "Thus, in order to be contemplated here below, the forms had to have been present during a pre-empirical existence. The awareness that we have of them is simply a recovery, or better, an awakening."[16] True knowledge is thus a remembering (*anamnēsis*), and the natural affinity of the soul derives from that previous life in which it contemplated the ideal forms.

In contrast, the present state of humankind is clearly a falling away from that pre-empirical existence and, imprisoned in the constant flux of the sense world, we are enmeshed in ignorance and perplexity (*aporia*). The famed allegory of the cave in *The Republic* depicts this condition as that of men chained from birth in a dark cave without the ability to move or turn toward the light that shines behind them.[17] That which really is (*ontōs on*)[18] is not the world of sensible things (*aisthēta*) at all, but rather the world of intelligible realities (*noēta*), which alone constitute the reality in which sensible phenomena simply participate in various degrees. Plato sets up a radical dichotomy between the changeable, evanescent world of sensible objects, which leads only to fallible opinion (*doza*) and confusion (*aporia*) and the unchanging, objectively real world of the intelligible ideal forms (*eidē*), which account for the possibility of true knowledge (*epistēmē*).

In discussing the immortality of the soul in the *Phaedo*, Plato pictures Socrates as arguing: "Must we not ask ourselves what that is which, as we imagine, is liable to be scattered away, and about which we fear? and what again that is about which we have no fear?"[19] Socrates proceeds to define the soul as simple, uncompounded and therefore not subject to change or dissolution, and thus the soul is incapable of being "scattered away" at death. The base problem is that the soul is polluted and engrossed by the corporeal, has no eye except that of the senses, and is weighed down by the bodily appetites. The soul is "dragged by the body into the region of the changeable."[20]

With such a radical dichotomy between the invisible (*aeides*) and the visible (*horaton*), the task of the wisdom-lover is to pass from sensible appearances to a contemplation of that which "really is," namely, the unchanging world of the ideal forms.[21] Although enmeshed in the sensible, the soul does have an organ for contemplation, the *nous*.[22] It is positioned midway between the sensible and the intelligible. But in order to mount from the sensible world of change to the intelligible world of being itself, the soul needs to purify itself from the foreign mud (*en borborō barbarikō tini*)[23] of the sensible. This process of purification (*katharsis*) is the path of salvation for the soul, for only thereby can it attain the goal of contemplation. As Festugière explains, "contemplation (*theōria*) is a seeing of the invisible. This seeing is possible only to the degree that the soul separates itself from matter. And this is *katharsis* (purification)."[24] One must then separate the soul from the body as much as possible; train the soul to leave the envelope of the body in order to gather itself together; concentrate on itself; be alone with itself, delivered from the ties to the body as from chains.[25] Thus purification means a holding aloof from the body and a practicing of dying.[26]

The first step in purifying the soul is a moral purification, for without the practice of the virtues and the control of the passions,[27] the *nous* is unable to approach the contemplation of the invisible. But such a moral purification, although necessary as a first step, is by itself inadequate to being about contemplation.[28]

A purification of the mind is also needed, which, carried out by dialectic (*dialezis*) unites the knower to the known.[29] The mark of this purification of the mind is "to always disengage oneself more and more from matter to attain a level more spiritual, closer to the invisible. In the measure that one has separated oneself from the body, in that same measure one approaches the absolute purity of the forms."[30] The soul mounts as on a staircase from an awareness of the sensible to an awareness of the soul itself, to an awareness of the intelligible in sequential, discursive movements, and then realizes the act of contemplation.[31]

The end point, contemplation (*theōria*, from *thea* and *horaō*), the act of seeing[32] (not to be confused with the modern use of the word "theory" as logical, consistent meaning) is a union of the soul with the invisible forms.[33] This contemplative seeing of the invisible is a return to the pre-empirical state of the soul. But it is not simply the highest state of discursive knowing, the apex of philosophical endeavor, for in the process of dialectic the *nous*, freed from passions by *katharsis*, purifies and strips its notion of the invisible, the *noēta*, from all sensible shape and all imagination (*phantasia*). The seeing of contemplation then has no identifiable content but, rather, is characterized simply as a "sense of presence."[34]

In the words of Festugière, "up until that [contemplation] the eye of the soul finds itself in the presence of delimited forms. Each represents a determined essence. . . . One can distinguish that which is seen. [But] at that hour [of contemplation] there is an ocean of light which envelops the spirit. The object is no longer limited, and such is the fullness of its light that the mind is blinded."[35] The object of contemplation cannot be defined except by negative affirmations, for "it is no longer possible to say what one has perceived. It is a contact beyond seeing, a union ineffable where the *nous*, lost in the object, touches it without being able to define what it has touched and has no other feeling than the very feeling of touching."[36]

It was this structure of Platonic thought, including its further developments in the Neoplatonism of Plotinus and the more popular thought of middle Platonism,[37] that was adopted as the conceptual form for the expression of Christian mystic insight into the meaning of Christ. Its intuitive affirmation of the existence of a separate reality beyond the sensed world seemed to echo Christian ideas about heaven and life with God. But, as before, the Christian use of the conceptual model consisted not only in adopting, but also in adapting these structures to meet the needs of Christian faith enunciation. Thus when Festugière states that Christians Platonize when they "think" their mysticism, one can hardly argue the point. But when he goes on to say that "there is nothing original in the edifice,"[38] one must demur, for what was new was precisely their experiences of faith and insight into the meaning of Christ. Thus the next section will turn to a consideration of the basic themes that form the common doctrinal background expressed by Christian mystics in that Platonic framework.

The ensuing mystic tradition developed within commonly accepted themes of salvation. These themes are summarized by John Meyendorff as "the patristic doctrine of the image of God in man and of his original destiny, its interpretation of original sin, and finally its interpretation of redemption."[39] In order, then, to lay a basis for an examination of the mystic thinkers themselves, one must first clarify these doctrinal themes, which form the common faith understanding of Christian mystic thought.

THE CHRISTIAN ADAPTATION OF MYSTIC PLATONISM

The Christian doctrinal understanding of salvation developed in tension with the Platonic structure outlined above, modifying it and being modified by it in crucial areas. The initial reaction of Christian thinkers to Plato was a somewhat polemical one. As early as Justin Martyr, Plato's idea of the natural immortality of the soul was refuted.[40] Although it is true that Origen did teach the preexistence of souls, fallen from their true state into bodies, yet most Christians never found such a teaching to be congruous with their faith understanding.[41] And with the firm adoption of the teaching of *creatio ex nihilo*, the notion of the divine nature of the soul or any essential likeness between the soul and its creator was excluded. As Andrew Louth explains, ". . . the Platonic notion of the soul's kinship with the divine . . . was destroyed by the doctrine of *creatio ex nihilo*."[42] However, although Christian thinking maintained this essential difference between Creator and creatures, yet it did admit almost without question the Platonic notion of a separate reality beyond the change and flux of the sense world. The soul was not simply chained to the world of sense and without prospect for rising toward God, for as Genesis 1:26 teaches, men and women were made "in the image and likeness of God." The quest for an unchanging reality beyond the constant flow of experience in the world was grounded upon the Patristic notion of the image of God within human beings, for God was defined as unchanging, unmitigated essence.

The first teaching on the image of God in humans is probably to be found in the deutero-canonical book of Wisdom, itself the product of a Greek milieu at Alexandria about 50 B.C.E. Wisdom 2:23, paraphrasing Genesis 1:26 states that "God did make man imperishable [and] made him in the image of his own nature."

The influence of Greek thinking is apparent here. Anders Nygren notes that "this doctrine of the image of God was first developed at a time when the Greek language was making its way into the religious literature of the

Jews."[43] Many modern theologians argue that, because of the lack of any teaching of the image of God in humans in the canonical books of the Old Testament, this doctrine does not belong to the essentials of Christianity.[44] Even Vladimir Lossky, who argues strongly for the validity of "the theology of the image" concedes that "in the purely Hebraic text of the Bible, interpreted in the context in which the books of the Old Testament were composed, there is nothing (or almost nothing) which would permit us to base . . . a religious anthropology on the notion of the image of God."[45] It seems reasonably clear, then, that in the fathers' treatment of the meaning of God's image in humans we are dealing with the adoption of Greek, Platonic thinking.

Athanasius appears to be the first Christian father to employ such a notion, for he spoke of the soul "being a pure mirror which, when pure, can reflect the image of God."[46] In his *Contra Gentes* he writes:

> So when the soul has put off every stain of sin with which it is tinged, and keeps pure only what is in the image, then when this shines forth it can truly contemplate as in a mirror the Word, the image of the Father, and, in him meditate on the Father, of whom the Savior is the image.[47]

For Athanasius, "man was created out of nothing in the image of God; he is not by nature immortal, but he was created so that it was possible for him to progress to an immortal fellowship with God through contemplation of the divine Word."[48] "The light of Christ, whereby men could see the father, can then be received by man because he is capable of imaging God in the depths of the soul."[49] Thus "Athanasius' metaphor of the soul as a mirror in which God is reflected suggests that there is a real similarity between the soul and God. . . . But it does this without suggesting that there is a *natural* kinship between the soul and God. There is no ontological continuity. . . . We have, then, an adaptation of a familiar Platonic theme, while the fundamental insight of Nicene orthodoxy into the radical significance of the doctrine of *creatio ex nihilo* is not at all blurred."[50]

But even though the fathers adapted the Greek teaching so as to harmonize it with Nicene orthodoxy on the distinction between Creator and creature, they adopted almost unchanged the Greek notion of salvation as an unchangeable state beyond the changing sense realm. The fathers mused at length and with various interpretations on the nature of the image that rendered immortality possible.[51] But, as explained by John Meyendorff, "there is an absolute consistency in Greek patristic tradition in asserting that the image is not an external imprint, received by man in the beginning and preserved by human nature as its property independently of its relationship with God. 'Image' implies *participation in the divine nature*."[52] Human nature has the potential to participate in the divine nature, is open to reflect the ultimate within, and is capable of realizing an unchanging state of sharing in God.

Cyril of Alexandria located that image in the fact that humans are reasonable (*logikos*) and taught that they could participate in the Divine Logos. Before the fall Adam "preserved in himself, pure and without stain, the illumination God had granted him, and did not prostitute the dignity of his nature."[53] Thus humans before the fall were capable of participating in divine illumination, were free to seek and find God. And even after the fall that possibility remained open.

But, alas, that blissful state of the original Adam is not the experience of living people in the changing world, for we do not live pure and free from stain, and divine illumination is not a fact of everyday reckoning. The fathers, basing themselves on Paul's reading of Genesis, taught the doctrine of the fall to account for such an apparent disparity. Again, in Meyendorff's translation, Cyril states:

> Adam was created for incorruptibility and life; in paradise he had a holy life: his intellect was wholly and always devoted to the contemplation of God, his body was in security and calm, without the manifestations of any evil pleasure, for the tumult of stupid propensities did not exist for him. But when he fell because of sin and slid into corruption, then the pleasures and impurities invaded the nature of the flesh, and the law of savagery which is in our members appeared (Rom. 7:5, 23). Nature fell ill through sin, through the disobedience of one (Rom 5:19), Adam. And the multitude was made sinful not through having partaken in Adam's sin—they did not exist yet—but through partaking in his nature under the law of sin (Rom. 7:23; 8:2). As in Adam, man's nature contracted the illness of corruption (*errōs-tēsen tēs phthoran*) through disobedience, because through disobedience passions entered man's nature. . . .[54]

The salient feature here is that the original nature of human beings was beyond change and corruptibility, much as was Plato's pre-empirical existence. It is the fall that brought about corruptibility and death. "It was death and corruption that stood in the way of man's participation in divine nature."[55] "As a result of the fall man returned in accordance with God's explicit judgment upon sin to that death, that corruption, that nonexistence from which God in his love had originally called man forth and created him."[56] If humans had been created out of nothing, by the fall they were destined to return to that nothingness.

This is why redemption through Christ, the risen One, was understood quite naturally as an overcoming of death, as the granting of immortality. Christ, both human and divine, reestablished the link with the original, immortal destiny of human beings. Christ restored the image of God to its fullness and changed the conditions under which human nature existed. In rising from the dead, Christ then saves all human nature. As Athanasius writes:

> The body of Christ was of the same substance as that of all men . . . and he died according to the common lot of his equals. . . . The death of all was being accomplished in the body of the Lord, and, on the other hand, death and corruption were destroyed by the Word which dwelt in that body.[57]

The central problem of death in the thinking of the fathers reflects the same concern that engrossed Qoheleth and Plato. The constant passing away of all things, the dread that the soul would be blown away like a wisp of smoke, elicits anxiety not only in Wisdom writers and Greek philosophers, but also in Christian fathers and thinkers. For Qoheleth there was no adequate answer. But Plato found that answer in the natural immortality of the soul, which, in the apt phrase of Festugière, "offered some compensation from suffering."[58] For the fathers that salvation from death and passing away remained the sought goal, but was achieved only by the dying and rising of the incarnate Christ.[59]

Besides adopting this notion of immortality as normative for Christian theology, the fathers also accepted almost without question the Platonic idea of a human being as composed of a material, changing sense body and a spiritual soul. In later times, once the doctrine of the radical dependency of humans upon the Creator was well established, Christian theology even reintroduced the notion of the natural immortality of the created soul.[60]

This teaching that humans attained an unchanging state beyond death through Christ was evolved within a philosophic position that held the essence of a human being to be more real than any individual, who simply shared in that essence, a notion that harks back to the ideal forms or essences of Plato. The fathers thought for the most part in essentialist categories. As Maurice Wiles explains:

> the important thing about Christ was not that the Word had become a man, but that the Word had assumed humanity in order to save it. . . . At the incarnation divine and human natures met, and human nature as a whole had received an injection of immortality. It was a way of thought congenial to those who, like the Alexandrians, thought in terms of natures as real entities. Cyril of Alexandria . . . found it essential to an adequate understanding of the unity of Christ's person to insist on the universal, as opposed to the individual, character of his human nature. That same emphasis on the universal nature of Christ's humanity fitted well with a presentation of the incarnation as the antidote to the universal problem of man's mortality.[61]

Furthermore, on what is perhaps an even deeper level, the fathers often adopted a Greek pattern of thinking in their assumption of confrontational understanding as normative. As Festugière explains, for the Greeks the focus in understanding was upon the object understood, which stood over against and confronted the understanding mind.[62] Following Festugière, Andrew Louth writes: "The Greeks were pre-Cartesians, we are all post-Cartesian. We say, 'I think, therefore I am,' that is, thinking is an *activity* I engage in and there must therefore be an 'I' to engage in it; the Greeks would say 'I think, therefore there is that which I think—*to noēta*. What I think is something going on in my head; what the Greek thinks, *to noēta*, are objects of thought that (for example, for Plato) exist in a higher, more real world."[63] Such an assumption of the existence of a known over against a knower might seem quite natural, for the tree that I see is different from the I who sees it. Yet this implicit epistemology is not accepted as normative for all understanding by many present-day thinkers, such as Bernard Lonergan.[64] And it is seen as totally inadequate by the mystics of other, non-Christian traditions, who were at least as good at loving wisdom as were the Greeks.

The acceptance of these four Greek ideas of the ultimate salvation being an unchanging state beyond the flux of the experienced world, of the human being as composed of body and soul, of the essentialist notion of human nature as more real than the individual person, and of the confrontational mode of understanding, whether theoretical, mystic, or commonsense, will form central questions in the ensuing discussions concerning the employment of a Buddhist perspective for Christian faith. Within the Christian mystic tradition the notion of the unchanging nature of final salvation was reevaluated by Gregory of Nyssa, but the notion of the person as body and soul is not questioned at all. It would also seem that the notion of the essence of human nature as more real than individuals was not doubted in the Patristic period. But the assumption of confrontational understanding as normative did, it would seem, cause tension in some of the mystic thinkers, for as soon as one realizes that thinking is a human constructive activity, a confrontational notion of understanding as being presented with real entities is inadequate to understanding understanding. This seems to have been particularly the case when the focus of attention was on mystic meaning, and Christian mystics, such as Gregory of Nyssa and Pseudo-Dionysius, have held that the meaning they thematize is beyond any such knowing. One of the principal concerns of the Christian mystic writers was with the nature of mystic understanding and, with Gregory of Nyssa, the fathers did indeed develop an understanding of mystic understanding that does not coincide with the image of an identifiable known object confronting a knowing subject.

Yet the issue of the nature of such mystic understanding has not yet found any general agreement among scholars, and different interpretations frequently lead to differing evaluations of the early mystic writers themselves. A brief excursion into that question will, then, sketch the understanding of mystic understanding herein employed.

THE NATURE OF MYSTIC UNDERSTANDING

It is one thing to experience a mystic participation in God, to experience God as Abba, to attain the wisdom of God, and quite another to think about that experience and develop explanations of its nature. Theoretical teachings can be handed down with some confidence that later generations can elicit acts of insight and judgment that enable them to reformulate in themselves a somewhat faithful understanding of the original intent. But mystic teachings labor under a further burden, for the content of mystic experience is consistently maintained to be beyond any words that might be used to express it.

William James in his *Varieties of Religious Experience* describes mystic states as "states of insight in depths of truth unplumbed by the discursive intellect. They are illuminations, revelations, full of significance and importance, all inarticulate though they remain. . . ."[65] It was with a like understanding that Maximus Confessor (d. 662) could sum up early Christian mystic writings by noting that "theological mystagogy" transcended the dogmas formulated by the councils, for the doctrines of the church were "transcended by their own content."[66]

Indeed it would then seem most appropriate that mystic experience should be expressed in a negative or apophatic fashion so as to emphasize the limitations of verbal, conceptual knowing. In fact, such an apophatic mystic theology did develop upon the base assertion that one actually knows God best by a "not-knowing," by a negation of the content of conceptual understanding. This apophatic theology has formed a persistent, if marginal, trend in Christian mystic thinking.[67]

Yet there are well-respected Christian scholars who downplay the ineffability of mystic experience and question whether there really is a valid Christian mystic experience that is not verbally interpreted and expressed. If one would allow the mystic to have full sway, then it seems impossible to state clearly just what Christian faith is all about, and all doubts about claimed mystic content can be discounted merely by arguing that the questioner does not have the requisite mystic experience to understand the ineffable. Edward Schillebeeckx writes that "experience is always interpreted experience," that "the content of every new experience is put into words: a new experience is also a speech event. Speech is an ingredient of experience." Thus, since an "interpretative identification is an intrinsic element, . . . there is no experience without 'theorizing,' without guesses, hypotheses, and theories. Specific, private, so-called direct experiences are always communicated by general terms. . . . This is also true of everything that we call 'religious experiences.' We experience reality . . . always through models of reality."[68]

On such an understanding, the nature of a given mystic experience can be surmised from the constituent explanation whereby it is interpreted.

Thus thinkers such as R. C. Zaehner can distinguish among nature, monistic, and theistic mysticisms by analyzing the mystics' interpretations of their experiences.[69] But such an insistence upon the unity of experience and interpretation runs counter to the thought of many of the early Christian mystics themselves, who regarded their "thinking" of mystic experience as not only discrete from the experiencing of that experience, but also as at base misrepresenting it, due to the weakness of language.

In speaking of religious experience, Bernard Lonergan explains that "to say this dynamic state is conscious is not to say that it is known. For consciousness is just experience, but knowledge is a compound of experience, understanding, and judging. Because the dynamic state is conscious without being known, it is an experience of mystery."[70] Words flow not simply and automatically from consciousness, but are evolved to express the content of acts of understanding. If that experience is not understood, then, although it is conscious, it cannot be judged, that is, known. Mystic experience is claimed to be ineffable because it is impervious to insight and thus to the language that might embody such insight.

Yet, just as human consciousness does move from experience to understanding and judgment, at times mystics also do attempt to understand their experience and offer judgments on its nature. But their interpretation is a separate act following upon the experience and not a constituent element of it, for it is not necessary to the experience itself. In the primal awareness, "the mystic withdraws into the *ultima solitudo*, he drops the construct of culture and the whole complicated mass of mediating operations to return to a new mediated immediacy of his subjectivity reaching for God."[71] Such immediacy of mystic experience is a withdrawal from the world mediated by verbal meanings and a recovery mediated precisely by the awareness of the inadequacy of words, "mediated . . . in the prayerful mystic's cloud of unknowing."[72] Thus the difficulty in expressing mystic meaning is that the very immediacy of the experience is both prior to and transcendent to the genesis of acts of verbal understanding and enunciation.

The immediacy of mystic experience is not simply prior to knowledge, for such an experience is not a return to the immediacy of the infant's nursery, where experiences are simply given "without any perceptible intrusion from insight or concept, reflection or judgment, deliberation or choice."[73] The mystic is driven to attempt to embody his experience in communicable words, however inadequate he or she may claim them to be. It is because of such failed attempts that mystic experience is deemed to transcend all verbalization and all acts of knowing. Although they consider them to be totally inadequate, mystics in all traditions have in fact produced extended treatises upon the nature and meaning of their experiences. Indeed if the nature of mystic awareness is to be discussed at all, words are obviously necessary, even if the base awareness is nonverbal. It would seem that the basic concern of writers like Edward Schillebeeckx is to counter the claims of a muddled mystic affirmation that, in discounting all verbal expression as beside the point, renders itself likewise irrelevant.

However, this quite necessary concern is amply protected by emphasizing, with Bernard Lonergan, that "there are two quite different modes of apprehension, of being related, of consciously existing, namely, the commonsense mode of operating in the world mediated by meaning and the mystical mode withdrawn from the world mediated by meaning into a silent and all absorbing self-surrender."[74] Here one should include in the world of mediated meaning not only commonsense, practical meaning, but also theoretical understandings, for its insights are expressed in mediating words and concepts. An understanding of these two modes not only allows for the primacy of mystic awareness, but also delineates the subsequent task of verbalization. After the withdrawal into the cloud of mystic unknowing, one again must reenter the world of language and custom in order to bring something of that unknown content to speech.

The distinction of these modes is affirmed by most of the Christian mystics themselves. Pseudo-Macarius, to cite one of many examples, writes:

It is impossible for one who has the spirit of the world and has not been born of the Holy Spirit to know in a conscious experiencing (*en peira gnōseōs*) and just as they are the things of the Spirit, and, if they dare to venture forth, they are puffed up with conceit in their carnal intelligence. If they rely upon worldly wisdom and pretend to comprehend spiritual realities merely by their own intelligence without the visitation and revelation of the Spirit, they will come to naught and perish due to the lack of a true foundation — which is the Lord.[75]

Such a passage echoes the thought of Paul in 1 Corinthians 2:11–14, who contrasts worldly wisdom with the wisdom of God, which is not the content of any theoretical position, for

the depths of God can only be known by the Spirit of God. . . . Therefore we teach, not in the way in which philosophy is taught, but in the way that the Spirit teaches us: we teach spiritual things spiritually. An unspiritual person is one who does not accept anything of the Spirit of God: he sees it all as nonsense; it is beyond his understanding because it can only be understood by means of the Spirit.

Mystic awareness moves in a realm of meaning different from commonsense and theoretical meanings, and its validation is had only in the immediacy of that awareness. Nevertheless, it must be examined by a perusal of what Christian mystic writers have actually said about their experience.

The overall pattern of Patristic mystic thought revolves around the two dominant themes of light and darkness. The first theme of a light mysticism is found in Origen (d. ca. 254), the pioneer of so much in early Christian thinking, in Evagrius Ponticus (d. 399), a Greek ecclesiastic who fled into the desert in search of perfection and who rather consistently follows the thought of Origen, and in Pseudo-Macarius (between 380 and 430), who represents an alternate strain of spiritual teaching known as Messalianism. This initial Patristic mysticism of light was expressed within the Greek philosophical assumption of the validity of the subject-object structure of knowing, and thus developed into an intellectualist approach to mystic experience — an approach that harmonizes closely with the theoretical understanding of the Incarnation and the Trinity outlined above.

The second dominant theme of darkness, which will be analyzed in chapter 5, below, focuses upon the thought of Gregory of Nyssa (d. ca. 395), the most orthodox of all the present thinkers and the father of Christian mysticism, and Pseudo-Dionysius (ca. 500), the unknown author who passed himself off as the disciple of Paul. This trend abandoned the intellectualist approach in favor of seeking contact with God in the darkness of unknowing, thus establishing a dichotomy between mystic thought and theory. This approach to mysticism presupposes and enunciates a different interpretation of mystic awareness and will be briefly outlined in the remainder of part I, to highlight the mystic tradition that it is the intent of this book to reclaim and deepen by the adoption and adaption of the Mahāyāna pattern of thinking.

LIGHT MYSTICISM

Origen and Evagrius are often described as proponents of an "intellectualist" brand of mysticism. Andrew Louth writes that

> we can see Origen as a founder of the tradition of intellectual mysticism that was developed and bequeathed to the Eastern Church by Evagrius. In this tradition, contemplative union is union of the *nous*, the highest point of the soul, with God through a transforming vision. And in such a union the *nous* finds its true nature; it does not pass out of itself into the other; there is no ecstasy. Also, the God with whom the soul is united is not unknowable. Consequently, darkness is a stage which is left behind in the soul's ascent: there is no ultimate darkness in God. We have a mysticism of light.[76]

This intellectualist tradition is heavily influenced by Platonic thinking. The *nous* (i.e., the intellect) that gains unitive vision is not a faculty of worldly understanding, but properly an organ of mystic insight. Thus the resultant vision achieved is similar to Plato's knowledge as *epistēmē*, which is contrasted with worldly opinion.

Origen sketches the process of mystical ascent by paralleling it with the content of the canonical Old Testament wisdom books attributed to Solomon. In his *Commentary on the Song of Songs*[77] he writes:

Thus [Solomon] first taught in *Proverbs* the subject of morals, setting regulations for life together, as was fitting, in concise and brief maxims. And he included the second subject, which is called the natural discipline, in *Ecclesiastes* (i.e., *Qoheleth*),[78] in which he discusses many natural things. And by distinguishing them as empty and vain from what is useful and necessary, he warns that vanity must be abandoned and what is useful and right must be pursued. He also handed down the subject of contemplation in the book we have in hand, that is *The Song of Songs*, in which he urges upon the soul the love of the heavenly and divine under the figure of the bride and bridegroom, teaching us that we must attain fellowship with God by the paths of loving affection and love.[79]

The aim of the first path of morals is the attainment of a purification from passion that leads to imperturbability and impassibility (*apatheia*), the attainment of "perfect purity and charity through the observance of the commandments."[80]

The state of *apatheia* is the condition of being imperturbable, of being beyond the fluctuation of the passions. It denotes the necessary calmness and quietude of the mind whereby, being rendered Godlike, one may gain insight into heavenly things. It is the restoration of the image of the impassible God in humans, whereby they might overcome the last enemy, death.[81]

Evagrius, a follower of Origen, in his *Chapters on Prayer* explains in a similar vein that "the state of prayer can be aptly described as a habitual state of impassibility."[82] As John Bamberger notes, "for Evagrius it is unthinkable that a man should aspire to be united with God in pure prayer without first cleansing his heart fully. Only when he has attained *apatheia*, a state of abiding calm derived from the full harmony of the passions, can he ... hope to know God."[83]

But, as with Plato, moral purification is not enough, for to attain contemplation, one also needs to purify the understanding and direct it away from sensible things. Again the goal is an overcoming of the transitory nature of the sensible world in favor of the unchangeability of ultimate reality, of sharing in the impassibility of God. Thus for Origen the second state is that of natural discipline, namely, "the good usage of all things as a means for a religious consideration of the world and the conviction of the vanity of everything visible."[84] Thus after the moral purification, one comes to the teaching of Ecclesiastes, which Origen explains in his *Commentary on the Song of Songs* as teaching "that everything visible and corporeal is transitory and weak. And when the person who is eager for wisdom discovers that this is so, he will doubtless despise those things."[85]

The parallel with Plato's notion of intellectual purification in its flight from the sensible through dialectic is striking. It is only when the soul has attained purification from all attachment to this world of sense in these first two paths that it becomes capable of the third path, that of contemplation of the Godhead by a genuine and spiritual love.[86] This contemplation is a return of the soul to its true nature and an experience of the light of the Word. In his *On First Principles* Origen explains:

> For the eyes of the mind are lifted up from their preoccupation with earthly things and from their being filled with the impression of material things. And they are so exalted that they peer beyond the created order and arrive at the sheer contemplation of God and at conversing with Him reverently and suitably as He listens. How would things so great fail to profit those eyes that gaze at the glory of the Lord with unveiled face and that are being changed into his likeness from glory to glory? For they partake of some divine and intelligible radiance. This is demonstrated by the wise, "The light of your countenance, O Lord, has been signed upon us" (Ps. 4:6).[87]

Here contemplation is a "gazing at the glory of the Lord face to face," for the mind is flooded with his radiance. For Origen, then, at this summit of the spiritual life God no longer remains unknowable, but is present to the soul "with unveiled face." This state of contemplation is also a return to the original nature of the soul, for, before the fall into the body, it preexisted in a blessed and pure state.[88] In his *On First Principles* Origen explains that God created a number of rational souls endowed with free will, who subsequently sinned and fell into this world of bodily existence.[89] He created this present world only as a punishment, binding those sinful souls to the body.[90] In this precosmic scheme of things, even after the fall into the body, the soul yet retains within itself the image of God, which is identified with the intelligent nature of the soul. Origen teaches that human beings have some affinity to God and

> can by progressing from small things to greater and from visible to invisible arrive at a more perfect understanding. For it is placed in a body and necessarily progresses from perceptible things, which are corporeal, to imperceptible things, which are incorporeal and intelligible.[91]

It is thus that the soul as a rational, intelligent nature "participates in the intelligible light" and "can understand and perceive God."[92] In *An Exhortation to Martyrdom* Origen continues:

> And it is clear that just as each one of our members is constituted by nature to preserve a relation proper to it, the eyes in relation to what is visible, the ear in relation to what is audible, so also the mind preserves a relation to what is intelligible, to God, who transcends the intelligible order.[93]

The mind, created as a rational, intelligent nature, is thus quite capable of returning to its original state and of knowing God, for it is made in God's image and preserves the ability to mount beyond the sensible to the knowledge of God.

However, Origen does not mean that this knowledge exhausts the divine nature in its knowing. In his *On First Principles* Origen explains that the mind "cannot arrive at the perfect end of what he seeks. No mind that has been created had the ability to understand completely."[94] As Rowan Greer points out, this dynamic and endless feature of contemplation is present in Origen only in germ and awaits Gregory of Nyssa for its fuller explication.[95] It would appear that the reason for this limitation in the soul's ability to know God comes from its created nature, for the uncreated God completely transcends all created natures. Origen does not focus upon an analysis of the mind itself in its search for knowledge, for to him it is axiomatic that the soul indeed has the ability to know God, since it was created at the beginning as a rational, intelligent nature.

Evagrius shared Origen's anthropological and cosmological ideas and followed them even more rigorously to their logical conclusions.[96] In his *Kephālaia Gnostica*, which formed the basis for the anathemas of Origenism at the Fifth Ecumenical Council in 558,[97] he also presents an account of the preexistence of the rational soul, the fall into the body, and the return to that lost primal state of immaterial existence. Light is natural to the soul and the attainment of "essential contemplation (*theōria ousiōdēs*), which is the activity only of those creatures who are totally purified of all passion of a disordered sort and of all images which could interfere with such an exalted form of understanding,"[98] constitutes a return to the original nature of the soul. Thus the highest contemplation is somehow of the essence of the soul. In his *Chapters on Prayer* Evagrius writes: "The proof of *apatheia* is had when the spirit begins to see its own light, when it remains in a state of tranquility in the presence of images it has during sleep and when it maintains its calm, as it beholds the affairs of life."[99]

This inner light appears to be the natural light of the mind, which derives from its natural kinship with God. Thus for the intellectualist tradition of Origen and Evagrius, the highest mystic awareness is one of light, of understanding, for the mind is naturally capable of regaining its original state as an immaterial intelligence. It is a small step from here to the opinion of Eunomius (d. ca. 395) that human intellect can know the essence of God.

However, the notion of a light mysticism in which the mind comes to know God face to face does not depend upon the cosmic speculations of an Origen or an Evagrius. Pseudo-Macarius presents a mysticism of light without any speculative flights about precosmic conditions. The works that go under the name of Macarius, the father of Egyptian mysticism, were written by an unknown author, possibly Symeon of Mesopotamia, in either Asia Minor or Syria-Mesopotamia.[100] He presents a series of homilies on the spiritual life. These homilies are identified by scholars as coming from the monastic group of the Messalians, a transliteration (*mesalianoi*) of the Syrian term, *mᵉsalleyane* (i.e., those who pray). This name apparently derives from their almost total focus upon the life of prayer to the exclusion of all else. The need for such constant prayer came from their acute awareness of the threat of ever-present demons. As Vincent Desprez explains, "for them, a demon was 'substantially' united to each man at his birth. Baptism, like a razor, indeed cut off past sins, but it was not able to pull out the roots, i.e., the passions. Rather, it is intense and continual prayer that chases away the demon and obtains the coming of the Holy Spirit, who brings impassibility."[101]

Although Pseudo-Macarius does not evince the speculative zest of an Origen, he does appear to have been influenced by him. Werner Jaeger notes that "he embraced with all his heart the mystical and ascetical theology that developed from Origen's speculations."[102] Although after the fall the soul is united to a demon and ensnared in the mud[103] of the passions, although imprisoned in darkness,[104] yet the soul is "a precious work, destined to be the dwelling of God and to be made in his image."[105] But in order to realize and recover that image condition, the soul has to be trained and reformed. It needs a "full formation" so that "it might receive the imprint of the perfect image of Christ."[106] Pseudo-Macarius teaches that the mastering of passion, which leads to realizing the image-nature in mastering bodily sufferings and fears, consists in overcoming all the animal poisons and in deposing the last enemy, death.[107] It is the role of the Spirit to unite the soul with Christ, which union is expressed under the image of light: "It is Christ that is kept in the soul in ineffable light; he is not known in truth except by the eyes of the soul, and for the man not initiated it is impossible to know the things of the Spirit."[108]

In the second path of Origen, that of natural discipline, which is aligned with the book of Ecclesiastes, the soul had to abandon its attachments to all created things. Above, in his *Commentary on the Song of Songs*, we read that all material and visible things are to be despised as transitory.[109] Pseudo-Macarius echoes this theme: "The constructions of the world are feeble and have no solid foundation, since, at the consummation of the world, all those constructions will be destroyed, 'the heavens will be rolled up like a book and the earth will pass away' (Mt. 24:25)."[110] But through the light of Christ the soul attains a state beyond the transitory world. "Perfectly illumined by the ineffable beauty of the glory of the face of Christ,"[111] one "feels his sweetness and enjoys in a real experience the goodness of the light of that ineffable enjoyment."[112]

But, not being of such a theoretical bent as Origen or Evagrius, Pseudo-Macarius shifts his emphasis away from rational intelligence to the human heart. As John Meyendorff explains, "the heart — and not the intellect — takes there the central place in the human composite. . . . The 'intellectual prayer' [of Evagrius] becomes 'the custody of the heart' and the result is a contemplation of the divine light."[113]

One must not, however, conclude that, because of their notion of the ability of the mind to know God in light, the mystic awareness of Origen, Evagrius, or Pseudo-Macarius is simply to be equated with the mediated meaning of conceptual, verbal knowing. Mystic understanding, even in the light, remains beyond words. In his *On First Principles* Origen explains:

Everyone who is concerned with truth should be little concerned with names and words, ... [but] should pay more attention to what is meant than to how it is expressed in words, ... [for] there are some things the meaning of which cannot in any way rightly be explained in any words of a human language, but are made plain by a purer intellectual apprehension rather than by any property words have.[114]

This purer intellectual apprehension of the mind is understood to function in a realm beyond words and language. Evagrius in his *Chapters on Prayer* concurs, for "the spirit that possesses health is the one which has no images of this world at the time of prayer."[115] At the time of prayer and mystic awareness of God, even the most pure thoughts are to be avoided, for "they do impress a certain form upon the spirit and draw one far away from God."[116] Thus, "in order to see the One who is beyond every thought and perception,"[117] "do not fancy the Divinity like some image formed within yourself."[118]

Pseudo-Macarius likewise stresses the ineffability of spiritual experiences, which are expressed only in metaphor under the direction of the Spirit. In his *Homilies* he says: "The spiritual realities are ineffable if the Spirit himself does not teach them through experience and make the soul brave and faithful through his action."[119]

One element in this understanding of the ineffability of mystic awareness on the part of Evagrius, and probably Pseudo-Macarius as well, is most likely the need to respond to the claim of the Arian Eunomius (d. ca. 395), who apparently taught that the divine essence was accessible to human understanding. Eunomius' thinking does clearly form a portion of the background against which Gregory of Nyssa wrote his mystical works, for he entitled a principal doctrinal work *Against Eunomius*.[120] It would appear that Evagrius also responded to such a rationalistic approach. In his *Kephálaia Gnostica* he writes:

He who sees the Creator as within the harmony of being does not actually know his essence, but rather knows his wisdom whereby he had made all things, and I do not refer to that essential wisdom, but to that which is manifested in beings. ... And if this is so, then how great is the madness of those who say that they know the nature of God.[121]

Thus, although for Evagrius mystic understanding is awareness of inner light, such an awareness, being beyond images and concepts,[122] is not to be confused with conceptual knowing. Pseudo-Macarius agrees, for that awareness is an "ineffable seeing that the language of the flesh cannot express."[123] But this is a knowing beyond language that enables men and women to apprehend the separate reality beyond sense images and conceptual names.

CONCLUSION

This trend of light mysticism appears to have been derived from an anthropology that saw in terms of cosmic drama the mind of humans as naturally capable of knowing God in some fashion, for the original image-nature assures the human potential to approach God and attain an unchanging immortality beyond the constant flux of the fallen, finite human condition. In conjunction with that original image-nature, the final goal was conceived in Platonic terms as an unchangeable state beyond the flux of the material passions. Although the knowing of the unchanging God and the experiencing of that state is embodied in a mystic awareness of light, yet it is to be distinguished from all empirical conceptual understanding.

The question this occasions is, then, just what kind of knowing we are talking about. If we do not know God through concepts and images, then just how do we know God? What is this superabundance of light that comes upon the mind? How can it be called knowing, when it is in no wise conceptually or verbally expressible? What is a knowing of God that has no words or concepts?

Central to this complex of ideas are the metaphysical assumptions inherited from Platonic thought. With its attention turned to the nature of the unchanging *noēta*, the object to be known, Greek thought patterns encouraged the early Christian thinkers to bypass any close examination of the consciousness that functions in mystic awareness. God is known because God becomes the object of knowing. God is beyond images and words not because the divine transcends the subject-object pattern of knowing, for that pattern was never subjected to critical analysis. Rather, God transcends language because of the august superiority of God's objectively real being. There is here no need to distinguish and delineate a mystic realm of meaning, for, with the proviso that God cannot be expressed in words and images, knowledge of God functions in parallel with theoretical knowledge. But it is this very proviso that drives one toward a clearer understanding of the nature of mystic meaning. With the further development of mystic thought by Gregory of Nyssa, a new understanding of mystic consciousness is attained, propelled, it would seem, by the need to explicate what that non-verbal knowing is in contrast to Eunomius' rationalistic approach, which could so easily be drawn from Origen's intellectual bent. In treating mystic knowledge, Gregory and Pseudo-Dionysius after him focus upon the disparity of such understanding with all empirical knowing. They will evolve a mysticism of darkness, for they seem to be more acutely aware that it is not only anthropomorphic imagining that is tied to images and words, but also all theoretical knowing as well. It is their mystic teachings that become crucial — although in the context of theoretical theology always peripheral — in the Christian mystic tradition. It is their thought that needs to be reclaimed.

5

A Mysticism of Darkness: Gregory of Nyssa and Pseudo-Dionysius

Chapter 4 offered a brief sketch of a light mysticism in which the underlying understanding of mystic consciousness was patterned after a confrontational model of a knowing subject reaching out to grasp the unchanging divine reality. This pattern of a knowing mind, the *nous*, being confronted with the *noēta*, the knowable objects, is implicit in the thinking of Origen, Evagrius, and Pseudo-Macarius.

But, in the mysticism of darkness a shift of focus takes place, for mystic meaning is found not in the knowing of God in any intellectual fashion, but in an immediacy that precedes the object-subject pattern altogether. Mystic meaning is not a knowing of the divine impassibility, but an awareness arising within a human consciousness that directly touches God. With Gregory of Nyssa's (335–394) mysticism of darkness and its further evolution in Pseudo-Dionysius, the stress of the unknowability of God implies not only divine preeminence, but also a greater awareness of the inability of empirical, confrontational thinking to attain any mystic consciousness. Although this mysticism of darkness is often relegated to the margin of Chistian thinking, Gregory is described by Jean Daniélou as the father of the Christian mystical tradition inasmuch as he modified the thought that he inherited from Origen and Clement, gave it definitive form, and bequeathed that thought to later Christian thinkers.[1] The marginality of Gregory and Dionysius does not derive from their unimportance in Christian theology, but from the felt tension that their writings elicited (and still elicit) among Christian theologians: the pattern of their understanding is in sharp discontinuity with the subject-object pattern implicit in both Christian theory and light mysticism.

Just as the development of the theoretical understanding of the meaning of Christ took place in contrast to Arian thinking, so the development of all mystic thought took place in contrast to the claims of the Arian Eunom-ius who, taking to an extreme the intellectualism of Origen, held that the human mind could know the essence of God. This notion is a logical pro-gression from the confrontational pattern of knowing. If God is an un-changing essence to be known, then it is a small step to conclude that the mind, when properly purified, can indeed know that essence. It would seem that implicit in Origen's threefold path through morals, natural discipline, and contemplation was the conviction that at the culmination one actually did know the essence of God, however imperfectly.

In contrast to such a notion, Gregory modified Origen's threefold path so as to include the understanding that occurs within Origen's third path of contemplation within his second path of natural philosophy, thus leaving Gregory free to describe the third path as a higher, nonconfrontational mystic realm of understanding. He thus clearly avoids any notion that at the summit of mystic consciousness one can know the essence of God. The third path for Gregory is one of darkness, which is the fruit of union issuing from an awareness of presence. "What is certain is that Gregory, taking cognizance of the errors of Eunomius, has more clearly disengaged the proper domain of mystic knowing, and it is in this regard that he is the founder [of mystic theology]."[2]

What is beginning to take place here is parallel to the rise of theoretical thinking and its bifurcation from commonsense meaning. In doctrinal un-derstandings, the fathers had to distinguish and delineate a realm of the-oretical meaning, wherein focus is upon the interrelation of concepts one to another, from the undifferentiated Christian affirmation of faith in Christ, wherein focus is upon the practical implementation of meaning in actual living. But the base gospel experience of meaning is not to be iden-tified simply with the theoretical, for the experience of God as Abba moves within a mystic realm. With the attainment of agreement upon the necessity and validity of theoretical thinking, it then became necessary to step back and delimit more clearly the realm of mystic meaning.

Gregory clearly attempts to delineate this mystic meaning. In his *Com-mentary on the Song of Songs* he follows Origen in aligning the three books of Proverbs, Qoheleth, and the Song of Songs with the three stages of the spiritual life: infancy, youth, and maturity.[3] The first stage represents an awareness of spiritual goods that leads one to strive for them. The second represents an awareness of the vanity of all the changing things of this world. The third is that stage where, after having been purified from all attachment in the awareness of the vanity of all things, the soul is led into the divine sanctuaries, wherein takes place a union of the soul with the divine.[4] In *The Life of Moses* Gregory presents a paradigm of this process in his description of the career of Moses: "The manifestation of God was first made to Moses in light (*dia photos*; Ex. 19:18), then He spoke to him through a cloud (*dia nepheles*; Ex. 20:21), and, finally, having become more perfect, Moses contemplated God in darkness (*en gnopho*; Ex. 24:15–18)."[5]

There is thus a progressive darkening of empirical, confrontational understanding until one contemplates God in the total absence of any mediating image or concept. Two themes seem central to an understanding of Gregory's thinking: his notion of the original nature of human beings and his understanding of the nature of mystic understanding.

GREGORY'S UNDERSTANDING OF THE ORIGINAL NATURE OF THE HUMAN BEING

In his understanding of human nature, Gregory does not take as his starting point a phenomenological description of human existence in the world, for to him that would not represent the true, original nature of human existence at all but, rather, the fallen state of humans bound by passion and illusion. Basing himself on the theme of the original happiness of humans,[6] Gregory outlines a notion of a real community between human beings and God. In his *On the Creation of Man* he writes: "The fact of being created in the image of God means that a royal character has been given to man since his creation. . . . But this dignity does not consist in external attributes, but in virtue, the beatitude of immortality and justice."[7] He goes on to explain that that image, which denotes the original nature of human beings, includes purity, impassibility, beatitude, and separation from all evil.[8] It is located in the mind, for the nature of humans is to think.[9] Thus the objective of Christian living is to regain this original nature and return to the original state of purity and happiness: "If the soul returns to itself, if it knows its true nature, it then contemplates its model in its own beauty, as in a mirror or an image."[10]

This state of original purity is also characterized by a primitive unity of consciousness, for mystic knowing is but a return to the consciousness that characterized the original nature. In his commentary on the passage from the Song of Songs, "You have ravished me with a single one of your glances," Gregory explains:

The soul has two possible orientations: one that regards the truth and one that is lost in illusion. But the pure eye of the bride [in the Song of Songs] is open only to the truth of the good and its other eye is never [open]. Thus the friends [in the Song] praise only that one eye through which alone she contemplates He who is unique, I mean He who alone is constituted in immutable and eternal being, the true Father, the only begotten Son, and the Holy Spirit. He is truly one, for he exists in one nature and the plurality of *hupostaseis* introduces no separation. But there are people whose multiple eyes turn foolishly toward the unreal and divide the one into multiple natures through the imagination of their distorted eyes. These are men who are said to have seen much, but in seeing so much they see nothing.[11]

The abandonment of a multiple consciousness is a precondition for insight into the one who is not dispersed into multiplicity. As Jean Daniélou explains, "in this text we see the identification of the multiple (*diapharos*) with that which had no independent existence and is unreal (*anuparktos*), and which exists only in imagination (*phantasia*)."[12] Mystic consciousness is opposed to empirical, confrontational understanding that would attempt to grasp in multiple concepts and images the essence of God. It does not discriminate one idea from another or waver in two minds, but abides in a primal unity prior to the genesis of standpoints.

The attainment of this unified mode of conscious awareness is a return to the original nature of the soul. Such a primitive unity of the spirit is expressed in the creation story by the command not to touch the tree of good and evil, which serves for Gregory as a symbol of division. "The first law confirms this doctrine [of simplicity], for in giving to man the use of all the trees of Paradise, they were forbidden only that one whose nature was a mixture of contrasts."[13] This primitive unity characterized the natural state of humans as the image of God, to which, according to Gregory, the sense and animal life are foreign. In the original state in which the human was created, unity is then equivalent to divinization and it constitutes one's true human nature: "When the soul becomes entirely simple (*aplē*), unified and entirely deified, she finds the truly simple (*aploun*) and immutable Good."[14]

Thus this original nature implies a realm of meaning and consciousness that does not serially pass from one thing to another, but abides in such a state of unified and simple awareness. The return to that original state involves the abandonment of the multiplicity that comes from the varied images and concepts of confrontational knowing. Gregory is here presenting a notion of mystic understanding as a proper characteristic of the original nature of human existence. One cannot then gain understanding of the mystic meaning of God through ordinary knowing, however purified, but must, rather, return to a more fundamental, simple mode of consciousness that does not engage in the work of observing images and gaining insight into them.

However, human nature is not characterized by either immutability or simplicity, but is, rather, under the tyranny of passion (*pathē*), which includes all the changes and sufferings that people undergo—birth, eating, sex, sickness, death, and so on—as well as mental activities, such as sense knowing, desire, anger, and so forth, and the entire complex of sinful tendencies.[15] But these *pathē* do not negate or eliminate the original nature. *The Great Catechism* explains that

> The liability to death, then, taken from brute creation, was provisionally made to envelop the nature created for immortality. It enwrapped it externally, but not internally. It grasped the sentient part of man, but laid no hold upon the divine image.[16]

Biological life, together with all the sinful passions, is then a covering over the divine image of the original nature, which renders it mortal and leads to the illusions that substitute confrontational knowing derived from sense perception for the simple mystic understanding that characterizes the unfallen nature. All the passions, the principal ones being the concupiscible and irascible appetites, "surround the soul, but are not the soul. They grow like warts on the thinking part of the soul."[17] They are also compared with the garments of skin with which Adam covered himself after having been expelled from the primitive garden, for they cover over the primitive nature of human beings.

In *On the Soul and the Resurrection*, Gregory writes: "That which constitutes the image of God and which belongs to man by nature is the contemplative, critical and overseeing faculty; in other words, the mind. The rest, anger and fear, are accretions from outside."[18] In a similar vein Gregory comments on Numbers 22ff., which treats the magical spells of Balaam: "By the magical spells of Balaam we understand the various delusions of the present life through which men, drugged through some philtre of Circe, leave their own nature to clothe themselves in the forms of animals."[19]

Passion then not only involves a fall to the level of beasts, but is also a magical illusion (*goēteia*). And so a return to the original nature is not only putting the passions under control,[20] but also a turning away from illusory appearances. In his *Commentary on the Song of Songs,* Gregory defines the intent of the book of Qoheleth, namely, of the second path of the cloud, as follows:

> Having condemned in this book the attachment of men to appearances and having proclaimed that all that is unstable and ephemeral is vain, by saying that all that which passes away is vanity, he raises up the natural elan of our soul above all that is known through sensibility to the invisible beauty.[21]

By purifying the soul of attachments to all that appears (*phainomena*) to the mind, one is persuaded of the vanity of all appearances[22] and attains the goal of the second path, which is "a more attentive awareness of hidden things which leads the soul beyond appearances to the world of the invisible. And this is a kind of cloud (*nephelē*) which overshadows all appearances, and slowly guides and accustoms the soul to look toward what is hidden."[23]

This need to see hidden things implies that appearances are indeed illusory (*apatē*),[24] for there is an awareness that goes beyond the biological orientation that sees objects as confrontational units of meaning. Such an insight and awareness is within the understanding of the second path, for by close consideration one can understand that no transient object can claim any firm, stable meaning of itself. But, for Gregory, in contrast to Origen, this awareness is not itself yet mystic understanding, which transcends all intellectual understanding and will be described not only as an overshadowing cloud, but as night, that is, the full and complete darkening and cessation of all mediating images and concepts.

Yet this shadowing of empirical knowing does play a pivotal role in leading one away from illusion and attachment and in preparing one for entry into the darkness of mystic meaning. In his *Commentary on Ecclesiastes*, Gregory writes:

> All the things which are beautiful to the sense are beautiful only in appearance through an illusion of evaluation (*dia tēs kata tēn oiēsin apatēs*), but in their nature they have neither existence nor constancy, but are of a flowing and transient nature. It is through an illusion and a false opinion that those who have not been formed believe that they truly exist. Thus, as they embrace unstable things and do not desire those which are eternal, the Ecclesiastes, taking a position as upon a high observatory, seems to cast down an appeal to human nature: "There is a time to love and a time to hate," i.e., there are other goods which are also beautiful and which are at last real and which render beautiful those who participate in them.[25]

Thus mystic understanding involves a leaving behind of the false opinion that sense phenomena, the appearance of confrontational objects, offers any stable meaning that might be clung to in security. Again, Gregory in his *Commentary on the Psalms* explains:

> [The Psalm] calls "hard of heart" those who do not discern the lie and vanity of reality, but who love that which is inconstant (*anuparkton*) and neglect that which is stable and worthy of being loved. It says in effect, that only holiness is truly admirable and all other things upon which men follow as good are so only in their minds (*en hupolēpsei*) and do not exist in themselves, but appear to have existence in the vain evaluation of men.[26]

The base source of such illusion is the sense nature of human beings, which leads one to assume that, just as objects confront the senses as real, so truth confronts the mind as real. But all such meanings are only mental constructs and have no lasting value. In the *Commentary on Ecclesiastes* Gregory writes:

> As sensibility is born with our first birth and reason in contrast waits upon the corresponding increase in age in order to appear little by little in the subject, because that mind is dominated by sensibility and accustomed to obey it through force, it judges beautiful or ugly that which sensibility adopts or rejects. This is the reason why the understanding of the good seems difficult and laborious to us.[27]

Because the pattern for all understanding is taken to be that of sense knowing being confronted by concrete objects—that is, because of the biological extraversion of consciousness—people imagine external things to be real and possessed of given meaning and fall into a dreamlike illusion. *The Commentary on the Song of Songs* states:

> The Lord has given his disciples many precepts by which their minds might shake off all material elements, like so much clay, and thus rise to a desire for the transcendent. And one of these is that all who are seriously concerned with the life of heaven must conquer sleep; they must be constantly awake in spirit, driving off, like a cloud of darkness, the deceiver of souls and the destroyer of truth. By drowsiness and sleep I here am referring to those dream-like fantasies which are shaped by those who are submerged in the illusion of life: I mean public office, money, influence, external show, the seduction of pleasure, love of reputation and enjoyment, honor, and all the other worldly things which, by some sort of imagination (*dia tinos phantasias*) are sought after vainly by those who live without reflection. All these things will pass away with the flux of time, their existence is mere seeming (*en tō dokein*) and they are not what we think they are, nor do they ever abide constantly in the conception we have of them. No sooner do they appear than they must pass away. They are like waves that raise their crest above the water, and for a moment are given a certain substance by the action of the winds: but the dignity they have cannot be permanent, for soon after they are raised by the wind's blast, they are restored once more to their place and reveal nothing but the flat surface of the sea. Hence, that our minds may not be subject to such illusions (*tōn toioutōn phasmatōn*), we are bidden to shake off that heavy sleep from the eyes of our soul, lest by our attraction toward the unsubstantial (*to anuparkton*) we slip away from those which have true being and subsistence.[28]

Here the root illusion is mistaking imagination (*phantasia*) for understanding, as if the mere appearance (*phainomenon*) of an image entailed the grasping of a concomitant reality. But human biological life, the source of these images, is itself a consequence of the loss of the original nature and covers over that originally pure nature like Adam's garments of skin, without ever being able to destroy it entirely.[29] In the *Commentary on Ecclesiastes* we read:

> We might object that since all is vanity, then none of those things which do not subsist (*ouch huphestēken*) exist at all. In effect, that which is vain is inconstant, unreal, and one should not include that which has no reality (*anuparkton*) among that which has reality. If things are not at all, then what is it that exists and remains? The

answer to this question is brief for Ecclesiastes: Know what you will become if you are raised by virtue. . . . If you know this, you will understand that which was at the origin, the creation to the image and likeness of God.[30]

As Jean Daniélou explains, this passage teaches that that which is real is the world of the image-nature, which is from the origin, and to which one is restored.[31] Gregory teaches that "the resurrection (*anastasis*) is nothing other than restoration to the original state (*apokatastasis eis to archaion*)."[32]

Gregory depicts the path of the cloud as a clouding over of empirical knowing in reaching beyond appearances, in going out from sensible knowing to an awareness of the divine reflected in the original image-nature. The result is a state of contemplation that is a negation of empirical words and images. Gregory's understanding of the original image-nature is that it does have a likeness to immutable being, to that which truly is. In the light of such an unchanging reality, empirical, biological life is an illusion and to be rejected. Yet this is still a stage on the second path and not the summit of mystic experience. This cloud is not a final point, for it leads and introduces one into mystic darkness in which no being of any kind can be identified, and there is nothing at all to be rejected. It is a realm of no-knowing, in which the presence of God is embodied as a "feeling of presence (*aisthēsis parousias*)."[33] Thus the nature of mystic understanding is described by Gregory within the context of the third path, that of darkness.

GREGORY ON THE NATURE OF MYSTIC UNDERSTANDING

In his *Commentary on the Psalms* Gregory states that the soul, "having passed beyond all appearances through the spirit, penetrates the heavenly sanctuaries."[34] The term *aduton*, sanctuary, refers to the most interior realm of consciousness, which transcends all empirical knowing.[35] This innermost mind is described in *The Life of Moses* in a series of negative terms: "The interior, which is called the holy of holies, is not accessible to the multitude. . . . For the truth of reality is truly a holy thing, a holy of holies, and is incomprehensible and inaccessible to the multitude."[36] Human beings, driven to react by passion and clinging to imaginative illusions, find the truth of their original nature beyond their ability to represent, and thus it is incomprehensible and inaccessible. In *The Life of Moses* this mystic realm is also described as "a storehouse, that is to say, the hidden and ineffable things of life."[37]

For Origen the third and final path of contemplation issued in *theologia* (i.e., knowledge of God). But Gregory teaches that knowing God is a not-knowing. Mystic knowing, *theognōsia*, is a knowing of the hidden things in the sanctuary, the innermost realm of mystic consciousness. The *Commentary on the Psalms* states that "this is truly a hidden thing, incomprehensible and invisible and beyond all imaginative knowing."[38] It would thus seem that the term *theognōsia* indicates specifically the mystic realm of meaning, for, as explained in *The Life of Moses*, one "is led into the hidden sanctuary of mystic knowing."[39]

Gregory develops this theme of darkness always in relation to the account in Exodus 20:21 of Moses entering into the darkness of Mount Sinai where he encounters God. In *The Life of Moses* Gregory asks:

> What does it mean that Moses entered the darkness and then saw God in it? What is now recounted seems to be contradictory to the first theophany, for then the divine was beheld in light, but now he is seen in darkness. Let us not think that this is at variance with the sequence of things we have contemplated spiritually. Scripture teaches us that religious knowledge comes at first to those who receive it as light. Therefore what is perceived to be contrary to religion is darkness, and the escape from darkness comes about when one participates in light. But as the mind progresses and, through an ever greater and more perfect diligence, comes to apprehend reality, as it approaches more nearly to contemplation, it sees more clearly what of the divine nature is invisible. For, leaving behind everything that is observed, not only what sense comprehends, but what the mind thinks it sees, it keeps on penetrating deeper until by the mind's yearning for understanding it gains access to the invisible and incomprehensible and there it sees God. This is the true knowledge of what is sought; this is the seeing that consists in not seeing, because that which is sought transcends all knowledge, being separated on all sides by incomprehensibility as by a kind of darkness.[40]

This same progression from light through the cloud to darkness is also found in the *Commentary on the Song of Songs*: "It is in light that God begins to manifest himself to Moses. Then he speaks to him through the cloud. Finally, when Moses rose higher and became more perfect, he saw God in the darkness."[41] Likewise, in the *Commentary on the Song of Songs*, the bride, after having arrived at the darkness, realizes that the Beloved "resists the grasp of our thoughts," and, when she questions the angelic hosts, "Their only answer is silence and by their silence they show that what she seeks is incomprehensible to them, . . . for what she seeks can be understood only in the very inability to comprehend its essence."[42]

The term "darkness" then indicates a break with all mediated meaning, whether undifferentiated commonsense, clearly defined theoretical meaning, or the confrontational intuition of light mysticism. It is an awareness of presence whereby one is conscious of God without being able to know or see God in any way whatsoever. In the *Commentary on the Song of Songs* Gregory describes this further:

> [After having passed beyond all that is sensible,] the bride is encompassed by a divine light (Song 3:1), during which her spouse ap-

proaches, but does not appear. How could that which cannot be seen appear in the night? But he gives to the soul a feeling of presence, even while he eludes her clear apprehension, concealed as he is by the invisibility of his nature.[43]

God never appears (*phainetai*) as one phenomenon, albeit the most preeminent, among others that can be imagined and apprehended. Rather, God comes or approaches (*paraginetai*) in the absence of images and names. This is a realm of meaning beyond empirical knowing (*ezō tōn phainomenōn, ou phainetai*).[44] It was Pseudo-Macarius' failure to distinguish between these two realms of meaning that led him to his description of the divine presence, in which God is pictured as encountering the soul in an empirical fashion.[45]

This mystic presence is variously described by Gregory. It is perceived as a perfume, a touch, a state of drunkenness. But by far the most central term for awareness of God is that of love (*agapē*). In contrast to Origen's intellectualism, love is placed at that summit of the spiritual ascent into darkness, for the soul by its original nature is drawn toward a participation in God beyond words and images. Gregory explains:

> Just as each nature is drawn to that with which it has kinship and as man has a certain kinship with God, since he carries within himself the image of his model, the soul is of necessity drawn toward the divine, with which it is conatural.[46]

Thus the experience of love is a state of fulfillment for the proleptic orientation of human existence toward the full realization of the original image-nature. In the *Sixth Homily in the Beatitudes* Gregory comments on the pure of heart seeing God:

> We must understand this phrase in the sense that it is not those who know something about God who are blessed, but rather those who possess him in themselves. . . . This is not a confrontational vision that God offers to him who has purified the eye of his soul. The deep meaning of the phrase is certainly what the Lord has declared elsewhere: "The kingdom of God is within you," and we understand that he who has purified his own heart of all creatures sees in his own beauty the image of the divine nature.[47]

The phrase "confrontational vision" above is significant because, in the thinking of Gregory, God does not appear as an objective reality over against a subjective knower. This is the basic reason why mystic awareness must occur in darkness. God is not here to be understood as an unchanging essence that actually confronts humans face to face (*antiprosōpou*), nor as an object of vision (*theama*). Rather, when the originally pure image-nature is purified from the superfluous and superadded garments of skin of the passions and illusions, then one becomes aware of God within. It is that awareness and participation that Gregory terms "love," and not any clinging to human images of God.[48] In the *Fourth Homily on the Beatitudes*, he explains:

> God at creation has imprinted the image of the good qualities of his own nature. But sin, in spreading over that divine likeness, has caused those good qualities to disappear by covering it in shameful garments. But if by a rigorous life you wash off[49] the mud[50] that has been splashed over your heart, that God-like beauty will shine anew in you. In effect, that which is akin to the good is good. Thus in seeing yourself, you will see within yourself him whom you seek.[51]

Similarly in *On the Soul and the Resurrection* he says:

> If the soul is liberated from the agitation of passions when it has returned to itself, when it recognizes itself in its true nature, nothing can obstruct it from participating in the [divine] good. It then contemplates the model in its own beauty, as in a mirror and an image.[52]

The original image-nature of human existence means that once the mud of sin has been washed away that image can reflect God as in a mirror, for awareness of God is gained not by seeking to confront a divine, external object, but by recognizing what is reflected in the pure mirror of the consciousness that participates in God.

This mystic awareness is indeed beyond words and images. But that does not render words and images simply useless, for the original nature includes critical faculties of thinking. The same Gregory who is termed the father of Christian mystical theology was also the most speculative of the Cappadocian Fathers and himself developed highly theoretical teachings on Trinity and Incarnation. In distinguishing mystic meaning from theoretical meaning, in depicting mystic awareness as beyond words and images, he does not mean to negate all value to language. But one must keep in mind that language itself can lay no claim to capturing absolute truth, for no words can ever grasp God. Gregory explains:

> The divine nature transcends all intellectual apprehension. Every concept that we form for ourselves of that [divine nature] is an imitation of that which we seek, because it does not show the [divine] form itself, which no one has seen or can see, but rather it sketches "in vision and enigma" a certain image of the object sought which our soul forms by conjecturing. All words which express such concepts have [their] validity from an ineffable point, which cannot express that which the mind intends to say. Thus the soul, led through these

concepts to an understanding of the unknowable realities says that it must make to abide in itself a nature above all understanding.[53]

Theoretical thinking is, then, symbolic and, through its limitations, serves to lead toward a darkening of empirical knowing, namely, into the mystic darkness.

Such mystic participation, although based upon the original image-nature of human beings, is yet an outflow from God and a participation with Christ,[54] for the original nature is created by God and redeemed through Christ. The entire tract *On Perfection* is dedicated to the theme of the imitation of Christ. Such an imitation leads to the purification of the image-nature and is the base for the familiarity of the soul with God whereby it can call God "Abba." Even in his first work, *On Virginity*, Gregory explains:

What happened in the stainless Mary when the fullness of the God-head which was in Christ shone forth through her, that happens in every soul that leads by rule the virgin life. No longer indeed does the Master come with bodily presence, "we know Christ no longer according to the flesh," but spiritually he dwells in us and brings his Father with him. . . .[55]

Even this indwelling is not a totally new reality, but rather, a characteristic of the image-nature, now regained. The *Homily on the Beatitudes* says that "God is in each one, unknown and hidden, and he is found when one turns to him."[56] The presence of Christ is experienced in the three stages of growth, for this presence is perceived in the fruits of mystic growth. The *Commentary on the Song of Songs* describes the seeing of the Master in terms of the awareness of the fruits of spiritual growth.[57] This growth is not the exact same for all, however, for it is adapted to the capabilities of each, and so he appears "in different way in the hearts of those who receive him. He is not the same in everyone, adapting himself to the capacity of each one."[58] The *Fourth Homily on the Beatitudes* summarizes Gregory's understanding of the presence of the word in the soul as the dwelling within the soul of God, the "tasting" of God by the soul:

Thus the great apostle Paul, who has tasted the fruits reserved for Paradise, seems to me to have been satisfied with what he had tasted and yet to have always thirsted: "Christ lives in me," and yet he always "stretches forth (*epekteinetai*) toward that which is ahead," until he states, "It is not that I already know that for which I search nor that I am already perfect."[59]

The presence of Christ is then a realization or fulfillment of the proleptic desire to discover God that flows from the image-nature of our original creation, which, upon completion, expands further the horizons so that a constantly renewed stretching forth and dynamic growth characterizes the awareness of that presence.

This mystic understanding of the meaning of Christ is described in terms of a conscious process of purifying the mind. It implies a going out of the self, a forgetting of empirical knowing, and ecstasy *(ekstasis)*[60] that is attained through a more intimate awareness of the nature of consciousness. This going out of self involves a quieting of the mind and a state of tranquillity *(apatheia)*. As Gregory explains in *The Life of Moses*:

> In the same way [as with Moses' solitude], we shall live a solitary life, no longer entangled with adversaries or mediating between them, but in the sole company of our thoughts and our dispositions with all the movements of our soul unified under the guidance of the mind as a flock of sheep guided by their pastor.[61]

Such a tranquil return to oneself is tied up with awareness of transcendence. In *On Virginity* he explains:

> The great David seems to me to have expressed the impossibility [of expressing the nature of God who is beyond all good]. He was lifted up by the power of the spirit out of himself and saw in a blessed ecstasy the inaccessible and incomprehensible beauty — he saw as fully as a man can see who has gone out from his coverings of flesh and penetrated by consciousness only *(dia monēs dianoias)* to the contemplation of the spiritual and the intelligible — and longing to say something worthy of that which he has seen, he bursts forth with the cry which all re-echo: "All men are liars."[62]

The scriptural passage here treated is Psalm 115, verse 11, which in the Septuagint version reads: *egō eipa en tē ekstasei mou pas anthrōpos esti pseustēs* (I said in my ecstasy, all men are liars). The Hebrew text as translated by the Jerusalem Bible has: "In my alarm I declared: 'No man can be relied upon!' " (Ps. 116:11). But Gregory takes the term *ekstasei* to refer not to a state of alarm, but to mystic insight and withdrawal. In such a state of going out from empirical knowing, all language falls away and misrepresents the content of that mystic understanding. Gregory continues: "I take that to mean that any man who entrusts to language the task of presenting the ineffable light is really and truly a liar, not because of any hatred on his part for the truth, but because of the feebleness of his expression."

It is interesting to contrast here Gregory's treatment with that of Origen and Philo.[63] For Philo, ecstasy implies an abolition of one's own mind, wherein a divine principle takes over and is substituted for human mental functioning. In reaction to the Christian version of Philo's thought as reformulated by the Montanists, Origen interprets ecstasy as a maintaining of the mind on a plane above the sensible. But Gregory evolves a new insight, for in his understanding ecstasy is above all empirical knowing, but yet is a state of human consciousness. At the same time that it is a going out from, ecstasy occurs only because one penetrates and is aware of mystic meaning through consciousness only (*dia monēs dianoias eiselthōn*), that is, when the mind, quieting the vast array of images and words, no longer is deluded by such images and words into thinking that mystic meaning can be grasped as a confrontational object, but, being conscious of itself as consciously striving and stretching forth, becomes aware of the original purity of the mind as reflecting God in simplicity. Thus the going out of ecstasy is again a return to the original image-nature of the pure mind and a rejection of the sense-patterned mode of eonfrontational knowing. This interpretation is further supported by a passage from *Against Eunomius:*

> Abraham at the divine command went forth from his own community and from his own kin, but his migration was such as befitted a prophet in quest of the knowledge of God. Indeed, there is not a physical migration, I think, that can prepare us for the knowledge of those things which are discovered by the spirit. But by going out of his native land, that is, out of himself, out of the realm of base and earthly consciousness, Abraham raised his mind as far as possible above the common limits of our human nature and abandoned the association that the soul has with the senses. Thus, unhindered by appearances, his mind was clear for the apprehension of the invisible, and neither the operation of his sight or hearing could cause his mind to err because of appearances.[64]

Here this going out of self is identified with a change from base and worldly consciousness, based upon and patterned after sense appearance, to a consciousness that, disengaged from such imaginative illusions, is capable of contemplating that which cannot be seen or imagined. The passage continues by explaining the stages of the conversion of consciousness:

> Abraham surpassed in understanding his native wisdom, that is, the philosophy of Chaldea, which rested merely in appearances. ... [He] passed through all the reasoning that is possible about the divine attributes, and, after he had purified his mind of all such concepts, he took hold of a faith that was unmixed and pure of any concept and he fashioned for himself this sign of knowledge of God that is completely clear and free from error, namely the belief that God completely transcends any knowable sign. And so, after this ecstasy which came upon him as a result of these lofty visions, Abraham returned once more to his human frailty: "I am," he admits, "dust and ashes," mute, inert, incapable of explaining rationally the God that my mind has seen.

Here Abraham's going out of himself, his ecstasy, is again a leaving behind of all images and concepts for an imageless faith, purified of concepts. The term "sign" (*sēmeion*), "borrowed from Epicurean thought, refers to sense data which serves as the basis for an inference to the invisible or meta-physical."[65] For Origen such a progression from sign to understanding would remain valid even in ecstasy, but the point for Gregory is that the sign of pure faith is to have no sign at all, and so to be imageless and conceptless.

This attainment of mystic consciousness is further equated with wisdom. In the *Commentary on the Song of Songs* Gregory treats the theme of the cup of wisdom, whereby the participant is lifted above empirical conscious-ness to a state of sober drunkenness. He also connects wisdom's call from on high with this cup of wisdom, for mystic consciousness is a transcending of concepts and images:

> The vine is "the wine that rejoices the heart of man," that fills one day "the cup of wisdom," and is offered to the guests from a call on high for the sake of that good and sober drunkenness.[66]

Such a wisdom is the result of a going out of empirical consciousness, whether commonsense or theoretical. In commenting upon the Song of Songs 5:1, "Eat, my friends, and drink, and become inebriated, my broth-ers," Gregory explains that "All intoxication causes an ecstasy of the mind by wine. Hence what is urged in our text actually is realized in the Gospel through the divine food and drink.[67] And with this food and drink there is constantly brought about a transformation and ecstasy from a lesser state to a better condition."[68]

Such wisdom is not, however, aimed solely at mystic insight for the par-ticipant, but also must somehow be expressed for the sake of others. Even though that state of mystic awareness implies that all people who speak are liars, yet Gregory, following Paul, knows that in some fashion it must be expressed to others. It is such a necessity that led the mystic writers to describe their understanding in the texts under consideration. In the *Com-mentary on the Song of Songs* he explains:

> It is [with this drunkenness] again that Paul ... was intoxicated when he entered ecstasy and declared: If we seemed out of our senses, it was for God, but if we are being reasonable, it is for your sake (2 Cor. 5:13). It is to God that ecstasy relates. But he (i.e., Paul) also affirms in answering Festus that he is not mad, but speaks words of truth and soberness (Acts 26:25).[69]

Here the being "out of our senses" is for God, and points to the ineffable experience of mystic meaning. But, if one is to communicate at all, there is also the need for "being reasonable" in order to speak to men and women. In answer to the Roman governor Festus, who shouted to Paul, "Paul, you are out of your mind; all that learning of yours is driving you mad," Paul rejoins that he speaks words of truth and soberness.

Such mystic understanding is not, however, a fixed, static acquisition that occurs once and for all. As Jean Daniélou has explained, a pervasive theme in Gregory's entire development of mystic thinking is that of the constant stretching forth of horizons.[70] The source for this theme is found in words from Philippians 3:13: "Forgetting what is behind and stretching forth to what is ahead." The term *epektasis* means a reaching forth or a stretching out and is aptly employed by Daniélou to highlight the basic thrust of Gregory's thought as a constant, perpetual progress that takes each and every attainment as the starting point for yet further progress. Even after entering the darkness of mystic awareness, one finds no final resting place. The goal of unchangeable, eternal being described by Origen and Evagrius is no longer seen as the end of the process, for Gregory does not present a system of static, self-enclosed stages leading to a state of blessed immobility, but rather, describes an unending process of expanding horizons.[71] The goal is not any final, definitive state of happiness beyond change, but a constant growth in consciousness of God, who can never be grasped or exhausted. These expanding horizons involve the constant leaving behind of images and concepts. Empirical knowing, intellectual insight, and particular mystic experiences are all left behind in a constant series of vertiginous departures. The starting point in empirical living is described in *The Funeral Oration for Placilla*:

> Like animals who labor and sweat in a mill with their eyes blindfolded, we go about the mill of life always going through the same motions and always coming back to the same place again. I mean that round of hunger, satiety, going to bed, getting up, emptying ourselves and filling ourselves—one thing constantly follows the other and we never stop going round in circles until we get out of the mill.[72]

All such going around in circles is a clinging to what is illusory and without stable basis. The *Commentary on Ecclesiastes* has: "All men's interests in the things of this life are like castles children build in the sand. The enjoyment is limited to the effort one puts into building them and as soon as you stop, the sand collapses and leaves not a trace of the work you put in."[73]

However, at its base, human movement is not merely fragmented into such vicious circles, but, in virtue of the purity of the original image-nature, one can break through to attain a constant mystic growth. In *On Perfection* Gregory explains that human nature is capable of changing and growing in good, so that

> We may constantly evolve toward what is better, being "transformed from glory to glory" (2 Cor. 3:18), and thus always improving and

becoming more perfect by daily growth and never arriving at any limit
of perfection. For that perfection consists in our growth in good, never
circumscribing our perfection by any limitation.[74]

Thus the notion of a constant "stretching forth" is present in all stages of
spiritual growth. In *Against Eunomius* Gregory teaches:

> Relying on what he had already found, he [i.e., Abraham] stretched
> himself forth to the things that were before. . . . And as he disposed
> all these things in his heart, he kept constantly transcending what he
> had grasped by his own power, for this was inferior to what he
> sought.[75]

After the initial drawing of the soul into light,[76] wherein one sets forth on
the path to mystic awareness, the mind is drawn to empty itself of all images,
names, and concepts. This emptying was the intent of Qoheleth, and Gregory is well aware of the mental vertigo it can occasion. His *Commentary
on Ecclesiastes* describes the feelings of mystic disorientation:

> Imagine a sheer, steep crag, of reddish appearance below, extending
> into eternity; on the top there is this ridge which looks down over a
> projecting rim into the bottomless chasm. Now imagine what a person
> would probably experience if he put his foot on the edge of this ridge
> which overlooks this chasm and found no solid footing or anything to
> hold onto. This is what I think the soul experiences when it goes
> beyond its footing in material things in its quest for that which has
> no dimension and which exists for all eternity. For there is nothing it
> can take hold of, neither place nor time, neither measure nor anything
> else; it does not allow our minds to approach. And thus the soul,
> slipping at every point from what cannot be grasped, becomes dizzy
> and perplexed.[77]

A like simile is found in the *Commentary on the Beatitudes*:

> Along the sea coast you may often see mountains facing the sea, sheer
> and steep from top to bottom, while a projection at the top forms a
> cliff overhanging the depths. Now if someone suddenly looked down
> from such a cliff to the depths below, he would become dizzy. So too
> is my soul seized with dizziness now as it is raised on high by this
> great saying of the Lord, "Blessed are the pure of heart, for they shall
> see God." But, "no man hath seen God at any time," says the great
> John. This then is the steep, sheer rock that Moses taught us was
> inaccessible, so that our minds can in no way approach it. For every
> possibility of apprehension is excluded by the words, "No man can
> see the Lord and live."[78]

The vision of God is not a confrontational seeing of God, but the ever-constant leaving behind of accustomed support and the expanding of horizons in the darkness of unknowing. Upon Sinai Moses asked to see God face to face, but God "granted what was requested in what was denied," for

> He would not have shown himself to his servant if the sight were such as to bring the desire of the beholder to an end, since the true sight of God consists in this, that the one who looks up to God never ceases in that desire. . . . The man who thinks that God can be known does not really have life; for he has been diverted from true being to something devised by his own imagination.[79]

Moses sees God in the darkness, but that darkness is meant to guarantee the never-ending realization of expanding mystic awareness in love and apart from the grasping of any set essence in concept or image. *The Life of Moses* declares: "That which is sought transcends all knowledge and is separated on all sides by incomprehensibility as by a kind of darkness."[80]

With this notion of unending progress, Gregory seems to be going beyond the idea of God as an unchanging, immutable essence, for that idea is treated only when he deals with the second stage of the cloud. Rather, he focuses on the mind of nonconfrontational wisdom that abides in an awareness of the ever-expanding dynamic of passing beyond and emptying all concepts and ideas. Gregory is the father of Christian mysticism precisely because he identifies this realm as a contentless and immediate awareness of God in darkness and thus differentiates mystic experience from mediated knowing, whether commonsense or theoretical.

THE PLACE OF PSEUDO-DIONYSIUS

Gregory's themes were taken up and developed by the author of the Pseudo-Dionysian works. The *Corpus Aeropagiticum*, a collection of four books and a set of letters piously but falsely attributed to Dionysius the Aeropagite, the Athenian convert of Paul mentioned in Acts 17:34, continues Gregory's theme of mystic understanding. From the content of these writings it is clear that their author was intimately schooled in the mystic philosophy of Proclus (410–485), who was scholarch at the Athenian School of Neoplatonism. Pseudo-Dionysius stands, then, in the line of Christian thinkers most indebted to Neoplatonic thinking and follows the models of Origen, Clement, and the Cappadocians in explaining Christian faith in terms of Greek philosophy. He felt no need to defend Christian faith against Greek philosophy.[81] In his "Letter Six" to Sosipatrus, a priest, he writes:

> Do not think this a victory, reverend Sosipatrus, to have treated spitefully a religion or an opinion which did not seem to be good. For even

if you refuted the opinion accurately, the opinions of Sosipatrus are not on that account well expressed. For it is possible that the truth, being one and hidden, should elude both you and others, while you are dealing with many false and apparent things. Nor indeed [is it true] that, if something is not red, it follows that it is white, or, if something is not a horse, it must of necessity be a man. If you trust me, you will do as follows: you will no longer speak against others, but you will speak in defense of the truth in such a way that the things you say will be completely irrefutable.[82]

For Dionysius, speaking in defense of truth is not defending one's position against another, for, as will become apparent, his basic understanding of Christian consciousness and theology is apophatic and not generative of affirmative standpoints. "Letter Seven" relates this ecumenical attitude to Greek thought:

I for one do not know that I have ever spoken against Greeks or others, believing it is sufficient for good men if they are able to know and to speak that which is true as it really is. ... It is superfluous, then, for the arguer of truth to do battle with these or those [partisans of this or that opinion]. For everyone says that he alone has the solid currency, yet he may have only a deceptive image of a certain part of the truth. And if you refute this, first one party and then another will want to contend about it. But when an argument has been well proposed through its own truth and remains unrefuted by all others, everything that does not correspond with it in every particular is of itself cast down by the indisputable status of the real truth. Having, I think, well understood this, I have not hastened to speak against Greeks or others. It is enough for me — may God grant me this — first to know about the truth and, having known, to speak as I must.[83]

This passage recommends the abandonment of all confrontational understanding that would line up opinions, Christian or Greek, against one another like horses at the starting line. Rather, it advocates another ground of understanding that would transcend such differences. As Hathaway aptly remarks, the thrust of the *Letters* is found "in the denial of the conflict of beliefs, whether Christian or pagan."[84] Such an understanding is possible only in the presupposition that one is able to move within a realm of mystic meaning, for, if thinking is restricted to theory or commonsense, opinions are clearly lined up against one another.

DIONYSIUS' UNDERSTANDING OF MYSTIC MEANING

Dionysius relies upon the Neoplatonic philosophy of Proclus for the framework of his thinking.[85] The basic teaching of Proclus is that there is a triadic development from the highest, primary One down through all the stages of being. This descending evolutionary process unfolds in three movements: immanence, progression, and turning back. Inasmuch as each being that proceeds from the One is similar to that cause, it has an identity with the causal origin, and thus each being remains in the Principle. But, inasmuch as each being differs from that causal origin, it is said to progress out from it. Thus, although separate from the ultimate One, each being has an innate tendency, eros, to turn back and be again united with the One.

But the primary principle transcends being and thus any predicate that can be applied to it, for "we can only say what it is not, realizing that it stands above all descriptive thought and positive predication."[86] The human soul, however, has a faculty above thought, the *nous* whereby it attains unity with the ultimate in ecstasy.

Dionysius in his *Divine Names* repeats the same threefold division.[87] In his *Heavenly Hierarchy* he describes the ordered stages of the world striving for "as much as possible assimilation to God and union with Him."[88] He describes that striving as eros,[89] love for the ultimate from which they have come and which remains, in the words of Proclus, "present to the mind."[90] Dionysius explains: "All things [are] in relation to it, for the sake of it, and it is present to all, and all things are maintained in it . . . and it is that which all things seek."[91] The ultimate is not treated in terms of conceptual knowing, for it is beyond all concepts. Rather, being present to all it is the original goal that draws forth all movement back toward itself. This process of "turning back" is described by Dionysius as purification, illumination, and union.[92] Here Dionysius seems to have been influenced by Gregory. His *Mystic Theology* begins with the question: "What is the divine darkness?" (*tis ho theios gnophos*), and Cordier in his accompanying commentary in Migne's *Patrologia* explains that "the fullest and most abundant theology consists in [understanding] what that darkness is and how to enter it."[93]

But just what is one purified from? To what is one illumined? What is Dionysius' understanding of mystic meaning? This becomes clear in Dionysius' introductory statement to his *Mystical Theology* and in Maximus' commentary[94] to that work. Dionysius writes:

Triad beyond essence, beyond deity, beyond goodness, . . . guide us to that highest point of mystic words, which is beyond knowing and beyond light, where the simple, unconditioned, and unchangeable mysteries of divine words lie hidden in the darkness beyond the light of the silence of hidden mystery, and in that darkness shine forth more than light.[95]

The first phrase of this passage identifies the Trinity in terms constructed purposefully to contrast with the Chalcedonian definitions. The sequence of the terms seems to imply that it is the Father who is "beyond essence" (*huperousie*) rather then being defined as immutable essence, the Son who is beyond deity (*huperthee*) rather than being defined as consubstantial with the deity of the Father, and the Spirit who is "beyond goodness" (*huperagathe*) rather than being defined as goodness itself. Yet it is not that Dionysius is refuting the doctrine of the Trinity. Rather, he is negating the mode of understanding Trinity as if it were a given essence to be understood by confrontational consciousness. In place of such an extraverted consciousness, turned outward on objects to be understood, divine wisdom is recommended as the true manner of understanding the divine mysteries. These mysteries are described as simple (*apla*), unconditioned (*apoluta*), and unchanging (*atrepta*), terms that echo Gregory's notion of the original unity and simplicity of primal consciousness, prior to the genesis of the subject-object pattern of knowing. Furthermore, just as Gregory described the highest knowing as a darkening, so here the mysteries lie hidden in darkness and silence, that is, beyond the range of any subject-object understanding or enlightenment that might take words and images to correspond to real, given essences. Maximus in his *Scholia on the Mystical Theology* explains in more detail:

> That which is simple and unconditioned are those things which are understood apart from signs and are not beheld in images. The word "unconditioned" is used to refer to those things not said by clinging to names and signs, but rather refers to those things realized through cessation and liberation from all things and concepts. This quiescence of all mental activities in regard to the holy has been referred to as the emptiness of thinking. Now [here it is called] a most obscure darkness in which one cannot see.[96]

Maximus makes clear that that extraverted consciousness, which is turned outward toward signs (*sumbolōn*) and images and which proceeds by clinging to names (*kata anaptuzin onomatōn*), is an obstacle to mystic understanding. All such mental activities must cease (*tē tōn noēseōn apopausei*) and the resultant quiescence (*anenergēsian*), that is, the nonfunctioning of such clinging to names, images, and concepts is precisely the emptiness of thinking (*anoēsian*),[97] or the most obscure darkness (*skoteinotaton*). It is because the mind abandons extraverted consciousness and does not cling to or interpose any idea, image, name, or concept that it opens up the possibility of mystic awareness. In *The Mystical Theology* Dionysius further explains how such cessation is to be attained:

> This is my prayer that you, beloved Timothy, in earnest exercise in regard to the objects of mystic contemplation, should leave behind sense and mental activities, all that is perceived or understood, all that which is not and which is, and in such an unknowing manner

strain toward union with him, beyond all essence and understanding. By the unceasing and unconditional separation from yourself and all things in purity you will be led upwards toward that ray of divine darkness that is beyond essence, leaving behind and being liberated from all.[98]

Gregory's notion of stretching forth (*epektasis*) is found here in Dionysius' statement that one should "strain toward" (*anatathēti*) union, and it is further explained that such a straining forward takes place precisely in the unknowing that is bereft of sense and mental activities. Again Maximus explains:

This [phrase about leaving behind all sense and mental activities] is made clear by comparing [sense and mental activity], for the ancients called what is sensed that which does not exist, since it shares in all manner of change and is not always the same, while they called what is understood that which is, since by the will of the Creator it is always being and does not change its essence.[99]

The dichotomy between sense experience of the changing world and the understanding of the unchanging and immaterial essences is that of Plato himself, for whom the really real (*ontōs on*) is attributed only to the ideal forms (*eidē*) and the world of sense experience is seen merely as an illusory shadow. But for Dionysius both sense and mental activities, both the sensed and the known, must be left behind and transcended in the darkness of unknowing. Plato mounted from sense objects to the intelligible, thus focusing not upon the mind itself, but upon objects of knowing (*noēta*). But Dionysius demands that the entire mode of extraverted, confrontational understanding be abandoned, for the understanding of essences as given units of meaning out there ready to be known constitutes a clinging to names and thus precludes union with an unknowable and unnamable God. Again Maximus explains: "In the phrase 'leaving behind and being liberated' that liberating separation means the abandonment of all attachments so that one might not be detained by any attachment, either to self or to any creature."[100] What was described above as grasping names and concepts is here identified as attachment (*schesis*) either to self (*pros auton*) or to any creature (*pros to tōn ktismatōn*). In the immediacy of direct unknowing, even ideas and concepts are reckoned as creatures, for they interpose a created medium between the understanding mind and the unknown God with whom it is united. It is because extraverted, confrontational consciousness leads to attachments to self and others that it blocks mystic awareness.

In *The Divine Names* Dionysius teaches the same understanding of mystic understanding. The first chapter clearly distinguishes extraverted, confrontational understanding of essences from nonverbal, nonconceptual wisdom. In the introductory heading to this first chapter Dionysius states that his purpose is to explain the tradition concerning divine names. He is not then attempting to offer any new doctrine, but rather, it would seem, to clarify the manner in which the traditional doctrine on naming God should be understood, that is, to identify the realm of meaning in which divine names attain their significance. He begins by contrasting "the per-suasive words of human wisdom" with "the demonstration of the power which the Spirit stirred up in the sacred writings," a distinction drawn from 1 Corinthians 2:4. He then goes on to describe in systematic fashion the nature of this "demonstration," and the entire treatise could well be termed a commentary on Paul's distinction between human knowing and divine wisdom. He explains how the power of the Spirit functions: "In an ineffable and unknowing manner we are joined together with the ineffable and unknowable in a union which exceeds our logical and intuitive facul-ties and abilities."[101]

Here the realm of meaning is mystic, for meaning flows not from logical or intuitive abilities, but rather, from the contact of being joined and united with the ineffable. Since such contact and union is beyond all thought and language, it is completely transcendent to extraverted understanding and this is what is termed "unknowing." He writes: "For an understanding of it (i.e., the Godhead) that is beyond words, mind, and essence is proper to that unknowing beyond essence."[102] Unknowing (*agnosia*) is then a negation not of all awareness, but of the verbal, rational understanding that would identify the name with what is named, the image with what is represented, that would intuit divine meaning as a property of an external essence. But, although the Godhead is beyond such knowing, yet it is not aloof from human understanding. "Divine things are uncovered according to the abil-ities of the minds of each ... through the workings of the goodness of the divine principle."[103]

The leaving behind of extraverted clinging and understanding is precisely the removal of the obstacles that allows those divine things to be uncovered (*anakaluptetai*), for, when images and concepts are taken to capture exter-nal meaning units, they become obstacles that cover over the mind and prohibit divine illuminations. Instead of coming into contact with the divine, the mind is engrossed in considering its own constructs. The removal of these obstacles and the uncovering of the abilities of the mind is the con-stant work of the divine principle, that is, of the goodness of God.[104] The central notion is that such divine workings, although present at all times, are covered over, obfuscated, and hindered by clinging consciousness. It is for these reasons that Dionysius so stresses the inability of any concept to represent God: "It is the cause of all that exists, and yet it is not being, for it is beyond all essence, and only it can validly and understandably shine light on itself."[105]

Maximus in his *Scholia on the Divine Names* comments upon the notion that God is completely unknowable and relates it to the doctrine of the Trinity:

> Only God himself understands himself, knowing himself just as he is. To all others he is unknown in what he is and how he is. "No one knows the Father, except the Son, and the Son, except the Father" (Mt. 11:27). For the Father, knowing his image, which is to be worshipped, that is, the Son, knows himself. The same is true of the Holy Spirit: "No one knows God, except the Spirit, who is of God." Therefore, everything that blessed man here presented is to be understood of the venerable Trinity.[106]

According to Maximus, then, Dionysius' notion of mystic unknowing points to the mystic realm of meaning in which the doctrine of the Trinity is to be understood. That doctrine is not exhausted by a theoretical explanation of divine essence and person, but rather, revealed concretely in the abandoning of all clinging awareness of concepts. The notion of the three persons as "objective presentations" does not mean that they are three objects of theoretical understanding, but rather, that they are presented to pure consciousness as three concrete presentations of the one God who is beyond essence altogether. The ineffable Father is made known by the Son and realized in the Spirit. Christ is the image of the Father, the word from the silence of the Father, inasmuch as in his life and teachings he manifests the Abba experience. The Spirit, who moves in our hearts, is the power whereby we are freed from imagining God as a given essence and realize a conversion of consciousness that attains the wisdom to understand Christ as image and word. Although the divine principle is totally beyond knowing, because of the goodness of that principle in communicating the teaching of the scriptures, by attending to them and removing all attachments to names and concepts, one can attain to that conversion of the mind and understand the scriptural images and their summation in the image of Christ as mediating God as Abba and leading to union. The divine image in humans (*theoeideia*) is not any aspect of empirical human nature, but rather, the pure consciousness in virtue of which one rejects clinging to extraverted meanings. Dionysius describes a progression in the realization of such a conversion:

> For that good is not completely unrelated to beings, but rather, while remaining in itself and having established its ray of light beyond essence, from its loving goodness it shines forth by means of proportionate enlightenments to each and every being and draws them upward to such contemplation, participation, and resemblance of itself.[107]

Dionysius goes on to explain that the first step is the contemplation (*theōria*) of God attained by the abandonment of extraverted consciousness. The second is participation and comes about because all along the good has been in participation (*ou mēn akoinōnēton esti*) with human understanding. The third step is resemblance (*homoiōsis*), whereby the inner divine image, namely, wisdom consciousness, mirrors God to the world. The basic causes for such attainments are the enlightenments (*ellampesin*) that shine forth from the goodness of God.[108]

Such a conversion is not, however, the attainment of a completely new state of mind, for all along the possibility of rejecting extraverted consciousness and returning to the pure consciousness of enlightenment is present.

> We learn that it (i.e., the good) is the cause and origin and essence and life of all. And it is a calling back and a rising back for those who have fallen away from it, a renewing and reforming for those who have stumbled into a corruption of the divine image within them.[109]

The terms "calling back" (*anaklēsis*), "rising back" (*anastasis*), "renewing" (*anakainismos*), and "reforming" (*anamorphōsis*) all imply a return to a lost state of consciousness and connote that the original mind was free from clinging and did mirror the divine. They not only reflect Proclus' notion of "turning back," but also echo Gregory's teaching on the original unity of consciousness and on the image-nature of human beings.

THE DOUBLE TRADITION OF THEOLOGY

The process of abandoning all names and images is what Dionysius terms "negative theology," for by negating each and every possible concept that might be applied to God, one realizes the emptiness of thought necessary for mystic insight. Negative theology thus has priority over any positive theology that would describe God in ideas and images. But thinking about God cannot remain silent in its mystic wonder, lest "divine ignorance" be mistaken simply for ignorance. In the development of thought in his *Letters*, Dionysius moves from an emphasis on negative theology, which ascends through negation to an awareness of the first principle in unknowing, to an emphasis on affirmative theology, which, once the firm insight into the incomprehensibility of God is attained, can then descend through words and thinking to positive statements about God.[110]

The structure of the *Letters* depicts this process. As Ronald Hathaway explains:

> . . . in the *First Letter* God is equivalent to *the* unknown; in the *Second*, this unknown transcends even the term "divinity" and has no relation to any other being. The *Third* and *Fourth Letter* treat the descent of God into the world. The *Fifth* through the *Seventh Letter* cautiously affirm the manifestation of God in perceptible things generally, then

in nature as the "cause" of such things as eclipses, the notion of the sphere, and other miracles. The *Eighth Letter* ends with a story about the descent of Christ as an act of justice, and deals with the manifestation of God in the world as justice. The theme of the *Ninth Letter* is the manifestation of God in "symbols," both in scripture and in the whole of visible nature, and the *Tenth* alludes to the manifestation of God (at the lowest level, below even shadow and dreams) in personal revelations to men, such as that of John.[111]

The movement of these *Letters* is first away from an extraverted, positive theology that would cling to and defend its names and images as expressing the real truth about God to a negative theology that rests in the cessation of conceptual thinking and divine ignorance. But, once having realized such "ignorance," thinking again proceeds to speak affirmatively through symbols, that is, through names and images. The crucial difference is that one no longer clings to these names and images or assumes that they represent any absolute essence that can be conceptually identified. Through the catharsis of negative theology positive theology passes over into symbolic theology, which is simply the nonclinging employment of symbolic affirmations. In "Letter Nine," Dionysius defines symbolic theology as the employment of "names from perceptible things applied to divine things."[112] Thus symbolic theology is affirmative theology in the "light" of the divine darkness and is thus apophatic, since it affirms from a context of prior negation. Names do not refer to their sensed images or understood concepts, but rather, meaning is understood as insight through names and images into what is beyond names and images. Theology does not fall from heaven, but is a mental construct reflecting the underlying consciousness of the one who theologizes. Extraverted theologians who imagine they are dealing with external meaning units called essences use positive statements to "explain" the mysteries, while symbolic theologians use names and images to introduce one into those mysteries. No one may be content to remain aloof in the cessation of all thinking, in the total embrace of divine darkness, for, as "Letter Nine" states: "All those who hear a clear theology without symbols weave in themselves a sort of model, which guides them to an understanding of such a theology."[113]

Thus Dionysius is led to propose a double tradition of theology, the one negative and the other symbolic. "Letter Nine" explains:

It must be understood that the theologian's tradition is double, being on the one hand not expressed in words (*arrētos*) and mystical (*mustikē*), and on the other public (*emphanē*) and a matter of common knowledge (*gnōrimōtera*); on the one hand symbolic (*sumbolikē*) and aiming at initiation (*telestikē*), and on the other philosophic (*philoso-*

phon) and aiming at demonstration (*apodeiktikē*); and what is not said is interwoven with what is said.[114]

These distinctions can be arranged in columns as follows:

What Is Said	What Is Not Said
not expressed in words	public
mystic	common knowledge
symbolic	philosophic
aimed at initiation	aimed at demonstration

The first series denotes the nonverbal awareness of mystic unknowing, which can be expressed only through symbols and experienced only through initiation, namely, a direct experience of the mysteries. The second series denotes verbal teachings, available to all and subject to discussion. If one were to rely only upon verbal theology, then positions are generated, clung to, and defended. But such clinging, albeit for valid apologetic purposes, constitutes an obstacle to mystic awareness. If, on the other hand, one were to rely only upon nonverbal awareness, he or she simply does not write or speak theology at all. The fusion of both means that theoretical theology must be done from an awareness of mystic meaning, for both theory and mystic insight are to be interwoven within the same consciousness. Dionysius continues:

> Theologians view some things as involved in this world (*politikōs*) and subject to custom (*ennomōs*) and others with a view to purification (*kathartikōs*) and non-defilement (*achrantōs*); some humanly (*anthrōpikōs*) and mediately (*mesōs*), but others as beyond the world (*huperkosmiōs*) and with a view to perfection (*telesiourgikōs*) . . . according to what is suitable to the sacred writings and to minds and souls.[115]

Whereas the first schema, above, emphasized the necessity for the double tradition of theology to be interwoven and interdependent, this schema stresses that each must be used in accord with the differing needs of the individual people to whom theology is directed. This schema can be charted as follows:

Involved in the world	Aimed at purification
Subject to custom	Aimed at nondefilement
Human	Beyond the world
Mediate	With a view to perfection

This last set echoes the theme of purification, illumination, and union stated above, for, after being made pure and undefiled, one attains illumination beyond the world and realizes perfection in union. But that awareness of mystic meaning must then be mediated to people in worldly recognizable terms, that is, in conventional words and images. The needs of each person determine whether the theologian speaks negatively or affirmatively.

THE RELATIONSHIP BETWEEN MYSTIC AND THEORETICAL THOUGHT

For Dionysius the mystic realm of meaning is a distinct and different realm from the theoretical, for insight into mystic meaning occurs not when one sees the systematic interrelation of a number of logically related ideas, but in the immediacy of direct contact. Yet the same mind that has mystic awareness also thinks theoretically. Gregory of Nyssa not only evolved a mystical theology, but also wrote numerous tracts on doctrinal, theoretical themes. Although Gregory did indeed delineate the mystic realm of meaning, it is not clear just how these realms of meaning are to be related one to the other. How does Gregory's highly precise and theoretical treatment of the *hupothaseis* and the *ousia* of God relate to the darkness of mystic awareness? Are they negated at some higher level? The emphasis on the double tradition of theology presented by Dionysius seems to be an attempt to relate these realms in some kind of intelligent fashion, for verbal, theoretical knowledge always follows upon and is evolved from an awareness of mystic unknowing. Hence, it would be of some interest to examine just how Dionysius treated the main doctrinal themes of Incarnation and Trinity, for he attempts to interpret all Christian teaching with a more consistent awareness of mystic meaning.

At first glance Dionysius' christology appears to be quite distinct from the theoretical outline presented in chapter 3, above. The technical terminology of those disputes is not central to his writings.[116] It is sometimes thought that this is due to his postulated monophysite understanding of Christ,[117] but there is a lack of even monophysite terminology and little attempt to demonstrate its superiority to the Chalcedonian definitions. It would perhaps be the case then that the main reason for this distinctiveness of Dionysius' christology is not his monophysite leaning, but rather, his attempt to alter the meaning realm in which the entire discussion takes place.

Dionysius does repeatedly and strongly affirm that Christ is both God and human. René Roques gathers together the relevant passages and concludes that Dionysius' christology is substantially orthodox.[118] But his thinking proceeds in a different key. If we interpret his christology in accord with the notion of a double tradition of theology, it becomes evident that Christ is, on the one hand, beyond words and mystic, while on the other being the enunciation of the divine silence to humankind. In *The Mystical Theology* Dionysius writes: "Jesus, who is beyond essence (*ho huperousios Iēsous*) has become essential in the truth of human nature."[119]

Christ is here interpreted not in the terms of the divine and human natures of the earlier christological discussion. Rather than working with notions of divine and human essence, Dionysius uses notions of no-essence and essence. It is difficult not to see this as implying a criticism of the earlier Nicene and Chalcedonian definitions. From the perspective of negative theology, Dionysius frequently stresses that the Incarnation is beyond words and inexpressible. In *The Divine Names* he states: "The most clear teaching of theology, the incarnation and birth of Jesus in human form is inexpressible in any words and unknown by any mind."[120]

Yet, although inexpressible and beyond verbal thinking, Jesus does become human and takes on human compound existence. As *The Divine Names* explains:

> And it [the divine Triad] is called benevolent because in one of its *hupostaseis* it truly and entirely shared in our human condition, calling to itself and uplifting the low human condition. Because of this in an ineffable manner the simple Jesus came into compound existence and the eternal took on temporal duration and he who, being beyond all essence entirely transcends all fixed natures, was born in our nature without change or confusion of his own abiding.[121]

Dionysius here repeats the general teaching that Christ is a divine *hupostasis* who has taken on human nature. But such a description is the coming of the simple Jesus (*ho aplous Iēsous*) into compound existence and must therefore be understood as the public, language-formed symbol for the unknown content of the Incarnation. According to Maximus' *Scholia* cited above, the term "simple" refers to "those things which are understood apart from signs and not beheld in images."[122] Thus to term Jesus *aplous* means that he cannot be properly understood by means of clinging to extraverted signs and symbols. However, he has come into compound existence, for Jesus is the speaking of God from silence. "Letter Four" again treats this theme:

> How is Jesus, who is beyond all essence, wholly and substantially in the same rank with men? It is not as though he were the cause of men [for then he would simply be God], but rather as though he were in himself in his whole being really a man. However, we do not define Jesus in human terms. For he is not a man only. [He would not be above being if he were a man only.] But [we define him] as being a man truly beyond men, a being beyond being made substance according to men out of the substance of man. But no less does he preserve his eternal transcendence of being in his superfluidity. In truly coming into being, made to be above being, he did the things of man [in a manner] above man. ... By seeing in a divine way one will come to know ... affirmative statements above [one's] mind about Jesus' love

of man, but not in the sense that he was not-man, but in the sense that, though from man, he was beyond man, and beyond man he truly became man. And for the rest he did not do the things of God as God or the things of man as man, but, when God was made man, he exercised for us a new kind of divine-manlike activity.[123]

Dionysius' refusal here to define Jesus in human terms reflects the negative approach of abandoning all names and images, for one can come to understand affirmative statements only in a divine way, that is, by unknowing. Therefore, there is no discussion of the union of natures, since Dionysius rejects the concept of nature as being truly applicable to God at all. Rather, Christ is the sum of the double tradition, the enunciation of the ineffable. This understanding of Christ is not the ontological picture evolved in the earlier disputes, but a mystic understanding in which Christ, as the enunciation of the ineffable deity, is described as simple and constantly related to the activities of purification, illumination, and union. In his *Ecclesiastical Hierarchy* he explains:

We know that the most divine Jesus is a perfume beyond essence (*huperousiōs euōdē*), who transmits himself to our minds in an intelligible manner and fills them with divine joy. . . . Jesus is the fertile source of divine perfumes and it is he himself who, in the measure appropriate to divinity, fills the minds which have attained to the greatest conformity with God.[124]

The approach of Jesus is a mystic experience, imaged forth here under the metaphor of perfume, for he comes to the mind unseen and apart from rational inquiry.

However, not all scholars agree that Dionysius' christology is orthodox. Many hold that, because of his total focus on nonverbal unknowing, he simply has no room for any teaching on the Incarnation. Dean Inge thinks that "Dionysius the Aeropagite describes the Father as 'superessential indetermination,' the unity which unifies every unity, the absolute no-thing which is above all unity." He then argues that this "philosophical" conception cannot satisfy "the requirements of religion," in which deity must be granted attributes of personality.[125] Similarly Christian Baur argues that the terms "beyond essence, beyond deity, and beyond good" represent philosophical abstractions and, since they have no reality, there is no room for any new relationship within God and thus no room for the Incarnation.[126] Étienne Vacherot repeats this criticism that "in place of the living God" Dionysius presents "an abstract Trinity, unintelligible," which cannot be related to the human in the Incarnation.[127]

But these critics do not seem to have fully appreciated the teaching of Dionysius on the double tradition of theology, according to which there is a clear separation between the symbolic, mystic, nonverbal negative theology, and the philosophic, public, conventional, affirmative theology. In Dionysius, divine ignorance is not to be equated with philosophical abstraction. Quite the contrary, its focus is upon bringing about an understanding of consciousness that functions not only in the verbal, philosophic mode of names and concepts, but also in the nonverbal mode of direct awareness, in which no attribute can be grasped as literally and absolutely true. The point is, then, not to uphold the divine incomprehensibility as an item of obscure theological lore, but to invite one to examine the nature of religious consciousness within oneself. Once the realm of mystic consciousness is clearly understood, then all kinds of appropriate images can be used to aid in the theoretical and philosophical understanding of the Incarnation and the Trinity, for all theologians weave in themselves models of that which they cannot express. Dionysius' intent, it would appear, was to weave a mystic model that would speak the words of christology only in the "light" of mystic darkness. His attempt was both to deconstruct the theoretical presentation of Christ and to reclaim it in terms of a symbolic theology, functioning in clear awareness of the emptiness of all thinking.

CONCLUSION

The mystic thinking of Gregory and Dionysius did indeed succeed in distinguishing and delineating the mystic realm of meaning as apart from all mediating images and words, as distinct from the extraverted, confrontational knowing of imagined essences. In the notion of a double tradition of theology, as explicated in Dionysius' *Letters*, an attempt was made to relate that mystic understanding to the doctrinal and theoretical meanings of faith. But the *Letters* themselves do not seem to have exercised much influence and they are seldom quoted by later thinkers. Even the teaching of *The Divine Names* and *The Mystical Theology*, which were cherished throughout the Middle Ages, was not accepted at face value. Rather than granting primacy to negative theology, from which one might proceed to develop a symbolic, affirmative theology, Christian thinkers, following Aristotle, affirmed the primacy of an affirmative understanding of religious meaning. Throughout the history of Western theology the themes of Gregory and Dionysius have remained apart from the dominant intellectualist pattern of thinking, marginal and confined to books on spirituality and devotion. They were marginal because they directly challenged the subject-object mode of thinking underlying that dominant theology and could not be adopted without raising fundamental problems about the validity of that theology.

For the Schoolmen of the Middle Ages truth is the *adequatio rei et intellectus*, the bridging over of the gap between the subjective knower and the objective reality. For Thomas Aquinas (1225–74), the paradigm of Scholastic thinkers, human beings essentially are contingent rational beings, contingent because it is not of their essence that they in fact exist. God, on the other hand, is a necessarily existent being, for God's essence is precisely to exist (*ipsum esse*).[128] Since it is God who is the cause of all created beings and because causality implies that there is an influx exerted in the beings created,[129] all created beings participate in being inasmuch as they share in the being granted by God through creation as an effect shares in the being of its cause.[130] Thus creatures in some degree resemble that divine cause, and therefore one can know God by ascending from the attributes of created beings to their uncreated cause. But the attribution of creaturely attributes to God does not mean that they retain the same sense in both cases, for we do not know how God contains goodness, truth, beauty, and so forth, only that in God they are identified with God's very being. As Étienne Gilson explains, "it is precisely as equivocal (i.e., as meaning two quite different things) that God contains the effects He creates and that, consequently, their perfections can be attributed to Him."[131] But, because of the relation binding cause to effect, what we say about God is not altogether equivocal, for creatures participate proportionately in the being from which they come.

For Dionysius, positive, symbolic theology is a weaving of affirmative models that flow from the awareness of unknowing, that is, from negative theology. The primacy remains always with negative theology. Thomas Aquinas also begins by refusing to attribute to God any of the qualities we see in the world (*primo quidem et principaliter in omnium ablatione*). But then, in explicit contrast to Dionysius, he develops a more positive evaluation of theology.[132] As Gilson explains, "the proper object of negative theology, therefore, is to prevent us from staying on the level where the names of creatures are uncritically understood as properly applying to God."[133] But, after that first step, a second step consists "in transcending those things and attributing them to God by excess (*secundario vero per excessum*)," for "we know God by way of causality when we consider that whatever is found in creatures proceeds from God as from its cause." Thus the names applied to God are valid in an analogical sense, and they "are said of the very substance of God; that is, of that which God himself is."[134] The analogical knowledge of God grounds, for Thomas Aquinas, the validity of applying to God positive, affirmative attributes, as long as they are shorn of their creaturely mode and understood to be in excess of whatever they mean in creatures.

Theoretical meaning becomes not a symbolic weaving of models to express the ineffable, but an analogic and valid affirmation of what in fact is true about God. Such a theology saw no need to relate itself organically to the mystic thought of a Gregory or a Dionysius. It considered that it had already incorporated and retained what was true in their teaching on mystic themes. But the point of mystic thought was not its content, but rather, its distinguishing between the realms of meaning and the underlying patterns of consciousness in which mystic meaning is understood. Thomas Aquinas knew well that negative theology cannot remain in its mystic silence, but he failed to understand the distinction between theoretical and mystic realms of meaning. In his *De Potentia* he writes:

> The meaning of a negation is founded in an affirmation, as appears from the fact that every negative affirmation is proved by an affirmative one; consequently, unless the human understanding knew something of God affirmatively, it could deny nothing of God; and such would be the case if nothing of what it says of God could be verified affirmatively.[135]

Gregory would demur, for his mystic unknowing did not flow from any surety of a prior affirmative knowledge about God, but from an experience of love and presence in the light of which all affirmations were totally darkened. The prior awareness of God, of ultimate meaning did not for him move in a realm of knowledge at all, but in one of the immediacy of mystic contact. Consequently Gregory's awareness, unable to be expressed conceptually, can hardly presuppose the validity of affirmative knowing.

The pattern of this Christian mystic thought has never been organically related to Christian theory because it was subsumed under and judged by the criteria of that theory. Christian mysticism tended to be a light mysticism, present in the realization of the truth already expressed in theoretical doctrines, rather than the source from which doctrine flowed. Faith is preached, then, not as the sharing in experience and insight, but as the announcing of the validity of religious truth claims. It would appear that in the history of Christian thinking the mystic teachings of Gregory and Dionysius have not been organically related to the mainstream theology. While deeply honored for their attainments, mystics are not considered to be serious thinkers. And, while theologians abound, their own religious experience is often considered not central to their theologizing.

Such an imbalance, whether to the one side or the other, can perhaps be redressed by understanding the religious consciousness that generates meaning in all realms. A critical understanding of consciousness could both identify and defend the genesis of both mystic and theoretical meaning by outlining their realms and procedures, and grounding them within the same religious mind.

An overemphasis on Christian theory tends to obviate the need to focus upon such a critical understanding of religious meaning, for it is tacitly assumed that mystics simply express in a poetic and metaphorical manner the content of that theory. But Gregory and Dionysius—together with the entire lineage of Christian mystics who follow them—are speaking in a different key and with a different understanding of what constitutes meaning, that is, direct, immediate experience. Theoretical Christian thought seldom finds itself seriously threatened by its mystics, who by and large think and speak outside its theoretical arena.

By contrast, historical circumstances in the evolution of Buddhist thought in India forced the Mahāyāna thinkers to deal directly with the relationship between mystic awakening and religious discourse, for Mahāyāna Buddhism began as a mystic movement that negated the validity of theory altogether. The Mādhyamika and Yogācāra schools, being of a philosophical turn of mind, were as a result faced with the problem of how to validate clear, logical thinking upon that mystic base. In their treatment of the problem, they evolved an understanding of consciousness that attempted to hold in healthy tension both mystic and theoretical meanings by identifying their realms within an understanding of human consciousness. Meaning is understood neither as logical, consistent theory nor as direct mystic insight. Rather, in Yogācāra, meaning is understood as a function of conscious operations, generated either from illusory or true consciousness. Besides the realms of commonsense, theoretical, and mystic meaning, they identified another realm of critical meaning wherein one understands not practical, logical, or mystic meaning, but the consciousness that generates each. In such a critical realm, meaning is constituted not by practical considerations, logical necessity, or direct insight but, rather, by understanding its genesis and ground within the mind.[136]

The subsequent discussion will shift, then, from outlining the developments in Christian thinking to a consideration of the understanding of consciousness evolved by the Mahāyāna thinkers, for that understanding of consciousness can perhaps serve as a basis for interpreting not only Buddhist experience, but also the Christian meaning of Christ as expressed in the Gospels—and for a reclaiming of the centrality of the Christian mystic tradition of darkness and unknowing.

PART II

Mahāyāna Thought as Theologiae Ancilla

6

The Developing Pattern
of Buddhist Doctrine:
The Mādhyamika Philosophy
of Emptiness

It is the argument of this book that Mahāyāna Buddhist philosophy, especially the Mādhyamika thought of Nāgārjuna and the Yogācāra thought of Asaṅga, can assist Christian theology both in reclaiming the centrality of its own mystic tradition and in maintaining a valid place for theoretical systematics. Yogācāra philosophy is suited for this purpose because it developed in response to questions about the grounding and criteria of religious meaning and was intended to validate both mystic awareness and conventional, language-formed presentations of that awareness. But the basic doctrines of Mahāyāna predate Yogācāra. The Prajñāpāramitā scriptures and Mādhyamika philosophy first presented the themes of emptiness, dependent co-arising, and the two truths, heightening the tension between theory and mystical awareness. In order to place Yogācāra in its context, we must sketch the history of Buddhist thought prior to the rise of Yogācāra, with particular attention to the evolving tension between theoretical, systematic thinking and mystic understanding.

THE NATURE OF THE BUDDHA'S AWAKENING

The foundational experience of all Buddhism is the awakening of Śākyamuni Gautama, who died about the year 486 B.C.E.[1] In the primitive Buddhist community, that awakening was expressed in terms of the four noble truths and the twelvefold chain of causes. But the initial movement of Indian thought did not begin with the Buddha, for he appears within the developing flow of Indian thinking. Earlier Indian texts, the *Upaniṣads*, contrast the constantly changing experience of human beings transmigrating through many lifetimes of suffering with the unchanging, ever-abiding reality of the *brahman*, identified with the self (*ātman*) of each individual, as in the famous phrase *tat tvam asi* (that [*brahman*] thou [*ātman*] art) from the *Chāndogya Upaniṣad*.² *Ātman* or *brahman* transcends time and is beyond all words and descriptions. This monistic teaching constituted the most popular worldview at the time of the historical Buddha.

The Buddha, however, did not accept this doctrine of an eternal *ātman* (self), but took all existence to be an unceasing flow of change and suffering. He taught that human beings from the beginningless beginning have been transmigrating in the wheel of suffering through endless lives (*saṃsāra*) and have no hope of ever being absorbed into or united with any eternal *brahman*. He did not offer an escape from the radical inevitability of empirical change. The Buddha's teaching of no-self (*anātman*) is meant to negate any notion of a self, either as the inner constituent core of a person or as the outer constituent core of the universe. It is grounded in insight into the impermanence of all things, an impermanence one cannot avoid by taking refuge in any theories of an eternal, unchanging self.³

For the Buddha the final goal is defined in terms of stopping this painful samsaric flow of constant change; *nirvāṇa* is precisely the cessation of that flow. But it is not any kind of an eternal state of self-abiding. It is, rather, the complete abandonment of all concern for self, even ultimate concern for self. In virtue of the compassion that arises from the wisdom of awakening, a buddha (an awakened one) abides in a nonabiding cessation (*apratiṣṭhita-nirvāṇa*). He dwells neither in cessation nor in transmigration, but maintains his or her presence among humans for the sake of performing the deeds of compassion.

The four truths are the outflow of such compassion, for they describe the content of the Buddha's awakening so that others might become so awakened. The first truth is that all is suffering (*duḥkha-satya*), that all joys and pleasures are fleeting and without lasting worth. The second truth is that there is an origin of suffering (*samudaya-satya*), presented in the twelvefold chain of causes: each element in our phenomenal experience arises in dependence on its predecessor in a cyclical and ongoing tedium and ennui. The third truth, the cessation of that suffering (*nirodha-satya*), as witnessed in the Buddha's awakening, means that suffering may be ended; while the fourth truth, the path (*mārga-satya*), preaches the concrete way human beings might realize that cessation for themselves.

In its full traditional form, the origin of suffering is described as a twelvefold chain of causes, each of which leads to the next. The full list includes ignorance, impelling conditions, consciousness, named forms, the six senses, sense and mental contact, sensation, thirst for what is sensed and known, the desire to possess those things, the experience of rebirth, rebirth itself, and old age/death.⁴ This series is intended to account for constant transmigration in the world of suffering and means that the self (*ātman*), either as the perduring reality of the person or as the participation in a transcendent self, is but an illusion; the consciousness of a self is simply a misunderstanding of the dependently co-arisen series of twelve causes.

This teaching is not, however, meant to be a philosophic account of life-in-the-world. It is more a phenomenological description of human experience than an attempt to relate causes one to the other in a logically consistent fashion. It is a mistake to subject these primitive Buddhist teachings to a rigorous logical analysis, a mistake made not only by modern scholars, but even by the ancient Buddhist disciples themselves. The Chinese *Āgama*[5] entitled *The Scripture on the Teaching of the Twelve Causes* presents an account of this causal chain that undercuts all attempts to identify systematically its components in clear concepts and consistent logic. The account begins with the disciple Ānanda meditating on the twelve causes. He opines that, though they are claimed to be truly deep and profound, he in fact does understand them quite well. So thinking, he begins to wonder why they are considered to be so profound. He bestirs himself out of his meditative posture, goes to the Buddha, and repeats his query.

> Then the Buddha spoke to Ānanda and said: Cease and desist! Don't say such a thing! The clarity of the doctrine of the twelve causes is indeed profound and difficult to understand. Ānanda, the twelve causes are difficult to see, are difficult to understand. All the gods and spirits, priests and hermits and brahmins have not yet gained insight into them. If they try to conceptualize, analyze, and reason out their meaning, they will all be lost in the woods and be unable to gain insight into them.[6]

With Ānanda consenting at each and every step, the Buddha proceeds to explain the chain of causes that result in suffering. It does indeed seem that Ānanda is well informed on this most basic of the Buddha's teachings. But the text then presents what is perhaps an older version of the causal series wherein one identifies the primal cause of suffering not as ignorance, but as the mutual interplay between naming things and consciousness:[7] "Thus it is, Ānanda, that consciousness has the naming of material forms as its cause and the naming of material forms has consciousness as its cause." The entire process that results in suffering is due to the arising of consciousness in the naming of material forms, which forms in turn confront and structure that consciousness. The Buddha continues: "If consciousness were not to abide in name and form, then it would have no abiding place. And, if it had no abiding place, then birth, old age, sickness, death, sorrow, pity, suffering, and anxiety would not occur."

Although Ānanda might have properly grasped the correct names and the literal meaning of the doctrine, this does not mean that he has actually understood its underlying meaning. If he merely abides in the names in which the doctrine is presented, his consciousness has not escaped the samsaric cycle of suffering. The Buddha goes on to explain that his intent in presenting the twelve causes was to bring it to speech, not to offer any theory: "Ānanda, I have presented this [doctrine] in order to verbalize it, in order to render it suitable [to human understanding], in order to arrange it [in an intelligible fashion], for the sake of wisdom insight, for the sake of sentient beings."

The presentation of the doctrine is not, then, a verbal disquisition to be learned by means of rational analysis, but a means of enunciating what cannot be grasped by such reasonings—verbalized only for the sake of aiding sentient beings to realize awakening. It is a mystic cessation of that naming consciousness that clings to words as pictures of reality. The famed refusal of the Buddha to engage in metaphysics is due to the mystic nature of his primal awakening. His doctrine (*dharma*) does not abide in names and is liberated from the clinging and suffering they bring in their wake. The primal awakening of Buddha takes on its significance only within a mystic realm of meaning.

The Greater Discourse on the Lion's Roar in *The Middle Length Sayings* explicitly describes the Buddha's insight as above all reasonings. It reports the Buddha as pronouncing the following anathema:

> Now, if of me, who knows and sees all this, anyone were to say that there is nothing superhuman about the recluse Gautama's ennobling gifts or his knowledge and insight, and that it is Gautama's own reasoning which has hammered out a doctrine of his own evolving and personal invention, if such a one does not recant these words of his, change his heart, and renounce his view, he will find himself hauled into hell.[8]

Thus the early Buddhist texts, the Pali *Nikāyas* and the parallel Chinese *Āgamas*, present the Buddha's awakening as a mystic awareness. The focus of the Buddha was upon the concrete, phenomenological experiencing of such mystic awareness. This is why he refused to engage in metaphysics, "for they do not conduce to . . . final cessation."[9] This is why he refused to indulge in any escape from impermanence in a doctrine of an eternal, unchanging *ātman*.

THE RISE OF BUDDHIST THEORY

But people do think, and, despite the advice not to engage in unprofitable questioning, many cannot quench the desire to understand what doctrines imply and how they form a consistent whole. Even in the early texts, the very same *Nikāyas* and *Āgamas*, there are passages which demonstrate a growing theoretical exigency, which finds its full development in the later Abhidharma scholasticism. The term *abhi-dharma* originally meant "in regard to the doctrine,"[10] and the Abhidharma tractates were meant as explanation and systematizations of the doctrine of the scriptures, the *sūtras* taught by the Buddha.[11] This theoretical thrust eventually resulted in a separate *Abhidharma* collection of commentarial texts alongside the *Sūtra* and the *Vinaya* (Discipline) Collections to form the three "baskets" (*piṭaka*) of the Buddhist canon.

In its final stage the Abhidharma masters not only organized commentaries on the scriptural teachings, but presented their own rearrangement and theories on the meaning of those teachings. Such theoretical teaching in fact constituted a Buddhist scholasticism, and the term "Abhidharma" came to mean "the higher or the special teaching." In the later commentaries of the Sthavira tradition, it was regarded as "the superior doctrine."[12] This superior doctrine was precisely a theoretical, philosophical understanding of the mystic awareness of original Buddhism.

The modern Theravāda master Nyanatiloka explains: "[the Abhidharma collection] is . . . in no way to be considered as a corruption or distortion of the Buddha's doctrine, but rather as an attempt to systematize all the doctrines laid down in the Sūtra [collection], and to elucidate them from the philosophical . . . standpoint."[13] Just as the Hellenization of the gospel entailed a bifurcation of meaning, so in Buddhist doctrinal history, the development of the Abhidharma scholasticism sharply distinguished theoretical meanings from the commonsense, mystic meanings of the earlier scriptures.

New technical languages were developed and the early Abhidharma texts devote much attention to defining their language "matrix" (*matṛka*),[14] for without a clear definition of terms, it was felt that the meaning of the doctrine might indeed be lost. *The Discipline of the Mūlasarvāstivāda* explains:

> The men of later times are of small wisdom and dull senses. They rely upon texts to understand and do not grasp deep meanings. . . . So I myself (i.e., Kāśyapa) will now present the definitions (*matṛka*), because I want to assure the preservation of the meaning of Scripture and Discipline.[15]

This passage not only highlights the development of theoretical thinking, but also identifies the underlying impulse as the felt need to preserve the integrity of the scriptures. Just as in the Christian West, it was feared that the meaning of the scriptures might be misconstrued and thus clear systematizations and definitions were aimed at preserving their original teaching. The Abhidharma commentaries were considered to constitute a discernment of that original teaching. Vasubandhu[16] in the *Commentary on the Abhidharma Treasury* defines Abhidharma as "pure wisdom with its accompanying elements. Wisdom is the discernment of doctrines."[17] This discernment is a serial investigation of all teachings and results in a theoretical grasp of absolute truth. Wisdom, objectified in the Abhidharma teaching, became an analytic understanding of the content of all teaching, of the *dharmas*, or the essences of all things.

Vasubandhu further explains the content of this discernment by distinguishing commonsense, relative truth (*saṃvṛti-satya*) from the absolute truth (*paramārtha-satya*) of philosophically analyzed concepts.[18] Absolutely true concepts here mediate absolute truth, which, if implemented and practiced, can lead to the cessation of suffering and the attainment of awakening. Conceptual analysis issues in a knowing of the essences (*svabhāva*) of things, the firm, stable, and perduring factors behind commonsense appearances. For example, when the Abhidharma masters treated the commonsense notion of a self, they found that there was no essence corresponding to the self and thus identified it as an illusion. But they did locate five stable elements underlying that illusion, the five aggregates of material form, sensation, conceptualization, karmic dispositions, and consciousness. These were deemed to exist absolutely (*paramārtha-sat*), and the knowledge of such freed one from clinging to the self. *The Abhidharma Treasury* presents a list of seventy-five such factors (*dharmas*).[19] All things could be philosophically understood as comprised of such *dharmas*, which are themselves absolute because they cannot be further reduced to more basic elements through any subsequent analysis. The Greeks were not the only thinkers who evolved an ontological pattern focused upon the content of what is known, for their *noēta* parallel the Abhidharma concept of *dharmas* as the *svabhāva*, or essence of things. In Abhidharma, wisdom is equated with theory and the differentiation between commonsense and theoretical realms of meanings is seen as the difference between the commonsense, relative truth, and the philosophically absolute truth. Nyanatiloka explains that "in the Sūtra the doctrines are more or less explained in the words of the philosophically incorrect 'conventional' everyday language understood by anyone, while the Abhidharma, on the other hand, makes use of purely philosophical terms in the absolute sense."[20] In a like vein the fifth-century Therevāda master Buddhaghosa states that "the Abhidharma is instruction in the absolute nature of things."[21]

The Abhidharma becomes the systematic objectification of the content of awakening, of absolute truth, and its unfolding of that content in theoretical terms. Although the original awakening of the Buddha was a mystic awareness, the Abhidharma enterprise became quite rationalistic. In terms similar to those of the Christian fathers who were most influenced by Plato, the Abhidharma masters drew a clear distinction between the changing impressions of the sense world, which offer only a conventionally valid, practical truth, and the realm of true knowledge, which exists absolutely and can be grasped in well-analyzed concepts. Beyond the changing world, there are stable and unchanging realities. One can indeed obtain the correct view (*samagdṛṣṭi*), which allows one to eradicate passion and attain awakening. One can become a saint through learning the path and implementing it in a lengthy series of meditations, until one reaches its final point wherein all passion is exhausted and cessation realized.

The Abhidharma presentation of the path system was highly scholastic and resembled more a curriculum of study than a set of directions for the faithful. As such it was aimed at an intellectual elite of monks who had the time and training to meditate, and it overlooked the needs of the less theoretically inclined lay Buddhists.[22] Throughout the entire system the only obstacle to awakening is passion, which leads to false views. But human knowing, when shorn of such mistakes, is understood to be capable of reaching the truth and attaining final cessation. Such an intellectual approach could not but force the less theoretically sophisticated to seek elsewhere, for not everyone is capable of, or interested in, unraveling the correct view from the many pretenders to that honor. A parable told by Nyanatiloka depicts the situation: "A soaring royal swan spied a lowland crane puddling in a mud pool. Of compassion he descended and told this inglorious feathered kinsman of the Himalayan heights, of cool mountain streams, of their shining jewels. 'But I live on mudfish. Are there any mudfish there?' asked the crane. 'No, there are no mudfush there, nor any mud,' replied the swan. 'Then I don't want your mountain and your jewels,' said the crane."[23] In their rejection of Abhidharma theory, the subsequent Prajñāpāramitā thinkers gloried in their status of lowland cranes.

In the Christian tradition, a thoroughgoing theoretical presentation of the content of ultimate meaning was not taken as the final word, for the Gospels themselves constantly insisted that God is beyond all concepts and words. In contrast, it would seem that in the Indian Buddhist tradition the Abhidharma model for a time all but usurped the place of mystic thought and thus brought forth in response a full-blown mystic reaction that negated not particular Abhidharma teachings or ideas, but the entire theoretical pattern in which those teachings were understood. The impact of such a reaction was far greater in Buddhist India than its analogue in the Christian West, perhaps because the preceding trend of Abhidharma intellectualism was, for a time, more assured of its ultimate validity. Buddhist mystic thought arose in full rejection of all theory. The Prajñāpāramitā scriptures constantly express their insight by negating and ridiculing the Abhidharma assumptions.

THE MYSTIC MOVEMENT OF THE PRAJÑĀPĀRAMITĀ SCRIPTURES

The composition of the Prajñāpāramitā scriptures launched the Mahāyāna movement in which mystic experience plays the central role. These Prajñāpāramitā (perfection of wisdom) texts (ca. 50 B.C.E.–150 C.E.) and their subsequent continuation in the Middle Path (*Mādhyamika*) thought of Nāgārjuna constituted a radical departure from and a consistent deconstruction of the previous Abhidharma endeavor.[24] The Abhidharma masters had bifurcated consciousness into a commonsense realm of conventional, relative truth and a theoretical realm of absolute truth. In contrast, the anonymous Prajñāpāramitā authors ushered in a new mystic movement that radically broke with that theorizing and championed the priority of mystic insight clothed only in commonsense language. These scriptures were written specifically to negate and counteract the Abhidharma assumption that intellectual understanding leads to a liberating knowledge of absolute truth. The mystic movement they introduced, canonized as the Great Vehicle (*mahāyāna*), stressed the ideal of the *bodhisattva* (wisdom being) who, in his realization and practice of nonconceptual wisdom, far transcended the Abhidharma saint (*arhat*).[25] Subsequent Buddhist history not only in India, but also in Tibet, China, Korea, and Japan, had to base itself squarely upon this mystic foundation.[26]

In contrast to the Abhidharma texts, which based their intellectual confidence upon their stated ability to know the essences (*svabhāva*) of things, the Prajñāpāramitā scriptures declared all things (*dharmas*) to be empty of essence and not amenable to theoretical knowing. The Abhidharma enterprise was personified in the figure of Śāriputra, who was painted as the consummate master of analytical knowledge, but who was subordinated to Subhūti, the master of nonconceptual wisdom, "whom he constantly asks for information, whose superiority he repeatedly acknowledges, who occasionally shows up his utter obtuseness, and 'reproves' him, although the venerable Śāriputra has taken hold of the matter as far as the words are concerned."[27] *The Large Sutra* expresses this theme as follows:

> If this continent of Jambudvīpa were filled with monks similar in worth to Śāriputra, . . . their wisdom would not approach the wisdom of a bodhisattva who courses in perfect wisdom by one hundredth part, not by one thousandth part, not by one 100,000th part.[28]

This same concern is evident in the Mādhyamika thinking of Nāgārjuna, who developed this basic insight of the Prajñāpāramitā into a rigorous dialectic of emptiness.[29] His intent in writing the *Stanzas on the Middle*, his most famed work, is described by Vimalākṣa in the introduction to the Chinese translation of that work as the refutation not only of false views, but also of clinging to the literal meaning of Buddhist views. Vimalakṣa criticizes those who seek "the definitive nature of the [twelve] causes or the five aggregates."[30] The Buddha's intention is described as the desire to cut off all "views" whatsoever, for they lead to a clinging to self that precludes insight into emptiness. Nāgārjuna proclaims: "I bow to Gautama who, taking compassion, taught the true doctrine in order to cut off all views (*sarvadṛṣṭi*)."[31]

This focus upon the inadequacy of all views, which parallels Paul's criticism of the Corinthian mind-set and Dionysius' advice to his friend Sosipatrus not to engage himself in refuting the Greeks, is aimed directly at the Abhidharma belief in the ability of theory to attain absolute truth. The central theme with which such theoretical views were overturned was that of emptiness (*śūnyatā*).

The Abhidharma thinkers were constantly engaged in "reviewing" *dharmas*,[32] and their goal was the attainment of a clear and distinct apprehension of the nature of reality. For them the term *dharma* referred to factors of existence deemed absolutely true through an analysis that determined their specific essence (*svabhāva*).[33] The word *svabhāva* literally means "own-being" and indicates the essence or nature of an object apprehended as the enduring meaning of the thing in question. It was the conceptual knowing of such essences that for Abhidharma constituted the basis for liberating views. But in the Prajñāpāramitā and later in Mādhyamika philosophy all things are empty precisely of such an essence. Thus any views generated from their apprehension are illusions. Not only are all the *dharma* lists of the Abhidharma brushed aside, but even the Abhidharma presentations of the Buddhist path system and the four noble truths are declared invalid and useless. *The Heart Sutra* states: "Here, Śāriputra, all things are characterized as empty. . . . There is no suffering, no origination, no cessation, no path. There is no cognition, no attainment, and no non-attainment."[34]

Pre-Mahāyāna Buddhists taught the doctrine of no-self, claiming that one's sense of personal continuity derives solely from the coming together of the five aggregates. But the Mahāyāna thinkers went a step further and denied validity even to these five aggregates, thus teaching the emptiness of all things. According to *The Large Sutra* "a bodhisattva who courses in the perfection of wisdom should investigate all things as empty in their essential nature."[35] *The Heart Sutra* echoes this theme:

> Avalokita, the noble Lord and Bodhisattva, moving in the deep course of the perfection of wisdom, looked down from on high and beheld but the five aggregates, seeing that they were empty of essence. . . . All things are to be characterized as empty.[36]

Having no essence that could be apprehended by analysis, things do not support the genesis of views. The notion of emptiness itself is not then to be understood as another view within the same analytical framework. It is, rather, the reversal of that framework. Even the doctrine of the Buddha is not to be taken as any kind of a "correct" view, for, as *The Diamond Sutra* teaches, the Buddha never taught any doctrine, "for there is no doctrine to be apprehended as the doctrine."[37] There is no doctrine because doctrine cannot be learned through signs and concepts. Indeed the attainment of cessation is "the very coming to rest, the non-functioning of perceptions of signs of named things."[38] Thus Nāgārjuna concludes his *Stanzas on the Middle* with the blunt assertion that "cessation is the coming to rest of all ways of taking things, the repose of named things; no truth has been taught by a Buddha for anyone, anywhere."[39] There is no valid apprehension of meaning as if the mind were confronted with a pre-existent, given unit of meaning in things themselves.

The candidate seeking wisdom should, then, not attempt to implement any scholastic path system. *The Accumulation of Precious Qualities*, a verse synopsis of *The Perfection of Wisdom in Eight Thousand Lines*, recommends that one should not engage oneself in any training, for "he who trains himself without discriminating between either training or not training trains himself in this Buddha doctrine."[40] Training as the learning of a set of objectified, codified meanings and as their implementation in practice is all to be rejected, because it reduces the immediacy of the experience of awakening to a programmed apprehension and implementation of mediated ideas. But he who trains himself without discriminating between any set of externalized meanings will learn the true Buddha doctrine through awareness of emptiness.

Words are not the means to learn the Buddha doctrine. *The Large Sutra* explains that "words are artificial . . . and are expressive in a conventional manner through agreed-upon designations."[41] *The Diamond Sutra* adds that "seizing upon a material object is a matter of linguistic expression without factual content."[42] Even the philosophically exact words of the Abhidharma reasoning, far from presenting any absolute truth, are merely conventional designations agreed upon as meaningful within the Abhidharma linguistic context.[43] They have no intrinsic relationship with the things indicated, for all things are empty. Thus *all* verbal teachings are relative truth with no absolute validity. In carrying out this radical deconstruction of Abhidharma confidence in theoretical knowing, the mystic Prajñāpāramitā authors delighted in presenting enigmas and conundrums to theoretical consciousness. By itself, however, it is doubtful if this mystic Prajñāpāramitā movement would have maintained its central position in Mahāyāna thought, for one cannot long abide silent in the direct immediacy of emptiness. If not for the subsequent Mādhyamika philosophy of Nāgārjuna, the Prajñāpāramitā movement would perhaps have developed on the periphery of Buddhist thinking, much as did the Christian tradition of mystic darkness in the West.

MĀDHYAMIKA PHILOSOPHY

Mādhyamika thought is the foundational standpoint of Mahāyāna teaching. Taking his inspiration from the Prajñāpāramitā scriptures, Nāgārjuna (ca. 200) developed a deconstructive strategy of rigorous reasoning to negate belief in essences, in whatever form that belief might appear. Mādhyamika thinking is presented through a patterned interweaving of two main themes. The first theme is the identification of emptiness with dependent co-arising, while the second is the complementary teaching of the disjunctiveness of the two truths of ultimate meaning and worldly convention. These two themes relate to the same awareness of lived experience, but they approach it from different aspects. They are themselves structured in mutual dependence to direct attention to our actual experiences in the quest for awakening.[44]

Emptiness and Dependent Co-Arising

Emptiness is a total rejection of selfhood, a nullification of essence and self-identity that can cause a shaking of one's most personal sense of stability. Insight into emptiness can induce emotions of vertiginous dread and anguish. The selfhood here negated encompasses the inner being of all things, including not only one's sensed inner identity, but also the inner stability of all the things we cling to in the hope of finding some rock-solid refuge from our fragile appearance in being. Negating the inner essence (*svabhāva*) of all things, the Mādhyamika masters undercut the very possibility of generating valid, fixed viewpoints, which draw their putative validity from an assumption of the reality of essences. The doctrine of emptiness is the presentation of a foundational standpoint that, negating the validity of any fixed standpoint, is itself no standpoint at all. It is a total rejection of all essentialist perspectives of thinking. Even the doctrine of emptiness is itself of no absolute validity.

> If there were something not empty, there might be something termed empty. But there is nothing not empty, and so where might there be an empty something? The Victors have declared emptiness as the expeller of all views, but those who hold emptiness as a view they have pronounced incurable.[45]

Not only is emptiness not a view, it is the expeller and deconstructor of all views. Through emptiness, Mahāyāna Buddhism shifted radically to a commitment to think constantly within a pervasive awareness of the illusory status of all beings. As evidenced in Nāgārjuna's *Stanzas on the Middle*, Mādhyamika is permeated with "a hundred negations and a thousand denials."

Yet Mādhyamika philosophy is not confined to refutation and denial; it is not merely a deconstructive strategy that rests satisfied at having refuted every essentialist viewpoint. Aimed at dispelling the pertinacious clinging to the assumed reality of essences and the constant projecting (*prapañca*) of illusory ontologies in the service of selfhood, the basic thrust of Mādhyamika is toward understanding our experience in its immediacy and interpreting it without constructing fixed positions that occlude and distort that experience. Emptiness is not simply nothingness (*nāsti*), but rather, insight into the absence of essence (*niḥsvabhāva*) in dependently co-arising beings. Such a deconstruction is not a pure negation that positions itself within the same realm of meaning that generates essentialist affirmation. It is a denial of the total context of essentialism and theory in favor of the immediacy of nondiscriminative awareness. The commentator Candrakīrti in his *Lucid Exposition* explains:

> Emptiness is taught in order to lay to rest all differentiation without exception. Thus the intent of emptiness is the laying to rest of differentiation in its entirety. But by [attributing] to emptiness the sense of non-being, one hypostatizes it.[46]

The Mādhyamika thinkers held that illusion is generated by the fabrication of language in virtue of which words are taken to represent the essences of things. Mādhyamika is not a negation of truth within that fabricated pattern of extraverted consciousness, but a negation of the entire pattern. Candrakīrti again explains:

> By not recognizing that all things have no essence, when people cling to things as real, they are caught in the net of fabricating. But, since things are really without essence and are empty, like the son of a sterile woman, if those burning with desire did not cling to things as real, then they would not be caught in the net of fabricating and regard such things as objects to be known. And, not being caught in the net of fabricating, neither would they be caught in the net of projected imaginings, which arise by taking such fabrications as objects. And, not being caught in the net of projected meanings, they would not give rise to the passions, which are based upon the belief in self, which in turn gives rise to clinging to "me" and "mine." Therefore, basing themselves on emptiness, upon the absence of essence, they sever fabricating, imaginings are exterminated. . . . Therefore emptiness, because it is the extermination of fabricating, is called cessation.[47]

Here fabrication (*prapañca*) indicates the construction of meaning in concepts.[48] It is conceptual, verbal expression based on the clinging to essences, as if they could offer a stable source of true knowing. Thus Candrakīrti continues to explain that "fabrication is characterized by [the dichotomy between] the speaker and the spoken, the knower and the known."[49] Once such a dichotomy has been set up within the mind, the subjective knower, overlooking the immediacy of mystic awareness, focuses totally upon the known, upon mediating knowledge through language to him or herself from outside. Such a person is in need of the antidote of emptiness, for he or she must first become disengaged from projected imaginings, no matter how religious or theoretically correct, in order to be open to the immediacy of awakening. Emptiness is then the negation of confrontational patterns of knowing. It is not pure nihilism.

It must, however, be kept in mind that insight into emptiness does not function in abstraction from experience. Rather, in Mādhyamika and throughout later Mahāyāna developments, it is always understood in synergy with the doctrine of dependent co-arising. The doctrine of dependent co-arising is central to all Buddhism. In its earliest formulation it was used in the primitive stages of Buddhist teaching—probably by Śākyamuni himself—to describe the twelve-staged cycle of factors that explain the genesis of transmigration (*saṃsāra*). In this pre-Mahāyāna usage, dependent co-arising expressed the closure of experience within a one-dimensional circle of primal ignorance (*avidyā*), unable to transcend that cycle of suffering and attain cessation (*nirvāṇa*).

Nāgārjuna reclaimed this notion of dependent co-arising from the earlier teaching, identified it with emptiness, and reinterpreted it to signify the being of that which is empty, thus giving the notion of dependent co-arising a transcendent dimension as the content of insight into emptiness. In this deepened understanding of dependent co-arising, Nāgārjuna no longer refers simply to samsaric confinement, but to an awareness that the entire world, expressed and known within consciousness, is the transient appearing of that which is empty of any stable essence. Emptiness, then, refers to the essence-free presence of dependently co-arising beings. In so identifying emptiness and dependent co-arising, Nāgārjuna avoids the extremes of both clinging to essences and clinging to nothingness. In its pre-Mādhyamika meaning, dependent co-arising action leads only to the samsaric cycle of suffering, but in Nāgārjuna's reinterpretation dependent co-arising denotes the liberating wisdom of insight into the essence-free being of all things. It is a liberated field of experience wherein one lives and dies by insight into the emptiness of life and death, namely, *saṃsāra*.

In the thought of Nāgārjuna the notions of emptiness and dependent co-arising are convertible.[50] Both refer to the same reality of human experience in the world. The radical nonbeing of things is expressed as their emptiness, absence of essence, and no-self, while the phenomenal being of the very things declared to be empty of essence is expressed as their dependent co-arising. Neither emptiness nor dependent co-arising taken separately expresses Mādhyamika philosophy. By itself emptiness leads to a negative mysticism that denies the phenomenal givenness of being-in-the-world and as such is of little interest to people living in the world. Similarly, by itself dependent co-arising can discern nothing more than the endless process of illusory conditioning that results in constant suffering and ennui. It is only in their identity and convertibility that emptiness and dependent co-arising form the foundational standpoint of Mādhyamika thought.

Yet negation maintains priority, because being is not presented to us in its pristine immediacy. It comes distorted through the lens of our language constructs and conceptual gestalts. Caught in the confines of samsaric passages, humans constantly seek security in the illusions they themselves fabricate. The primary thrust of Mādhyamika, indeed of all Buddhism, is to negate and undermine that security and the ideas it uses to justify its illusions. This priority is clearly evident in the invocational stanzas of *The Stanzas on the Middle*:

> Not arising, not passing away; not eternal, not terminable;
> Not one, not many; not coming, not going;
> I pay homage to the Buddha, the foremost among teachers,
> Who has taught this dependent co-arising
> In order graciously to uproot all fabrication.[51]

Here Nāgārjuna presents an understanding of dependent co-arising in which negation has priority. The intent of dependent co-arising, stated above, is to uproot the fabrication (*prapañca*) that projects essences upon things and regards the discrete beings of our experience as essentially present to themselves. In contrast, in the light of emptiness, dependent co-arising signifies beings as coming into being and empty of self-identity. Because enfolded in emptiness, dependent co-arising is an affirmation of being as a negation of a negation, affirming the dependent co-arising (being) of that which is empty (nonbeing). For Nāgārjuna, this awareness of the identity of dependent co-arising and emptiness constitutes the middle path, not as a balancing act halfway between being and nonbeing, but as a rejection either of being in favor of emptiness or of nonbeing in favor of dependent co-arising. Thus in his *Overcoming Vain Discussions* Nāgārjuna identifies the middle path with both emptiness and dependent co-arising:

> I pay homage to the unequaled Buddha,
> Who taught that emptiness, dependent co-arising,
> And the middle path are one in meaning.[52]

The middle path is not a path of moderation or balance, but the practice of insight into the empty being of that which phenomenally occurs. Likewise, the notion of suchness (*tathatā*) refers not to any essential ground behind or underlying beings. Suchness is not the inner being of beings. Rather, it is the spontaneous immediacy of dependent co-arising beings wherein emptiness has "hollowed out" (the root of emptiness, *śūnyatā*, is *śvi*, to hollow out) any inner selfhood.

Dependent co-arising is not a theoretical explanation of how real things are causally interconnected, for it is quiescent of all conceptual fabrications. It is not a theory of causality. It is not any kind of a theory. Dependent co-arising is an awareness of the changing flux of existence free from the fabricating process of imagining and imputing essences to these existents. In his *The Sixty-Verse Treatise on Logic*, Nāgārjuna states: "I give salutation to the Lord Śākyamuni, who, in negating the arising and passing away [of all things] by the principle of the path, deigned to explain dependent co-arising."[53] Similarly, in what is perhaps the most quoted stanza of *The Stanzas on the Middle*, he says: "It is dependent co-arising that I term emptiness. Taking on this designation (*prajñapti*), it (emptiness) is established. It alone is the Middle Path."[54]

Here dependent co-arising is termed a *prajñapti* (designation), a technical term of crucial import in Mādhyamika. Mervyn Sprung argues incisively that it is a "non-cognitive, guiding term which serves to suggest appropriate ways of coping with the putative realities on which it rests for its meaning and to which it lends meaning."[55] It would thus appear that Nāgārjuna, in his refusal to employ theory as a valid meaning realm, enjoins the adoption of commonsense meanings in order to teach one how to deal with the fabricated illusions that block understanding. Hence the doctrine of dependent co-arising is used by Mādhyamika in a commonsense realm of meaning as a method of coping with the overbearing assertions of theorists.

Dependent co-arising is a commonsense term embodying a practical and mystic awareness of things as having no essence apart from the overall flux of changing phenomena that might serve as a starting point for the genesis of absolute views. It is the starting point of Plato and the early Christian fathers, who saw sense things as constantly in flux, but at the same time it is the rejection of their idea that behind that flux there is any stable or constant point to take hold of, for there are no ideal forms and no divine immutable essence. Thus a search for such forms or such an essence, an evolving of a centrist philosophy or a theology,[56] offers no hope of attaining ultimate meaning. The dual notions of emptiness and dependent co-arising point to an awareness of existents in their immediacy and prior to the genesis of explanatory viewpoints and negate the assumed stability of essences as the starting point for understanding. They imply the abandonment of conceptual knowing as a path to awakening. *The Stanzas on the Middle* state: "There never has been any existent that has not dependently co-arisen. Hence among all existents, there is none that is not empty."[57]

The meaning of dependent co-arising is, then, identical with that of emptiness, for it turns upon an awareness of the world that is free from the conceptual fabrication of essences that can lead to views. Such an awareness is apart from conceptual and verbal signs and is nondiscriminative. Is, then, the Buddhist mystic thinker simply rendered mute? Such is not the case, for these thinkers have in fact produced lengthy treatises upon these mystic themes. What then is the relationship between mystic awareness and verbal expression? In Mādhyamika the doctrine of the two truths addresses this question.

The Two Truths

The first Mādhyamika theme of the identity of emptiness and dependent co-arising is only half the story, for it directs our attention to the experience of being-in-the-world, declared to be the dependent co-arising of that which is empty. The complementary teaching of the two truths of ultimate mean-

ing (*paramārtha-satya*) and worldly convention (*saṃvṛti-satya*) turns attention to the constant and total otherness of the truth of ultimate meaning
from any worldly and conventional embodiment of that truth. This notion
of two truths (*satya-dvaya*) was used by the Abhidharma thinkers to distinguish between their absolutely true theory and conventional, commonsense
understanding. But it was Nāgārjuna who explicated its meaning for Mahāyāna thinkers.[58] The same terms as used by the Abhidharma thinkers,
paramārtha-satya and *saṃvṛt(t)i-satya*, were used in Mādhyamika, but their
interpretation was quite different. Ultimate truth, literally the truth (*satya*)
of ultimate (*parama*) meaning (*artha*), reflects not any conceptual embodiment of meaning, but the ineffable (*avācyatva*) and silent (*tūṣṇīṃbhāva*)
immediacy of awakening, which cannot be circumscribed or indicated in
any word or concept. Yet, just as emptiness is always understood together
with dependent co-arising, so ultimate truth, while being completely other
and transcendent, is not apart from conventional truth. *The Stanzas on the
Middle* state:

The Buddha's doctrine relies upon two truths: the worldly, conventional truth and the ultimate truth. Those who do not know the distinction between these two truths, do not know the deep reality in
the Buddha's teaching. Without reliance upon conventions, the ultimate is not taught. And without arriving at ultimate truth, cessation
is not reached.[59]

The theme of the identity of emptiness and dependent co-arising moves
horizontally to include the totality of our experience, issuing in a heightened
awareness of being in its transient immediacy and fleeting beauty. The
theme of ultimate meaning and worldly convention moves vertically to express our awareness of transcendence and otherness, an otherness that goes
beyond any identifiable presence in the horizontal plane of experience. One
must then maintain insight into emptiness and dependent co-arising in
synergy with an understanding of the two truths, for neither theme in itself
constitutes Mādhyamika philosophy.

The doctrine of the two truths is rooted in insight into emptiness. Since
all things and all words are empty and without inherent character, the
construction of strategies to embody truth always fails and self-destructs
before the disjunctive otherness of ultimate meaning. Ultimate meaning
remains other in silence and is always distinct from human constructs. In
this sense the entire path description of graded stages is itself a construct
(*kṛtima*) and the entire journey toward awakening is worldly, conventional,
and dependently co-arisen. Ultimate meaning transcends the entire process
and is not the final step attained at the peak. Cessation is present not as
something one can earn and accomplish as the final reward of sustained
effort, but as both present in its otherness at the very inception of the path
and as beyond any termination point indicated by the path.

Ultimate meaning is here the emptiness of things in their inexpressibility and silence, in contrast to which all dependently co-arising things come to expression as worldly and conventional. The positing of any identifiable truth as ultimate meaning self-destructs and tumbles from its august position, for there is no conventionally perfected state of any ultimately meaningful selfhood. Nevertheless, just as emptiness is not simply the negation of dependent co-arising, so ultimate meaning is not simply the negation of worldly convention. Rather, having gained silent insight into ultimate meaning, one becomes reengaged in worldly convention and restores selfhood, not now as an absolute, but simply as worldly and conventional.

In the absence of insight into ultimate meaning, worldly convention is the language-formed functioning of deluded understanding, which, while attempting to manifest ultimate meaning, occludes that ultimate meaning. It attempts to bring ultimate meaning to speech, for its spontaneous exigency is toward the complete fulfillment of human questioning in a realization of ultimate meaning. Yet, clinging to that ultimate meaning as if it were a supernal essence, it occludes ultimate meaning by misidentifying it as an expressible something. Worldly conventional understanding is simultaneously enmeshed in unconscious ignorance and ascendant in its spontaneous thrust toward goodness and truth. Yet no ascendant thrust of verbal consciousness ever reaches anything, for one continually searches within the context of selfhood for that which is not a self. It is only when wisdom negates its own content and recognizes its inefficacy in the face of the silence of ultimate meaning that one awakens to ultimate meaning as completely other than and disjunctive from worldly convention.

Awakening entails a leap from every explanation and every description of ultimate meaning to an awareness of its total otherness, in virtue of which, no longer trying to confine ultimate meaning within the context of worldly convention, one is freed to reenter the realm of worldly convention and reclaim its pristine spontaneity as simply worldly convention, aware that all human thinking is a clouded and occluded attempt to bring to speech and identify that which forever escapes such effort. It is in this context of reengagement in the world that Mādhyamika speaks of the identity of ultimate meaning and worldly convention. This identity is never a matter of verbally understanding ultimate meaning. Rather, it lies in realizing that worldly convention is never anything more than worldly convention, in not supposing that worldly convention ever rises above being worldly and conventional. It is a conscious identification of opposites that remain opposites, not an admixture of truths in a graded hierarchy of high and low. On the one hand, the sage abides in the silent awareness of the total otherness of ultimate meaning; on the other, by that same awareness he or she engages in the worldly articulation of that silence. It is not a question of perspectives, as if what is true in worldly convention is not true in ultimate meaning. All perspectives are worldly and conventional, in the face of which ultimate meaning is perspectiveless and silent.

There is no continuity between ultimate meaning and worldly convention and their identity remains that of opposites. If the expression of worldly convention is seen as an emanation from ultimate meaning, the otherness of ultimate meaning is rendered meaningless, since ultimate meaning would then reach down and become delimited within the context of worldly and conventional selfhood. Not emanating from or directly based upon ultimate meaning, worldly convention is always and only worldly convention, remaining always clouded and occluded understanding that can never lay claim to any final validity. Yet it is only when one has realized the otherness of ultimate meaning that, liberated from clinging to illusions and reengaged in the realm of worldly convention, one discovers the limit and validity of worldly convention. Mādhyamika affirms the validity of worldly convention not because of some ultimate viewpont, but by reclaiming the conventional validity of dependently co-arisen standards that do not fill the silence of ultimate meaning with the babble of conceptual "absolutes."

In this schema of the two truths (itself worldly and conventional), both ultimate meaning and worldly convention are termed truths. The truth of ultimate meaning is the silence of ineffable awakening, without any mental activity. It is the realm of nonimaginative wisdom that abides in no abiding point. Ultimately meaningful truth is never propositional truth that would capture emptiness in a verbal sack and allow one to glimpse inside the mystery of the universe. But neither is worldly convention simply the truth of propositional statements, as if that were a lower level of truth. There is no gradation of levels between the two truths, for they are absolutely discontinuous and other. There is no mounting from worldly convention to ultimate meaning or descent from ultimate meaning into worldly convention, since they are at the same time both completely other and already identical. The performance of such a move from a worldly conventional level to an ultimately meaningful level, by the very fact of identifying ultimate meaning, confines ultimate meaning within the cycle of selfhood, that is, worldly convention. The obverse move from ultimate meaning to worldly convention leads to a spurious affirmation of the validity of a worldly convention transmuted into something mistakenly deemed to be ultimately meaningful. Indeed, the negations of Mādhyamika thinking are grounded on the absolute otherness and disjunctiveness between ultimate meaning and worldly convention, not on the negation of one proposition by another. Ultimate meaning is the negation of the final validity of the entire dimension of worldly and conventional propositions; it is an exploding of all horizons and an evaporation of all viewpoints.

The interplay between the two truths and the theme of emptiness and dependent co-arising is seen in the identity of ultimate meaning with worldly convention, which signifies the simultaneous presence of an awakening to empty ultimate meaning and of reengagement in the conventional world of dependent co-arising and verbal affirmation—in full awareness of the complete discontinuity between ultimate meaning and worldly convention. Since worldly and conventional understanding, although reaching out toward ultimate meaning, attains nothing ultimately meaningful, the truth of worldly convention is found in the awareness of the mutual self-estrangement and negation between the two truths, in the refusal to find ultimate meaning within worldly convention. In such a context the truths enunciated by conventional understanding always stand on the brink of falsification and maintain their validity not as statements of reality, but as trace images that for a time may harmonize with that silent awareness and indicate ultimate meaning before they fade out into nothingness. Insight into ultimate meaning is not a mystical vision reserved for the spiritual elite. It is not a gnosis refused to common deluded people. It is mystic not because of its extraordinary nature, but only in the sense that it has no mediated and identified content. One cannot center one's life activity on ultimate meaning, for it is not a centering point. Insight into ultimate meaning throws one back constantly upon worldly convention, whose exigency for ultimate meaning is a knocking at an eternally unopened door. But the practice of differentiating the two truths makes that knocking itself an awareness of the otherness of ultimate meaning and a reengagement in worldly convention. Such worldly convention, functioning in harmony with ultimate meaning, weaves verbal statements that maintain their validity as skillful methods of signifying the process of awakening to the otherness of ultimate meaning.

When mystic insight occurs, the language meant to express it falls away. Here the parallel with Dionysius' double tradition of theology is striking, for in Dionysius mystic awareness is inexpressible in any positive, public, custom-formed manner, and yet one must weave language models to express that negation. It is only when the silence of emptiness and ultimate meaning has laid to rest all ideas of being that these ideas are resurrected in a mind freed from clinging to ideal essences and reengaged in the dependently co-arising world as the field for bodhisattva practice. This is the restoration of worldly convention. Expressed in language, emptiness signifies an awareness of the transience of things, a realization not of empty nothingness, but of the suchness of beings as originally empty, namely, as dependently co-arisen. The practice of emptiness is, then, a reengagement in dependent co-arising, not as the samsaric cycle of suffering engendered by attachment to essences, but as a dependent co-arising convertible with emptiness. The central focus of an enlightened person, that is, a bodhisattva, is upon the dependently co-arising and conventional world, for emptiness and ultimate meaning cannot be objects on which to focus. Thus the bodhisattva is one who is reengaged in the concrete world as his or her *total* concern. Here one's ultimate concern is not directed toward any transcendent object, but toward the world in all its fallibility.

This reengagement is an entry into history and society, which, in virtue of emptiness, functions not through emptiness or because of ultimate meaning, but through worldly and conventional reasoning. The reasoning of reengagement (i.e., the dialectic of emptiness), in its Mādhyamika presentation, is not a refutation of falsehood by truth. In its deconstructive phase, Mādhyamika reason refutes both truth and falsehood and signifies a worldly convention wherein both truth and falsehood — always judged by worldly and conventional standards — alternately appear and disappear, never able to maintain any fixed stability. In its constructive phase, Mādhyamika reason both weaves models to indicate the otherness of ultimate meaning and functions within the world through worldly and conventional thinking to embody intelligently and skillfully the works of compassion. The only focus of a bodhisattva is the concrete, historical world in which we live. Compassion is directed toward fostering awakening in this world, toward intelligent action in this world. A bodhisattva's activity is oriented single-mindedly toward worldly convention; ultimate meaning is never an object of human activity. Reengagement in worldly activity is not, then, a matter of doing-what-you-can-until-*nirvāṇa*; rather, the world as it is, in its suchness, is the total field of engagement and compassion.

The human (worldly convention) and the numinous (ultimate meaning) do not become mixed or commingled. Reengagement in worldly convention is possible precisely because ultimate meaning and worldly convention are discontinuous. If ultimate meaning were drawn into and fused with worldly convention, no reengagement would be possible. When the numinous becomes the principle of a society, the result is a theocracy that sees its idea of God or its truth as essentially true and beyond question. From a Mādhyamika perspective, this is an arrogant assertion of a worldly and conventional self as ultimate. The realm of enlightened reengagement does not function by religious pronouncements, for, in its perspective, rendering pronouncements is not religious but secular.

Worldly convention is always and only dependently co-arisen and never ruled or directed by any divine principle. In its own sphere of language-formed insight and verbal construction, worldly convention is autonomous. Ultimate meaning does not oversee the world as if it occupied some august, hierarchical position within that world. It is present only as completely other, as escaping every attempt to circumscribe it within the world, even for the betterment of the world. Its presence is felt in a silent wonder at that which can never be homogenized as an object among objects. In worldly activity, its function is experienced in deconstructing arrogant attempts to capture absolutes within conventional nets and in constructing programs and plans to fulfill the tasks of compassion — judged, however, not by anything ultimate but always by intelligent application of worldly and conventional insight. The belief in an ultimate that actively oversees the world and directs its course through an all-seeing, if incomprehensible, plan is an illusory assertion of religious selfhood. Such an ultimate, whether a supernatural God or a materialistic dynamic directing historical development, is but a projection of one's own selfhood. Reengagement in the world is not an application of divine principles of emptiness to worldly affairs. It is not an incursion of ultimate meaning into the territory of worldly convention. Rather, reengagement is a discovery of dependent co-arising as that which has been present from the beginning; a being-at-home in the transient and fragile world. It is only in this context of secular thinking and reasoning that new life can be breathed into worldly convention and its statements can be validated as contextually and provisionally true. The heightened dimension of reengagement in the dependent co-arisen world is itself worldly and conventional, not a direct outflow from ultimate meaning. Thus the reengagement of a bodhisattva in the dependently co-arising world does not come with a set of instructions. It is realized only through the practice of differentiating worldly convention from ultimate meaning, through particular practices that imply decision and commitment to particular goals. Social and historical liberation occur through the historical and social actions of persons aware that they are and remain estranged from ultimate meaning. In such social action, ever adaptable to changing needs, the silence of ultimate meaning takes on the sound of thunder. The sound of that thunder is not a millennial quest or an ideological revolution, but always human decision reached in awareness that all decisions are always clouded and occluded by primal ignorance.

The obvious objection to all this is that if ultimate truth is totally ineffable, then nothing the Mādhyamikas say has any validity either. Such objections were indeed leveled at Nāgārjuna. In his *Overcoming Vain Discussions* he contrasts the notion of emptiness with the ideas of the Nyāya school of logicians who held that words are valid because they have intrinsic meaning. The logicians argue: "If all things are entirely without any essence, then words have no essence. In that case you cannot negate the essence [of all things by using words]."[60] The logicians adduce an essentialist perspective and argue that Nāgārjuna is caught in a contradiction by affirming that things are essence-free. Similarly, as noted earlier, Thomas Aquinas argued that all negations presuppose some prior affirmation.[61] But Nāgārjuna responds to such critics:

> Negating by means of emptiness is like one magically-created man negating another magically-created man. The magically-created man who negates the other magically-created man is [himself] empty. . . . Just in the same way, my words are empty, like everything else which is created by magic or illusion. Words therefore can negate the essence of all things.[62]

The words that Mādhyamika employs claim no absolute value and remain throughout symbolic and conventional. Their function is to express the inexpressibility of ultimate, mystic meaning by cutting off all viewpoints, all pretenders, just as for Gregory the sign of the presence of God in darkness is that there is no sign. They use words provisionally to negate that there is any other way of using words. They derive their negative force not from some prior affirmative content, but from the nonverbal immediacy of mystic experience. And so Nāgārjuna argues, "If I formulate any proposition, then I would be in error, but I do not formulate any proposition."[63] In the realm of mystic meaning propositional truth is simply beside the point and its criteria are meaningless. Arguing with Nāgārjuna must have seemed to his opponents to be very like reasoning with Alice in Wonderland, who made words mean anything she wanted them to mean. But throughout, the same shifting of meaning realm, and therefore the value of language, is apparent. Upon superficial inspection, Mādhyamika thinkers are shifty and slippery. After negating the views of others, they retreat into unassailability by claiming that they themselves have no statement to offer, presenting instead an at times overly subtle and bewildering discourse on emptiness, dependent co-arising, and the two truths. But in Mādhyamika the proposing of clear theories precludes an understanding of mystic meaning, since that involves clinging to concepts. In the Christian West, the initial exercise of the medieval Scholastic manuals was to define the terms used in the questions at issue. In Mādhyamika even this apparently innocent attempt at clarity would be treated with suspicion, lest it lead to an unnoted conceptualism, as indeed Scholasticism is inclined to do. Emptiness is not the negation of any particular theory within the horizon of conceptual meaning, but the negation of the validity of the entire horizon in the face of ultimate meaning. It is no wonder, then, that they slip out of any pattern of confrontational knowing.

However, the goal of the Mādhyamika philosophers was not to leave people confused; they wanted to denude people of their mental coverings and were clearly committed to the use of dialectical reasoning to drive home their deconstructive point. The earlier Prajñāpāramitā authors had expressed their mystic awareness in commonsense terms. When they focused on the intellectual pretensions of the Abhidharma masters, they were generally content to make sport of their theories. They delighted in presenting conundrums and paradoxes to negate the Abhidharma mind-set and did not bother to treat any theory seriously (a practice brought to perfection by the Chinese Ch'an masters). In contrast, the Mādhyamika thinkers elected to fight fire with fire by evolving a rigorous negative dialectical method whereby one might incisively refute any would-be theoretician.

Mādhyamika logic and dialectic themselves are not unusual, for they are based upon the principles of contradiction and the excluded middle. Their logic functions within the realm of worldly convention and claims no special status or peculiar logic beyond what is worldly and conventional. The dialectical application of this logic proceeds "to dichotomize the possible views on any matter into a formal, final, either/or. . . . Having set up a rigid either/or, Mādhyamika then exhibits the untenability of both, either by showing each to be self-contradictory, or contrary to experience, or incompatible with the possibility of enlightenment."[64] The point of such exercises is to refute all views and to show that any possible theoretical position, if pushed far enough, is necessarily false. Logic for Nāgārjuna serves as a method of falsification, without thereby implying that there is a contrary correct view, for the aim is not to refute this or that opinion, but to negate the entire realm of theoretical meaning. The words of logic are like one cartoon character (Nāgārjuna's magically created man) refuting another, for in the context of emptiness, no words have any essence that might validate their logical relationship. Nāgārjuna, awakened to the direct, immediate emptiness of all words, participated in the theoretical disputes of his day with the intent of offering a logical method of coping with the truth claims of all theory. In the logical analysis of any positive statement, the logical consequences (*prasaṅga*) of any proposition, if pushed far enough, leads to the falsification of that proposition.

Such a procedure was sure to evince strong objections, for, to the theoretically minded, it seemed to be recommending meaninglessness. But those objections were, the Mādhyamika thinkers maintained, based upon illusion and name-clinging. The adversary was always in a compromising position, for it was the adversary who was making the positive statements. By contrast, the Mādhyamikan made no such assertions and could not be proved wrong. Candrakīrti explains:

> The adversary is bound to a conclusion which is perverse by logical necessity. We are not so bound because we advance no thesis of our own. It is therefore impossible to invalidate any argument of ours. Our intention is fully satisfied so long as a multitude of logical faults, due to internal contradictions, descend on our adversary.[65]

The point of the Mādhyamika dialectics is to free the mind from mediating words and concepts to an awareness of unmediated truth. "This non-mediated presence of truth . . . was known in the religious literature (sūtras) of Nāgārjuna's time as *prajñā-pāramitā* — the surpassing or consummate *prajñā* (wisdom)."[66] It is precisely the fabricating of views that prevents one from realizing such wisdom, for, as Paul knew, no position or *Weltanschauung* can substitute for the awareness of the ultimate through direct contact. No theoretical explanation can hope to reverse the process, for, by its affirmation of essences, it moves totally within the very illusion that it might seek to remove. If the empirical world is a magical illusion, then "metaphysicians are, as it were, attempting to give a reasoned account of the emergence of rabbits from empty hats or of coins from nostrils,"[67] rather than uncovering the illusion.

Religious meaning cannot be expressed in theoretical terms, for when things are empty of essence, language has no valid objectifying function. Nāgārjuna argues that "when the object of thought is no more, there is nothing for language to refer to."[68] The inability of language to make affirmative assertions is because it presupposes that words actually do refer to essences. In the absence of words that can explain anything, Mādhyamika presents its teachings as pointers to direct experience.

TATHĀGATAGARBHA AS MYSTIC MONISM

Mādhyamika is in no sense nihilistic and its goal of freeing the mind from illusory concepts was directed to a reengagement in the world in all its transcience and endless interrelatedness. Yet it did seem quite nihilistic to those who could not follow the subtlety of its deconstructionist mode of thinking. It is thus not surprising that a more affirmative mystic trend should have arisen to counter that perceived negativism.

The Participation in the Jeweled Lineage records a series of objections to Prajñāpāramitā and Mādhyamika thinking, the main one of which seems to be that it makes one despondent.[69] Thus the Tathāgatagarbha thinkers found the teaching of emptiness to be unacceptable.

> It has been said here and there that all things are to be known every-where as unreal, like clouds, [visions in] a dream, and illusions. But then why has the Buddha declared here that the Buddha nature exists in every sentient being?[70]

The teaching referred to here is that of the Prajñāpāramitā and Mād-hyamika texts. *The Stanzas on the Middle* states: "It is like an illusion, a dream, or an imaginary city in the sky. In such fashion are [the ideas] of origination, duration, and cessation described."[71] Mādhyamika dialectic had swept away all theorizing as an obstacle to awakening. The Tathāgatagarbha thinkers, having learned that lesson well, swept away even the Mādhyamika dialectic as too overbearingly pessimistic, or perhaps as simply too over-bearing.

In contrast to this supposed negative tone of Mādhyamika, the Tathā-gatagarbha texts all present the Buddha realm, the realm of the *garbha* (womb, seed, matrix) of a Buddha-Tathāgata, in an affirmative and positive fashion. The principal theme of *The Sutra on Neither Increase nor Decrease* is the identification of the reality of experienced life, the realm of being (*sat-tva dhātu*),[72] with the ultimate Dharma Realm (*dharmadhātu*), the ul-timate Dharma Body (*dharmakāya*).

> The Dharma Realm is not different from the realm of being and the realm of being is not different from the Dharma Realm. The realm of being is precisely the Dharma Body and the Dharma Body is pre-cisely the realm of being. Śāriputra, these two states are one in mean-ing, differing only in name.[73]

Here the Tathāgatagarbha thinkers simply identify the ultimate realm with the reality of the experienced world in a monistic fashion. All *dharmas*

are not empty, for the Buddha realm, the Buddha-nature is really real, as is evident in the attribution to it of the four perfect attributes of eternity, constancy, purity, and immutability,[74] attributes that Nāgārjuna would have immediately negated as conceptual fabrications. In the Tathāgatagarbha tradition the world is indeed illusory, but the Buddha-nature is really real behind the changing appearances of everyday living.[75] In a manner similar to the early Christian fathers who saw an immutable God behind and above the changing flux of the unstable and unreal world, these Buddhist thinkers regarded the single ultimate, monistic reality of the Buddha-nature as the one, immutable, eternal reality. *The Lion's Roar of Queen Śrīmālā* expresses it as follows:

> The Tathāgata seed (*garbha*) is empty (*śūnya*) of all the defiled coverings, which are all different from and distinct from that Tathāgata seed. But the Tathāgata seed is by no means empty (*aśūnya*) of the Buddha attributes, which are not different nor apart from it.[76]

All defilements are adventitious (*āgantuka*) and do not pertain to the original essence of that seed. The scope of emptiness is restricted to the defiled coverings and not to the underlying *garbha* or to its intrinsic attributes. Emptiness is no longer all-inclusive, for after negating all the defilements of experienced life as illusions, there remains left over (*avaśiṣṭa*) the eternal, immutable, already pure reality of the Buddha-nature.[77]

Such a reality, however, is not accessible to human understanding and when *The Lion's Roar of Queen Śrīmālā* raises the question of how one can gain insight into this essentially pure Buddha-nature, the answer given is simply a restatement of the original purity of the mind, for "the highest truth of the Buddhas can be understood only by faith."[78] Thus the faith-conversion to that reality is not a radical break with previous awareness, but a turning back and reclaiming of one's original nature, much as it was with Origen and Gregory. Conversion is a recovering of the already present, but unrecognized, original nature of the mind, a conversion that brings a monistic realization that being (*sat-tva*) in the world is actually not different from the ultimate Dharma Realm, which is identical with the *garbha* in which all exist and which exists in all.

Tathāgatagarbha was not an attempt to analyze theoretically the nature of the mind or the nature of reality, but rather, a mystic encouragement to practice the path, an encouragement bolstered by faith in the real possibility of attaining Buddhahood, since at the base of one mind that seed already existed. Yet such a stress upon this positive mystic meaning scarcely allows one to develop any awareness of human experience in the world. There was little interest in articulating the Mādhyamika notion of a field of reengagement in which ultimate meaning is identified with worldly convention and the focus of a bodhisattva is totally on the dependently co-arising tasks of compassion — all that is swept away as unnecessary.

The Mādhyamika thinkers attempted to refute theory through a negative dialectic of falsification. The Tathāgatagarbha thinkers simply ignored theory altogether in favor of a commonsense affirmation of the ultimate reality and validity of the Buddha-nature. Although the Tathāgatagarbha tradition maintained the primary focus on mystic meaning, as did the Prajñāpāramitā movement, their affirmation of the Buddha-nature reintroduced into Mahāyāna thinking themes similar to the *brahman/ātman* doctrine of the *Upaniṣads* against which the historical Buddha himself had reacted.

But there was a felt need to allow some validity to doctrinal discourse and some avenue toward becoming reengaged in the world. Thus the necessity for examining experiential consciousness became more and more a pressing exigency. How is the mind now defiled, if it is/was originally pure? What kind of fall has it experienced? Even if defilements are adventitious warts on that pure nature, even warts must have a cause! Can a defiled mind speak doctrine? How does the awakened mind enunciate doctrine? How does a bodhisattva fulfill the tasks of compassion in the world? One of the first texts to address these questions was *The Ornament of the Scriptures of the Great Vehicle*.

A TENTATIVE TURN TOWARD INTERIORITY

The Mādhyamika doctrine of emptiness and the Tathāgatagarbha insistence on the reality of the *garbha* were both mystic teachings, but both left unanswered questions. Where did insight into emptiness come from? If all things are empty, why do people consider them real with an insistence that is almost instinctual? And if the *garbha* is the one true reality, then why does illusion ever arise? In a word, how does consciousness come to be either awakened or deluded? Both Mādhyamika and Tathāgatagarbha agreed that illusion characterizes the everyday life we all experience. Both set out to counter that illusion—Mādhyamika through a rigorous reasoning about views and Tathāgatagarbha through the inculcation of faith and practice. But what is the genesis of that illusion? The insistence of the Tathāgatagarbha masters on practice and realization drew them away from any consideration of consciousness as experienced in the world. The entire phenomenal world falls away to insignificance. But that is the world in which we live and in which we become awakened. Even the Mādhyamika reasoning, to some at least, seemed far removed from the actual experience of their lives.

It was the Yogācāra philosophers who attempted to deal with these questions and to explicate the ramifications of emptiness through their understanding of consciousness, both defiled and awakened. But they did not spring from a vacuum. They were obviously of a questioning nature and committed to restoring theory in a context of emptiness. They probably were also influenced by the Tathāgatagarbha tradition and its insistence on the pure mind of the *garbha*. They accepted the teaching of emptiness from the Prajñāpāramitā scriptures and from the Mādhyamika treatises and tried to develop a new Abhidharma philosophy in that context. The history of the early development of Yogācāra is far from clear, but one can detect a transitional stage in Maitreya's *Ornament of the Scriptures of the Great Vehicle*, which is included within the doctrinal lineage of Yogācāra, but which represents a transition from the previous Tathāgatagarbha texts to the more theoretically attuned Yogācāra attempts to offer clear and incisive explanations of the mind of wisdom and the genesis of illusion.[79] Here we shall consider it briefly in order to bring into focus the problematic that engaged Asaṅga and the other classical Yogācāra thinkers, which will be treated in the following chapters 7 and 8.

The basic teaching of *The Ornament of the Scriptures of the Great Vehicle* remains quite close to the Tathāgatagarbha themes. The original purity of the mind and the adventitious nature of defilement are affirmed, for "the mind is luminous at all times, but blemished by adventitious faults."[80] It teaches the reality of the *garbha*: "Although suchness is not differentiated in regard to all [sentient beings], when it has been purified, it is Tathāgatahood. Therefore, it is said that all sentient beings are that seed (*tadgarbha*)."[81] This is a clear affirmation of the basic theme of the pure *garbha*, and Vasubandhu's accompanying commentary explains that this does indeed mean that all sentient beings are possessed of the *tathāgata-garbha*.[82] The basic focus of this text is upon the one reality of the Buddha-nature, already pure and always present. When discussing the ultimate Dharma Realm, the monistic theme of *The Sutra on Neither Increase nor Decrease* is repeated: "Indeed there is nothing else in the world, and yet the world is unconscious of it. How has this kind of worldly illusion come about, whereby one clings to what is not and entirely ignores what is?"[83]

But even with this focus on the really existing Buddha-nature, *The Ornament of the Scriptures of the Great Vehicle* takes a step beyond the Tathāgatagarbha texts and attempts to answer the question of how the mind becomes defiled. That attempt is couched in terms of the three patterns of consciousness (*trisvabhāva*), a theme that will be treated in detail in chapter 7. When Maitreya uses this theme in *The Ornament*, he presupposes the reality of the pure mind of the *garbha* and then tries to explain just how empirical consciousness has devolved away from that purity. The three patterns are regarded as modes of reality or suchness (*tathatā*), for consciousness in any of its patterns is seen not as it is actually experienced, but as the arising (*vṛtti*) of suchness in the world.

> Reality (*tattvam*) is that which is always devoid of duality, that which is the basis for confusion, and that which can never be verbally expressed, for its being is not conceptualizable. It is to be known, to be rejected, and to be purified, although it is originally undefiled.[84]

Vasubandhu's commentary identifies these three states with the three patterns of consciousness as presented in classical Yogācāra: that which is entirely imagined (*parikalpita*), that which is dependent on others (*paratantra*), and that which is fully perfected (*parinispanna*).[85] The focus of *The Ornament of the Scriptures of the Great Vehicle* is not on experiential consciousness, but on the reality of the pure mind of suchness, the fully perfected mind, which always underlies such illusions and in the light of which all duality is nonexistent. This is the mind of the *garbha*, originally present in its pristine state, yet needing to be purified from the adventitious defilements of the other two patterns. The description of the other-dependent pattern as the basis for confusion (*bhrāntescá samnisrayah*) identifies it as the source of the illusion of imaginary consciousness, the source of the adventitious defilements of the imaginary pattern, which is devoid of any reality at all (*dvayena rahitam*).

In this explanation the starting point is not consciousness as experienced, but an affirmation of the pure *garbha*, and the only function of the other-dependent pattern of consciousness is to identify the source of the confusion of everyday consciousness. When one has indeed understood the fact that duality does not exist, then its underlying source, the nature of consciousness as dependently co-arisen, is to be rejected. The consistent tension here is between the pair of the imaginary and the other-dependent patterns over against the fully perfected pattern. Conversion, then, is a returning to that original nature in rejection not only of imagined illusions, but also of the other-dependent pattern of everyday consciousness. The basic weakness of the Tathāgatagarbha tradition was its failure to understand adequately the nature of experiential and defiled consciousness, a weakness not fully corrected in *The Ornament of the Scriptures of the Great Vehicle*, despite its attempt to account for the genesis of defiled consciousness.[86]

The schema of the three patterns in *The Ornament of the Scriptures of the Great Vehicle* is but an initial attempt to evolve an understanding of consciousness. But it still begins with an affirmation of an originally pure reality, hardly accessible to consciousness as we experience it, and, in the light of this pure mind, brands the consciousness we do experience as illusory and to be rejected as merely dependent on others. This leaves scant room for Nāgārjuna's notion of emptiness, since the pure mind is not empty and really exists behind the coverings of defilement. It further negates his emphasis upon reengagement in dependent co-arising, for the other-dependent pattern of consciousness is to be rejected as the source for such illusions.[87] In the Yogācāra thought of Asaṅga, which will be examined shortly, this doctrine of three patterns of consciousness will be reinterpreted and deepened. Here the point to note is that soon after Mādhyamika and Tathāgatagarbha, Mahāyāna thinkers began trying to ground the themes of emptiness (and dependent co-arising) within an understanding of the structure and development of consciousness. A shift took place away from Mādhyamika reasoning about emptiness and away from the Tathāgatagarbha practical inculcation of practice toward an examination of conscious interiority, the mind of illusion and the mind of wisdom.

CONCLUSION

This sketch of Buddhist philosophical development highlights the problematic involved in understanding meaning in all its realms: mystic, commonsense, and theoretical. If Abhidharma was the sole carrier of meaning, then no mystic insight was necessary. But if the Prajñāpāramitā texts embodied the meaning of awakening, then there was no room for theory at all. The back-and-forth swings from the commonsense mystic awareness of early Buddhism to theory, back to commonsense mystic insight in the Prajñāpāramitā and to dialectic deconstruction in Nāgārjuna, and on to the affirmative mystic monism of the Tathāgatagarbha teaching, witness to the need to develop some understanding of mystic meaning that can function in tandem with some understanding of theory. The Abhidharma pattern of theory based upon confrontational, essentialist thinking was rejected by the Prajñāpāramitā scriptures and Mādhyamika philosophers, who tended to equate all theory with delusion. But was that the only possible way to theorize? In order to ground both mystic and theoretical meaning in the same consciousness, one had to examine the nature of consciousness itself. In the West, theory admitted the mystic tradition of darkness only on the periphery of serious theology, for affirmative theology could and did proceed quite well without any mystic darkness. But in Buddhist India, theory seemed to have come a cropper, for, with the agreed-upon priority of mystic insight in Mahāyāna, it seemed to have no valid role to play in doctrinal discourse. Yet, although theory was under such a mystic interdiction, people continued to think and continued to systematize their thoughts into coherent wholes. The Yogācāra thinkers were forced by this problematic about the nature of religious meaning and discourse to turn inward and discover a new, yet unidentified realm of meaning: conscious interiority. From an understanding of the conscious genesis of meaning, they hoped to ground both mystic emptiness and consistent, verbal theory within an understanding of consciousness and thus to offer a hermeneutic for the interpretation of religious speech in all its previous manifestations.

7

Yogācāra:
A Critical Understanding
of the Genesis of Meaning

INTRODUCTION

The Yogācāra thinkers were influenced by all the currents of doctrinal thinking that had preceded them. As Mahāyānists they placed priority on the mystic meaning of the Prajñāpāramitā scriptures and accepted Mādhyamika teachings on emptiness and dependent co-arising as basic principles. Asaṅga wrote commentaries both on the Prajñāpāramitā scriptures[1] and on Nāgārjuna's *Stanzas on the Middle*.[2] Vasubandhu turned his commentarial skill to *The Diamond-Cutter Scripture*.[3] Sthiramati composed an extensive commentary on *The Stanzas on the Middle*,[4] and Dharmapāla composed a Sub-Commentary on Āryadeva's *Hundred Stanzas*.[5] However, while they remained faithful to the Mahāyāna doctrine of emptiness, the Yogācārans were also committed to philosophical understanding and resurrected Abhidharma-like attempts at theoretical analysis within their understanding of emptiness. Tathāgatagarbha thinking on the original purity of mind also played an important role in their endeavors, as we saw above in Maitreya's *Ornament of the Scriptures of the Great Vehicle*. However, being averse to its monistic and nonexperiential tone, they were constrained to reinterpret it too in the context of their understanding of emptiness.

The main thrust of Yogācāra thinking was toward working out the implications of insight into emptiness in terms of philosophic discourse so as to avoid both Abhidharma realism and Tathāgatagarbha monism. This attempt to explicate the ramifications of the Mādhyamikan principles of emptiness and dependent co-arising led Maitreya, Asaṅga, and Vasubandhu to develop a critical philosophy of consciousness.

The Yogācārā philosophers begin neither with a deconstructive dialectic of emptiness nor with an assertion of a pure mind, but with an examination of consciousness as we experience it. They try to evolve an understanding of the themes of emptiness and dependent co-arising in terms of the everyday processes of understanding and misunderstanding. Nāgārjuna had thematized illusory fabrication (*prapañca*) and refuted the supposed truths of verbal propositions by his deconstructive dialectic, identifying all views as obstacles to wisdom. Asaṅga and his school turned their attention to the structure of such illusory consciousness and how it may be reversed and transformed into wisdom. In so doing, he expanded Buddhist thinking into a new realm of meaning: conscious interiority, wherein all meaning is identified by understanding its conscious genesis.

Dramatis Personae: People and Texts

Yogācāra, as does any well-developed system of thought, gladdens the reader with an array of personages and a formidable assemblage of texts. Its explanations are at times abstruse and its argumentation often prolix. While its overall point of departure from the preceding currents of Buddhist thinking is rather clear, the specific *Sitz im Leben* of individual texts often remains somewhat opaque. As with any system, its terms tend to define themselves by cross reference, thus precluding easy access. The difficulties are such that to date Yogācāra has made little impact outside Buddhist philosophical circles. The few Western books on the subject, and the more numerous monographs,[6] tend either to be wide of the mark or to devote themselves to narrow questions of philological and textual meanings. Unlike Mādhyamika, which has received insightful attention from Western scholars,[7] Yogācāra remains for the most part the preserve of an inner circle of (mostly Japanese) Buddhologists. Thus, although it is the present writer's contention that Yogācāra constitutes a valid and insightful way of philosophizing, any attempt to reclaim its relevance may well be hampered by its lack of familiarity to Western thinkers. Before we embark on our brief excursion through Yogācāra thinking, it might be profitable to identify the principal thinkers of the school and their main works.

The foundational text of Yogācāra is a scripture (*sūtra*), *The Scripture on the Explication of Underlying Meaning*.[8] As a scripture, it is considered to be the word of the Buddha. Like many other scriptures, however, it does not date to the time of the Buddha, but was composed around 250 c.e. by someone who evidently believed that he wrote under the inspiration of the Buddha, and thus entitled his composition a scripture. It is divided into three sections: an introductory discourse on ultimate truth in the Prajñā-pāramitā style, a brief but crucially important section on consciousness, and a long section drawing out practical implications for novices. This work is frequently quoted in the following discussion.

Another body of root Yogācāra texts is attributed to Maitreya, the teacher of Asaṅga.[9] In the traditional accounts Maitreya is portrayed not as an ordinary human being, but as a celestial bodhisattva, dwelling in the

Tuṣita heaven. Asaṅga ascends into the presence of Maitreya and there his perplexity over the doctrine of emptiness is assuaged. It is recounted in the biographical literature that Asaṅga, initially an Abhidharma student, had become perplexed at his inability to understand emptiness from his Abhidharma perspective. In a distraught state of mind, he resolved to commit suicide. Although dissuaded from this course by a friend, he remained confused about emptiness until, in a state of deep concentration, he ascended to the Tuṣita heaven, received instruction from the Bodhisattva Maitreya, was converted to the Great Vehicle, and gained insight into the emptiness of all things. He subsequently wrote down and presented this teaching, becoming, as it were, the earthly amanuensis for the heavenly Maitreya. Maitreya is thus reputed to have been the author of *The Ornament of the Scriptures of the Great Vehicle*,[10] *The Analysis of the Middle and Extremes*,[11] and *The Stages of Yogic Practice*.[12]

It is understandable that many scholars reject the historical status of Maitreya and regard him as Asaṅga's "tutelary deity," that is, as his heavenly inspiration.[13] But the fact remains that a number of pre-Asaṅgan texts do exist. Asaṅga often cites *The Ornament of the Scriptures of the Great Vehicle* and *The Analysis of the Middle and Extremes* as authorities for his teachings. The defense of the historicity of Maitreya by the eminent Japanese Buddhologist Hakuju Ui is based upon the existence of these texts. He maintains that, behind the obviously hagiographic embellishments of the traditional account, there did exist a historical Maitreya who was Asaṅga's teacher and who did indeed author the texts in question. In the following discussions, without deciding the question, we shall use the name of Maitreya simply to refer to the author of these pre-Asaṅgan texts.

Asaṅga (ca. 310–ca. 390) was the systematizer and first historically verifiable figure in Yogācāra thinking. His principal work, referred to frequently below, is *The Summary of the Great Vehicle*.[14] This is an attempt to systematize and present in a logical form the basics of Yogācāra thinking. This text is perhaps the most important and seminal Yogācāra work, setting the standard for later Yogācāra thinkers. Asaṅga is also associated with *The Stages of Yogic Practice*, a voluminous compendium of Yogācāra philosophy.

Vasubandhu (ca.320–ca.400) was the younger brother of Asaṅga. According to his biography, he was an ardent follower of the Sarvāstivāda, one of the principal Abhidharma schools. Indeed, the *Commentary on the Abhidharma Treasury* is attributed to him.[15] He is reputed to have "slandered" the Great Vehicle until Asaṅga managed to convert him, whereupon he offered to tear out his tongue in repentance. Asaṅga recommended that he use it, rather, to propagate the Great Vehicle, and so he did, authoring several treatises. The best known is the brief *Thirty Stanzas on the Establishment of the Doctrine of Conscious Construction Only*. This text, however, is imbedded in a larger commentary, which is attributed to Dharmapāla, and is preserved only in a Chinese version, which reflects later Chinese

Yogācāra thinking (the Fa Hsiang school).[16] Vasubandhu also composed a *Commentary on the Summary of the Great Vehicle.*[17]

Asvabhāva (450–530) was a later commentator on the work of Asaṅga and the author of *The Exposition of the Summary of the Great Vehicle.*[18] He is reckoned as the precursor of the Dharmapāla lineage of Yogācāra and in places does offer new and exciting insights into Asaṅga's texts.

Sthiramati (ca.470–ca.550), another later commentator, is rather dogged in his dedication to present full explanations in his commentaries. He was evidently more of a straight commentator than an original thinker, as becomes apparent in his commentary on *The Ornament of the Scriptures of the Great Vehicle,*[19] which is almost twice as long as Asvabhāva's commentary on this text, but certainly not twice as insightful. He also composed a *Sub-Commentary on the Analysis of the Middle and Extremes.*[20]

Dharmapāla (530–561), although he passed on to an early nirvāṇa, is considered to have been the founder of a distinct lineage of Yogācāra thinking, which was transmitted to the Chinese pilgrim monk and translator, Hsüan-tsang (600–664), and systematized in China by his disciple, Ch'i, to constitute what became the orthodox Fa Hsiang school of East Asian Yogācāra. Dharmapāla seems to have been influenced by Dignāga (ca. 400–ca. 480), the great Yogācāra logician, and to have championed a limited but true validity for conventional thinking. But the exact lines of development are difficult to trace, since his writings are preserved only in Chinese translations and viewed only through a Chinese perspective. The Chinese *Treatise on the Establishment of the Doctrine of Conscious Construction Only* is the main source for his line of thought,[21] but, although this text accurately presents his interpretations, it often misrepresents the opinions of other Indian masters.[22] Dharmapāla is regarded as the author of the foregoing text, although it may be that Hsüan-tsang actually composed it according to his understanding of the place of Dharmapāla in Yogācāra thought. Dharmapāla also wrote a commentary on the Mādhyamikan Āryadeva's *Hundred Stanzas.*[23]

The Indian monk Paramārtha (499–569) had been the first major Yogācāra missionary to China. He labored under adverse political conditions and, although desirous of returning home, finished his years in China, translating numerous Yogācāra texts into Chinese.[24] He was fond of Tathāgatagarbha ideas and often worked them into his translations, at times adding entire sections to the originals. His translation of Asaṅga's *Summary of the Great Vehicle* and of Vasubandhu's *Commentary* on the same led to the establishment of the She-lun school of Yogācāra in China with its emphasis on the originally pure mind. It was these translations which so perplexed Hsüan-tsang that he set off to seek the true Yogācāra teachings in India, found them in the Dharmapāla lineage, and by bringing them back to China eclipsed Paramārtha's She-lun school.

Śīlabhadra (529–645), a contemporary of Dharmapāla, wrote a commentary on *The Scripture on the Buddha Land* entitled *The Interpretation of the Buddha Land*, which is preserved only in Tibetan. Bandhuprabha (fl. ca. 700) is identified as the author of a work of the same title preserved in Chinese, which in fact was based on Śīlabhadra's work but also includes a large amount of material from the Dharmapāla-Fa Hsiang tradition.[25]

Having identified a few of the trees in this particular forest, it is time to embark upon an exploratory foray into the thickets of Yogācāra philosophy.

YOGĀCĀRA THOUGHT

Yogācāra is based on the Prajñāpāramitā scriptures and attempts to rethink Mādhyamika thought in terms of a critical understanding of consciousness. Yogācāra philosophy is expressed in three interlocking themes: the structure of consciousness; its functional patterns (*gestalten*) and their etiology; and the ramifications of this critical understanding of consciousness for the understanding and interpretation of scripture.[26] These three themes are summarized in the affirmation that all things are only constructs of consciousness. Each point needs explanation.

The Structure of Consciousness

The Abhidharma theortists had regarded the mind (*citta, vijñāna*) as a subjectively real knower of objectively real entities (*dharma*). The Prajñā-pāramitā scriptures and Nāgārjuna's Mādhymika philosophy negated this subject-object pattern of knowledge, but did not offer any explanation of consciousness that might ground mystic insight into emptiness within our everyday thinking and understanding. The Tathāgatagarbha preachers then reacted against the supposed negativism of emptiness, asserting the nonempty reality of the pure *garbha*: the pure base of consciousness that enables everyone to become an awakened Tathāgata. But again, they offered no critical understanding of this pure mind, contenting themselves with appeals to faith in its existence. Such mystic claims, whether the negative variety of emptiness or the affirmative sort of the Tathāgatagarbha, stood in need of explication, for they could easily be rejected merely by disclaiming the presence of any such mystic insight. In emphasizing the difference between ultimate meaning and worldly convention and insisting on the complete otherness of ultimate meaning, the Mādhyamika philosophy of emptiness ran the risk of being simply ignored in the ongoing attempts to bring the Dharma to speech. In asserting the original purity of the mind, the Tathāgatagarbha tradition tended to drift into a nonverifiable and nonexperiential monistic theory of the one, ineffable reality behind all appearances.

The Yogācāra response to these doctrinal dilemmas was to focus upon the structure of consciousness, since it is consciousness from which Abhidharma theories, Mādhyamika negations, and Tathāgatagarbha faith assertions arise. In so doing, the Yogācārins succeeded in resurrecting theory and placing it in the context of insight into emptiness. The Abhidharmists had assumed the normative validity of the subject-object dichotomy between the real existence of consciousness and real external things. In contrast the Yogācārans applied the ideas of emptiness and dependent co-arising to consciousness and understood it to be itself dependently co-arisen and thus empty. They rejected both the naïve belief in objective essences and the uncritical assumption of a subjective mind that confronts those essences. Rather, they argued that consciousness is structured upon the constant interplay between a latent, fundamental container consciousness (*ālaya-vijñāna*) and the manifested, active consciousnesses (*pravṛtti-vijñāna*) of sensing, perceiving, and thinking. *The Analysis of the Middle and Extremes* explains:

> [Consciousness arises, on the one hand, as a latent, causal consciousness and, on the other, as the resultant, manifest phenomenal consciousness.] The container consciousness is consciousness as cause, because it is the basic cause for all the other [seven] consciousnesses. Thus caused [in a manifest manner], the [seven] active consciousnesses are related to [that container consciousness as a store of] experience.[27]

The earliest Yogācāra text, *The Explication of Underlying Meaning*, introduced the notion of the container consciousness as a seminal consciousness and understood it to be a latent and preconscious accumulation of karmic seeds from past experiences within the transmigratory cycle.[28] In virtue of this seed accumulation, the entire growth and development of consciousness is karmically defiled. This text presents the seminal container consciousness as underlying the six active consciousnesses of the five senses and perception and resulting in a proclivity toward the illusory fabrication (*prapañca*) of names and images in discriminative language.[29] There is no mention here of any undefiled or pure mind from which one might validate the Tathāgatagarbha teaching, for all conscious activity and experience arise in virtue of the underlying seeds of the container consciousness and function in an illusory pattern of imagining entities as real and fabricating views. All experience is then molded and programmed by the force of recurrent karmic defilement.

This schema of the active consciousnesses as consisting in the five sense consciousnesses plus perceptive consciousness (*manovijñāna*) outlined in *The Explication of Underlying Meaning* is drawn from the previous Abhidharma division of consciousness into the sense consciousnesses and thinking (*manovijñāna*). According to this schema, one simply analyzed sense data to arrive at the true knowledge of the essence (*svabhāva*) of things. Further reflection, however, led the Yogācāra thinkers to find this schema inadequate. Asaṅga reduced the *manovijñāna* of *The Explication of Underlying Meaning* to the perception of sensed objects and introduced a seventh consciousness, called *manas*, thinking, which he identified as the proximate source for defiled and illusory thinking. It is such thinking that, programmed by the latent seeds in the container consciousness, sees fleeting and transitory things as a fixed and stable continuum and evolves a false belief in the selfhood both of the inner subject and of outer things.[30]

Consciousness occurs, then, as a discriminating extraverted awareness that mistakes appearances for solid and abiding realities. Asaṅga outlined the genesis of such illusory fabrication as beginning with the seemingly neutral but actually illusory presentation to the mind of objects as external meaning units already given in the environment. In contrast to the supposed reality of things, one then conceives of and clings to one's own body as a sensing and perceiving being. Hence the apparent validity of our biological response to the world, that is, the subject-object pattern of knowing, is here described as illusory, for the reality of both poles is empty of any essence whatsoever.

Upon the supposed reality purveyed by this sense pattern of subject-object, one then fabricates the "clear" notion of an inner self, "the notion that I am" (*aham iti vijñapti*). But far from being a primal and self-validating Cartesian starting point, such thinking results from the defiled thinking that would cling to self as to a firm and enduring reality apart from and standing against the outer world. Just as the body is seen to house a self, so the total environment is seen to house discrete and independently existing realities that are to be sought and clung to or avoided and fled from.[31]

In this illusory manner of understanding, meaning is then externalized by illusory fabrication, and our insight into the emptiness and fleeting pattern of appearances is occluded by our attachment to the ideas assumed to represent the essences of things. Because of the apparently given validity of our biological extraversion, we set our own bodies and selves off against the environmental world and attempt to manipulate it. The sense-patterned mind is mistaken for an inner and subjective self confronting those external and objective realities.

Such a process functions, however, in forgetfulness of the underlying presence of the permeating force of the karmic seeds, which are accumulated in the latent container consciousness. It fails to understand the genesis of illusion and defiled clinging to illusory objects, rests satisfied with a truncated understanding of consciousness, and militates against insight into emptiness and the abandonment of attachment to illusions.

The structure of consciousness, the Yogācārans claim, is not this independent and self-sufficient *tabula rasa* inner mind looking out at external things. Rather, the constant interplay between the container consciousness and the active consciousnesses of sensing, perceiving, and thinking means that all conscious understanding is dependent upon the latent seeds that program and mold its initial response to the surrounding world. But it is not simply that our experience and understanding arise out of a store of latent karmic defilements, for the interplay between the container consciousness and the active consciousnesses is not a one-way street from the latent to the manifest. Rather, it is a two-way process, for simultaneous with the permeation of the latent seeds from the container consciousness into thinking and understanding, the very misunderstandings and illusions of extraverted knowing plant new seeds in the container consciousness, propelling onward the ever-cyclical progression of samsaric life.[32]

Here Asaṅga applies the Mādhyamika notion of dependent co-arising not only to the transient appearances of our everyday experience, but to the structure of consciousness itself. The mind then becomes the focus both for emptiness, since the subject-object pattern is actually empty of any valid reality, and for dependent co-arising, for its structure is itself dependently co-arisen, or in the Yogācāra term, other-dependent. All meanings that result from mental functioning are thus structured in dependency both on the latent container consciousness and on the errors of thinking consciousness.

However, consciousness is dependently co-arisen not only by virtue of this constant interplay between the latent container consciousness and the manifested active consciousnesses. It is also dependently co-arisen because the manifested mental activities of sensing, perceiving, and thinking depend upon the presence both of a sensed image (*nimitta*) and of insight (*darśana*) into that image.[33] Hence the Abhidharma view—which assumes that understanding is a looking out at the world of realities, a faithful picturing of the images of things, whether inner or outer—assures no true understanding. Without the occurrence of insight into the meaning of that image, it remains a nonunderstood picture-image, falsely taken to package and present meaning in its sensed givenness. Things then appear to be solid and real on the film of the cameralike mind and one is compelled to manipulate and cope with them in an illusory quest for the security of a nonexistent self.

The illusions of samsaric thinking and the attachments that follow in their train plant ever more seeds in the container consciousness. Thus, *saṃsāra* is not merely a description of the reality of things, but of this constantly renewing cycle of illusory fabrication projected upon the empty and dependently co-arising world by deluded consciousness. Both the latent seeds and the manifested activities are cause and result to one another, their synergy issuing in the sufferings of the samsaric life cycle. Neither the container consciousness with its defiled karmic seeds nor the manifested activities of self-assertion exist independently. If there were no store of karmic seeds, then consciousness would arise clearly as an originally pure, or at least neutral, mind. If there were no defiled mental activities, samsaric illusion would never become manifested in the existential sufferings of this fleeting world. In synergy they produce the human experiences of fragmentation and suffering. One cannot then eliminate suffering and enter *nirvāṇa* simply by guarding one's thoughts and reforming one's behavior. One must also root out the inner, preconscious seeds lurking in the container consciousness.

The Three Patterns of Consciousness

The doctrinal theme of the three patterns (*trilakṣaṇa*) of consciousness is the hallmark of Yogācāra thinking, for it expresses the overall intent of these thinkers to examine consciousness both in its defiled, empirical pattern, and in its potentiality for the attainment of wisdom and awakening. Indeed, in China this theme was seen as so central that the "orthodox" lineage of Yogācāra was identified as Fa Hsiang, literally, the school of "the patterns of mental states."

These three patterns denote three different modes in the functioning of consciousness. The structure of consciousness remains, as explained above, an interdependent interplay between the latent container consciousness and the active consciousnesses, and within the active consciousnesses between image and insight. The three patterns differ inasmuch as these structured relationships function differently.

The three patterns are (1) the imagined pattern (*parikalpita-lakṣaṇa*) wherein consciousness fabricates illusions and clings to them as if they were stable realities, (2) the other-dependent pattern (*paratantra-lakṣaṇa*) which, being the basic structural functioning of consciousness, initially supports the imagined pattern, but which can be converted into (3) the perfected pattern (*pariniṣpanna-lakṣaṇa*), the absence of illusion and clinging within the other-dependent structure of consciousness. The force of the underlying seeds of defiled karmic actions is the prime mover in the defilement of consciousness and its devolution into the illusory, imagined pattern. Only when the permeating influence of these seeds is negated and the seeds themselves eradicated, can other-dependent consciousness become purified and illusory knowing converted into wisdom-consciousness. But from within the imagined pattern it is difficult to explicate the relationships between the container consciousness and the active consciousnesses because the seminal container consciousness is latent and preconscious and functions through words that themselves are permeated by karmic seeds. Hence, the Yogācāra analysis of the three patterns focuses instead on the manifested interdependent structure of active understanding. Asaṅga in his *Summary of the Great Vehicle* sets the context for this examination by saying: "The mental states that characterize the active consciousnesses have as their essence constructed ideas (*vijñapti*) endowed with image and insight."[34]

The three patterns differ inasmuch as the same basic interdependent structure of consciousness, whereby image and insight manifest our preconscious and latent experience, may function differently either to bring about illusory fabrication or to be liberated from such illusory fabrication. Ye Shes sde, the Tibetan translator of Asaṅga's text, is apodictic on the point: "It is because they are endowed with image and insight that the mental states have three patterns.[35]

Asanga then presents his teaching on the three patterns in the context of this understanding of the interdependent image-insight structure of the active consciousnesses as manifesting the latent store of karmic experiences in the container consciousness. As noted earlier, the other-dependent pattern is the basic structure of consciousness. It serves as the pivot around which turn both the defilement of the imagined pattern and the purification of the perfected pattern. *The Abhidharma of the Great Vehicle* explains: "There are three states [of consciousness]: that which consists in the defiled aspect, that which consists in the purified aspect, and that which is both at the same time."[36] It is the other-dependent pattern that consists in both defilement and purification, inasmuch as its initial arising is yoked with the imagined and its awakening with purification.

Asanga begins in the second chapter of his *Summary of the Great Vehicle* by moving from a consideration of the other-dependent pattern as the support for the imagined, illusory pattern to a consideration of the other-dependent pattern as liberated from such illusion and imagination. The other-dependent pattern is the pivotal state. It can function either in the weaving of illusion or in liberation from such illusion. He describes its illusory functioning as "the conscious construction which germinates from the container consciousness and which consists in unreal imagining."[37]

The occurrence of fabricated and unreal imaginings results from the construction within the mind of ideas imagined to capture and represent the essences of things. Unreal imagining is the mistaking of images for pictures of the real, just as for Gregory of Nyssa imagination led one into the illusion that stability could be found in the unsubstantial world. The same point is made in a famous and tightly packed passage from Maitreya's *Analysis of the Middle Path and Extremes*: "Unreal imagining (*abhūta parikalpa*) does exist, but in it the two [imagined aspects of subject and object] do not exist. However, herein, emptiness does exist, and in that [emptiness], this [unreal imagining] exists."[38]

The unreal imagining that takes images to be pictures of external meaning and constructs ideas of real entities does indeed exist, for it is the illusory functioning of other-dependent understanding as the constant fabrication of illusion. But its illusory pattern of confrontational knowing, which dichotomizes real external things over against an equally real internal knower, does not represent any reality, for the duality between subject and object is empty. The imagined reality of the subject-object pattern of knowing is a superimposition of constructed ideas upon experience, a reality imagined to be given in sensation and validated in concepts. It operates without any awareness of the dynamic pull of the seed store of karmic experiences in the container consciousness toward the constant objectification of and attachment to phenomena. It is not just that the transient things of experience are empty of any firm essence to which one may securely cling; the subject and object pattern is itself empty and without any abiding meaning. Nevertheless, the other-dependent pattern, which here gravitates downward under the force of imagining, does itself exist in emptiness.

Understanding, as other-dependent in its basic structure, is dependently co-arising, and thus empty of any set essence. The imagined pattern of illusion takes place upon the other-dependent pattern and dependently co-arisen structure of consciousness and is a distortion of that structure. But it does not thereby negate the possibility of dependently co-arisen and illusion-free understanding. To borrow a term from Gregory of Nyssa, it is a "wart" on the other-dependent functioning of true understanding. In his *Sub-Commentary on the Analysis of the Middle Path and Extremes*, the commentator Sthiramati explains the meaning of the passage above:

> Unreal imagining is the discrimination of subject and object. The word "two" [in the passage] refers to subject and object. . . . Emptiness, however, is apart from this dichotomy of subject and object, [which arise] from unreal imagining. . . . Thus unreal imagining exists in emptiness.[39]

Unreal imagining does indeed exist, for images do appear and seem to imply their own meanings. Nevertheless, it is unreal and illusory since the dichotomy of subject and object is tacitly assumed as valid and the patterns of sensed images are taken to be normative, even though they are programmed by the underlying seeds in the container consciousness. Insight into the emptiness of all inner and outer essences negates the validity of such a pattern of understanding. By emptiness here is meant a conscious understanding not caught in the net of illusory fabrication, an understanding that the driving thrust behind the seeming validity of the imagined pattern comes from the karmic store of defiled experiences accumulated in the container consciousness. The oft-repeated Yogācāra theme that all things are only conscious constructs is intended to negate the validity of imagined realities corresponding to an equally imagined self. Thus Asaṅga defines the imagined pattern as "that which appears as an object, even though there is no object, but only a conscious construct (*vijñaptimātra*).[40]

To emphasize the point, Vasubandhu in his *Commentary on the Summary of the Great Vehicle* interprets the passage above: "The phrase 'appears as an object' means that it appears as an object that is apprehended or as a self that apprehends."[41]

Once images in the active consciousnesses are taken to imply the valid givenness of really existent essences as set and stable units of meaning, whether external things or an internal self, then the other-dependent pattern of understanding functions within an entirely imagined and illusory horizon, for insight is frozen at the image as if that image itself had already grasped reality. Openness toward understanding beings in their dependent co-arising, and thus in their emptiness, is aborted and wisdom becomes impossible.

A crucial point of the analysis above is the distinction drawn by the Yogācārans between the basic other-dependent pattern and its imagined mutation. Not only were they attempting to develop a critical understanding of consciousness and its operations that would account for the genesis of the illusory fabrication that had been negated by the Mādhyamika thinkers, but they also intended to allow scope for a limited but valid role for clear and consistent doctrinal discourse as an expression of wisdom. Once freed from the illusion that meaning resides in any reputed "purity" of an original mind, one is freed to think and construct theory in full awareness of emptiness, namely, of the dependently co-arisen structure of all understanding. Thus Vasubandhu could explain the character of emptiness (*śūnyatālakṣaṇa*) as the nonexistence of the imagined pattern, but the existence of the other-dependent pattern functioning in its fully perfected pattern,[42] and Asaṅga defines the fully perfected pattern as "the complete absence of all characteristics of real objects in the other-dependent pattern."[43]

These three patterns of consciousness are not, then, to be taken as three distinct and separate layers of consciousness. Rather, they describe the one other-dependent structure of consciousness that issues in the genesis of defiled consciousness but is also capable of a reversal toward the attainment of wisdom.[44] When the question is raised as to whether the three patterns are different or identical, Asaṅga responds: "They are neither different nor identical. In one mode of being (*paryāya*), the other-dependent [pattern] is itself dependent on others. In another mode, it is the imagined, and in another mode it is fully perfected."[45]

The other-dependent pattern is present in both the imagined and the perfected, for it plays the pivotal role in the definition of the three patterns. In illusory consciousness it serves as the support for imagined essences, for in that case it functions as unreal imagining. But in the perfected mode, it ceases to imagine illusory realities and, no longer programmed by the underlying seeds of karmic defilement, supports the wisdom insight of full perfection by bringing emptiness insight into dependently co-arisen speech. In this perfected pattern the other-dependent and fully perfected patterns critically ground the Mādhyamika theme of the two truths wherein the truth of ultimate meaning, namely, silence, comes to speech in skillfully woven words of wisdom—a theme to be treated more fully in the next chapter. Liberation from the imagined pattern means not only the attainment of full perfection, but also a recovery of the already present but now undistorted pattern of other-dependency. Thus the passage above speaks of the other-dependent pattern in one mode being dependent on others—being freed from illusion and functioning in emptiness as the awareness of the dependent co-arising of images and insights and hence being capable of weaving endless conventional discourses on the meaning of ultimate meaning.

The Yogācārans refer to this transformation, from the imagined pattern to the perfected pattern of wisdom and awakening, as a conversion of the support (*āśraya-parivṛtti*), that is, of consciousness, for the basic other-dependent structure of consciousness that supports both is turned around (*parivṛtti*) from illusion to wisdom. In awakening, the defiled seeds of the container consciousness are eradicated and the underlying mind of awakening becomes a mirror wisdom that reflects the suchness of things in their ultimate emptiness. In awakening, images are not seen as pictures of the essences of things, but call forth wisdom insight in a purified and conventional awareness of things as they arise and pass away co-dependently. In his *Summary of the Great Vehicle* Asaṅga describes this conversion as the attainment of the ultimate Dharma Body:

> What is the character of the Dharma Body of awakening? It is characterized as the conversion of support, because, having eradicated the other-dependent pattern in its defiled aspect, it is liberated from all obstacles, is assured of mastering all states, and is transformed into the other-dependent pattern in its purified aspect.[46]

Such a conversion is not only insight into emptiness. It does not rest content with a negation of essences, but asserts a valid and true understanding of things in a context of emptiness, that is, in the true functioning of the other-dependent pattern of consciousness. *The Treatise on the Establishment of the Doctrine of Conscious Construction Only*, reflecting Dharmapāla's position, rejects the opinion that the other-dependent structure of insight into image is itself imagined and illusory:

> The mind and its mental states, because of the force of its propensities, develop in the two aspects [of image and insight]. Because these two aspects arise from causes, they are other-dependent. . . . But because of illusory clinging, people universally imagine set [ideas] of being and non-being, identity and difference, both [being and non-being, both identity and difference], neither [being nor non-being, neither identity nor difference], and such like [views]. It is thus that these two aspects are termed imagined.[47]

The appearance in the mind of an image and the insight into that image are dependently co-arisen, and thus other-dependent. But clinging to the images that appear as if they themselves represented the fixed essences of things in imagined insight results in the fabrication of illusory views. This same theme is repeated by Dharmapāla in *An Extensive Sub-Commentary on the Hundred Stanzas*:

> It is because of clinging to what is entirely imagined that the developments of consciousness appear externally as all the defilements,

and that, due to these defilements, unstable clinging arises. Because of unstable clinging, [people] cling to and imagine the real existence of a self and others. But all impure and pure states, whose essences are taken as subjects or objects, are actually dependent on others.[48]

The theme of the three patterns presents then a critical understanding of the dynamics of conversion and enables one to discourse critically on the nature of wisdom awareness. In validating other-dependent understanding, it proffers the possibility of resurrecting theory, of recovering the basic, nonimaginative functioning of other-dependent understanding, in a context of emptiness.[49] Thus the third summary point of Yogācāra is identified by Asaṅga as the interpretation of the meaning of what has been handed down in the tradition, that is to say, in doctrinal interpretation and discourse.

THE YOGĀCĀRA HERMENEUTIC

The Interpretation of Scripture

The aim of Yogācāra was to develop a consistent understanding of conscious understanding which would do justice to the mystic awareness of the Prajñāpāramitā texts and Mādhyamika deconstructive thought, while at the same time leaving room for theoretical explanations of doctrine. Since all words are empty of any specific essence and take their meaning only within the dependently co-arisen context in which they occur, interpretation cannot proceed in a literal manner. One must not engage solely in analyzing the words of the scriptures, but must also uncover their underlying meaning. *The Explication of Underlying Meaning*, as its title suggests, outlines the method:

> Through a wisdom born from [hearing] the doctrine, the Bodhisattvas base themselves upon the words [of the scriptures], take the text literally, and do not yet understand the intention. . . . Through a wisdom born from reflecting [on those words], the Bodhisattvas do not base themselves upon the words or take the meaning literally, and do understand the intention. . . . Through a wisdom born from meditation, the Bodhisattvas either base themselves on the words or do not, either take the text literally or do not, but, in understanding the intention, they see the heart of the matter through the images understood in concentration. . . . [50]

Only when the experience of wisdom has uncovered the heart of the matter can interpretation truly express the intent and meaning of the scriptures. No literal reading that would refuse to seek that intention suffices. No philosophic approach, such as the Abhidharma method, which sought to uncover the essence behind the "inexact" words of scripture, is adequate. Only when one has experienced conversion from imagination to full perfection and recovered the basic operational structure of other-dependent understanding can interpretation truly reflect the wisdom with which the scriptures were proclaimed. The notion of taking the intent of the author into account when interpreting texts is perhaps a commonplace among modern Western exegetes and they might thus find the profound impact this recommendation had for third-century Buddhist thinkers somewhat difficult to appreciate. But such a proposal was indeed revolutionary in light of the then current options of either taking the word of the scriptures as literally absolute and self-validating, or of accepting the well-analyzed categories of Abhidharma theory as defining the essence of things. Asvabhāva in his *Exposition of the Summary of the Great Vehicle* explains: "Up until now, explanations of the meaning [of the scriptures] have not taken into account the intention of [their] author. But it is in taking into account that intention that one should explain the meaning of what has been declared [in the scriptures]."[51] One must then constantly question the text and seek to understand its underlying meaning.

Such a method necessitated a clear understanding of meaning in all its contexts and led the Yogācārans to see that doctrinal meaning develops. A famous passage from *The Explication of Underlying Meaning* presents the Yogācāra understanding of the development of doctrinal meaning:

> The Bodhisattva Paramārthasamudgata said to the Buddha: "In the country of Benares at the Ṛṣipatana in the Deer Park the Bhagavat first turned the Wheel of Doctrine, demonstrating the Four Noble truths for the followers of the Word Hearers' Vehicle. The turning of that Wheel was marvelous and wonderful, such as nobody, whether god or man, had ever turned before in the world. Nevertheless, there were superior doctrines. This [first turning] gave rise to criticism, had to be interpreted, and became an object of controversy. Then the Bhagavat with an implicit intention turned the Wheel for the second time for the sake of the followers of the Great Vehicle, explaining that all things are without essence, do not arise, are not destroyed, are quiescent from the beginning, are originally in cessation. Nevertheless there are teachings superior to this, for it also gave rise to criticism, had to be interpreted, and became an object of controversy. Then the Bhagavat with an explicit intention turned the Wheel a third time for the sake of the followers of all vehicles, explaining that all things are without essence, do not arise, are not destroyed, are quiescent from the beginning, and are originally in cessation. This turning of the Wheel of Doctrine is absolutely marvelous and wonderful. It is unsurpassed, does not give rise to criticism, is explicit, and does not become an object of controversy.[52]

This passage highlights the Yogācāra understanding of doctrinal development. The first turning of the wheel includes both the early commonsense teachings of the *Nikāyas* and the *Āgamas*, and the theoretical Abhidharma presentation of those teachings, both of which took the four truths as their central theme. These teachings are characterized as imperfect and in need of the Prajñāpāramitā mystic negation that all things are without essence. Even though theoretically elaborated in Abhidharma theory, they still need to be interpreted (*neyārtha*), for their meaning (*artha*) needs to be drawn out (*neya*), since it has not been rendered explicit and identified in terms of its critical genesis in consciousness. But even the second turning of the wheel, the Prajñāpāramitā, does not explicate its critical grounding and it too must be interpreted, for it does not identify the genesis for its negations within consciousness. Instead, its mystic teachings remain an object of controversy and criticism. It is only the third turning, which is Yogācāra, that renders explicit (*nitārtha*) its critical basis, for its meaning has been drawn out (*nita*) and made manifest by identifying it within the operations of conscious interiority.

But Yogācāra does not hereby claim to offer a deeper or more profound doctrinal content. The Mahāyāna themes of the third turning are identical with those of the second: emptiness and the nonarising of essences. Yogācāra does not attempt to offer any new doctrinal content, but, rather, seeks to render explicit the implicit ground of the Prajñāpāramitā and Mādhyamika teachings by analyzing the genesis of such insights in terms of the patterns of our conscious understanding. Yogācāra is a critical validation of Mādhyamika, a reclaiming of theory in the context of insight into emptiness applied to the functioning of conscious understanding. In the apt phrase of the Japanese Buddhologist Jikidō Takasaki, Yogācāra "was really a successor to Abhidharma Buddhism, but it was Abhidharma based upon the teaching of Prajñāpāramitā, and hence deserves to be called 'Mahāyāna Abhidharma,' as shown in the title of one [of its] scriptures."[53]

The passages above show that the Yogācārans did not understand meaning to be univocal. Rather, their hermeneutic functions in an awareness of the differences in dependently co-arisen meanings. In their critical understanding of the conscious genesis of all meaning, they came to differentiate distinct realms of meaning and, as critical philosophers, to recommend their understanding of critical meaning as a method to validate insight into emptiness and carry forth the tasks of doctrinal discourse. The chapter "On Knowing Reality" in *The Bodhisattva Stages* offers a fourfold schema of meaning realms, which consist in "that which is accepted in the world, that which is accepted by reasoning, that which is the sphere of wisdom purified from the obstacle of passion, and that which is the sphere of wisdom purified from the obstacle to the knowable."[54]

The first meaning, that which is accepted in the world (*lokaprasiddha*), is explained as meaning that is accepted through habit or convention without being deeply considered or pondered. As such it signifies a realm of commonsense meaning whose criterion is relevance to practical living. The second realm, that which is accepted by reasoning (*yuktiprasiddha*), is explained as well-analyzed knowledge derived from proof and demonstration. As such it corresponds to theoretical meaning whose criteria are the reasonableness of the judgments made and the logical consistency of the analyses performed. This is the realm of meaning of the Abhidharma philosophers, for whom logical analysis and demonstration were sufficient to validate theories of essences. The third realm of meaning, that which is the sphere of wisdom purified from the obstacle of passion (*kleśāvaraṇa-viśuddhijñānagocara*) is defined as the wisdom obtained through purification from impure outflows of passion. This is the wisdom of practitioners who abide in quiescence without any further concern for understanding the knowable world or carrying out the tasks of compassion. Meaning here is validated only in direct, mystic insight without any need for conventional truth. It is the realm of the solitary hermit who, alone like the rhinoceros, attains mystic insight without any felt need to communicate that experience to others in doctrinal discourse. The fourth realm of meaning, that which is the sphere of wisdom purified [also] from the obstacle to the knowable (*jñeyāvaraṇaviśuddhijñānagocara*), is the wisdom of buddhas and bodhisattvas who have realized the emptiness of both self and others in a critical awareness of the genesis of all meaning, and thus are in no danger of functioning in an illusory, imagined pattern or of neglecting dependently co-arising and conventional meanings as simply useless fabrications. The Yogācārans insist that one must be purified not only from the obstacle of passion that flows from the defiled seeds in the container consciousness, but also from the obstacle to the knowable that issues from aborting the other-dependent pattern of insight into image.

To interpret scriptures, then, is not simply an exercise in insight into ultimate emptiness. It also necessitates insight into the dependently co-arising insights into particular images at particular times and an explication of the underlying meaning the words of scripture are meant to embody.

THE DOCTRINE OF CONSCIOUS CONSTRUCTION-ONLY

These three basic themes are capsulized in the doctrine that all things and all mental states are only conscious construction (*sarva-dharmaḥvijñap-timātra*). This Yogācāra refrain is meant both to affirm the mystic negation of essences in the immediacy of insight into emptiness and to ground conventionally valid doctrinal discourse by understanding other-dependent understanding as constructive of mediated meaning.

The central term *vijñapti* is an abstract noun formed from the causative root of *vi-jñā*, to know, and denotes that which causes knowing to occur. It thus comes to mean a sign or symbol that brings knowing about, such as a letter imparting information. In its technical Yogācāra usage, it refers to that which causes conscious knowing to occur, and signifies the mental construction of ideas and words that mediate meaning. Such words and ideas, although appearing as if reflecting the external reality of things upon the inner reality of the mind, in fact are formed through the influence and permeation of the seeds in the container consciousness. Their construction is molded by those seeds and the assumed realities they purport to convey are empty of any essential reality. The fact that ideas and words are not impressed upon the mind through the causality of external essences is emphasized by the term "only" (*mātra*). The teaching of *vijñapti-mātra* signifies the genesis of meaning through the construction of ideas in virtue of the prior programming of the seminal consciousness and without any appeal to the putative realities of confrontational knowing.

Because of the permeation of the active consciousnesses with the defiled seeds of past action (*karma*), words and ideas are taken to picture realities that can be clung to by imagination and desire—precluding not only the necessity, but even the possibility, of insight into the meaning of sensed images. Rather than understanding that all meanings are dependently co-arisen in a host of cultural and language contexts, meaning is frozen at the givenness of images in the imagined pattern. Thus the Yogācārans proclaim that "the functioning of the wisdom of conscious construction-only implies that wisdom is objectless."[55] The intent of the doctrine of conscious construction-only is to negate the validity of the imagined pattern of conscious understanding, to negate the imagination that clings to ideas and tries to bridge the gap between an illusory real subject and its projected real objects. The affirmation of this doctrine is a denial that there are meaning units "out there" awaiting apprehension and an assertion that all mediated meaning is a constructive exercise of understanding.

The Yogācārans were insistent on this point, for they saw the imagined pattern of subject-object knowing as a most tenacious illusion, rooted as it is in the biological response of embodied persons to the physical environment. When *The Explication of Underlying Meaning* treats the question of whether meditative images are different from or the same as the mind that knows them, it answers that "They are not different because those images are only constructs. I have declared that all the objects of consciousness come forth only as constructs."[56] Although images appear as distinct from the thinking that considers them, as if they represented real meaning units, in fact they are simply one factor in a conscious process of interdependent insight into image. But the subject-object pattern is hard to see beyond, and the objection is pressed that, if the images that occasion knowing are not different from the thinking mind, then how can thinking see (*utprekṣata*) what is thought? Indeed, if knowing is an inner subject looking at real objects, then there must be a difference between what is seen and the seer. *The Explication of Underlying Meaning* depicts the Buddha as denying that understanding is any kind of looking or seeing.

No mental state ever comes to look at anything.[57] Rather, thought, arising [dependent on conditions], does come forth in such a manner that it has the double aspect of subject and object. . . . The thinking that comes forth thus and the images known in concentration seem to be distinct things, but they are only two aspects [of the same process of understanding].[58]

The appearance of subjective thinking reaching out toward objective reality is not self-validating, but only the process of constructing mediated meanings in a context of emptiness.

Despite assertions to the contrary, Yogācāra is not here propounding a form of subjective idealism that would negate the validity of true knowing. Rather, the intent is to transcend the dichotomy of subject and object (*grāhyagrāhaka*) by negating the validity of both poles, for that dichotomy is simply the inner form by which the mind gains insight into images and constructs mediated meanings. If one stops short at the image as a picture of the real, then imagining aborts the process and blocks the possibility of dependently co-arisen understanding.

The intent of the doctrine of conscious construction-only is to negate the imaginings of the imagined pattern and is an alternate statement of the foregoing theme of three patterns of conscious knowing. Other-dependent understanding functions through insight into image. But when that process is broken off and frozen at an imagining of images as already containing meaning, then the imagined pattern obtains. When freed from such imagining, the mind is liberated and both perfected insight into emptiness and other-dependent insight into mediated meaning can occur.

The point is crucial, for without meditating upon the words and images of scripture (mediated meaning), illusions cannot be removed and understanding cannot be attained. Asaṅga treats the theme of conscious construction-only under the heading of penetrating the meaning of the knowable, that is, consciousness in its three patterns. He begins by stressing that a true understanding of these patterns cannot derive from the container consciousness, for on its own that seminal consciousness only engenders the karmic imaginings that cling to its own projections, to images and ideas as reality pictures. True understanding comes only for states of consciousness that counter these imaginings by becoming imbued with the teachings of the scriptures, states "imbued with much hearing of the doctrine of the scriptures." It is then of central importance not only to understand the structure and patterns of conscious understanding, but to turn that awareness to an examination of and meditation on the scriptures. In his commentary Asvabhāva explains:

These states are characterized by a continuity of mind and mental states imbued with much hearing of the doctrine and meaning of the Great Vehicle. Those whose hearing of [and familiarity with the scriptures] are weak are incapable of arriving at full comprehension. Remember what the Bhagavat said in *The Noble Rāhula Scripture*, for when Rāhula said to him, "I would like it if the Bhagavat would simply teach me full comprehension," the Bhagavat answered, "Do you already know the collection of the good doctrine?" "No, I do not, Bhagavat." Whereupon the Bhagavat said to him, "You must first know the collection of the doctrine."[59]

The stress is here not upon nonverbal, mystic insight into emptiness, but rather, on establishing images and insights within other-dependent understanding. Initial awareness must be mediated by insight into images and, lacking the appropriate images, none can occur. It is thus the doctrine of the scriptures that counteracts the illusory imaginings that flow from the container consciousness. Scriptural understanding is not merely a scholarly exercise, but is crucial for constructing a store of mediated meanings that can occasion insight into the Buddha's underlying intent. In the words of Nāgārjuna, ultimate meaning can be expressed only in reliance upon words. Both inner words and the written words of the scriptures are constructs that embody meanings understood by the mind.

If one understands that all mediated meaning is a conscious process of constructing ideas upon images, one can avoid clinging to imagined fantasies and proceed to valid doctrinal discourse. Nāgārjuna's statement that emptiness takes on the designation (*prajñapti*) of dependent co-arising is here reinterpreted, in terms of the doctrine of conscious construction-only, to mean that all ideas and images of emptiness are only constructs (*vijñapti*) woven by the mind of wisdom upon scriptural meditation. Such words, being other-dependent, are valid, even as theory, as long as they are not taken to imply the reality of essences or the absoluteness of mediated meaning. Thus the bodhisattva can penetrate consciousness both as a unity, because he or she understands the ultimate emptiness of the duality of subject and object, and as a duality, because he or she understands that in mediating conventional meaning, understanding does appear as dual.

The Yogācāra hermeneutic is then a recommendation to make explicit the intent of the scriptural tradition within the critical realm of meaning expressed by the theme that all things are only constructs. It constitutes a radical deliteralization of verbal teachings and scriptures and a radical deconstruction of all pretensions to absolute verbal validity, while insisting upon the necessity for valid thinking about and meditation on the scriptures.

Wisdom is not, however, limited to the understanding of the other-dependent validity of doctrine. First and foremost, it is entry into a realm of nondiscriminative insight. Asaṅga teaches that "the perfection of wisdom (*prajñāpāramitā*) is not different from nondiscriminative wisdom."[60] Beyond the attainment of insight into mental words and images, by rejecting in Mādhyamika fashion even the concept of "conscious construction-only," by direct experience, one abides in the Dharma realm of nondiscriminative awareness. By severing the germination of the container consciousness into the imagined pattern, one develops seeds of contact (*sparśa-bīja*) with that ultimate Dharma Realm. Thus wisdom is both a direct, unmediated contact with the ineffable that is attained through basic nondiscriminative wisdom (*nirvikalpa-jñāna*), and, based on that experience, a subsequently attained wisdom (*pṛṣṭhalabdha-jñāna*) that can validly enunciate doctrine without misunderstanding. The horizons of experience are not encompassed within the karmically defiled store of the container consciousness but, upon conversion, open to the direct experience of and contact with ultimate meaning.

CONCLUSION

In the three points above (and their expression under the theme of conscious construction-only), Yogācāra comes to terms with the mystic insight of the Prajñāpāramitā scriptures and, taking its departure from the teaching of emptiness and dependent co-arising, expands its understanding of consciousness into a realm of conscious interiority. The understanding of the container consciousness in its constant interplay with the active consciousnesses of sensing, perceiving, and thinking allowed the Yogācāra masters to present consciousness as illusory, on the one hand, and yet open to perfection. The basic structure of consciousness is other-dependent, for experience and thinking are mutually dependent, as are image and insight in verbal thinking. It is by taking the appearance of the subject-object dichotomy as normative that it arises in its distorted, imagined pattern. It is by eliminating those karmic seeds and attaining insight into the emptiness of both one's self and other things that that distortion is eradicated and consciousness is converted to the perfected pattern.

But questions remain, for, if consciousness is empirically defiled and tends on its own to generate only imaginative illusions, then how can it ever be open to a conversion by hearing the doctrine? Even if its basic structure is open to such a conversion, how in fact is that effected? Does this not imply some notion of an originally pure mind? of a basic potential within consciousness for awakening? Do all sentient beings share in an original Buddha-nature and have within them the embryo of a Tathāgata (*tathāgatagarbha*)?

The next chapter will consider the Yogācāra understanding of the originally pure mind and the nature of awakening (*buddhatva*) as the three bodies of Buddha (*buddha-trikāya*). It will, however, begin with a discussion of the theme of the two truths as understood in Yogācāra, for this notion embodied the actual application of the Yogācāra hermeneutic to a scriptural interpretation of the nature of mystic awakening.

8

The Structure
of the Wisdom Mind

The basic Yogācāra understanding of consciousness sketched in chapter 7 focused on empirical consciousness and laid the ground for a reaffirmation of the value of doctrinal discourse and theoretical thinking. However, Yogācāra was not only concerned with examining everyday thinking and maintaining the validity of theory as other-dependent. It was also committed to upholding the priority of mystic awareness. The Yogācāra thinkers embraced the Prajñāpāramitā notion of emptiness and the Mādhyamika identity between emptiness and dependent co-arising, not only in terms of a recovery of the original other-dependent structure of consciousness (and thus of the limited validity of conventional theory), but also in terms of the fully perfected pattern, of an unmediated, contentless awareness of ultimate meaning.

The Yogācāra thinkers were influenced by the Tathāgatagarbha tradition, but, in place of that tradition's notion of an originally pure mind, they argued that the other-dependent structure of consciousness is that which is originally present. Asaṅga does not restrict the scope of emptiness quantitatively, limiting it to the "adventitious defilements" that cloud the originally present pure *garbha* mind. Rather, he understands emptiness to apply to all mental acts, whether truly understood as signifying dependently co-arising being or mistakenly thought to imply the real being of beings in the imagined pattern. The Yogācāra masters realized the centrality of mystic insight and, spurred on by the Tathāgatagarbha objections to the perceived nihilism of the notion of emptiness, they attempted to explicate mystic meaning within the framework of their critical theory of consciousness.

Mystic meaning, by Mahāyāna definition, is a matter of unmediated, nondual awareness. It is not then amenable to an easy analysis or to consistently logical presentation. Consequently, the task of explicating in doctrine its mystic structure was carried out using a number of doctrinal themes: the two truths, the structure of full perfection, the three bodies of

Buddha, and the five factors of awakening. In all these themes, however, there is a recurrent structural motif that will engage our attention.

THE TWO TRUTHS

The Prajñāpāramitā and Mādhyamika texts had presented the theme of the two truths with stress upon the ineffability of ultimate truth. Conventional truth (*saṃvṛti-satya*) was a "covering over" (*saṃ-vṛ*) and occlusion of truth. By contrast, the Yogācāra thinkers attempted to evolve an understanding of the two truths that would accord relative yet valid status to conventional truth and at the same time maintain the mystic immediacy of insight into ultimate meaning.

Asaṅga agreed with the Prajñāpāramitā insistence on the ineffability of wisdom and its recommendation that the bodhisattva should maintain his mind "unsupported by form, sound, smell, taste, touch, or mind-object, unsupported by doctrine, unsupported by no-doctrine, unsuppported by anything."[1] In his *Commentary on the Diamond Scripture*, Asaṅga states:

> Although suchness is always and everywhere, still it cannot be realized by those who, on account of ignorance, have their mind supported, but, on the contrary, it is realized by those whose minds, on account of right understanding, are supported nowhere.[2]

Conventional truth is valid as a provisional method for realizing ultimate meaning. It is truth only *sub specie vacuitatis* as a skillful expression of an awakened mind that recognizes its provisional nature. Yet without conventional expression, the truth of ultimate meaning remains silent and detached in absence of compassion and soon becomes regarded as trivial and irrelevant to human living. A true enunciation of doctrine entails a prior awareness of ultimate meaning and a commitment to construct provisional discourse.

It was the task of the Yogācāra thinkers to explicate the structure of conventional enunciations about ultimately meaningful silence, a task they attempted to carry out through their critical focus on the three patterns of conscious understanding. Upon the conversion of consciousness, the basic other-dependent structure of insight into image begins to function in the service of the perfected pattern of wisdom insight into silent, ultimate meaning, constructing wisdom images and offering wisdom insights. The illusory programming of the container consciousness is now no longer frozen at the projected essences of things, but is transformed into wisdom consciousness, engendering images that serve to suggest and trace the content of unmediated insight. Wisdom understanding derives not directly from the words or images of conventional discourse, but indirectly from the immediacy of nonverbal and unimaginable insight. In the Yogācāra analysis, such a fully perfected pattern of wisdom consciousness comes to speech, by reaffirming its dependently co-arisen operation in the service of bringing silence to speech. All conventional discourse is seen as a weaving of models upon the silence of ultimate meaning and all doctrinal literalism is banished totally. An example of this can be seen in Asaṅga's commentary on the following passage from *The Diamond Scripture*:

> The Bhagavat said: "If any bodhisattva would say, 'I will create harmonious Buddha lands,' he would speak falsely. Why? The harmonious Buddha lands, the harmonious Buddha lands, Subhūti, have been taught by the Tathāgata as no harmonious Buddha lands. Therefore, he spoke of harmonious Buddha lands."[3]

Here mystic insight negates the validity of speaking about the pure Buddha lands, for such a concept can preclude the possibility of realizing wisdom. Buddha lands can then only be affirmed through a negation that declares their emptiness. Asaṅga in his *Commentary on the Diamond Scripture* draws out the implications of the passage above in concise terms: "One cannot grasp Buddha lands because they are only ideas constructed from wisdom. They are not physical locations, but are preeminent [wisdom descriptions, and thus] their harmony is a no-harmony."[4]

It was stated earlier (chap. 6, above) that worldly convention can be "in harmony" with ultimate meaning. Here Asaṅga explains this harmony as consisting in a recognition of the absence of harmony between any constructed idea and ultimate meaning. Like Nāgārjuna before him, Asaṅga affirms the complete otherness of ultimate meaning, locating the validity of discourses on the Buddha land within wisdom consciousness as a meaningful idea, which, if not clung to as an imagined reality (a literal harmony), has an other-dependent validity in the service of the full perfection of wisdom (a harmony of no-harmony).

Maitreya's *Analysis of the Middle Path and Extremes* offers a schematic understanding of the two truths, describing ultimate meaning as the objective (*artha*), attainment (*prāpti*), and practice (*pratipatti*),[5] while worldly convention is depicted as enunciating truth, functioning in other-dependency, and expressed in words.

The first and prime meaning of ultimate meaning is that it is the objective of the mind of wisdom. The word *artha* comes from the verb *arth*, to strive to obtain, and here refers to the objective of the mind that reaches toward ultimate meaning.[6] It is this striving of the mind that accounts for the ascending movement of worldly convention in its attempts to realize ultimate meaning. But ultimate meaning is not an object like other objects, for it transcends the subject-object polarity of mediated knowing. This striving is perhaps similar to Gregory's notion of an unending "stretching forth" toward ever-expanding horizons, toward a goal that is never attained, for even in its second meaning of attainment, what is attained is an awareness of ultimate meaning as silent and unmediable. The attainment of ultimate meaning does not reduce it to an object among objects, but abides in insight into emptiness and in the patience not to force words upon the ever-receding horizon of silence in an onrush of human words. The word *pratipatti* signifies ultimate meaning as practice, for it is wisdom realized in and witnessed by the practice of differentiating the two truths and engaging in acts of compassion.[7] It is this practice that signals the transition from silent attainment to verbalized doctrine, and which, in the Yogācāra scheme of things, brings conventional truth within the sphere of truth as the enunciation of silence.

Maitreya's presentation of the threefold understanding of conventional truth is grounded upon and formulated in light of the three patterns of conscious understanding. He says: "There are three kinds of convention: the convention of words (*prajñapti-saṃvṛti*), the convention of functioning (*pratipatti-saṃvṛti*), and the convention of manifesting (*udbhāvana-saṃvṛti*)."[8] Sthiramati in his *Sub-Commentary* on this text explains that the first convention is thinking in words, that is, establishing things as really existent units of meaning. As such, the convention of words corresponds to the imagined pattern of consciousness, the fabricating process of imputing meaning to assumed essences that is an occlusion of meaning. The second kind of convention indicates the actual operations of conscious understanding, the imagining of those imagined realities. As such, it corresponds to the other-dependent pattern. The third convention is meaning as manifested in the words and images about nonverbal and unimaginable emptiness, that is, in words and images that issue from the wisdom of the perfected pattern of consciousness.[9]

The most basic of these three kinds of convention is that of functioning, for it indicates the other-dependent structure of consciousness. Nagao explains that "the first, thinking in words, and the third, manifesting [ultimate meaning], are not themselves conventional, but are different states comprised within conventional [consciousness]. That is, the world of everyday conscious discriminating and judging is conventional truth and it occupies the central position. Thinking in names, which establishes clinging to the imagined, and manifesting full perfection develop from that [other-dependent functioning], the one downward and the other upward."[10] The Yogācāra masters here interpret the basic nature of conventional truth as the structure of other-dependent consciousness, which, as long as it does not cling to names as essences, is capable of manifesting truth, of being converted to a pattern wherein words can themselves manifest truth in their dependently co-arisen validity.

Asaṅga describes the other-dependent pattern as "a mirage, a dream, a reflection, a trace image, an echo, the moon reflected in water."[11] In its imagined pattern, such a description denotes its illusory character, but in its perfected pattern, words take on another significance, for the words and images of wisdom are trace images and phantomlike reflections of ultimate meaning. Other-dependent consciousness does not then lose its dependently co-arisen character in being converted from illusion to wisdom. Rather, those same appearances of things come to serve a wisdom consciousness fully aware of the emptiness of all things.

Yogācāra thinkers such as Dharmapāla stress the continuity between ultimate meaning and its conventional manifestation, for the two truths meet in the verbal expressions of wisdom teaching.[12] Words, having an other-dependent validity, express the emptiness of ultimate meaning in dependently co-arisen enunciations. In his *Extensive Sub-Commentary on the Hundred Stanzas* of Āryadeva, Dhamapāla states: "In ultimate meaning, the speaker, his words, and the meaning of those words are all non-existent, but they do exist conventionally. . . . This means that they are established as other-dependent. . . . All that which is not validated as other-dependent is [unreal], like horns on a hare."[13]

Other-dependent thinking, aware of the emptiness of all dependently co-arisen discourse, does issue in conventional, logically valid meanings, which are not, like the hare's horns, simply to be swept away as illusion. They retain a limited, relative validity, and can support the evolving of doctrinal discourse. Other-dependent insights into images ground and validate doctrinal presentations and theory about ineffable, ultimate meaning. It is only when one clings to ideas as representative pictures of "the way things actually are" that meaning is not constructed by insight into image, but assumed to be already given in the presence of picture images. Clinging to the conceptual form even of doctrine becomes an obstacle to realizing wisdom, to understanding the very content of doctrine.

Nevertheless, other-dependent understanding can never capture ultimate meaning in words, for ultimate meaning remains always completely transcendent to and other than speech. Ultimate meaning is grounded in consciousness only by the experience of attaining wisdom, an experience that forever goes beyond its "embodiment" in speech and in which ultimate meaning remains forever unattained. Upon attainment of wisdom, the programming of the seminal container consciousness is eradicated and the mind is drawn forth into a realm of nondiscriminative emptiness, which is subsequently expressed through the skillful practices of constructing doctrine to manifest the trace images of ultimate meaning. In the final analysis all words are empty, for they can never substitute for the direct experience of wisdom. Dharmapāla further explains:

> From of old the Doctrine Masters [have said that] we establish the two truths because of the differing dispositions [of sentient beings]. Conventional meaning is mediated by words and reveals [meaning] to the conventional dispositions [of those sentient beings]. But the truth of ultimate meaning, which is completely other than words, manifests the absolute. Although worldly conventional doctrine is addressed to conventional dispositions, yet in reality it is empty. Thus it is not truly real.[14]

The only image that can express the ultimate is the lack of image. The only word is silence. The only ground for silence is the realization of the emptiness of other-dependent thinking, the nakedness of a primal experience of wisdom. One can never take doctrinal teaching as a road map to awakening. All words, being simply conventional and constructed descriptions of the ultimate, serve as skillful means (*upāya*) for enunciating that ineffable ultimate. They are, in Dionysius' terms, theological models that flow from an awareness of unknowing. Yet, even as skillful means, even granting the primacy of the Mādhyamika insistence on mystic meaning, the Yogācāra thinkers argue that words and thoughts are subject to both logical argumentation and theoretical development, valid as long as they do not usurp their own content, the ultimate truth which is their objective and which is always present as silent and other to wisdom awareness. In speaking of wisdom, Bandhuprabha in his *Interpretation of the Buddha Land* writes:

> Although the essence [of wisdom] is one, yet its activities of manifesting meaning are many. It is distinguished into both [nondiscriminative and discriminative] wisdom without any logical inconsistency. [But] it is only when one has reached to the truth of ultimate meaning that one can understand the truth of convention.[15]

Thus for the Yogācāra thinkers conventional truth is the mediation of wisdom, the "coming to be" (*vṛt*) of truth in words, understood always to be empty in the final analysis.[16]

THE STRUCTURE OF FULL PERFECTION

Yogācāra also talks about mystic understanding in explaining the structure of the conscious pattern of full perfection. In his *Summary of the Great Vehicle*, Asaṅga draws doctrinal discourse even closer into the structure of wisdom by including the function of doctrinal "disclosure" within the perfected pattern of consciousness. When there has occurred a conversion from the defiled aspect of other-dependent consciousness to its purified aspect, then words, which had previously served merely to entrap one in imagined illusions, become capable of manifesting images of the ultimate.[17] Asaṅga expresses this in his treatment of the four pure factors that constitute the perfected pattern of consciousness:

> Among these four, the first is original purity (*prakṛti-vyavadāna*), that is, suchness, emptiness, reality, the imageless, ultimate meaning. It is equivalent to Dharma Realm. The second is undefiled purity (*vaimalya-vyavadāna*), that is, that same [original purity] inasmuch as it is freed from all obstacles. The third is the purity of the path (*mārga-vyavadāna*), whereby one attains that [undefiled purity], that is, all

the virtues favorable to awakening. The fourth is the purity of the object understood (*ālambana-vyavadāna*), which gives rise to that [path]. This is the doctrine of the Great Vehicle. Because this doctrine causes purity, it is not merely imagined. Because it is the outflow of the pure Dharma Realm (*viśuddhi-dharmadhātu-niṣyanda*), it is not dependently co-arisen.[18]

This notion of doctrine being an outflow from the ultimate Dharma Realm echoes the Prajñāpāramitā theme that doctrinal discourse is the result of wisdom, the direct experience of awakening as it overflows into discourse.[19] It does, however, differ from the Mādhyamika emphasis on the complete silence of ultimate meaning and is much more confident of the validity of doctrine. By including the purity of doctrine within its discussion of the fully perfected pattern of consciousness, Asaṅga stresses not only the necessity of first realizing wisdom before coming to speak doctrine, but also the fact that doctrine thus enunciated is itself in full harmony and conformity with ultimate meaning realized in awakening; not a second-grade truth, but the verbalization of silent ultimate awakening. This outflow of doctrine is not dependently co-arisen, for it flows directly from ultimate meaning, that is, from the Dharma Realm. But Asaṅga does not say that the verbal expression of doctrine is such an outflow. Rather the intent and meaning that is the object (*ālambana*) of discourse, not its literal formulation, flows from ultimate meaning.[20] Doctrine is, then, not merely insight into images in the purified other-dependent pattern, for its dynamic flow is from an awareness of the ultimate Dharma Realm, just as in defiled other-dependent consciousness illusion flows from the seeds within the container consciousness. Doctrine is the nonverbal, unmediated, and purified content of nondiscriminative wisdom, embodied in skillfully constructed teachings and enabling one to practice the purity of the path toward the attainment of awakening, that is, undefiled purity.

The first of the four purities above is original purity and constitutes a Yogācāra reinterpretation of the Tathāgatagarbha theme of the *garbha*. In his *Commentary on the Summary of the Great Vehicle*, Vasubandhu comments on original purity: "Original purity is the original nature of all worldlings. Suchness, being unchangeable, is the common trait of all things. It is because of suchness that the adage affirms: All beings are the seed of Tathāgata (*tathāgatagarbha*)."[21] This explanation repeats the very terminology of *The Participation in the Jeweled Lineage* and seems to be affirming its notion of the originally pure mind of the *garbha*. But in Yogācāra the meaning of these terms has shifted, for the mind is not regarded as being of any pure essence. Rather, the original purity of consciousness is its conventional structure of other-dependent striving toward the ever-unfilled objective of ultimate meaning. In the imagined pattern, it remains karmically defiled and entrapped in the illusions of clinging to essences. But even upon conversion, it does not attain that ever-receding and completely other objective, but, entering into the silence that is aware of the otherness of ultimate silence, in compassion it turns toward the construction of doctrinal models to trace the image of that which remains beyond its verbal purview.

The originally present consciousness has no innate ability to bring about its own awakening,[22] yet in its illusory search for an absolutely unrestricted being, upon hearing and pondering the doctrine and becoming imbued with the meaning of that doctrine, consciousness is open to the experience of converting the imagined pattern into the perfected pattern of wisdom. The *garbha*, or seed of awakening, is found not in any innate purity of consciousness, but in its very defiled and illusory imagining of absolute essences, that is to say, in the other-dependent pattern.

The point is made clearly in the commentary on a famous verse preserved from *The Abhidharma of the Great Vehicle*, which states: "The beginningless realm is the common support of all things. Because of this, there exist all the destinies [of transmigration] and the access to cessation."[23] The Tathāgatagarbha tradition interprets the phrase "the beginningless realm" (*anādikāliko dhātuḥ*) to refer to the pure *garbha* present in all sentient beings. But the Yogācāra thinkers refer it to the container consciousness, which on its own develops into samsaric defilement — "all the destinies of transmigration,"[24] — but which can also support awakening if one ponders the doctrine that flows from the pure Dharma Realm and practices the path toward undefiled purity. In his *Explanation of the Summary of the Great Vehicle*, Asvabhāva explains:

> The phrase "the beginningless realm" means that, because there is no initial point, it is without beginning. Realm here means cause or seed. It is the cause for defiled states, but not the cause for pure states. As afterwards explained [in Asaṅga's text], the support which becomes imbued with the hearing [of doctrine] is not included within the container consciousness. But just as the container [matures], so this [hearing] germinates and becomes included in correct reflection [upon the doctrine]. These seeds [of hearing] arise in regard to the doctrine and its meaning. Because [the container consciousness] can support them, it is the support for all things, but it is not their cause. The notion of support (*dhṛti*) does not imply that of cause (*hetu*).[25]

Although karmically defiled and patterned to accept illusion as truth, the other-dependent structure of the container consciousness can be converted and opened to an originally pure horizon of wisdom. Yet, in its empirical functioning, without reflecting on the doctrine and receiving its influences, the karmically enmeshed container consciousness is totally incapable of such a realization.

Direct, immediate awareness of ultimate meaning is the prime content of the perfected pattern of consciousness, which, being freed from imagined illusions, recovers its originally other-dependent structure and weaves conventionally valid models of doctrinal discourse. Although such other-dependent conventional models are a recovery of the original structure of the mind, the attainment of ultimate meaning remains nondiscriminative and beyond words and images in a total discontinuity from any modeled understanding. Even valid conventional models of discourse remain empty and Asaṅga and Vasubandhu place no quantitative restriction on the scope of emptiness, as did the Tathāgatagarbha thinkers who held that while all the defilements are empty, the one reality of the *garbha* is not empty. Rather, the Yogācāra masters reinterpreted emptiness in terms of conscious understanding, and assert that all understanding either in the imagined pattern or in the other-dependent pattern is empty, the first in denial of the reality of imagined essences and the second in awareness of the ineffability of ultimate meaning.

THE THREE BODIES OF BUDDHA

Enterprises in doctrinal understanding not only must present their basic ideas in a consistent, logical manner, but also have to reflect on and incorporate the practices and devotions of the faithful. A religious tradition is grounded on the practices and experiences of its members, not just on their theologizing. The Yogācāra understanding of the structure of consciousness, the three patterns, and the grounding of emptiness in an understanding of the two truths and the four purities represents a well-articulated philosophy of conscious interiority. By contrast, the doctrine of the three bodies of Buddha (*buddha-trikāya*) does not derive from a philosophical exigency, but reflects cultic practices of worshiping buddhas. It was the Yogācāra thinkers who took earlier ideas about Buddha bodies and developed them into a three-body doctrine. But the roots of the doctrine lie in a more distant Mahāyāna past. The Yogācāra masters received them and attempted to incorporate them in their understanding of emptiness and dependent co-arising, that is, in their understanding of conscious interiority. The theory of Buddha bodies is closely interwoven with the Mahāyāna understanding of the role and function of the historical Buddha Śākyamuni and with cultic worship directed to him and other buddhas. In contrast to the teachings above on the ascendant attainment of ultimate meaning and full perfection, it presents an awareness of the descendant action of the Buddha in the world, and its intent was to explain the nature of Buddha as remembered and worshiped in cultic practice in terms of the reality of awakening (*buddhatva*). The Buddha bodies representing awakening embodied the Buddha figures of popular devotion. They constitute a Mahāyāna buddhology, a doctrinal understanding of the Buddha similar to the Christian attempt to evolve christology. To be sure, the mind of each and every sentient being is the mind of wisdom, endowed with these bodies. But, because of the social origin of the doctrine of Buddha bodies in popular devotion, the constant focus is not on experiential consciousness, but on the ideal forms of that consciousness exemplified in those who have already become buddhas.

An earlier two-body doctrine, meant to emphasize the reality behind the appearance in the world of the historical Buddha, distinguished an underlying reality of the Dharma Body from the magically created appearance (*nirmāṇa*) of Śākyamuni's form body (*rūpakāya*). The historical Buddha was then regarded as one in a series of awakened ones through whom the Dharma-reality is manifested in different ages. He is not really a historical being, but only appears as such in order to preach the doctrine to sentient beings. In its classical form in the Mahāsaṃgika sect, this explanation was developed into a thoroughgoing docetism. In contrast to the Dharma Body, the empirical body of the Buddha was a derived and magically transformed fiction meant to express the underlying reality of the Dharma Body of ultimate meaning and emptiness.

However, at and before the time of Asaṅga, Mahāyāna devotion was directed not only to the historical Buddha, but also to a host of other buddhas and bodhisattvas. The earlier docetic evaluation of the Buddha, regarding him simply as a representation of the Dharma Body, allowed for many other such representations. Many buddhas were conceived and many "Pure Lands" depicted in a host of visualization scriptures, each describing and recommending the qualities and merits of its particular buddha in assisting through his vows suffering sentient beings, and enjoining meditation practices of visualizing that buddha and taking refuge in his vows. These devotional cults increased to such a point that sometime before Asaṅga, *The Lotus Blossom of Compassion* had to be written to bolster weakening devotion to Śākyamuni Buddha.[26] It was in this context that the Yogācāra masters expanded the two-body teaching to include the enjoyment body (*saṃbhoga-kāya*) as the bodies in which these buddhas and bodhisattvas enjoyed and experienced (*saṃbhoga*) the Dharma as the reward for their previous practices and in which they were visualized by the practitioners of their cults.[27] The development of the notion of the enjoyment body is a Buddhist example of the Christian maxim *lex orandi lex credendi*, whereby the rule of faith evolves from devotional practice. Asaṅga clearly presents these themes:

The excellence of wisdom is to be understood as the three bodies of Buddha, which are the essence body, the enjoyment body, and the transformation body. Among these, the essence body is the Dharma body of all Tathāgatas, because it is the support for mastering all things. The enjoyment body is characterized by the various Buddha assemblies and is supported on the Dharma body, because it tastes the complete purification of the Buddha land and enjoys the doctrine of the Great Vehicle. The transformation body is also supported on the Dharma body because it manifests itself [in many perceptible manners, such as] residing in and descending from the Tuṣita palace, being born [in Kapilavastu], indulging desire, leaving home, going to the heretics' place, practicing asceticism, attaining perfect awakening, turning the wheel of doctrine, and entering into final cessation.[28]

Here the transformation body refers direcly to Śākyamuni Buddha and depicts his life course from his descent to his final departure. The enjoyment body refers to the buddhas worshiped in the many devotional cults, such as the Pure Land Amitābha Buddha in Sukhāvatī. These enjoyment bodies differ from the transformation body inasmuch as they are not identifiable in history, but are encountered in states of visualization and meditation. As such they are manifestations of Dharma Body to bodhisattvas, that is, to the Mahāyāna practitioners who actually practiced those meditations, while the transformation body, having a perceptible form, is manifested to all sentient beings. Both transformation and enjoyment bodies are supported on the Dharma Body and derive from it as its compassionate evolutions and manifestations.

Although enmeshed in this particular cultural context, this Yogācāra doctrine of the three bodies does present an understanding of the structure of mystic awakening and wisdom that parallels the foregoing themes of the two truths and the structure of full perfection. The Dharma Body parallels ultimate meaning in its complete otherness from all concepts and images, but the other two bodies, flowing from it, do embody that ultimate in perceptible fashion. Maitreya's *Ornament of the Scriptures of the Great Vehicle* describes the structure of the Buddha bodies as follows: "In the various world realms he is seen through the transformation body and in the assemblies [of bodhisattvas] he is seen through the enjoyment body, but he is never seen in the Dharma body in any manner whatsoever."[29] The Dharma Body is then empty of any identifiable content. Rather, it is the ineffable content of awakening. Commenting on the passage above, Sthiramati explains: "The sentence 'Dharma body is never seen in any manner whatsoever' means that, because its essence is internally realized, it is inconceivable. Because it transcends the sphere of thinking, it cannot be expressed in any worldly metaphor."[30]

Asaṅga in his *Summary of the Great Vehicle* devotes the whole of the last chapter to the three bodies. He understands Dharma Body as the silent and ultimately meaningful realization of awakening and characterizes it as consciousness converted from the karmic defilement of the container consciousness to the realization of the perfection of wisdom.

It is characterized as the conversion of support, for, having destroyed all obstacles and the other-dependent pattern in its defiled aspect, it is freed from those obstacles, assured of mastery over all things, and is transformed into the other-dependent pattern in its purified aspect.[31]

Here again it is the basic other-dependent pattern, which, now converted, is not only capable of valid conventional discourse, but is opened up to the ineffability of silent emptiness. In Asaṅga's treatment the focus is always on the Dharma Body, since it is the nondiscriminative wisdom of emptiness and the support for the manifestations of the enjoyment and transformation bodies, arising in accord with the needs of sentient beings. Just as wisdom implies both a nondiscriminative awareness of emptiness and a subsequently attained, discriminative awareness of things in their dependent co-arising, so Asaṅga describes the Dharma Body: "How is Dharma body attained for the first time by contact? By means of nondiscriminative wisdom and subsequently-attained wisdom."[32]

The structure of mystic meaning, although here descendant, remains one of an ultimately meaningful awareness of emptiness and the Dharma Body, which is disclosed through perceptible and conventionally identifiable manifestations of the enjoyment and transformation bodies. In this fashion the Yogācāra thinkers incorporated the three bodies of awakening within their understanding of mystic meaning and conscious interiority.

THE FIVE FACTORS OF AWAKENING

Mādhyamika and Yogācāra are the principal *śāstra* traditions of Mahāyāna Buddhism, but they do not exhaust its many-sided expressions. Alongside these more intellectual endeavors, more everyday approaches to awakening flourished. One of the popular approaches is found in the Pure Land tradition, an approach that remains relevant in East Asian Buddhism to the present day. It is in this Pure Land tradition that the five factors of awakening were first developed, in *The Scripture of the Buddha Land*. This short work was probably composed by a practitioner of Pure Land visualization and constitutes a very early attempt to interpret the Pure Land(s) in terms not of its mythical characteristics, but as the functioning of wisdom.[33] Pure Land, a symbol for awakening, is presented as comprised by the pure Dharma Realm, mirror wisdom, equality wisdom, discernment wisdom, and duty-fulfillment wisdom. The pure Dharma Realm is the ineffable content of insight into emptiness and is described through the metaphor of empty space, without characteristics or identifying qualities. Mirror wisdom and equality wisdom are both nondiscriminative awareness of the suchness of all empty things and their consequent nondual equality. Discernment wisdom and duty-fulfillment wisdom are subsequently attained and discriminative awarenesses that enable one to function in the dependently co-arisen world through conventional knowing and acting.

These ideas were soon adopted by the Yogācāra thinkers and elaborated within a Yogācāra context. Asaṅga adopts the later four wisdoms in his *Summary of the Great Vehicle* as descriptions of the converted mind.[34] He further equates the Dharma Realm with original purity as synonymous with emptiness and suchness.[35] But he did not explicate their relationships within the Yogācāra understanding of consciousness or its three patterns of functioning.

Asvabhāva, however, in his *Exposition of the Summary of the Great Vehicle*, reinterprets the four wisdoms as descriptions of the conversions of the different levels of consciousness. Mirror wisdom is the conversion of the container consciousness, for it gains insight into the suchness of things without obstacle. Equality wisdom is the conversion of the thinking consciousness, for it abandons the notions of "I" and "mine" and the entire illusory discrimination they entail. Discernment wisdom is the conversion of perceptive consciousness, for it is able to discern clearly the needs of beings to be saved. Duty-fulfillment wisdom is the conversion of the sense consciousnesses, for it deals in the concrete world through deeds of compassion.[36]

The same structure of silent ultimate meaning coming to expression is again evident here, emphasized as a conversion of the basic other-dependent pattern of consciousness. No longer programmed by delusions of imagination, the dynamic of wisdom consciousness flows from awakening into suchness and emptiness to the concrete insights and deeds of compassion.

A further step is taken when Śīlabhadra and Bandhuprabha composed *The Interpretation of the Buddha Land*, describing the three bodies in terms of these five factors. Again the Yogācāra intent is clearly aimed at grounding and identifying in conscious awareness the ultimate meaning realized in awakening. Dharma Body is equated with the pure Dharma as the ineffable content of wisdom. The enjoyment body is supported upon mirror wisdom and equality wisdom, for, as the realized body of a buddha, it has penetrated to the complete nondifferentiation between self and others and, imbued with insight into emptiness, turns to the world in compassion. That compassion is not, however, an aloof and detached feeling of pity, but is directed to the particular circumstances of suffering beings through the later two wisdoms. Thus the transformation body is supported by discernment wisdom and duty-fulfillment wisdom, for it carries out the actual deeds of compassion and fulfills the bodhisattva career in the world.[37]

Again we see the same structural motif: mystic meaning coming to be embodied in the dependently co-arisen world. Even in the doctrine of the bodies of Buddha, emptiness implies dependent co-arising and ultimate meaning still needs conventional discourse in order to be manifested.

CONCLUSION

In all these themes of mystic meaning the same structural pattern obtains. In their treatment of the two truths, the Yogācāra masters not only argue for a limited validity for other-dependent thinking and speaking, but also insist on the total mystic conversion of that other-dependent mind away from the defiling influences of the container consciousness and toward insight into ultimate meaning and silence.

In their description of the structure of the perfected pattern they emphasize not only the openness of consciousness to hear doctrine and be converted by that hearing to ultimate meaning and insight into emptiness and suchness, but they also stress the subsequent embodiment of that awareness in doctrine as the purity of the object.

The three bodies of Buddha (awakening) further describe the structure of mystic awareness as the experience and enjoyment (*saṃbhoga*) of ultimate meaning (*dharma*) issuing in the manifestations (*nirmāṇa*) of compassion within the world.

The five factors of awakening insist once again that the nondiscriminative insight into the pure Dharma Realm of emptiness must be embodied in the subsequently attained wisdoms of conventional understanding and action in the dependently co-arisen world.

If the early Christian proclamation of the gospel had fallen on ears accustomed to hearing such doctrines, the understanding of Christ as wisdom would have been an obvious avenue toward understanding what Christ means. But it is not too late; perhaps the Christian community is still in its adolescence. Hence this Buddhist analysis of consciousness and its wisdom structure is potentially useful in the ongoing Christian task of recovering the meaning of the Trinity and the Incarnation. It is to this task that the next chapter now turns.

9

Removing Objections
to a Mahāyāna Theology

The aim of this endeavor is to arrive at an understanding of Christian faith in the Incarnation and the Trinity from a Mahāyāna philosophy of emptiness and conscious interiority (Mādhyamika and Yogācāra). With this goal in mind, the first part of this work examined the Christian development of these doctrines, while the second part has turned to the task of delineating the Mādhyamika teachings on emptiness, dependent co-arising, and the two truths, as well as the Yogācāra understanding of conscious interiority, both defiled and awakened. The intent of all the preceding chapters has not been simply to present these developments, but to set the stage and marshal the requisite insights to enable one to interpret Christian faith within a Mahāyāna perspective. All the preceding research, interpretation, and historical judgment are meant to converge on this objective.

But before we launch into sketching a Mahāyāna theology of Incarnation and Trinity, it would be well to clear the ground, for there are objections, both general and specific, against such a hybrid Mahāyāna theology. Some claim that basic Mahāyāna teachings are simply incompatible with Christian understandings. Such an adoption of alien philosophical ideas, they hold, are precluded by the central affirmations of Christian faith. In the history of Christian doctrine some philosophical models have been adopted and adapted. The fathers employed Neoplatonic ideas freely and the medieval scholastics found a welcome philosophical model in Aristotle. More recently, some theologians have adopted the existential philosophy of Martin Heidegger, while others employ Marxist categories in explicating a theology of liberation. But this does not mean that all philosophies are amenable to the articulation of Christian faith. Elements of Stoic thinking did find their way into early Christian thinking, but there developed no theology based on the Stoic model, for the basic equation of *deus sive natura* found no resonance within Christian minds. And, far from reading Christian theology in terms of the skepticism of the Greek Sophists,[1] some of the early fathers aimed their apologetic at defining faith in contrast to the errors of the Greeks. Furthermore, after long and arduous battles, Gnostic patterns of thinking were banished from the arena of Christian doctrinal consideration. Might not the adoption of Mahāyāna prove to be as impractical as these examples?

In the past such objections to the adoption of philosophies in theologies came mainly from theologians themselves, committed to their confessional embodiments of truth. Today other objections also come from philosophers of religion, committed to constructing philosophies of religion and religious experience in clear and logical fashion. The great increase of disciplined insights from the phenomenology and sociology of religion bring new light to religious ideas and practices and raise important questions about traditional notions of religious experience and interpretation. Some of these issues were treated briefly in the first part of this book under the rubric of "The Nature of Mystic Understanding," but here must be raised again within the broader context of the Mahāyāna themes presented in chapters 9–11. Some philosophies of religion are not consonant with the argument of this book; some plainly contradict it. Thus, for purposes of clarity and precision, we shall delve briefly into a few examples of the philosophy of religion and treat two claims often offered as overviews of religious experience.

THE PHILOSOPHY OF RELIGION: TWO OPTIONS

The *first option*, represented by thinkers such as W. T. Stace, Arnold Toynbee, Hajime Nakamura, and Friedrich Heiler, is that religious experience, no matter how differently it might be interpreted, centers around a common core.[2] At their mystical center, all religions are "saying the same thing." If one looks discerningly at the descriptions mystics give of their religious experiences, it is argued, then one can detect common features in all experiences of ultimate meaning. For example, Friedrich Heiler points out seven common areas: (1) the existence of a transcendent reality, (2) the immanence of that reality in human hearts, (3) the characterization of that reality as supreme beauty, truth, righteousness, goodness, (4) the characterization of that reality as love, mercy, compassion, (5) the way to that reality is by repentance, self-denial, prayer, (6) the way is love of one's neighbor, even of one's enemies, and (7) the way is love of God, so that bliss is conceived as knowledge of God, union with God, or dissolution into the divine.[3]

An obvious problem for this affirmation of a common core in all religious experience is that in fact the world's religions often describe that experience in ways that appear directly contradictory. As will be discussed later, Buddhists make the specific claim that there is no God to save us and no soul that may be saved, while Christians usually insist on both. Jews and Muslims hold fervently to the oneness of God, rejecting Christian notions of Trinity as a lapse into a special kind of polytheism. Even when religions do present common descriptions, it often is the case that they mean different things by the same term. Thus, even if Buddhism and Christianity speak of a transcendent reality, this is no proof that they understand that reality in the same fashion.[4] This school of a common core must somehow account for the presence of such diverse descriptions.

A frequent way to do this is to relegate all interpretations of religious experience to a subsequent step of interpreting a primal, uninterpreted, mystic experience, and then to claim that this pure experience binds all religions together. Differences in interpretation are then explained as due to cultural and linguistic factors. Thus the content of the Buddha's awakening and the content of Jesus' resurrection may be held identical on the mystic level, but described differently because the cultural and linguistic patterns of India focused on the nature of awakening and liberation, while those of Palestine centered on a concrete overcoming of death.

Support for affirming the presence of a pure, unmediated, and ineffable experience in all religions is found in the almost universal claim of mystic writers that their descriptions are not to be taken literally. Gregory says that all people are liars when they seek to articulate the meaning of God. Dionysius claims that all knowing of God is in fact a not-knowing. The common Mahāyāna dictum has it that, although Buddha preached for sixty years, he never uttered a single word. Asaṅga describes the realization of Dharma Body as an experience of contact, bereft of all language constructs. The *Tao-Te-Ching* sums up the point: "Those who know do not say; those who say do not know."[5]

The *second option* is found among thinkers such as Steven Katz, R. C. Zaehner, and George Lindbeck, who reject the foregoing claim and argue for the diversity of religious experience. Understanding the argument for a common core to rest on the affirmation of an ineffable, pure experience, these thinkers deny that there is ever such an experience. They argue that all experience is shaped and formed by the cultural and social images, ideas, and values in which it is interpreted. R. C. Zaehner insists that there are three distinct and different mystical experiences — natural, monistic, and theistic — which can be shown from a close inspection of the way in which these experiences are interpreted.[6] Steven Katz puts the basic point concisely:

> There are no *pure (i.e., unmediated) experiences*. Neither mystical experience nor more ordinary forms of experience give any indication, or any grounds for believing, that they are unmediated. That is to say, *all* experience is processed through, organized by, and makes itself available to us in extremely complex epistemological ways. The notion of unmediated experience seems, if not self-contradictory, at least empty.[7]

There is, then, no valid distinction between experience and interpretation, as if interpretation were performed only at a later date on the data of pure experience. Interpretation determines the nature of all experience, including mystic experience, both prior to, during, and after its occurrence.[8] One does not experience the rapture of divine love unless that experience is prefigured in images of God and theistic expectations. One is not awakened to suchness and emptiness, unless one's mind has been prepared by the understandings and practices of the Buddhist tradition. This position represents a modern restatement of the Scholastic axiom: *"nihil amatum nisi praecognitum,"* which may be understood to mean that "nothing is experienced mystically (i.e., loved), unless first known." The ideas, images, and ideological values a person has "define, *in advance* what the experience *he wants to have*, and which he then does have, will be."[9] The differences in the language used to describe one's experiences indicate a difference in "the ontological claims that lie beneath and are necessary correlates of language."[10]

This option reacts strongly against the uncritical assumption that all religious experiences are the same and that they constitute an ineffable, pure experience. It characterizes the proponents of a common core beneath all religious experiences as motivated more from ecumenical concern than from a commitment for precision and clarity. The charge does seem to have some validity, for quite often when one meets and becomes friendly with persons from other religious traditions, the feeling engendered is that what separates us pales before our shared human and religious experiences. Yet, the affirmation of differences in religious experience does often pay closer attention to the contextual meanings of the descriptive evidence. According to the evidence gathered by the Religious Experience Research Unit at Manchester College, Oxford University, from written accounts of religious experience from thousands of volunteers, although a distinction between cognitive and affective elements "was originally thought to be a reasonable distinction . . . in practice, any such distinction breaks down."[11] One cannot then bracket the cognitive content of religious experiences to focus on any pure core common to all.

But, although this option pays closer attention to the diverse contextual webs of meaning behind the descriptive evidence, its rejection of the occurrence of "pure" experiences runs counter to the omnipresent insistence of those descriptions on the ineffability and uninterpretability of mystic experiences. They serve as warnings that the experiences, however one might understand them, are not accessible to language or rational thought. The mystics of all traditions warn constantly against taking their descriptions at face value and insist that not only do they inadequately represent what is experienced, but they actually falsify it. But, to these philosophers, if such claims were allowed to stand, one would be unable to use descriptions of mystic experiences as data for philosophical reflection and thus be unable to specify just what "ontological state of affairs" a particular experience might indicate. Again Katz presents the argument clearly:

> The terms "paradox" and "ineffable" do not function as terms that inform us about the context of experience, or any given ontological "state of affairs." Rather they function to cloak experience from investigation and to hold mysterious whatever ontological commitments one has. As a consequence, the use of the terms "paradox" and "ineffable" do not provide *data* for comparability, rather they eliminate the logical possibility of the comparability of experience altogether.[12]

On this reading, the ineffability and unknowability of mystic experiences can mean only that they are inadequately known. Claims for ineffability that are intended to deconstruct language are themselves deconstructed and interpreted figuratively. Indeed, it is argued that if the content of mystic experiences was literally unknowable, one would never hear anything about them in the first place.

Both of these philosophic options are incompatible with the argument of this book. At first glance the first assertion of a common core might appear congruent with an attempt to construct a Mahāyāna theology. After all, such a theology adopts an alien descriptive terminology for the expression of Christian faith and might be understood as implying that all religious descriptions converge on a central experience. In fact, however, the desirability of such a Mahāyāna strategy for Christian theology derives from a recognition that Mahāyāna categories of thought are indeed different and are not saying the same thing as the traditional Christian theologies. If they were, the endeavor would hardly be worth the effort. The second assertion of ontological diversity among religious experiences would invalidate the strategy altogether, because different descriptions, being constitutive of experience itself, could not be employed to refer to different "ontological states of affairs."

In a Mādhyamika perspective, however, both options are case examples of essentialist thinking and to be rejected. The first equates the basic experiences of all religions with a central core. Underlying all religions is this one essence, in which all participate and to which all in their various cultural paths tend.[13] This option is to be rejected because all things, descriptions included, are empty of any essence. The silence of ultimate meaning is neither amenable to demonstration nor usable as proof for anything. Dependently co-arisen interpretations function only within given contexts, which indeed differ markedly and can hardly be employed as proof for any central core experience. But a rejection of this first option does not entail an affirmation of the second. As Dionysius remarked to Sosipratus, just because something is not black, it does not follow that it is white. Even the second option is to be rejected. Those who hold that language and interpretation are constitutive of experience claim they are more sensitive to the differences in linguistic and cultural expressions of religious experience; but in denying that there is a pure, ineffable, and thus contentless experience, they are forced to dismiss the mystics' own descriptions of ineffability—admitted by all to be present in the textual evidence. Faithfulness to the evidence cannot be maintained by ignoring such descriptions nor by interpreting them to mean the opposite of what they in fact state, claiming that they mean that mystic experience is really (at least partially) knowable in language. If the evidence is accepted, one must assent that mystic thinkers, each in his or her own context, do issue such warnings and do restrict the sphere of verbal knowledge. In such a case interpretations of mystic experience cannot be used as signposts that refer to corresponding ontological entities.

Mahāyāna thought bases itself squarely on the occurrence of awakening, which it understands to be a nonimaginative and nondiscriminative wisdom. Such awakening is described as "the silence of the saints" and is considered to be ineffable and known only through personal, direct experience. That experience has no identifiable content and must not be reified as an ultimate something. In Nāgārjuna's expression, those who reify emptiness are incurable; because they take the antidote to views as itself another view, they lack the means to heal their illness. This does lead to the conclusion that, since the empty experience of awakening has no identifiable content, it cannot be employed as a proof of anything. One cannot center on awakening, because it has no center. One cannot base affirmations of a common essence among all religions on an ineffable common core, for, as Katz clearly realizes, an ineffable experience proves nothing one way or the other. It is not a source of data for further reflection. But Katz seems to shrink from this conclusion because that would imply that "pure" religious experiences are not amenable to comparative analysis. Not to be data for further comparative analysis is equated with not to exist at all. There is, it would seem, a *horror vacui* in philosophy also. By contrast, Mahāyāna admits a pure and uninterpreted experience of awakening and wisdom, and it affirms a distinction between mystic experience and interpretation. The two basic wisdoms of Mahāyāna are characterized as nondiscriminative (*nirvikalpa*) and subsequently attained discriminative (*pṛṣṭhalabdhavikalpa*). Neither Mādhyamika nor Yogācāra draws philosophical conclusions directly from pure experience. There are in Mahāyāna no mystical propositions. That is why Mādhyamika employs a dialectic of deconstruction and Yogācāra a critical theory of consciousness.

In Yogācāra, experience is constituted by fabricated language (*prapañca*). But such experience is deluded and its propositions about ontological entities function in an imagined pattern of misunderstanding. The fabrication of experience through the permeations of language is to be rejected because it uncritically takes images to contain insight, not because it fails to find a mystic center. Yet the Buddhist texts constantly assumed the occurrence and validity of a pure and immediate experience of awakening beyond the sphere of language and reference. That is what makes one a buddha. It does not appear that anyone in either Christian or Buddhist traditions ever makes the claim that language is constitutive of experience. Yogācāra dialecticians like Dignāga even describe more ordinary experiences as direct perception, prior to language and as yet unmediated.[14] Indeed, it is difficult to understand how one can deny, as Katz does, that there are no ordinary unmediated experiences. In everyday living one often has experiences that obviously have no mediating image or conceptual structure. Take, for example, the unpleasant occasion when one touches a hot stove. The interpretation that mediates that experience and identifies the stove as hot follows almost immediately but not soon enough to avoid having a finger burned. No interpretation is given prior to or during the initial duration of the experience itself. It is only after the direct sensation has been experienced that one realizes the sad mistake. Direct sensations are clearly not always prefigured by cultural or social ideas and images. To walk outside on an August day and feel a cool breeze is hardly determined by prior expectancies, unless one had heard a weather forecast. The Japanese Zen master Bankei often drew attention to such unmediated experiences—sounds heard but not attended to, such as the barking of dogs or the calls of crows—to indicate the presence of pure consciousness in each member of his audience, all of whom, the record states, were hanging on his every word.[15] We seem to move in a world of immediacy, which only gradually, over the course of one's life, and only in part is ever mediated. If no pure experiences are present without interpretation, then how would a newborn child experience anything?[16]

The question of mystic experiences is perhaps more problematic than these more ordinary direct experiences. But they are to the point, for the mystics often employ them as metaphors for that mystic awareness. Gregory speaks of the fragrance of God, for God cannot be known in any confrontational vision. Asaṅga describes realization of Dharma Body as taking place through contact (*sparśa*). Sexual union is a common metaphor for mystic experience, from the Song of Songs to the Esoteric Buddhism of Kūkai.[17] (Sexual union does indeed seem to be universally the same, arising in all cultures and all traditions.) Such metaphors indicate that awakening is more like these direct and unmediated experiences than any conceptual knowledge about a putative ontological state of affairs.

Furthermore, it is not true that different interpretations and descriptions always refer to different entities. The proponents of essential differences between religious experiences often note that if similar descriptions are interpreted contextually, they will be seen not to refer to the same entities at all. But the same move can be made in the other direction. Ninian Smart reports an example: "If Siberians think of wolves as grey spirits of the dead and if Italians think of them as dangerous animals, reports from both quarters would reasonably raise the question of whether it is the same sort of being that is being spoken of."[18] Further examples can be drawn from the vast array of metaphors for sexual union. Hemingway's "Did the earth move for thee too, daughter?" (*For Whom the Bell Tolls*) might describe an earthquake. Alan Paton's "And he possessed her" (*Too Late the Phalarope*) might refer to slavery. The Old Testament phrase, "And he knew her" might denote a relationship of casual friendship. Chinese descriptions of "entering the jade palace" might indeed refer to jade palaces. But of course they do not. Insight into contextual meanings does not always show that similar descriptions do not mean the same thing, but just as often indicates that different descriptions refer to the same thing.

The claim that such experiences do not exist often derives from a desire to be more logically consistent than the proponents of a common core. But, as Lonergan often comments, philosophic differences frequently reflect more basic epistemological understandings. To one who holds a positivist understanding of understanding, no mystic experience ever refers to anything because no mystic object can be empirically specified. To one who holds a naïve realist view of the matter, all language must correspond to objective entities, and mystic experience must, if valid, have its mystic object. Often, however, that epistemology remains itself implicit or barely expressed. Katz seems to be working within a Kantian model in which experience is always in part constituted by "synthetic operations" of consciousness, that is, discrimination and integration.[19] But he merely suggests the presence of this underlying epistemology without presenting any clear discussion of its shape. It is no aid to clarity to claim that "all experience is processed through, organized by, and makes itself available to us in extremely complex epistemological ways," when he offers no insight into what these complex ways might be. Indeed, in terms of clarity this is scarcely an advance on uncritical claims about the mysteriousness of religious experience.

By contrast, Bernard Lonergan argues that mystic experiences are precisely those that are conscious but unmediated. They are, he writes, experiences of mystery precisely because they are both conscious and unknown. In his understanding of conscious interiority—often in harmony with Yogācāra—consciousness refers to experience, while knowledge is a composite of experience, insight, and judgment. Knowledge occurs only when experience is mediated by images and ideas and brought to reflective awareness. Thus Lonergan writes:

> To say that dynamic state [of mystic awareness] is conscious is not to say that it is known. What is conscious is indeed experienced. But human knowing is not just experiencing. Human knowledge includes experiencing but adds to it scrutiny, insight, conception, naming, reflection, checking, judging. The whole problem of cognitional theory is to effect the transition from conscious operations to known operations. A great part of psychiatry is helping people to effect the tran-

sition from conscious feelings to known feelings. In like manner the gift of God's love ordinarily is not objectified in knowledge, but remains within subjectivity as a dynamic vector, a mysterious undertow, a fateful call to a dreaded holiness. Because that dynamic state is conscious without being known, it is an experience of mystery.[20]

The difficulty in getting hold of the issues comes from the fact that as soon as one attends to mystic experience and begins to examine it, those experiences are mediated. No unmediated experiences even come to expression, for once expressed, they are mediated.

The Mādhyamika theme of the identity of emptiness and dependent co-arising explains awakening as awareness of emptiness, beyond words and images, but expressed conventionally in the dependently co-arisen words of our making. Those words are valid when they are in harmony with ultimate meaning, that is to say, when uttered in full awareness of their dependently co-arisen and empty status. The Mādhyamika insight of Nāgārjuna drew the conclusion that since all words and all ideas are empty and do not refer to stable essences, the rigorous use of reason, itself wholly worldly and conventional, could expose the provisional and conventional character of all thoughts. All philosophical systems would, if pushed far enough, implode of their own accord, for all engender problems and questions unanswerable in terms of the system. Philosophies, then, are seen not as presenting any assured view of the ontological state of things, but as making provisional attempts to mediate and bring to speech the totality of experience. Mādhyamika is both a deconstruction of philosophy as ontology, and an affirmation of philosophy as provisional, dependently co-arisen, and conventionally valid.

The impact of all this is that one cannot go beyond a phenomenology of mystic experience to construct an ontological account. Typologies will remain provisional and more or less adequate inasmuch as they focus on the descriptive data available to them—the actual accounts of mystic experiences. "Mystical experience is not and logically cannot be the grounds for *any* final assertions about the nature of truth of any religious or philosophical proposition nor, more particularly, for any specific dogmatic or theological belief. Whatever validity mystical experience has, it does *not* translate as evidence for a given religious proposition."[21] If the only evidence is what is phenomenologically available in accounts and descriptions, one can go only as far as that evidence allows. Despite feelings of brotherly unity, despite the presence of authentic mystic experiences, one cannot logically move beyond the description of similarity by ignoring or negating the conflicting evidence of differences. Despite one's belief in ontological entities and their correspondence with language, despite a desire to render an account of mystical data, one cannot conclude beyond the descriptive differences by ignoring the descriptions of similarity. The evidence presents both clear parallels and stark differences. One must here practice Chuang-tzu's "fasting of the mind" and refuse to construct ontological explanations that trivialize the evidence.[22] The main criticism theologians level against the phenomenology of religion is not that phenomenologists practice phenomenology, but that they do not, that they adopt, often without saying so, philosophical frameworks that, however adequate to certain sectors of religious phenomena, reduce other sectors to data congruent with the chosen framework.

The same criticism may perhaps be leveled against the present endeavor. Is not a Mahāyāna theology a reduction of Christian faith awareness to the framework of a philosophical system? If Mahāyāna is to serve as the handmaid of Christian theology, does this not also level Christian thought to a preset complex of ideas—about emptiness and dependent co-arising, the two truths, conscious construction-only, etc.?

Indeed, Mahāyāna philosophy is a set of interconnecting themes and does indeed interpret the meaning of faith within that framework. In so doing, Mahāyāna, no less than any other philosophy, does reduce faith awareness to the terms of that philosophy. Faith always goes beyond theology. The validity of a theology is clearly affected by the philosophical framework adopted. This is why it is crucially important to understand the traditional Greek development of Christian thought, both strengths and weaknesses. The particular merit in adopting a Mahāyāna philosophy is precisely that it functions within an awareness of its limitations. The themes of emptiness and dependent co-arising, the two truths, and the theory of conscious construction-only mark a step back from essentialist thinking toward an understanding of religious and theological consciousness. The deconstructive thrust of emptiness and ultimate meaning offers some assurance against a naïve theology that would mistake its ideas for descriptive accounts of divine ontological affairs. The constructive direction of conscious construction-only in its understanding of the structure and functioning of consciousness, both defiled and awakened, insists that one must evolve theologies in the context of emptiness.

SPECIFIC QUESTIONS

Beyond these general issues about the nature of religious experience and interpretation, specific Mahāyāna doctrinal themes may indeed seem to contradict Christian faith awareness. We shall attempt to unravel the principal areas and to determine whether the clear differences between Mahāyāna interpretations and Christian interpretations are mutually contradictory and fundamentally opposed. Bernard Lonergan, often appealed to as our guide before, presents a schema for adjudicating whether such differences are (1) fundamentally and dialectically opposed and thus call for mutual repudiation, (2) perspectival differences entailing a different historical and cultural manner of expression, (3) genetic differences resulting from varied stages of progress in an analogous process of understanding, or (4) differences that evolve from a differentiation of the meaning realm employed.[23] Only if the differences belong to the first category will the present attempt at a Mahāyāna theology be deemed unfeasible. But its feasibility cannot be proved, as noted above, by appealing to any differentiation between ordinary language and a mystic realm of meaning, for that is a realm of silent experience.

The most obvious areas of potential conflict are (1) the doctrine of no-self, which seems to negate Christian ideas of a soul, (2) the impersonal nature of the ultimate, which appears to negate a personal God, (3) the Mādhyamika doctrine of emptiness that renders all discourse suspect, (4) the Mādhyamika and Mahāyāna understanding of the two truths, which seem to dichotomize the unity of truth, (5) the idealistic nature of Yogācāra philosophy, which appears to undermine the very basis of creedal affirmation, and (6) the Yogācāra teaching on the three bodies of Buddha which, if adopted as a model for understanding Trinity, would issue in a docetic understanding.

No-Self and Christian Anthropology

The Buddhist teaching of no-self (*anātman*) appears in the earliest layers of Buddhist doctrine and is a basic insight present in all later traditions. It is obvious that in its denial of selfhood this doctrine differs starkly from the Christian notion of human beings as having a soul, a self. In Christian thinking, it is this soul that is created in the image and likeness of God and that is saved by Christ. These two doctrines indeed appear to be dialectically opposed and mutually exclusive, with the consequence that one could hardly adopt the Buddhist notion of no-self as any part of a model for Christian thinking. How can one save or lose her soul, if she really never has a soul to begin with? How can a personal relationship with God be nurtured, when there is nobody on the receiving end? Does not the Buddhist doctrine of no-self contradict the basic Christian understanding of human existence?

That, however, is not the case. The Buddhist teaching of no-self is directed against the idea that human beings possess a set, fixed self that can serve as one's refuge in a constantly changing and transient world. It is opposed to the Greek notion of a self as a permanent, unchanging essence. Buddhists deny that self-awareness can lead to any valid affirmation of the being of the subject. But they do not deny subjectivity as experienced phenomenologically in the world. The awareness of an "I" leads to no affirmation of "therefore I am." The Yogācāra thinkers taught that the entire dichotomy of subject-object does indeed appear (*pratibhāsa*) within consciousness, but that this appearance does not validate the ontological status of either subjects or objects. *The Analysis of the Middle Path and Extremes* teaches that although other-dependent, unreal imagining does exist, this does not imply that the subject-object structure of that imagining actually reflects reality. Sthiramati comments that the unreal imagining that leads to the imagined pattern of consciousness consists precisely in the discrimination of imagined objects over against an imagined subject. But insight into the emptiness of all things negates the real existence of that entire dichotomous pattern of consciousness.

That insight, however, is not content with remaining aloof in empty contemplation. After the dawning of an awareness of no-self, one becomes reengaged in the world of dependently co-arisen selfhood in a new pattern of purified other-dependent consciousness in which subject-object thinking takes on conventional but valid meaning. The awakened subject, after awakening to no-self, searches for appropriate words and images skillfully to lead other subjects to share in the direct experience of wisdom. As Gadjin Nagao explains, Buddhism negates not the notion of an existential, other-dependent subject/self, but the idea of a fixed, essentialist self, clung to in imagination and illusion, as if anyone could escape the rising and falling of all things in the dependently co-arisen flow of time.[24] The doctrine of no-self is then diametrically opposed to a notion of Christian personhood that would affirm the final, ultimate structure of human beings as a fixed, secure essence, which can then be related to other essences in inter-essential-subjectivity. It is not, however, opposed to the Christian understanding of human life as contingently experienced, as constantly in flux. True, Buddhists share little interest in phenomenological descriptions of the value of the person and do not move within the personalist context of any modern psychology. They evidently mistrust those categories and shy away from the love-talk so dear to Christian devotion. But they do thematize compassionate engagement in the service of others and they do present an understanding of the other-dependent subject tending toward awakening and compassion. And that may just be more to the point for a Christian analysis of interiority than any examination of the polyvalent phenomenology of love.

Moreover, such notions of no-self are not absent from the Christian tradition. It is a mistake to think that Christians always and everywhere have upheld an essentialist idea of selfhood. The common Christian assertion of human contingency means that human beings do not possess their being, but only participate in it from moment to moment. Paul declares that in mystic awareness, he no longer lives, but Christ lives in him. Similarly, the fathers often counterpose the original image-nature of humans to their illusory, empirical personalities. In descriptions of mystic encounter, not only do Christians refuse to objectify God. They also frequently claim that one is raised out of self in ecstasy. Such descriptions are often relegated to the sphere of the unusual or the weird. But the experience so described does parallel what the Buddhist means by no-self and can perhaps be reclaimed for serious theological thought. In the experience of no-self, as of ecstasy, the entire pattern of objectifying insights and knowing their meaning as mediated is abrogated in a withdrawal from all mediated meaning.

Even subsequently mystics do not always attempt to reestablish that pattern. After descending from Sinai, Moses does not subject his experience to the criteria of verification and falsification. A mystic experience is not a datum for further cognitional operations. It is not a known experience, but simply a conscious experience. It would then be rash to claim that Christian faith experience somehow demonstrates the Greek Christian doctrine of a soul underlying the changes of our lives. Faith experience is independent of the theoretical explications of Christian personalism. The love of God occurs in the first instance, and only at a second remove does one at times develop explanations of its nature and implications. Indeed the fathers themselves did not develop a consistent theory of Christian personalism. For them even God was not defined in terms of modern personhood, for the term "person" did not then imply such notions of personality and intersubjectivity.

The differences between Buddhist teaching on no-self and Christian teaching on selfhood are derived from historical and cultural factors. The early Christian thinkers evolved their understanding of human nature as composed of body and soul in a Platonic context that assumed the objective validity of essences. Their concern was to develop a Christian anthropology that would present an explanation not only of human nature but also of the nature of Christ. That task was not accomplished easily or all at once. The Mediterranean world found itself in agreement on the immutable nature of God, but evinced no such unanimity about human nature. The New Testament presented no developed theory about just what constitutes a human being, and it was not until many centuries had elapsed that the Aristotelian notion of humans as composed of a body and a soul found general agreement. Greek notions of the human soul were developed in a context of debate over the humanity of Christ and did not question the essentialist pattern that was part and parcel of all Greek philosophy. By contrast, the Buddhist teaching on no-self was developed in opposition to earlier Indian ideas of an eternal *ātman* present in each and every human, beyond any change and essentially one with the absolute *brahman*. In this context they were concerned that human beings would attempt to take refuge in their own selfhood in disregard for the actual conditions of everyday living. Ethical action in the *Bhagavad-gita* derives not from the actual, dependently co-arisen situation of an imminent battle, but from firm adherence to the eternal and immutable *ātman* within and the demands of Arjuna's status as a warrior. The slaughter in warfare of relatives and beloved mentors is seen as Arjuna's duty (*dharma*).[25] It was in this context that the Buddha presented his doctrine of no-self. One cannot, he preached, escape from the suffering of transmigration simply by negating change and seeking the security of a transcendent selfhood.

Therefore, the differences between the Buddhist teaching of no-self and the Christian doctrine of the soul are not mutually exclusive, but derive from different historical and cultural contexts. This is not to claim that they really are saying the same thing. It is only to claim that there is no valid reason for rejecting the adoption of this Buddhist theme for Christian understanding. The adequacy of that endeavor can be judged only from its performance, a task to be done in the remainder of this book.

The Dharma Realm and the Personal God

Perhaps, a Christian apologist might adduce, the Buddhist theme of no-self is acceptable in Christian discourse, since Christians also negate the value of a fixed and permanent self. But Buddhism also denies the existence of God. From the very beginning the Buddha's doctrine rejected the notion of a personal God. In its Mahāyāna development, Buddhism continued to deny that any such being oversees our lives. The textual evidence is crystal clear on the point. In Mahāyāna, the ultimate Dharma Realm (*dharma-dhātu*) is never characterized as a personal being. How can a model that refuses to understand wisdom and awakening in personalist terms be employed to express Christian faith in a personal God? Again it seems that these differences are dialectically opposed and mutually exclusive. The adoption of one must, it would appear, exclude any theology constructed on the other.

But again things are not as obvious as they seem. The Mahāyāna understanding of the Dharma Realm is not meant to affirm that ultimate meaning and truth are impersonal, but to negate that they can be characterized in any way whatsoever — as either personal or impersonal. The Dharma Realm is not a knowable essence, the features of which can be expressed in mental words. The ultimate is described as realized only through personal awakening, not through ratiocination. Thus, when Buddhists refute the being of God, they are rejecting the notion of God presented in essentialist philosophy. The question of the existence of the Almighty (*Īśvara*) is refuted in Buddhist texts as but another example of clinging to the essences of things (*dharmagrāha*). *The Establishment of Conscious Construction-Only in Thirty Stanzas* presents the traditional argument:

Some claim that there is one Almighty God, whose nature is real, omnipresent, and eternal, and who can create all things. But this opinion is illogical for the following reasons: (1) if he creates all things, he cannot be eternal, and thus, not being eternal, he would not be omnipresent, (2) if his nature were eternal, omnipresent, and endowed with all capabilities, then at all times and in all places he should instantaneously create all things, and (3) if he is able to create only by relying on his desire or on other conditions, then that contradicts the teaching of a single cause, for then that desire or those conditions would also have to arise simultaneously, because they would be eternal [also].[26]

The early Buddhist had to reject not only fixed belief in a permanent self, but also theistic beliefs that regarded God as the highest being (*dharma*) among beings. In point of historical fact the early Christian fathers seldom faced objections about the being of God, whose existence was affirmed not only by Christians and Jews, but also by their pagan critics. It seemed here at least that a common ground could be found between Christians and pagans. In fact, the Greek notion of God was particularly attractive because it had already undergone a process of demythologization that stood in contrast to the anthropomorphic descriptions of the Old Testament God. The normative idea of God in Christian discourse was not derived from the New Testament, but from the Greek philosophic notion of an eternal, all-powerful, and unchanging essence behind the transience of life in the world.

The Buddhist argument does apply to this Greek notion of God as essence, for that notion is open to the criticism that if God is related to the transient world as its Creator, he too must share in its transience. This notion failed to offer any argument why the creation was not a constantly reenacted event and it constantly appealed to extrinsic factors, such as prime matter, used by God in bringing about that creation. But Christian thinkers, even working within Greek philosophical ideas, were not unaware of these problems. The idea of *creatio ex nihilo* was meant to exclude any notion of a demiurge who created the world by forming it out of unformed matter. Christians insisted that God was not simply the most august being among beings but the source and ground for the very being of beings, always transcendent to that which he created. The first criticism given above, that creation necessitates temporal change in God, and the third, that God needs to rely on other conditions, do not apply to a creator God who creates *ex nihilo*.[27] Many Christian theologians would further agree that the creative act is not a once-and-for-all action of a divine being making and sending a universe spinning off into space, but a continuing activity that grounds the existence of all things. Thus they would admit the second point that God does create at all times and in all places. The Christian notion of God is not identical with the notion of the Almighty negated in the Buddhist texts, even when expressed by Greek Christians. But the Christian notion of God is not confined to Greek philosophy. In fact many contemporaneous Christian theologians would find the Buddhist argument acceptable. The basic assumption of that argument is that the Almighty is a being within the universe, that is, an identifiable essence. Given that assumption, the Yogācāra argument follows logically, for any *dharma* within the universe could scarcely be argued to be the creative ground of the universe. Despite regarding God as Creator, Christians never equate God with one *dharma* among many, even the highest.

In the Mahāyāna tradition, all descriptions of the ultimate are accommodations to human speech, skillful means for bringing the ineffable to verbal awareness. In a similar fashion, the apophatic tradition of Greek thought sought to free itself from the essentialist pattern of Greek thought and insisted that God is completely unknown and inaccessible. God transcends both affirmation and negation and is beyond both being and nonbeing. "It was no less accurate to identify God as 'nothing,' for one did not use the verb 'to be' univocally in speaking of the Creator and creatures. Therefore Dionysius teaches that God is unknown—not in the sense that the name 'God' has no meaning, but in the sense that it transcends all meaning and understanding."[28] Maximus explained that God participates in the reality of his creatures, but "in a non-participatory way," retaining his absoluteness even in his sovereignty as Creator. In fact, "negative statements about divine matters are the only true ones."[29] Even the name "God" refers not to the essence of God, which cannot be named, but to God's loving kindness toward humanity.[30]

In such an apophatic tradition, theologizing can reach no further than language-truth and God never becomes an object of investigation, for God is not an object proportionate to human knowing. Hence, theology is conventional discourse about the ultimate meaning that is God. Similarly, Lonergan makes a distinction between the primary nonobjectifiable meaning of God and a secondary level of meaning, which takes God as the object of its inquiry and teaching. He writes:

> In what I have called the primary and fundamental meaning of the name, God, God is not an object. For that meaning is the term of an orientation to transcendent mystery. Such an orientation . . . is not properly a matter of raising and answering questions. So far from being in the world mediated by meaning, it is the principle that can draw people out of that world and into the cloud of unknowing.[31]

God is the term or objective of an orientation to transcendent mystery. In Yogācāra terms, the objective (*ālambana*) of the pure mind.[32] God is the ultimate meaning that transcends all worlds and all ideas. But one does not remain in that cloud of unknowing, for ultimate meaning, although totally other than and disjunctive from all worldly convention, is embodied in conventional meaning. Lonergan continues:

> However, withdrawal is for return. Not only can one's prayer consist in letting lapse all images and thoughts. . ., but also those that pray in that exhausting fashion can cease to pray and think back on their praying. They then objectify in images and concepts . . . the God that has been their concern.

God thus becomes an object inasmuch as God is an object of conventional and worldly (*saṃvṛti*) meanings. God becomes an object only after the divine presence has passed, only in a reflection on remembered states of contact. God is known not by affirming the divine essence as the Almighty, but only in unknowing, by emptying the mind of all images and words. God can be characterized neither as being nor as nonbeing, neither as personal nor as impersonal. Doctrinal discourse that objectifies God is a matter of skillfully using conventional theological language, not of identifying absolute categories. The Buddhist notion of the ultimate is in deep harmony with this apophatic tradition of Christian theology. Far from being contradictory to Christian concerns, its insistence on otherness is a needed method for abandoning the anthropomorphic musings that Christians are fond of and their consequent entanglement in imaginary and debilitating constructs. The differences between Christian and Buddhist understandings of the ultimate are cultural and historical, not mutually exclusive.[33]

Emptiness and Being

Throughout the preceding issues the Mahāyāna doctrine of emptiness comes up again and again. The teaching of no-self and the negation of the Almighty are both grounded in the rejection of essential being in favor of the emptiness of all things. Emptiness rejects the attribution of objective reality to things and brands such notions as imaginary fabrications. But the role of emptiness is not restricted to a simple negation. Nāgārjuna's rejection of Abhidharma essentialism was not a negation of an incorrect position in favor of a correct position. Rather, that rejection was aimed at a pattern of consciousness that pretended to have attained the truth by apprehending correct positions. His intent was to encourage people to abandon theory in favor of the immediacy of their own personal experience of awakening.

But how, one might ask, can a theology be built on a model that proclaims the absence of all positions? How can theology not be involved in evolving and defending positions? Is that not exactly what we are presently doing? How can theology function within a context of emptiness? The argument against emptiness is concisely put by Ninian Smart:

If we say that the religious ultimate, whether this be *śūnya* (Void, i.e. emptiness) or God, is indescribable (and/or incomprehensible, etc.) and mean this literally and rigorously, then how can either the Buddha or Christ be specially connected with it? For if it is just an X then everything and nothing bears its imprint equally. Thus as a position it is empty, and cannot hope to explicate the tradition which it is used to illuminate. And if it could it could exclude no other tradition, and all religions would become equally valid including those whose positions are attacked, e.g. in the Mādhyamika, dialectically. In brief it is one thing to say X is incomprehensible, indescribable, etc., in that there is something about it which transcends description, comprehension, etc., and another thing to say that it totally eludes any sort of human grasp.[34]

How can one do a theology with a philosophy that negates doing theology? Again, appearances are deceptive. Emptiness does indeed constitute the basic philosophical stance of Mahāyāna, a stance that in its deconstructive insistence is no stance at all. Nāgārjuna, Asaṅga, together with most of the Mahāyāna masters, insist that emptiness is to be applied rigorously to all positions whatsoever. But emptiness is never to be reified as an absolute itself. It is not Smart's "religious ultimate," but a descriptive term for the mind of wisdom that sees the illusory status of all verbal statements. To the question of how could the Buddha be specifically connected with emptiness, Nāgārjuna would have responded: How could he not? Where is the slightest anything that is not empty? Christ, no less than Buddha, lived and moved in a context of emptiness. Indeed, in Mahāyāna everything is empty, not only the propositions of opponents, and Mādhyamika reasoning is intended precisely to elicit this insight.

The above quotation further errs by asserting that emptiness cannot hope to explicate a tradition. In Mādhyamika philosophy, emptiness always functions in identity with dependent co-arising. It does not negate the dependently co-arisen status of religious statements and considers it quite adequate to adjudicate their validity through dependently co-arisen criteria. One weighs evidence, offers reasons, and comes to conclusions always in concrete situations and contexts, all of which are empty because dependently co-arisen and dependently co-arisen because empty. Emptiness itself does not exclude anything. Even the arguments presented by Nāgārjuna in *The Stanzas on the Middle* function not in virtue of emptiness but in and through a conventional reasoning that points out the untenability of each and every attempt to think essences.

Furthermore, it is a mistake to identify Christian thinking with essentialist philosophy. Christian examples of nonessentialist patterns of thinking abound. In 1 Corinthians Paul contrasts the mind that generates positions with the wisdom of God. He is unconcerned with establishing any correct position, but counterposes an understanding of Christ and the cross that negates all the Corinthian factional positions. The teaching of Gregory of Nyssa on knowing God in darkness and of Dionysius on unknowing both witness to the emptying of the mind of all images and ideas. God, who is beyond being, is known only through unknowing. Gregory's description of humans going around in circles of tiresome motion day after day like blindfolded animals tethered to a mill reflects the Buddhist notion of *saṃsāra*, while his description of the vertigo one experiences when the mind has nothing to "take hold of" brings to mind the teaching of emptiness in the Prajñāpāramitā scriptures. His assertion that all things are "unsubstantial" (*anukpartos*) is directly parallel to Mahāyāna teachings that all things are empty.[35] All is vanity and the only reality is found in what we might become when the original image-nature is restored. We need then to practice "an emptying of our thinking" (*cogitationis vacuitas*), to turn away from illusion and seek by unknowing that which alone is real. This tradition of mystical darkness in Christian thought presents clear analogues to the Mahāyāna theme of emptiness.

The Scholastic axiom has it that one can validly conclude the possibility of something from its actual occurrence (*ab esse ad posse valet illatio*). One can scarcely claim that the adoption of the doctrine of emptiness renders one incapable of explicating any tradition. In point of historical fact, the Mahāyāna masters did explicate their tradition from this standpoint of no-standpoint. And the Christian proponents of a theology of mystic darkness were not rendered simply speechless.

The teaching of emptiness is dialectically opposed to the assertions of naïve realism or conceptualism. Any essentialist ideas are negated if things have no essence. But its differences from the Christian tradition of mystic darkness are only cultural, perspectival, and historical. In the West the implications of Gregory's and Dionysius' understandings of unknowing were not developed into a philosophy of interiority and remained peripheral to the mainstream assumptions of Greek ontology. The philosophic shift to an analysis of conscious interiority did not take place within theological circles. Rather, it was evoked by tensions engendered from the bifurcation of consciousness into realms of commonsense and scientific theory, and occurred only in modern philosophy, when Immanuel Kant set out to examine the transcendental a-priori structure of knowing, both pure and practical. By contrast, in Buddhist India that shift was evoked within religious discourse by the tension engendered from a bifurcation between Abhidharma theory and Mādhyamika emptiness. Yogācāra philosophy set out to examine the inner structures of religious consciousness—how illusion comes about and how it might be reversed in awakening. Because of this emphasis on religious experience and consciousness, Mahāyāna philosophy can serve as a corrective to overconfident attempts at theology.

The Two Truths and the Oneness of Christian Truth

In the Middle Ages, Christian theologians attacked the Parisian scholar Siger of Brabant (ca. 1266) for affirming a doctrine of two truths: that what is true in philosophy is not necessarily true in theology, and vice versa.[36] The same issue is seen today in the insistence of scholars that one cannot demonstrate the truth of propositional claims in virtue of a higher, ineffable, and unknown truth. It would thus appear that the Mahāyāna doctrine of the two truths cannot be employed in an account of Christian faith awareness, for it too is a "double decker account of truth,"[37] and allows that what is true on the conventional level be adjudicated untrue in ultimate meaning, and vice versa.

This, however, is simply not the case. The two truths are not two distinct levels of statements presented as true: one in virtue of immediate experience and one in virtue of worldly experience. Rather, this doctrine thematizes the relationships between a silent, ineffable truth and conventional articulations of mediated truth. That silent truth can never prove anything and can never be expressed in any proposition. By contrast, conventional truth functions in its own autonomous sphere of language and reasoning, without any appeal to any nonrational experiences. Both, however, are empty of essence: ultimate meaning in the silence of nondiscriminative awakening and worldly convention in the formation of dependently co-arisen judgments.

Yet there is still a hesitancy about adopting a Mahāyāna doctrine of two truths because they seem to relativize theological discourse. The Mādhyamika interpretation of two truths regards all verbal statements as a covering over and occluding of the truth of ultimate meaning and has until recently found little acceptance among Christian theologians.[38] For the most part, despite their awareness of the Christian tradition of mystic darkness, Western theologians have remained convinced that Christian doctrine, rightly understood, is not an obstacle to the realization and awareness of God. Nāgārjuna's notion of doctrinal enunciation as only commonsense language (*prajñapti*) ill accords with the development of Christian theology and, it would seem, could hardly have supported the vast theoretical syntheses and the medieval theologians. It is, some would argue, ill equipped to deal with the needs of a Christian theological endeavor.

The Mādhyamika philosophy evolved in contrast to the inadequacies of Abhidharma conceptualism. To be sure, the criticisms of Nāgārjuna were trenchant in characterizing theorizing as an obstacle to understanding and awakening, for any system that substitutes concepts for acts of conscious insight renders the occurrence of insight less likely. His negation of theory forced mystic meaning to be expressed only in commonsense terms. But even within the context of emptiness, theoretical attempts were evolved, such as to rival any systematic theology in the West. Even mystics continue to think and to question the meaning of their experiences. Mādhyamika thinkers like Candrakīrti and Yogācāra scholars like Asaṅga addressed the issue directly. The Yogācāra thinkers discovered a new realm of meaning: conscious interiority. This philosophic advance allowed them to maintain the primacy of direct, mystic meaning and to uphold a lesser, but nevertheless valid, status for verbally expressed truth. The Mahāyāna understanding of truth is directly opposed to those Christian thinkers who hold that creedal statements do actually express, however imperfectly, the absolute truth. The doctrine of the two truths rejects all literalism and biblicism that would treat words or concepts as capturing and embodying the truth. Mahāyānists claim that such ideas result from mistaking imagination for understanding. But the doctrine of the two truths is not opposed to more modest Christian understandings of theoretical truth. The oneness of truth excludes the simultaneous truth of contradictory statements within the same realm of meaning. Indeed, in light of the at times prevalent Western adoption of a muddle-headed ecumenism that accepts all religions as "saying the same thing," we should insist that the principle of contradiction not be neglected. But such an insistence in no way negates the Mahāyāna notion of the two truths, for its central insight is that the two truths of ultimate meaning and worldly convention do not belong to the same realm of meaning. The truth of ultimate meaning is experienced in a mystic realm in which the only criterion is direct contact. The truth of worldly convention is found only in mediated realms of meaning, judged by commonsense, theoretical, or critical norms.

Moreover, the same differential structure of truth is found throughout Christian thinking. The New Testament often expresses the role of Christ as embodying and mediating the silent truth of God. Christ is the image of the invisible God (Col. 1:15; 2 Cor. 4:4). "No one has ever seen God. The beloved Son, who is in the bosom of the Father, he has enunciated him" (Jn. 1:18). The Logos is the word of the Father from silence. Gregory of Nyssa well realized that "all divine names were invented by human custom" and "represent our conceptions of the divine nature." Christians assent to the truth of faith not because they think that their language-formed ideas represent God just as God is, but because the life and words of Christ mediate to them an awareness and experience of God, subsequently expressed in creeds and in theology. Irenaeus can then say that "the Father is that which is invisible about the Son, and the Son is that which is visible about the Father," for "the Son is the measure of the Father."[39]

Maximus Confessor interprets the scriptures as expressing "the ineffable and hidden counsels of God in a bodily manner, so that we might be able to know divine matters on the basis of words and sounds that are cognate; for otherwise the mind of God remains unknown, his words unspoken."[40] Nevertheless, he claims, although those hidden counsels are expressed in language, all Christian doctrine is transcended by its own content. True fidelity to scripture consists not in claiming that its "language was a disclosure of the inner being of God, but in recognizing that it spoke about the saving will of God toward the world."[41] The early fathers distinguished the economy, which can be understood in words and images, from theology, which, because it deals with God, cannot be so understood.

These themes appear explicitly in Dionysius' double tradition of theology, in terms almost identical with the Yogācāra explanation of the two truths. Conventional truth is indeed public, common, philosophic, aimed at demonstration, involved in the world, subject to custom, human, and mediated. Ultimate truth, by contrast, is not expressed in words, is mystic, symbolic, aimed at initiation, purification, nondefilement, perfection, and beyond this world. (It is symbolic inasmuch as symbols in Dionysius' tradition function not in a realm mediated by verbal meaning, but in a realm of mystic meaning.)

Thus the differences between the Mahāyāna doctrine of the two truths and this Christian understanding of truth lie in their cultural emphases and perspectival approaches. The Mahāyāna thinkers stressed the ineffability of ultimate meaning against the overbearing theory of Abhidharma. Their problem was not to champion verbal truth but to question its presumptive claims. By contrast, the early Christian fathers, for the most part, did not have to respond to any parallel insistence on the adequacy of theory, for they understood theory in a Platonic way as itself issuing in a mysticism of light. Most felt no compelling need to seek its reversal in terms of a negative dialectic. This is perhaps why the mysticism of darkness of Gregory and Dionysius has remained marginal in Christian thinking. But, with the passing of the assured value of theory and metaphysics, this tradition becomes more and more attractive. Both the Mahāyāna understanding of truth and the mysticism of darkness present similar accounts of truth as both ineffable and expressed. Neither can be understood if the ultimate realm of silence is reduced to theory or if the conventional use of language is raised to an ontological status. The adoption of a Mahāyāna perspective for Christian theology can perhaps guard more securely against both errors.

Vijñaptimātratā and Christian Philosophy

The Yogācāra thinkers developed their theory of conscious construction-only (*vijñaptimātratā*) in order to articulate emptiness and dependent co-arising within a critical understanding of consciousness. They declared that all things are empty because they are only ideas in the mind without any corresponding essence that might assure their validity. At first glance it would appear that this affirmation that ideas (*vijñapti*) do not refer to objective realities implies that one can have no firm assurance of the objective truth of doctrine. Christian thinkers have not been inclined to affirm that they are merely thinking about ideas. The idealist philosophy of Bishop George Berkeley never became a framework for theological endeavors. Kantianism did have theological spin-offs, but they derived from Kant's ideas about practical reason, not pure reason, and were not, in any event, of lasting significance. It would seem that a philosophy of idealism is incompatible with Christian theology, and therefore that Yogācāra with its thesis of conscious construction-only is dialectically opposed to the objective truth claims of Christian theology and cannot possibly serve as a vehicle for its expression.

Let us grant the claim: an idealist philosophy presents almost insuperable problems for theological discourse. The question then becomes whether Yogācāra is indeed an idealist philosophy. And the evidence is not altogether conclusive. There are two options.

A number of Yogācāra passages seem to assert a purely idealist view. To take but one example, in *The Establishment of the Doctrine of Conscious Construction-Only in Twenty Stanzas*, Vasubandhu states that "if constructed ideas have no objective referent, . . . they cannot be validated,"[42] and goes on to explain that sense impressions do not correspond to sense objects. The obvious objection is that, if our impressions do not correspond to external objects, then why do all people confronted with the same object similarly perceive that object? Everyone climbing Mount Fuji seems to agree that there is a mountain there. Vasubandhu's answer is that all people are asleep in a similar dreamlike illusion because the karmic seeds in their individual container consciousnesses develop in a similar manner. They are each separately but identically deluded. Such an answer, however, rings false to mountain climbers.

But a second interpretation is recommended by many other texts. In *The Establishment of the Doctrine of Conscious Construction-Only in Thirty Stanzas*, Vasubandhu reflects further on this question and does not adopt a pure idealist position. There the objection is raised that "The external sphere of material forms is clearly and immediately apprehended [by the five sense] consciousnesses of seeing, hearing, etc. How can you deny the existence of what is known by direct perception?"[43] The reply, which seems to draw upon the epistemological theory of Dignāga, distinguishes the intent of the Yogācāra denial of objectivity: "When direct perception occurs, it does not apprehend [objects] as external. It is only later that thinking discriminates and falsely generates the idea of externality."

Here it is not a question of the validity of sensing the mountain, but the question of the pattern of subject-object in which that sense experience is interpreted as an external reality confronting the internal mind. In Yogācāra, as in later Ch'an, mountains are just mountains and do not themselves challenge the would-be conquerer. The intent of the Yogācāra doctrine of conscious construction-only is to negate the validity of the pattern of extraverted, sense-patterned knowing that fails to distinguish sense images from insight into those images. There is no need to negate the givenness of sense impressions, only to negate the equation of understanding with perception of such givenness. *The Thirty Stanzas* continues:

> Thus, objects immediately apprehended are the developments of consciousness into its image aspect and can be said to exist, [just as the insight aspect that understands those images exists]. But, inasmuch as their external objectivity is apprehended by the thinking consciousness and sense objects are falsely imagined to exist, we say that they are non-existent. . . . They are like objects in a dream, which cannot be apprehended as objectively real.

Sensation of itself is just sensation and does not relate the meaning of the sensed to the person sensing. What is denied is not the givenness of the sense image, but the subsequent step that would validate conceptual knowing by some capturing of those images in concepts. Conscious construction-only implies the rejection only of naîve realism and conceptualism.[44] Meaning is not given simply by sense impressions. One must engender insight into those images. Without such insight, knowing is indeed dreamlike, for in dreams images float by and elicit all kinds of feelings without the occurrence of insight into their meaning. Until one has awakened from insightless dreaming, the conscious activity of understanding does not occur.

Furthermore, the Yogācāra masters negate not only naïve objectivity, as if it were enough to abandon attachment to "objective" things. They also negate naïve subjectivity, because the inner self is only conventional and dependently co-arisen, empty of any abiding reality that might serve as a stable support for attachment. The meaning of *vijñapti-mātra* (conscious construction-only) is not the rejection of an illusory objectivity in favor of a really existing subjectivity, but a denial of the validity of the entire pattern of imaginative knowing (*parikalpita-lakṣaṇa*) with its assumption of the validity of that pattern of a subjective knower (*grāhaka*) confronted with the objective known (*grāhya*) and taking an imaginative look out from within.

Once, however, that imagined pattern has been broken, once the conversion of support has occurred, then wisdom insight arises and true knowing becomes possible. Bandhuprabha in his *Interpretation of the Buddha Land* explains that discernment wisdom is able to "know all objects, because it is the cause that gives rise to a consciousness of images."[45] He says:

> This means that the discernment wisdom of all Tathāgatas is able to understand all objects and has a multitude of images in which appear these knowable objects, just as a colored painting has a multitude of visible markings. In its insight aspect this wisdom is able to cause the arising of such a consciousness with its images.[46]

This discernment wisdom understands its inner images through insight into them and is freed from the pattern of imaginative fabrication. "This wisdom is able discriminately to manifest images of all objects. If it were not discriminative, it would be unable to examine causes and results or to enunciate doctrine without doubt for the various assemblies."[47]

In awakened wisdom, one does not abide in the silent emptiness of an imageless ultimate meaning directly experienced, but brings to speech a conventionally valid, subsequently attained wisdom of discriminative understanding and verbalization. Such discrimination and expression flow not from extraverted consciousness, but from a dependently co-arisen understanding drawn from concrete concerns and aimed at concrete goals. This dependently co-arisen, other-dependent understanding itself issues from a prior awareness of the undiscriminated meaning of suchness as the emptiness of all things. "Although not apart from suchness, yet, because it is discriminative, it does not realize the essence of suchness, for it takes as an object the image of suchness."[48]

Grounded on a direct, unmediated realization of ultimate truth, of the imageless Dharma Realm, the converted mind of wisdom mediates conventional meanings through images and words, attaining a certainty and awareness of its teaching that derive from that direct experience. Objectivity is not, then, a property of external objects or a quality of imaginative knowing but, rather, the conventional and valid understanding of conventional truth. The Yogācāra texts not only reject the naïve realism of Abhidharma conceptualism, they also affirm a conventional validity to language, freed from the pattern of imagining. They sketch human understanding as composed of both the image derived from sense perception and the insight that actually understands that image. It is insight (*darśana*) into image (*nimitta*) alone that issues in understanding meaning. One does not know by looking at images, but, rather, by the synergistic conjunction of both insight and image. The criterion for objectivity is not the obviousness of what confronts the subject,[49] but the occurrence of insight into image.

In affirming validity to conventional truth, the Yogācāra thinkers distinguished between rational and irrational thinking. *The Explication of Underlying Meaning* outlines four kinds of reasoning procedure and takes care to differentiate the valid and pure from the invalid and impure.[50] Reasoning from looking (*apekṣa-nyāya*) is the process of engendering karmic entanglements, for it takes imaginative looking as its criterion of truth. Reasoning from what has already been done (*kṛtakāra-nyāya*) reflects upon past karmic experiences and assures one of future rebirths within the realm of transmigratory suffering. These first two types of reasoning pertain to illusory, imagined consciousness. But the third kind admits of both illusion and truth. It is reasoning from the validity of evidence (*upapatti-siddha-nyāya*), the process of correctly establishing and understanding statements. Such reasoning can be either pure or impure, either valid or invalid, for it depends upon the pattern of consciousness in which reasoning and inference take place. The fourth kind of reasoning is reasoning from reality (*dharmatā-nyāya*), exemplified by Nāgārjuna's dialectic of falsifying all claims to absolute truth in awareness of the silence of ultimate meaning. These last two kinds of reasoning, the constructive functioning of reasoning based upon evidence and the deconstructive reasoning from reality, represent a Yogācāra interpretation of conventional and ultimate truth. While the thrust of reasoning from reality is toward the negation and emptying of all views, reasoning from evidence is worldly and conventional thinking that functions through language and judges the truth of its conventional claims. Based on well-argued claims, this reasoning underlies the entire Yogācāra attempt to reclaim theory in a context of emptiness.

The central concern of Yogācāra with reason and logic is seen in the fact that Vasubandhu is credited with writing four different tracts on these subjects.[51] He was recognized as a consummate logician in India.[52] Yogācāra developments after Dignāga focused principally on questions of the validity of knowledge and developed a critical epistemology and logic to undergird its understanding of consciousness.[53]

In sum, the evidence suggests a development of Yogācāra thinking toward a critical realism whose criteria are not the supposed objectivity of external realities but the adequacy of internal operations. The doctrine of *vijñaptimātra* is not then diametrically opposed to the needs of critical realism. If the first option is affirmed that Yogācāra is a philosophy of idealism, then one can argue that it represents a genetic stage toward the development of critical theory. If the second option is asserted, then Yogācāra is not idealist at all, but itself an affirmation of critical realism. The doctrine of *vijñaptimātra* is indeed opposed to and incompatible with naîve realism in its Christian version, such as expressed by Étienne Gilson,[54] but it is not opposed to a critical realism, such as that of Bernard Lonergan. Indeed, Yogācāra can perhaps assist Christian thinkers to recover the priority of their own mystic tradition, while hastening with all due speed toward their philosophical goals.

The Three Bodies of Buddha and the Christian Trinity

The Yogācāra doctrine of the three bodies of Buddha (*buddhatrikāya*) was meant to describe the nature of a buddha, one who has attained awakening. The doctrine began with the Buddha's early followers pondering the nature of the historical Buddha and passed through later stages of supernaturalizing that Buddha and distinguishing his apparitional body from the true eternal Buddha body. From the first, theories of the Buddha bodies have had a strongly docetic emphasis: the transformation or apparitional body is the fictive, magical body of the actual, historical Buddha, created to abide among sentient beings in order to carry out the works of compassion. Even when the Yogācāra thinkers added the enjoyment body to account for the buddhas experienced in (Pure Land) meditation, the docetism remains, for enjoyment bodies are the appearances of buddhas seen only in those meditative states.

As it stands, such a model cannot serve in a Christian understanding of the Incarnation or the Trinity, for it would simply repeat the docetic option. Hence, the doctrine of the three bodies as stated in the Yogācāra texts is diametrically opposed to Christian doctrine.[55]

However, it may perhaps be adapted to Christian use. The Christian doctrine of Trinity was not articulated in terms of wisdom, but in terms of the objective reality of the triune God. After many struggles and vicissitudes, the fathers of the church and the later medieval theologians finally hammered out a theoretical understanding of Trinity whose crowning achievement was the presentation of a logically consistent trinitarian theology. In Thomas Aquinas that movement reached its apogee, for he proceeded by establishing clear definitions of the terms "nature," "person," "procession," and so forth, and then succinctly and masterfully delineated a Christian understanding of God as three in one. But precisely because of its theoretical acumen, that very achievement engenders problems and tends to preclude other approaches. To the less theoretical such meanings are inaccessible — and most people are not theoreticians. The Gospels themselves do not move within such a theoretical pattern. Karl Rahner's insistence on reaffirming the doctrine of an economic Trinity seems to have been elicited from such a need to enunciate the doctrine of the Trinity in less theoretical and more generally available terms.[56]

In an adapted form the Yogācāra doctrine of the three bodies can perhaps serve as a model, enabling one to explicate not the nature of the ultimate itself but, rather, the structure of awakening to that ultimate. In their traditional presentation, the doctrine of the three bodies focused on the buddhas worshiped in visualization and encountered in history, grounding these appearances of buddhas in the Dharma Body of emptiness. The emphasis, however, was less on experiential consciousness than on the ideal figures of the buddhas presented in cultic practices. The subordination of the enjoyment and transformation bodies to the Dharma Body brought them firmly within the context of emptiness. In its Indian context, Yogācāra did not move beyond this understanding of Buddha bodies, but there are examples in later Mahāyāna doctrinal development where the Buddha bodies are more thoroughly demythologized. *The Platform Sutra* understands the Buddha bodies not as ideal buddhas, but as one's own mind (Dharma Body), one's own experience of change (transformation body), and one's own future reward and enjoyment of good practices (enjoyment body).[57] In contrast to the Greek account with its stress on ontological categories, such a usage of the three bodies focuses upon the experience of becoming aware of the ultimate.

To be sure, in order to be so employed as a model for Christian thinking, the Buddhist doctrine of the three bodies must be shorn of all docetic implications. A transformation body meant to account for a succession of historical buddhas serves no purpose in a Christian context. For the sake of the task at hand, we shall alter the traditional Yogācāra understanding of the three bodies and shift them into a Christian perspective. The meaning of *nirmāṇa-kāya* will then be modified to mean the embodiment (*kāya*) of transformation (*nirmāṇa*), and will refer to the transforming experience of living in the Spirit. The meaning of the enjoyment body (*saṃbhoga-kāya*) will be modified to mean the embodiment of the experience (*saṃbhoga* is often glossed as "experiential") of God as Abba. The meaning of the Dharma, or Essence, Body (*dharma-kāya; svabhāvika-kāya*) will indicate the embodiment of ultimate meaning as grounded upon its ineffable content. These meanings are not given in the Yogācāra texts. They are, rather, an adaptation of that teaching aimed at providing a model for the interpretation of the base Christian experience of the Trinity.

The particular value of using a Mahāyāna model for Christian theology lies in its ability to insist on the priority of mystic meaning, while engaged in constructing theologies. In its Prajñāpāramitā and Mādhyamika expressions this takes the concrete form of the doctrines of emptiness, dependent co-arising, and the two truths. In its Yogācāra presentation the implications of these insights for a critical theory of conscious interiority permits one both to differentiate mystic meaning from conventional discourse and to maintain the validity of that discourse as conventional. These themes are the elements that constitute the model to be employed in chapters 10 and

11. That model does not entail the adoption of Buddhist cosmological or metaphysical theory. Christians have had enough problems getting rid of their own Western cosmological and metaphysical baggage and have no need to take over anyone else's burdens in this regard. Specific Buddhist notions, such as transmigration, the twelvefold chain of causality, and the aggregates, form no essential part of the present model, for they do not directly relate to the analysis of conscious interiority. It is not, then, the intention of this endeavor either to affirm or to negate these notions. They represent the ever-evolving tradition of Buddhist thinking and as such fall outside the present purview. In a word, this Mahāyāna model can be employed for Christian theology because it is an "interlocking set of terms and relations."[58] To adopt Bernard Lonergan's terms, these insights will form the general terms that explain the dynamic nature of faith consciousness, which, combined with the special terms of Christian belief (Incarnation and Trinity), will present a Mahāyāna Christian theology.[59]

It would thus appear that Mahāyāna thinking has much to contribute to Christian thinking, ever struggling to bring to speech the Christ meaning. But, in order for one to assert to such a possibility, a broad agreement with the comparative analysis above is requisite. That analysis, however, has not restricted itself to logical, theoretical meanings, but often appealed to a realm of mystic meaning, a realm of direct experience. Its underlying foundation lies in the understanding of that experience, without some idea of which the entire analysis will seem to be equivocal and hedging whenever pressed. Thus, our discussion will turn to an examination of the nature of the conversion of the basic support of consciousness (*āśraya-parivṛtti*) and bring it into close relation with Christian notions of conversion (*metanoia*), for such an experience is the attainment of mystic understanding and the foundation for all subsequent theologizing.[60]

CONVERSION AS THE FOUNDATION

The foundational experience from which any faith understanding comes is the experience of its founder, participated in and recreated by the believers of that faith. Christians trace their lineage back to Jesus' Abba experience and his compassionate concern for the realization of the rule of God among humans. Buddhists trace their lineage back to the awakening of Gautama Siddartha. Such experiences are paradigmatic, for Christians and Buddhists try to reenact and recreate those experiences within themselves. No religious tradition maintains itself for long if those experiences are not reenacted and recreated. The point of faith commitment is not merely to understand the historical Jesus or the historical Buddha, but rather, to realize a parallel experience oneself. The regathering of the scattered disciples and their awakening to the meaning of the risen Lord constituted the original Christian church, as the Buddhist realization of awakening did the Buddhist *saṃgha*. Everything is understood in a new light, in a new dimension, for those experiences are experiences of conversion, of turning away from the fragmented, alienated life of sin and pride, and of turning to a full participation in the all-encompassing reality of ultimate meaning and wisdom.

Since it is such a conversion that constitutes the basis of religious teachings and traditions, a presentation of any doctrinal thinking presupposes an understanding of conversion. At its foundational level such a presentation should attempt to thematize and objectify the nature of religious conversion.[61] Without a clear statement of that foundational reality, religious teachings can hope for little resonance within the minds of people not yet converted. An apologetic that would argue that faith affirmations are at least not unreasonable hardly serves this function; the fact that one might be unable definitively to falsify any number of possible claims scarcely elicits assent to their validity. It is only from some understanding of the nature of the original experience, from some inner resonance with the descriptions of such experience, that one might be drawn to a deeper consideration of religious traditions. Teachings that are claimed to flow from direct, mystic insight and to mirror faith experiences can be understood only if one has some notion of what that experience is all about. Both Christian and Buddhist thinkers constantly declare their teachings to be beyond the sphere of logical verification, appealing to a mystic consciousness and calling for a reorientation of consciousness. Paul's presentation of wisdom, Dionysius' teaching on knowing by unknowing, Gregory's notion of meeting God in a complete darkening of all confrontational knowing, Nāgārjuna's insistence upon the emptiness of all things, Asaṅga's emphasis upon pure suchness — none of these doctrines can be understood if reduced to levels of commonsense or theoretical data. They find their validity only in the reality of mystic meaning, whether proleptically anticipated or actually realized. Any theological attempt that would try to bring to speech an Abba experience or the realization of awakening must base itself upon some understanding of conversion as the reorientation of consciousness to mystic understanding.

The issues raised above in the comparison of Yogācāra and Christian teachings can hardly be evaluated simply by an analysis of their logical consistency. Necessary as that is to detect false statements, doctrine presented as leading to mystic awakening can be understood only with some notion of what that awakening might be. If one were to deny that awakening occurs at all, then obviously no understanding of mystic teachings will ever occur. Religious teachings have been propagated by the saints and thinkers of all traditions not as cool statements of fact, but as injunctions to practice, demanding in the hearers a conversion to that practice. A thematization of conversion is needed not merely to delineate the type of base experience lying behind the verbal teachings, but to encourage practice that might bring about a personal conversion in the hearer.

The Yogācāra thinkers did not neglect the task of objectifying the experience of conversion, for the main thrust of their thinking is placed upon the realization of awakening. In his *Summary of the Great Vehicle*, Asaṅga thematized awakening as undefiled purification (*vaimalya-vyavadāna*) attained within a consciousness that has become purified from passionate clinging and imaginative knowing. Such an attainment comes from pondering upon and understanding the doctrine (*ālambana-vyavadāna*) and from practicing the path (*mārga-vyavadāna*) that springs from such a reflective awareness of doctrine. This endeavor is not wrought by analytical thinking or self-effort. Rather, doctrine itself is an outflow from the realm of mystic meaning, from an experience of the realm of ultimate truth.

However, for that teaching to evoke resonance within the mind of its hearers, there must already be present a predisposition, a readiness to listen, an ability to recognize mystic meaning. People do not set out on the long journey toward faith awareness merely because an idea sounds plausible. They are moved by God, they are grasped by ultimate concern, they are made aware of the unquestioned validity of awakening. No apologetic that recommends its teachings as not demonstrably untrue entices people away from the more secure pleasures of the present moment. No monks swarm upon the desert, no saints face martyrdom, no ascetics practice their austere art, no householders retire into the deep forest because of the possible validity of some idea or other. Rather, drawn by the example of others' realization, the desire personally to enter into ultimate meaning takes over one's total attention. In Gregory's terms, one enters the light and begins to practice the path.[62]

For Asaṅga the very possibility of initiating the process implies the original purity (*prakṛti-vyavadāna*) of the mind. Its *a-priori* structure is oriented toward an ultimate objective. Unless blocked by passion or illusion, that orientation leads one forth toward realization and wisdom. Clinging to sense satisfactions and comforting illusions is not abandoned merely because of the logical attractiveness of verbal teachings. Rather, those teachings, which flow from prior realizations of that originally pure orientation by others, find resonance at the center of one's consciousness and lead one forth in an unending progress of further insight and experience. Such is Gregory's "stretching forth," for the center of consciousness, lying at times unnoticed beneath the affairs of everyday living, resonates with the truth of the teachings and begins to direct its attention to them. It is for this reason that the Chinese translators of the Buddhist texts rendered the term *sūtra* as "matching scripture," for their teachings correspond to the basic orientation of the mind toward wisdom.

The process whereby mystic awakening occurs is treated by the Yogācāra masters as the conversion of the support that is consciousness. *The Ornament of the Scriptures of the Great Vehicle* explains:

> One reaches the highest meditation and is inaugurated into the attainment of diamond-like concentration, not disturbed by a tendency

to discriminate. And then, having been fully purified from the obstacles of passion and to knowing, one realizes a conversion of the final support.[63]

Such a conversion of support occurs within the other-dependent mind, for the mind is not of any set and fixed essence. Rather, it is open to both the illusion of imagining and the wisdom of perfection. Asaṅga explains:

What is the characteristic of the Dharma Body of awakening? It is the conversion of support, because, having destroyed all obstacles and the other-dependent pattern in its defiled aspect, it is liberated from all obstacles, assured of mastery over all doctrines, and is converted to the other-dependent pattern in its purified aspect.[64]

Such a conversion is away from the imagined pattern toward the perfected pattern. The wisdom so attained is not, however, simply the cessation of all human activity. In all Mahāyāna thought, the goal shifts from cessation to wisdom, that is, the practice of wisdom, which is its perfection (*prajñā-pāramitā*). *The Ornament of the Scriptures of the Great Vehicle* presents a stanza that describes the nature of this wisdom: "Suchness in all things is characterized by purification from the two obstacles. Mastery in reality wisdom, that which objectifies reality, is characterized by inexhaustibility."[65]

In their respective commentaries both Sthiramati and Asvabhāva explain that suchness (*tathatā*) is the emptying of the mind through a conversion that attains not only silent, ineffable, nondiscriminative wisdom (*mi rtog pa'i ye shes*), but also subsequently attained, purified, worldly wisdom (*rgyab bas thob pa dag pa 'jig rten pa'i ye shes*). It is this subsequently attained wisdom that objectifies the ineffable experience of nondiscriminative awakening and expresses it in verbal teachings.[66] In his *Sub-Commentary on the Ornament of the Scriptures of the Great Vehicle*, Asvabhāva explains: "Reality wisdom (*dgons po shes ba*) is subsequently attained wisdom. The word 'reality' here refers to the other-dependent pattern that is the container consciousness."[67]

Wisdom engaged in the world through language and teaching is subsequently attained because it is the other-dependent understanding of mediated meaning that flows from the direct, immediate awakening to suchness and emptiness. After that experience of direct contact (*sparśa*), wisdom mediates that experience and, however obliquely, objectifies it in teaching. In his *Commentarial Notes on the Ornament of the Scriptures*, Sthiramati explains that: "The phrase 'that which objectifies reality' (*dgnos bo shes pa la dmigs*) refers to the purified worldly wisdom subsequently attained."[68]

True doctrinal teaching is, then, a wisdom objectification that harmonizes with that ineffable, nondiscriminative experience. "It is because one focuses single-mindedly upon the Dharma Realm in all things by means of non-discriminative wisdom that one explains the essence of that Dharma Realm [by subsequently attained wisdom explanations]."[69]

Even this Yogācāra objectification of the nature of conversion claims no more than being a linguistic objectification of an ineffable experience. It functions in the other-dependent realm of conventional truth, which is a drawing into speech of a nonverbal awareness of ultimate meaning. The wisdom attained by the conversion of support includes a vertical dimension meaningful only in its immediacy, always disjunctive from any verbal expression, and a horizontal dimension filled out by the skillful employment of appropriate teachings.

This explanation of conversion does not stress the objective content to which one is converted, for that content is in the end not objectifiable. Any description of the content of conversion is regarded at best as a conventional description, at worst as a clinging to an imagined illusion. Such descriptions, functioning through purified other-dependent operations of insight and judgment, retain a valid but conventional truth. They are expressed not to capture that experience, but to avoid saying nothing at all. They are the functioning of wisdom in the world to lead all sentient beings toward salvation.

The Yogācāra masters further treat conversion under three constituent aspects of the total process. In his *Compendium of Abhidharma*, Asaṅga says:

> What is the final stage of the path [that leads to awakening]? It is the conversion of support without remainder. . . . What is this conversion of support without remainder? It is the conversion of the support of the mind (*citta-āśraya-parivṛtti*), the conversion of the support of practice (*mārga-āśraya-parivṛtti*), and the conversion of the support of the depraved drives (*dauṣṭhulya-āśraya-parivṛtti*).[70]

Sthiramati, in his *Commentary on the Compendium of Abhidharma*, explains this passage:

> The conversion of the support of the mind means that, when one has attained the state of nothing more to learn, the true mind, which is originally pure, is freed from the adventitious drag of the passions and there is a conversion to suchness. The conversion of the support of practice means that a conversion to a transcendent practice is realized after one has severed all covetousness and eliminated entirely all that has to be eliminated, for then a conversion of support in regard to practice is completed. The conversion of the support of depraved drives means that the container consciousness is freed from all passionate proclivities.[71]

Here the conversion of the support of the mind parallels the theme of the undefiled purification of original purity in *The Summary of the Great Vehicle*. It is the full realization of the originally pure orientation of consciousness to suchness. It is the fulfillment of the proleptic structure of the mind that is completely unrestricted and goes beyond any horizon, since it does not mediate meaning in any manner whatsoever. Rather, it is a completely unlimited horizon in which one is aware of ultimate meaning by direct contact.

The conversion of the support of practice is a transformation of practice that takes as its horizon both horizonless nondiscriminative wisdom and the subsequently attained wisdom that functions within particular horizons within history. It can so function without distorting mediated meaning because it is based upon an other-dependent awareness of direct awakening.

The conversion of the support of the depraved drives is the transformation of basic consciousness away from its propensity to mistake mediated meaning as itself ultimate, away from clinging to such meaning in passionate delusion, to the attainment of the conventionally true functioning of other-dependent thinking and affectivity necessary to embody wisdom in language and practice. In his *The Difference between Existents and Existence*, Vasubandhu writes: "Understanding existence entails a conversion to suchness, expressed as a constructed idea in the world."[72] All doctrinal discourse is, then, as Dionysius says, a weaving of models that more or less express the intent of mystic meaning. An overemphasis on theoretical meaning can obstruct the central function of doctrine to embody base mystic experience precisely because its success in logical consistency tends to usurp the less rigorous expression of mystic themes. Then, even if one has attained a true theoretical understanding, awareness of the basic, direct experience is lost.

This Yogācāra account of conversion is to be recommended as an explanation useful in Christian theologizing precisely because it objectifies conversion within the central context of mystic meaning and experience. It neither reduces mystic meaning to theory or commonsense levels, nor attempts to examine it under either the cool light of reason or the spiritual heat of preaching. It is an objectification, a theoretical attempt to express mystic experience in mediated words, which confesses all along the impossibility of the endeavor.

CONCLUSION

The intent of this chapter has been to answer both general and specific objections against the adoption of Mahāyāna philosophy in the understanding of Christian faith. Two options from the philosophy of religion were discussed: that all religious experiences, being ineffable, converge upon a central core, and that all religious experiences, not being ineffable, are predetermined by their social, cultural, and linguistic background and reflect different ontological realities. Both of these options were rejected as case examples of essentialist thinking. Many of the specific issues have been treated cursorily, for that suffices for our purpose. The questions raised about no-self, the Dharma Realm, emptiness, the two truths, and Yogācāra philosophy were all aimed at clearing the ground for what follows, the actual development of a Mahāyāna theology. The criticism of the doctrine of the three bodies as incompatible with Christian theology was admitted. In order to employ this doctrine in Christian thinking, as will shortly be done, it has been adapted and modified to avoid docetic implications.

The section on conversion is intended to stress the need for transformative experience. It too answers an objection: some claim that their experience reflects nothing about emptiness, ultimate meaning, or awakening. In response, the Mahāyāna asserts that experience reflects what the operative pattern of one's consciousness allows it to reflect. The Yogācāra account of conversion describes a transformation into wisdom consciousness and outlines the differences between the mind of a saint and the mind of a sinner, between a buddha and a common worldling. It does not explain just how one is to attain such a conversion. There is an immense literature on the concrete practices of the path: the practice of the ten perfections, practices of meditation and contemplation, the visualization of buddhas and bodhisattvas. But these themes lie beyond the scope of the present discussion, which is content merely to remove difficulties in preparation for the discussions to follow. The remaining chapters of this book will attempt to weave a Mahāyāna interpretation of the basic Christ meaning as expressed in the traditional doctrines of the Incarnation and the Trinity.

10

A Mahāyāna Interpretation of the Meaning of Christ

It has been argued throughout the preceding chapters that Christian theological insight could well profit from engagement with the Buddhist wisdom tradition. The often neglected riches of the Western Christian mystical tradition can, it is hoped, be reclaimed through such an endeavor. This does not imply that Christians must discover their mystics as if they had been entirely forgotten and lay in the dustbin of some ancient cave of Christian awareness. As in the past, Christian mystics are read and do enliven the minds of followers of the gospel. Many passages from the New Testament itself can be understood only in such a mystic realm of meaning: in the immediacy of direct experience. Christian mystics have been the objects of historical research and of numerous scholarly tracts on spiritual theology, as evidenced in the notes to the preceding chapters on Christian mystic thought. Hence the recovery of the Christian mystical tradition is not an introduction to anything new. Christians have not totally forgotten their mystics, but Christian theologians have shunted them to the periphery of serious theology.

There is indeed an entire genre of Christian mystical literature that goes under the name of spiritual or ascetical theology. It treats the ascent of the mind to God and focuses on the practices of Christian spirituality. Handbooks on meditation have long been popular. Classics like Thomas à Kempis' *Imitation of Christ*, John Bunyan's *Pilgrim's Progress*, or Francis de Sales' *Introduction to the Devout Life* retain their appeal for some, and year by year a host of new works on Christian prayer and practice appear. These books, however, are seldom regarded as central to the doing of theology. They are seen as applications of an already understood theological doctrine to practical living, not as themselves constitutive of that doctrine. The maxim *"lex orandi lex credendi"* (the rule of prayer is the source for doctrine) is warmly admitted when discussion turns on Patristic topics, but quietly ignored in many contemporary applications. One might with profit read

Francis de Sales, but it is to Thomas Aquinas that one goes for serious theological study or, in the modern day, to Karl Rahner's *Theological Investigations*.

There is a split in the Christian mind, such that the author of the *Imitation of Christ* can chide that at judgment day one will be asked not what one has read, but how one has lived. Christian thinkers are aware of this split and many attempt to remedy the situation and heal the broken mind in search of Christ. Figures like Thomas Merton spring to mind—individuals who have been unsatisfied with the seemingly arid approach of the theologians and who have dedicated themselves to bring into being a "new" theology that might address the whole of human consciousness, not just its intellectual, academic propensities.

As was argued in part I of this book, the causes of this dichotomy in Christian thinking go back to the very beginnings of Christian theologizing. The very adoption of Greek patterns of thought, necessary and desirable as it was within that cultural context, served to assure that the articulation of the main stream of Christian theology was enmeshed within the Greek metaphysical *gestalt* and, in its progressive developments, to tie theological endeavors to a "Christian" ontology of being. To be sure, the drive to understand Christian doctrine clearly demands an approach more systematic and rigorous than the imparting of spiritual advice or maxims. The need for theoretical acumen and exact discourse has been felt throughout the entire development of Christian thought. It has continued to engender penetrating responses and deep insights into the significance of Christ and the doctrines of the church.

The split continues to exist, however, for Christian thought has not been successful in organically relating theory to mystic and ascetical practice. Ascetical theology remains a poor stepsister to doctrinal endeavors, a second-stage application of theological insight to the practice of being Christian in the world. It is here that Buddhist Mahāyāna thinking can perhaps be of service, for in its Mādhyamika and Yogācāra forms it achieved a critical understanding of religious consciousness that could maintain in healthy tension both theory and mystic practice. The theologizing of Nāgārjuna constantly recognized the centrality of the ineffable experience of awakening, from which his entire tradition draws its sustenance. In the themes of emptiness and dependent co-arising he outlined an approach quite distinct from ontological systems. In his exposition of the two truths he allowed one to pursue conventional and rational discourse without losing in the plethora of words needed for that discourse one's awareness of the silence of ultimate meaning. The Yogācāra masters Asaṅga and Vasubandhu evolved a philosophy that attempted with significant success to draw together all the realms of human meaning around that central insight into emptiness, while allowing each realm to maintain its proper validity. Their philosophical doctrine of the three patterns of consciousness identified the mental genesis of imaginary clinging and outlined its conversion to perfected awareness of ultimate truth in the furtherance of other-dependent patterns of understanding. In the doctrine of the three Buddha bodies, the Yogācāra masters recognized diversity in the concrete presentation of ultimate meaning and distinguished those presentations as the Dharma Body, the enjoyment body, and the transformation body, although with the docetic implications noted above.

This is not to claim that Buddhist thought always embodied a perfect balance between academic theory and the practice of mystic insight. It did not; often the works of Mādhyamika and Yogācāra were seen as too scholastic to be of much use in the quest for awakening. In the scholastic monasteries of India, Tibet, and East Asia, great systems were evolved that in their complexity could hardly have appealed to anyone other than professional monks and scholars. But underlying these attempts at systematization, Mahāyāna Buddhist literature and practice maintained their basic focus on emptiness and dependent co-arising. The Prajñāpāramitā scriptures were always popular and, whenever theory tended to usurp the place of the silent practice of emptiness, called forth reform movements to refocus the attention of practitioners away from arid speculations and toward the concrete realization of wisdom. The Ch'an movement in China reacted to the T'ien-t'ai, San-lun, Fa-hsiang, and Hua-yen philosophies (that is to say, to the Chinese inheritors of Mādhyamika and Yogācāra) with a freshness and humor that still tends to sweep the mind clear of cherished intellectual ideas. Indeed, the introduction of Ch'an (Zen) into the West has addressed itself to a modern awareness that the deepest spiritual understanding and enlightenment is not contained in any words. With the Christian mystical tradition reserved for professional monks and nuns, Western Zen masters have seldom been aware that Christian thought was anything more than its doctrines and creeds. In its original Chinese setting, Ch'an was a deconstructive strategy that, aided by humor and irony, exploded the pretensions of Chinese scholastic Buddhism. In its advent to the West, Zen applies the same strategy to deconstruct Western minds from their attachment to doctrinal positions and sectarian formulas. Its appeal highlights the split in Christian consciousness and calls one to discover the "original mind" before its encumbrance with fixed ideas and specific concepts. The basic Zen texts are funny, a claim that can hardly be made for the more serious theology books of Western theologians. The stories and *kōans* of *Wu-men's Barrier* and *The Blue Cliff Records* abound in mind-twisting metaphor. Edward Conze once characterized Zen as Prajñāpāramitā with jokes. One does not "work through" these texts, but reads them avidly to see just what will happen, whether or not one appreciates their deeper meanings.

Mahāyāna Buddhist thought is deconstructive of all ontologies and metaphysics, and it will be its deconstructive themes that aid in deepening Christian insight into the gospel. It might be helpful here to summarize in a few paragraphs the themes to be employed. Mahāyāna regards any ontology, Western or Eastern, as the objectification of illusory conceptualization and rejects its underlying notion of essence (*svabhāva*) as the projection of the mistaken desire to identify a firm refuge from the impermanence and transience of the dependently co-arisen world. Hence the use of Māhayāna as a model for Christian theology entails the rejection of the metaphysical basis of Western theology. This indeed is a central prerequisite for thinking in the Mahāyāna mode, stressing as it does the articulation of a philosophy of emptiness and no-essence. As expressed by Nāgārjuna, emptiness is the destroyer of all views. It is not an alternate view within the field of metaphysics, but a shift to a totally disjunctive horizon in which all views are seen to be empty of essence and unable to sustain any claim to final validity. In place of clinging to views, Nāgārjuna recommends insight into dependent co-arising: awareness of the total mutuality among things and the total contextuality behind and within all doctrine (and all things). In the light of these notions, Mādhyamika reinterpreted the theme of the two truths of ultimate meaning and worldly convention. The difference between this theme and the doctrine of emptiness and dependent co-arising is one of perspective. The latter expresses insight into the reality of things as they appear "horizontally" in our experience and thinking, while the former presents a "vertical" insight into the totally ineffable and transcendent otherness of ultimate meaning and its dependently co-arisen manifestation in the world. In both of these main Mādhyamika ideas all notion of an essentialist ontology is expurgated and the world accepted in its dependently co-arisen givenness.

The Yogācāra thinkers Asaṅga and Vasubandhu worked out the implications of these insights in terms of a critical theory of consciousness. In their exposition of the three patterns of conscious understanding, the imagined pattern mistakes dependently co-arisen images for external objects and ideas for essences, clinging to things as if they were stable and really real. The other-dependent pattern is itself dependently co-arisen through the interplay of the different levels of consciousness (the container consciousness and the active consciousnesses) and through the interplay between insight and image in mediating experiences through ideas and words. In its empirical functioning in the world, without insight into its own emptiness and dependent co-arising, this other-dependent pattern supports the projection of ideas and views as if they were validated by the reality of essences encountered by the subjective mind taking a look out at objective things. But once consciousness is converted from its imagined pattern, the other-dependent pattern both supports the fully perfected pattern of awakening to suchness in which mediated meaning is totally absent, and recovers its own basic dependently co-arisen structure in which mediated meaning does occur. It is thus that the bodhisattva functions in the world of ideas and words in cognizance of the all-inclusive contextuality of language and thinking. The fully perfected pattern is awakening to the silence of ultimate meaning and awareness of the immediacy of the direct experience of enlightenment.

These are Buddhist notions to be employed as a "handmaiden" (*ancilla*) to Christian theology, a theology based not on an imagined grasp of essences given in any faith "deposit" or "contained" in any set tradition, but on the converted mind of faith that understands and asserts commitment to the meaning of life in the wisdom of Christ. Mahāyāna theology is not focused on the content to be understood, the Greek *noēta*, but on the mind that understands, for wisdom is a mode of conscious awareness and the wisdom of theology issues from minds familiar with the emptiness and ineffability of all doctrines in their co-arising articulation. Mahāyāna theology argues that all theological models (even a Mahāyāna model) are valid only within their contextuality in terms of the particular conditions in virtue of which they arise. In the words of Maximus Confessor, "the doctrines of the Church are transcended by their own content."

The remainder of this chapter and the next will be devoted to the task of unfolding a Mahāyāna understanding of the Incarnation and the Trinity.

A MAHĀYĀNA CHRISTOLOGY

A Mahāyāna christology will employ the themes of emptiness, dependent co-arising, and the two truths as philosophical insights. The doctrine of emptiness and dependent co-arising focuses on the "horizontal" experience of Christ, interpreting Christ as empty of any essence and engaged in the dependently co-arisen world in all its radical contingency. By itself this doctrine does not present an adequate christology because it fails to articulate Christ's ultimacy and otherness. The doctrine of the two truths emphasizes these "vertical" aspects and presents the meaning of Christ as both ultimate and manifested in the conventional world. A Mahāyāna christology rests on both themes and cannot stand if either is neglected.

Jesus as Empty

In a Mahāyāna understanding of the person of Jesus Christ, he is empty of any essence that might identify him and serve as a definition of his being. This does not mean that one is unable to form any notion of what he was like. The Gospel remembrances of how he acted and what he said serve well enough to depict his person. Yet he has no identifiable selfhood beyond those dependently co-arisen actions and words. There is no selfhood to Jesus at all, for all human beings are empty of any self (*ātman*). Christian doctrine on the person of Christ cannot then be expressed by attempts to define his dual nature or divine personhood.

This does not mean that the Nicean and Chalcedonian doctrines are simply illusory. It is true that the fathers of the church often expressed their understanding of Jesus in terms that a Mahāyānist would immediately reject. But within their Greek philosophical context, the affirmation that Christ was consubstantial with the Father expressed in rather well worked-out language just what Christ meant to the church: Christ is as ultimate and thus as divine as the Father. In terms of theoretical articulation the Chalcedonian teachings have gone about as far as words can go. A Mahāyāna christology would, however, understand the philosophical ontology in which these doctrines evolved not to be binding on all Christians, non-Greek as most of them are today. It would further caution one to be aware of the tendency of Greek philosophic language toward essentialist categories. In a world in which no alternative philosophic paths lay open, the fathers had to express their understanding of Christ in these terms. But to insist on the continuance of their Greek philosophic language in a world of myriad philosophies hardly serves to communicate their original insights. The Chalcedonian doctrine does today tend to encourage a naïve conceptualism about the person of Jesus Christ and hence to preclude direct awareness of meaning in Christ by engaging one in the fabrication of views. It reflects a confidence in words as meaning units that are regarded as secure and beyond falsification, a confidence that many modern philosophers and Christians from other cultures do not share.

The Gospels themselves do not define Christ. He is depicted as completely unconcerned with establishing any self-image or any self-identity. The center of Christ's "being" is constituted by a deep consciousness of the presence of Abba and by a dedication to the rule of God in the world. Jesus can scarcely be understood apart from his relationships to others. Thus Edward Schillebeeckx writes that "there is no a priori definition of the substance of Jesus."[1] Jesus is transparent and never sets himself up as "a second subject" alongside the Father and his coming rule.[2] His total focus is to mirror the presence of God as Abba and to embody the rule of compassion. His being is found in that continuing transparency as the mirror of the Father.[3] In this light one should not expect to be able to uncover the Christ of history from the Christ of faith, and as Albert Schweitzer taught. The success of discovering the true Jesus is not in scholarly reconstructions, but in abandoning such fabrications and following the example of Jesus in serving others, as Schweitzer himself did in serving as a medical missionary in Africa.[4]

Jesus' being is not to be understood as an objectively real essence set over against the believer (or the historian). Rather, his being is the being of emptiness, the negation of all clinging to selfhood and essence in an awareness of the dependently co-arisen being of life in the world. His experience of Abba (direct awareness of ultimate meaning) and his preaching of the rule of God in the world (the urgency of conventional reality) are not just external qualities of his subjectivity. They are constitutive of Jesus as person. That is who he is. The true self is defined not in terms of essence, but only in terms of emptiness and relatedness. *The Ornament of the Scriptures of the Great Vehicle* describes the self of the awakened as follows: "In pure emptiness the awakened acquire the supreme self (*mahaātman*) of selflessness and realize the greatness of the self by discovering the pure self."[5] Vasubandhu explains that this refers to "the highest self in the undefiled state," that is to say, in the realm of meaning in which no discrimination between subject and object occurs.

Rather than seeking an understanding of Jesus in terms of identifiable metaphysical essences or natures that define precisely what we are talking about, we might better be served by concentrating on themes of emptiness and no-self. Nowhere did Jesus as portrayed in the Gospels cling to self (*ātmagrāha*). Neither, then, should doctrine cling to definitions of his being lest, by precluding his mirroring of the Father, one might put ideas of his divine, immutable essence in the place of Abba. The role of Jesus as mediating and bringing faith to speech is often overlooked in a metaphysical disquisition on his dual nature. The mediating of an essentially conceived Christ is not the mediation of the word of the Father from silence, but a mediation between two entities, one human and one divine. Christ becomes a kind of ombudsman pleading the human cause before a divine, managerial presence.

As treated in chapter 2, the Gospels of Matthew and John, the writings of Paul, and the Epistle of James all identify Jesus with wisdom, understanding wisdom to be an immediate awareness of Abba before and beyond all mediated knowledge. Matthew identifies receptivity to wisdom with a childlike disposition unspoiled by learning. Paul understands the wisdom that is Christ to be beyond the development of worldviews, to be the negation of any worldview that attempts to capture salvation in its verbal net. In preaching Christ, he "speaks the wisdom of God in mystery." For him, those who boast in appearances fail to understand because they try to interpret spiritual things in an unspiritual manner. James echoes the Mahāyāna theme of unmediated, nondiscriminative wisdom in its teaching that wisdom does not waver or make distinctions between alternatives. One must not, James writes, be in two minds, trying to figure out for oneself in which direction the proper answer lies. Rejecting the need to ascertain and grasp truth for oneself, James recommends that we receive wisdom from the Lord in simplicity and gratitude. The redaction to the *sēmeia* source in John criticizes the mind that seeks for signs and is a direct refusal to present empirical evidence for the claims or personal status of Jesus. Wisdom in these New Testament authors becomes meaningful only in direct contact with God and cannot be realized through an examination of words that impose an identifiable element between human consciousness and the direct action of God. Wisdom consists, rather, in awareness of Abba, a direct awareness that goes before and comes behind all linguistic attempts to express the gospel. It is an awareness of being in Christ which makes us cry out "Abba, Father!" In none of these examples is there any emphasis on Jesus as "a second subject" beside the Father. His action is always to manifest the Father in the deeds and actions of his life. It is significant that Jesus never wrote anything. It was his life and actions that are remembered and shared in through the Gospel accounts and the earliest liturgies.

The constant motif of the Gospels is to call for conversion away from a sign-clinging mind that would equate faith with any one, correct position, to a mind that is receptive of the Spirit and aware of Abba. Jesus disappears in the face of the reality he proclaims. In Ch'an terms, he is a finger pointing at the moon. Look then at the moon; do not investigate the structure of the finger, examining its length and width, whether it is well formed or arthritic. Propositional theology has often played the role of a manicurist, sprucing up the human nails and trimming the divine cuticles without taking notice that the moon of Christian awakening was fast setting. Jesus remains silent even in the face of his accusers. Encounters with Jesus recorded in the scriptures do not portray him as demanding a theoretical assent to his own privileged position among people; he even refuses to accept the appelation of goodness. The constant stress is on radical conversion to the rule of Abba in the world. The meaning of Jesus is not found in analysis of his constituent nature, any more than that which is mirrored can be discovered by analyzing the nature of the mirror.

Neither is Jesus' resurrection to be interpreted as an empirical validation of his divine status. The risen Christ in all his glory does not once again confront the assembled Sanhedrin to demonstrate the validity of his life. The accounts of the appearances of the risen Christ are not intended to demonstrate the empirical truth of Christian claims. Rather, they are modeled on Jewish conversion motifs and represent the disclosure experiences of the ultimate validity of Jesus, who now comes, not in his empirical presence, but as "the light of the world."[6] They are the final disappearance of Jesus in the face of the reality he proclaimed.[7] The Easter experience is one of disclosure and enlightenment, and the Gospel accounts follow a Jewish conversion model of illumination. Schillebeeckx writes:

> In view of this already existing Jewish tradition of conversion by way of illumination (frequently pictured in a light-vision), the notion — or the possibility — is already here that the marvelous occurrence of a conversion, not now to the revelation of God in the Law but to the revelation of God in Jesus, has been expressed in the model of a conversion vision, which in essence signifies a "disclosure of God," epiphany and thus "enlightenment."[8]

This does not mean that the Easter experience was a purely subjective, psychological experience without any basis in life. Just as any objective interpretation is confined within the imagined pattern of illusory consciousness, so is any subjective interpretation. Mystic meaning is not understood within the subject-object pattern of consciousness: the experience of the Christ meaning is a direct, mystic experience of God who acted in Jesus, and an experience of Jesus as alive and exalted beyond death.[9] But that reality was not and is not a manifestation of the empirical Jesus as having "reconstituted his molecular structure,"[10] as having revivified his physiological and psychological being. If the presence of Christ is not the presence of an essence, then the resurrection is not the restoration of that essence. Its reality is eschatological and definitive, issuing in his exaltation by the Father and the practice of the rule of God's compassion in the world.[11]

The resurrection is, then, not a proof of this empirical victory over the grave in terms of an imagined pattern of consciousness. Its victory is precisely in the abandoning of that pattern through the attainment of enlightenment and wisdom in Christ. Death has no sting because Christ as risen and exalted is ultimate and not bound within the samsaric world of constant suffering and fear. The me-consciousness that worries over its future security is overcome through Abba and the practice of the rule of compassion.

The manifestation of Jesus to Paul on the road to Damascus is empty of any doctrinal content, for "the substance of the manifestation is remarkably 'vacant' or at least extremely meager; it has to be filled out by the subsequent account of the concrete, historical series of events in the life of Paul itself" (Schillebeeckx).[12] The conceptual attachment to images and ideas of who Jesus is remains just that, an attachment to images and ideas. It issues out of an imagined pattern of understanding that would demand a "factual" basis for its assent. Functioning within such an illusory pattern, the mind's constant demand is for a firm and solid assurance that goes beyond this fleeting world to uncover some religious certitude not subject to the verbal change and development entailed in all doctrinal understanding. While Christian thinkers have been quick to refute the naïve empiricism of the nineteenth century, they themselves often indulge in a variety of supernatural empiricism, demanding to have a supernatural assurance of the facts of the case, facts that if discovered would obviate the immediacy of awareness of Abba and cloud the mirror that is Jesus. To live in Christ is to live in that grace by which one abides in the world of change and impermanence, even to suffering and death, in awareness of Abba.

The Greeks could think of nothing more appropriate than to define the being of Jesus as both human and divine. "Divinity" was their term for ultimate meaning, an ultimate they themselves had experienced in their liturgical and personal participation in the life of Christ. But as contexts change and worlds shift their cultural patterns, other notions may express the ultimacy of Jesus with at least an equal validity. In a Mahāyāna christology the deepest insight into the meaning of Christ is articulated in terms of emptiness (and dependent co-arising). In this philosophical context any attribution of essence to the being of Christ is a denigration of Christ's meaning and would immediately be characterized as illusory fabrication. To declare Christ empty is not then to negate Christ's ultimacy, but to affirm it.

Jesus as Dependently Co-Arisen

In Mahāyāna thought, emptiness is articulated through the doctrine of dependent co-arising. As Nāgārjuna taught, emptiness is identical with dependent co-arising. To use the terminology of Western Scholasticism, emptiness and dependent co-arising are convertible: both describe the identical reality from different, complementary aspects. Because all things arise in mutual dependence, they are empty of any set essence; because all things have no essence and are empty, they exist in dependency on one another. The empty Jesus takes on his historical meaning through the dependently co-arisen course of his life and death. It is this meaning, expressed by the passion and resurrection accounts and experienced in the liturgies, that took form in the Gospel remembrance of Jesus and the gathering of Christians as church to do the Eucharist. The identity of Jesus was constructed from what he taught and did, from how he died and rose from the dead.

Those events were dependently co-arisen. They arose from the context of human affairs and reflected the culture in which Jesus lived. There has been a tendency to subtract the concrete historical and cultural context from considerations of the life of Jesus so as to discern an overarching divine plan guiding his every act and word. With the passage of the persecuted church from its primitive eschatological world-negation to its post-Constantine acceptance of world history,[13] Christian thinkers increasingly came to interpret the life of Christ in the light of a prearranged divine plan. From a Mahāyāna perspective such a teleological arrangement would be an example of the illusory projection of human desires to identify the clear and essential reality of things and to find security therein. The construction of such a plan and the placement of the death and resurrection of Christ as the key elements within that august project witness only to the tenacity of human attempts to keep things well arranged and in control. Indeed, if the divine Jesus were not in control, how then can human beings ever hope to be in control? In this view his passion is not really brought about by the Jewish religious hierarchy or the Roman authorities. It is the fulfillment of God's plan in which Jesus dies as a sacrifice for sinful humanity to right the balance between God and the devil. The Father becomes the sacrificer of his Son, albeit for the altruistic reason of saving erring men and women. In such a theology, no matter how one might define the humanity of Jesus, it necessarily remains above the flux and contingency of human experience.

If, on the other hand, Jesus is empty, then his being is dependently co-arisen. As human he was subject to the web of human contingency, change, and suffering no less than any other human being. All things arise in mutual dependency and Jesus was as immersed as any other in the flow of human history. As Christian Duquoc notes, "an absolute ideality, with no consideration of the concrete historical contingency and limitation in it, cannot be a foundation for christology."[14] Jesus' living and, more pointedly, his dying are not the unfolding of some supernatural plan, as if all the varied people in the happenings of his life were moved by the unseen hand of a divine presence. No programmed divine drama unfolds in the course of his life. Indeed it is climactically in Jesus' dying that God "silently reveals himself in Jesus' historically helpless failure on the cross."[15] At the mercy of the events of his times, Jesus preaches a conversion that entails a leaving behind not only of wealth and power (*atmya*), but also of all the psychological underpinnings of self-consciousness (*ātman*), whether they be financial security, fame, or a comforting theological position.

All this seems perplexing, for it leaves no firm peg on which to hang our theological hats. It offers no assurance that our lives, Christian though they may be, will not end in similar failure. One might suffer all for the sake of the assured value of faith, but when that value itself offers no identifiable assurance, when one has to rely solely on an ever-silent God, one is tempted to substitute the imagined security of cherished beliefs in the place of abandonment to Abba in the web of dependently co-arising events. The temptation is to cling to false security under a veil of imagined divine approval in order to escape human contingency in a dependently co-arisen existence. There is, however, no escape from humanness, from the utter contingency of who and how we are. The first truth taught by Śākyamuni is that all is suffering, that nothing can escape from the constant flow of being toward nothingness. As Karl Marx clearly saw, religion can dull the mind to its predicament by erecting a superstructure of eternal values and truths over against men and women, who are then assured of an eventual reward for present pain and distress. But such a religion has little to do with the Jesus who met failure in both his living and his dying, who converted but few to his ideal of the rule and kingdom of God, and who died a condemned criminal.

Absolute thoughts are illusions that negate the dependently co-arisen structure of all human endeavors. We are bound within our particular languages and particular cultures. We not only form those languages and cultures, but are in turn formed by them. Neither the dying of Jesus on the cross nor his rising from the dead are reversals of cultural relativity or of physical contingency: the fact is that our bodies grow old, become sick, and literally fall apart. Paul presents his theology of the cross to the Corinthian factions not as an alternate and more Christian viewpoint that might assuage their troubled and contentious minds. Rather, he rubs their fractious noses in the bare fact of dying—of Jesus' undeserved death on the cross and of our own unavoidable dying. In the light of such dependently co-arisen facts, the boasting and claims of the Corinthian factions to be already glorified and fulfilled ring false and presumptuous. Jesus himself was unable to avoid the karmic web of political necessities imagined by the Jewish hierarchy and the Roman authorities. He was quite simply murdered, one of that vast number of the "disappeared" who throughout history have fallen victim to the lust and hatred of truth-clingers. Dom Gregory Dix writes:

> It is the teaching of the New Testament that the kingdom of God among men comes in and through the events of history, through what

men make of real life as it has to be lived "here and now." Jesus of Nazareth was not a remote and academic sage teaching a serene philosophy of the good life. A man who would be Messiah handled the most explosive thing in Near Eastern politics. The world misunderstood Messiahship; but he died on a "political" charge and so did every Christian martyr in the next three centuries.[16]

If Jesus had not been so immersed in the conditions of his time, he could not have been human at all. There is no "independent" human existence apart from one's society and culture. Even the solitary hermit constructs his or her social identity in opposition to some cultural situation — the world of alienation and sin. The teachings and career of Jesus take on their meaning (and serve to "define" who he is) within the web of human history, within the milieu of cultural illusions, greed, and anger.[17] Jesus did not die because of some preordained plan. He died as the victim of society's clinging to an imagined religious truth, perceived as a dangerous prophet who might upset the delicate balance of social and political forces. As Israel before him suffered in the political struggles of its more powerful neighbors, he fell to that hard-headed *realpolitik* that reduces all meanings to the functional illusions of power.

Jesus' eschatological meaning is found both in an awareness of the ultimate validity of Abba consciousness and in the rule of God's compassion in the world, despite the recognition that such wisdom in fact does not hold sway. Christian eschatology is not simply an attempt to avoid human contingency in the hope of a millenarian reversal. Rather, it is an attempt to maintain the Christ meaning as ultimate and definitive despite cultural denials of human contingency in favor of ideological faith (whether religious or political). It is an affirmation of that meaning as relevant and true within an awarensss of our being as dependently co-arisen.

A Mahāyāna Christology sees Jesus not in terms of any essence or any dual nature. The notions of essence and nature are, within this philosophical culture, branded as illusions and seen as projections of a deluded consciousness that has failed to gain insight into the reality of life just as it is. Emptiness and dependent co-arising are coextensive, both describing the suchness of human existence. But this is not all there is to say. A christological model of emptiness and dependent co-arising sketches a rather Antiochene model of Jesus' humanity, since they focus on the "horizontal" understanding of Jesus as he appears in our history and experience. But, as Mādhyamika philosophy insists, the horizontal theme of emptiness and dependent co-arising must be complemented by the doctrine of the two truths. The two truths of ultimate meaning and worldly convention express the "vertical" dimension in which the silence of ultimate meaning remains completely other from worldly convention but is articulated by worldly and conventional language. Hence an interpretation of Jesus through the doctrine of the two truths complements the discussion above.

Christ as Embodying the Two Truths

The Mahāyāna masters attempted to understand the relationship between direct, mystic awareness and its articulation through the doctrine of
the two truths. In both Mādhyamika and Yogācāra the "two truths" refer
to the manifestation of truth in human experience and thought. They do
not address the question of whether one could attain truth. All Buddhists
assumed that one could indeed realize truth and embody it in practice —
that is precisely what Śākyamuni had done. The question entertained by
Nāgārjuna was that, since ultimate truth is empty and not identifiable in
terms of essences, how then can dependently co-arisen discourse manifest
it at all?

The truth of ultimate meaning is understood to be ineffable and yet
experienced. It is always the central contentless content of awakening. Verbal conceptualizations of doctrine always presuppose and draw on this non-
thematized experience, and conventional truth is the skillful enunciation
of that experience. But conventional ideas, images, and words do not draw
upon that ultimate experience as if they were properties of it. Their source
lies not in the experience itself, which remains always beyond ideas, images,
and words, but in the dependently co-arising world of discourse with its
myriad of historical and cultural signs and symbols. There is no direct
continuity between the ultimate experience of awakening and the skillful
doctrines evolved to lead others to that experience. Doctrine is not a road
map because awakening is not a final destination. Doctrine is not an upward
trail because awakening is not a mountain peak to be scaled. Doctrine gains
its validity by being skillfully articulated by an awakened bodhisattva or
buddha in the light of particular circumstances and based on particular
contexts to lead others toward awakening and peace.

The New Testament understanding of meaning in Christ was that he
embodied ultimate meaning in his contingent, dependently co-arisen living
and dying. Hence Jesus was confessed as Christ and God, for to religious
Jews God alone could be conceived as ultimate. The ultimacy of Jesus as
Christ flows from this identification with the Father and constitutes Jesus
as Spirit-filled and as the word and wisdom of God. He is seen as the
concrete speaking (*sermo*) of the ineffable God, the enunciation of God to
humans.[18] To repeat the incisive remark of Ignatius of Antioch, "There is
one God, who revealed himself through Jesus Christ, his son, who is his
word emerging from silence."[19] In the Johannine theme it is Jesus who
enunciates God whom nobody has ever seen (Jn. 1:18), for although "God
is ineffable, the Word declares him to us."[20]

Nevertheless, the word of the Father is not a representation of the divine
being, which remains in silence, unheard by any ear and unseen by any eye.
Jesus' identity with the Father does not imply that his spoken words derive
directly from the Father. They come from the dependently co-arisen and
conventional world of his engagement with others. Jesus' speaking does not

domesticate God and fit his Abba experience into linguistic packages.

It is in this context that the church fathers distinguished between theology and economy.[21] Theology referred to God and, since God is beyond human knowing, cannot be expressed in words. Economy referred to the divine dispensation of the Incarnation, for Jesus is the speaking of God, the verbal embodiment of ultimate meaning. In a Mahāyāna interpretation this dispensation is not any divine plan that might be discerned under the events of human affairs. There is no divine hand moving events from the backstage of the human drama. Rather, the economic dispensation is the dependently co-arisen world itself in all its fleeting emptiness. The dependently co-arising world is a hidden dispensation, not because it lies behind the world of experience but because the imagined pattern of understanding covers over that dependently co-arisen world with its illusions, and occludes insight into its impermanence and emptiness. In Mahāyāna terminology, worldly convention (*saṃvṛti*) covers over and hides (*vṛ*) the original dispensation of the world as dependently co-arisen and, in the absence of awakening, establishes images of a projected world that simply does not exist.

It was Jesus as embodying the presence of God as Abba and as calling for commitment to the practice of the rule of compassion in the world that gathered the scattered disciples into a community. The basis of that community was, however, empty of doctrinal content, which had to be "supplied out of the concrete life of the Church."[22] The basic experience of Jesus as the risen Christ is ultimate, ineffable, and witnessed in the confession that Jesus is Lord, the only doctrinal content of the Gospel of John. Subsequently, the full implications of that experience were fleshed out in the kerygma and modeled on the remembered preaching and career of Jesus in the individual communities of the first Christian century. The resurrection was presented by these early communities as a doctrinally empty, vertical experience of ultimate meaning in Jesus alive as Christ and enunciated horizontally in the kerygma.[23] The transcendent dimension of Jesus, expressed through his experience of Abba, is ultimate truth as an awareness of existence-just-as-it-is (*yathāvad-bhāvikatā*), shorn of theoretical constructs. Such an awareness is a joyful celebration of the meaning of Christ in the face of death, for it is an acceptance of the reality of Christ as empty. The incarnational dimension is conventional truth as an awareness "as-far-as-the-limits-of existence" (*yāvad-bhāvikatā*), expressible in a host of languages and cultural philosophies, all of which may serve as words from silence. The understanding of Christ as the worldly and conventional speaking of God entails the acceptance of Christ as dependently co-arisen in both his full historical particularity and our ever-changing historical situations.

In chapter 8 (above), *The Analysis of the Middle Path and Extremes* was discussed as offering a philosophical model of conventional truth as a manifestation of the ultimate. Its theme of "worldly convention as manifestation" (*udbhavanā-saṃvṛti*) denotes a contingent expression of silence. Because embodied in the historical, contingent person of Jesus, the meaning of the Incarnation is itself *saṃvṛti*, for how else could truth be realized except through particular events and ideas in all their relativity? One must, however, be constantly vigilant: in a Mahāyāna philosophical perspective, conventional expression (*saṃvṛt(t)i*) is both the embodiment of truth (*vṛt*) and the occlusion (*vṛ*) of truth. Words not only disclose but, in the imagined pattern of consciousness, cover over and occlude the experiences they intend to express, precluding others from participating in that experience. The presence of Jesus in history shares in the ambiguity of all concrete and particular words, but that does not imply any scandal of particularity, for ultimate meaning is never without embodiment in dependently co-arisen and historical words. The ultimate truth of the gospel, as of the Buddha-dharma, is not an aloof universal essence that transcends all particular expressions. Rather, it is realized and becomes true only in concrete events and persons.

Yet this interpretation of the contingent, conventional expression of ultimate truth does not express the full meaning of the Christian confession of Christ as the wisdom of the Father. Here it is simply a question of a conventional expression of truth, of an understanding that is freed from the pattern of imaginative knowing. Such an interpretation reminds one of early christologies like that of the Q tradition, which depicted Jesus as the last in a long line of prophets. It recalls the Nestorian theology of the indwelling Logos, which taught that Jesus became the Christ by the presence of the Spirit. Such a thesis has recently been reaffirmed in the christology of G. W. H. Lampe, the eminent Patristic scholar.[24] He presents Jesus as a man with a particularly deep experience of God, but in no wise himself ultimate or definitive. Such explanations disregard or minimalize the traditional confession of Christ as ultimate and divine.

A more adequate Mahāyāna model can perhaps be found in Asaṅga's *Summary of the Great Vehicle* (in the passage given in chap. 8, above). To repeat: "Because this doctrine [of the Great Vehicle] causes purity, it is not merely imagined. Because it is the outflow of the pure Dharma Realm, it is not dependently co-arisen."[25] Asaṅga thematizes the enunciation of ultimate meaning as the purity of doctrine flowing from the ultimate realm (*dharmadhātu-niṣyanda*). Such doctrinal discourse flows from a preverbal and direct experience of ultimate meaning. The focus here is not on conventional, human understanding but on the harmony of doctrine with the ultimate. Although such doctrine is not absolute in terms of its verbal expression, yet it is the direct outflow from the realm of ultimate meaning. A theology that adopts this model would interpret Jesus as the word of God flowing from silence and as one with the Father. The significance of Christ is not then merely conventional or culture-bound, for the experience of meaning in Christ flows from the wisdom of nondiscrimination. The identity of Christ with the Father is clearly entailed by the adoption of this interpretation of doctrine, the word, flowing from the ultimate realm, the Father. Thus the Christ meaning will transcend every christology, but that transcendence will be found only in specific theological attempts to embody verbally the Christ meaning, and never in an ideological clinging to any one system of thought.

CHRISTOLOGY HIGH AND LOW

This sketch of Jesus as empty of self and dependently co-arisen, as the embodiment of the two truths, does not necessitate a "low" christology, which would understand Jesus merely as a great man, a prophet, a beloved son of God. Much of the problematic in christological thinking turns upon the apparent contradiction of affirming Jesus' actual historical life with claims that he is also somehow divine. Attempts to treat his humanity honestly often have in fact led to reductionist christology, for they refuse, with reason, to function in the supernaturalist or metaphysical framework of the traditional christologies,[26] and cannot then avail themselves of the theoretical tools of that tradition to hold in healthy tension the two dimensions of Christ.

One such attempt is that of S. W. Sykes, who states that the structure of christology is not one of two storeys, one natural and one supernatural, but of two stories, two languages, the historical and the theological interpretations of that history.[27] The confession of Christ as divine was arrived at, Sykes claims, by theologically interpreting the bare fact of history. In order to maintain one's "intellectual honesty," the first task is seen as determining the historical picture of Jesus as clearly as possible, and then superimposing a theological language on that basis as "second level statements."

But such an approach does not seem to reflect the faith confession of the primitive or later communities, for they do not simply weave theological positions about Christ upon the empirical, historical Jesus. Rather, these confessions as presented in the New Testament and in the church fathers are based upon disclosure experiences whereby people come to share in the experience of God as Abba and commit themselves to the rule of God in the world. The faith confession of Jesus as Christ, as Spirit-filled and divine, does not take place in two separate moments, but in one disclosure and manifestation of ultimate truth in Jesus Christ. In the light of such experiences, Christians indeed interpret Jesus as divine, but that is not therefore a second-level affirmation from any bare bones of history. It is, rather, the verbalization of an experience of God as Abba realized through Jesus.

By contrast, the faith interpretation of Jesus as empty of essence and enmeshed in the contingent world does not imply a reductionist christology, for it is by understanding Jesus as empty and transparent that he is allowed to be Spirit-filled and to mediate the Spirit experience to others. It is not by hypostatizing Jesus that his functioning as divine word is allowed to operate upon human understanding. The Spirit was not sent until Jesus was exalted because it was only then clear to the disciples that Jesus was indeed empty and transparent. Only then was his life and death actually experienced as mirroring God as Abba.

A high christology does not necessitate the metaphysical terms of Chalcedon, although it does not negate them either. The present Mahāyāna christology takes that explanation as theory, Christian theory to wit, but theory nevertheless. It constantly stands guard against any imagined interpretation of that theory and demands that Jesus be understood as both empty and dependently co-arisen.

The basic concern of traditional christology has been to maintain focus on Jesus as both truly God and truly human. As the latter apparently is not as problematic as the former,[28] the emphasis of the church has most frequently been upon the divine nature of Christ, to the point where it has at times subsumed the human. Even within the New Testament this emphasis is at times evident, and E. Käsemann can intelligently argue that the Gospel of John presents Jesus as a God striding through human history.[29] Such a tendency, brought to logical term by Apollinaris, was rejected as docetism by church councils. But although rejected as explicit doctrine, the image of Jesus as some kind of divine personage (*theios anēr*) remains.[30] The traditional doctrine has been unable to identify these two dimensions within the same Jesus, for, even though defining him as one person in two natures, that person remains a divine person, and hence the human nature is the human nature of a divine person, although it thereby renders him also a human person. The balancing act can be at times dizzying.

The Mādhyamika identification of emptiness and dependent co-arising can perhaps offer an approach to express faith in Christ in a clearer and more meaningful manner. Jesus as empty of any essence whatsoever is an ineffable outflow from the ultimate realm. But as emptiness is identical with dependent co-arising, so Jesus is enmeshed in the web of the constantly flowing and changing events of his time. He is ultimate and absolute inasmuch as he is totally empty, and human and relative inasmuch as he is totally interrelated with the world. Here the two notions of emptiness and dependent co-arising need not be grounded within any concept of divine personhood, for in Buddhist Mahāyāna thinking they are already identical descriptions of the same wisdom insight and there is no need of any *tertium quid* to bring them together. The doctrine that flows from such wisdom, however, is a verbally expressed, conventional doctrine. The heresy of docetism, rejected in regard to the person of Christ, still sneaks in under the guise of doctrine presented as absolute statements of the way things are with God. According to this mind-set, words do not function in human other-dependence, but are taken as semantic images of the divine.

In their analysis of truth the Mahāyāna thinkers tried to maintain a balance between ultimate truth and conventional expression. So the interpretation of the Incarnation through the two truths confesses that Jesus is ultimate meaning embodied in contingently arisen circumstances. It need admit no literal or supernatural virgin birth or divine cohabitation to bolster the "divinity" of Christ, for Christ is divine and empty only in virtue of being fully and completely dependently co-arisen. Whereas the pair of terms, divine and human, function as opposites in the traditional account, emptiness and dependent co-arising are convertible, complementary, each fully interpenetrating the other.

Any picture of Jesus as a divine figure standing over and externally confronting the believer clouds over the gospel remembrance of Jesus as mirroring the Father and as totally committed to the rule of God on earth. An imagined understanding of Jesus serves not to open up the mind toward Abba and one's neighbor, but to chain it within the religious prison of an illusory orthodoxy. It is, rather, by pondering the gospel and identifying with Jesus in conversion from me-consciousness to a commitment to others in awareness of Abba that the meaning of Jesus as Christ is experienced, not by clinging to religious ideas under the disguise of defending tradition. By internalizing the Christ meaning within one's own interiority through contact with Abba, one embodies that meaning—not by imagining personal encounters with an imagined Jesus figure. Divine hero worship remains as illusory as any other kind of hero worship.

Such an understanding can be seen as a reductionist christology only by those who judge the absence of the traditional metaphysical terms to be an essential defect and who tie all Christian thinking to Greek ontology. A Mahāyāna christology does not reduce Jesus to a prophet in whom God dwells, or to a humanitarian preacher of universal values, but affirms his ultimate significance as word and wisdom of the Father precisely in, and not in contrast to, the actual historical events of his living and dying, for emptiness implies dependent co-arising. That ultimate meaning could not and does not derive from those ambiguous historical events, but only from the center of historical events is its meaning and truth ever realized. The Christ meaning as Abba-centered and committed to others, as empty of essence and dependently co-arisen, derives from the center of his being as empty, as the "non-being" of any imagined essence, and from his total immersion in the sufferings and dying that all humans experience. There is no need to define the specific difference between Jesus and other human beings. That would entail once again a metaphysics of essence. Rather, all human beings, including Jesus, are empty of essence. The mystical body of Christ, that is to say, the community of believing Christians, recognizes Christ's ongoing Lordship as head of that body in which all participate. Through realization of no-self and life in Christ, the focus is on Abba and his rule in the world, not on the philosophical differences between a metaphysical Christ and metaphysical human nature. Jesus as Christ is not the mediator of divine nature to human nature. Jesus does not bring a predetermined verbal revelation about divinity to human beings, but announces a preverbal mystic awareness that reverses and challenges others to reverse all self-clinging (*ātman-grāha*) and to live in the body of Christ, the conventional and dependently co-arisen community of the church. In the Gospels and the liturgies of the community, Jesus mediates the direct, immediate experience of God as Abba. Rather than being defined as "consubstantial" with the Father, Jesus may better be described as "nonsubstantial" with the Father.

The Christ preached by the church is, then, definitive because ultimate and not because Christ's historical contingency was better than any other historical contingency. A Mahāyāna christology holds the "divine" and the "human" within Jesus in the same dynamic tension as expressed through the identification of emptiness with dependent co-arising. Thus Christian doctrine, so understood, is ultimate as the embodiment of awareness of Abba, but as verbalized and language-formed it can make no such claim. The ultimacy of Jesus as Christ does not then imply the ultimacy of Christian teachings among all world religions. Arnold Toynbee correctly remarked that, until Christianity abandoned its exclusiveness, it would gain no hearing outside its own circle.[31] Such an option of affirming ultimacy for the meaning of Christ, while not claiming the same for any particular Christian enunciation of that meaning, is not open to the traditional theology of the hypostatic union, for that theology attempts to define the way things actually are in the deity, and Jesus is thus identified as the second person of a rather static Greek God. By contrast, a Mahāyāna interpretation of the meaning of Christ will transcend every christology, but will be enunciated only within totally conventional attempts to bring it to speech, and never in the ideological clinging to any one system of thought.

The meaning of Christ is not, however, exhausted by the doctrine of the Incarnation. It further led the early Christian church to express its understanding through the doctrine of the Trinity, the topic of the next chapter.

11

A Mahāyāna Understanding of the Trinity

The Christian doctrine of the Trinity was not a late addition. It grew out of the early Christian awareness of meaning in Jesus as Christ. In the early Jewish church of apostolic times, insistence on strict monotheism was too strong to allow for any direct equation of Jesus with God. The experience of meaning in Christ led the early apostolic fathers to offer the trinitarian model of "a man putting forth his thought and his spirit in external activity."[1] This model of an "economic" Trinity focused on the experience Christians had of God in this new "economy" or "dispensation" of salvation. But it did lessen Jesus' deity in comparison with that of the Father: God the Father contained the Logos as an inner word, which he expressed in the person of Jesus. This word was directed to human beings as the speaking of the hidden things of God. "What is invisible in the Son is the Father, and what is visible in the Father is the Son," states Irenaeus.[2] In this schema, the Spirit was conceived as the wisdom of the Father enlivening human beings by raising them to life in God.

"Economic" trinitarianism did not in the end carry the day, for it seemed to imply that the Son and the Spirit were subordinate to the Father, who alone was really God, just as a person's thought and spirit were not quite as real as the person. Nevertheless, this model does seem to have caught the basic pattern of the early Christian experience of life in the Spirit through Jesus as manifesting Abba. It did not, however, prove adequate in the context of Greek thinking with its emphasis upon defining essences, for this interpretation attributed a lesser share in the divine essence to the Son and the Spirit. An ontology of essences can think only in terms of essences and attributes of those essences; thus the Son and Spirit could be only attributes of God. The emerging trinitarian theology shifted to focus on the essential "being" of God and attempted with increasing success to construct a philosophical framework to objectify in clear terms the felt experience of meaning in Christ. But the Greek context is only one among many, and

perhaps the use of different conceptual tools may make it possible to reclaim economic trinitarianism as a valid reflection on the meaning of God
as Trinity. In order for this to happen, however, Christian trinitarian understanding must avoid all implication of subordinating Jesus or the Spirit
to the Father. Again Mahāyāna can perhaps provide some assistance,
through its understanding of the mind of wisdom.

As described in chapter 10, the experience of ultimate meaning in Christ
flowed from Christ's being completely empty and transparent, as the mirror
wisdom of the Father. In Yogācāra terms, the pattern of such an understanding of wisdom is thematized in the doctrine of the three bodies of
awakening (*buddha-trikāya*). The ultimacy of the experience of that awakening, of wisdom is the embodiment of the essence (*svabhāvika-kāya*),[3]
experienced by direct contact and never expressible in language. The joyful
experiencing of that ultimacy is the embodiment of experiencing (*saṃbho-
gika-kāya*) that essence, which flows into compassion and teaching. And the
transforming aspect of that experience is the embodiment of transformation
(*nirmāṇika-kāya*) in the actual occurrence of conversion, both social and
personal.

This Yogācāra scheme of understanding ultimate meaning functions not
by analyzing concepts of what wisdom might mean, but by identifying and
grounding the genesis of such meaning within religious consciousness. As
such, the employment of this pattern can clarify the Christian experience
of the Trinity.

Central here is the understanding of Jesus as the embodiment of the
experience of awakening (*buddha-saṃbhogika-kāya*): his life and meaning
were identified both with the experience of God as Abba and with commitment to the rule of God's compassion in the world. This is the understanding sketched in chapter 10—Jesus as empty and as dependently co-
arisen, as the embodiment of the two truths of ultimate meaning and
worldly convention. In terms that parallel the doctrine of the two truths,
The Interpretation of the Buddha Land explains the two aspects of this embodiment of experience: "There are two aspects to the embodiment of
experience. The first is the embodiment of one's own experience, . . . while
the second is the embodiment of experience for others, so that . . . all others
might experience joy in doctrine."[4]

In the New Testament confession of Jesus as Lord, not only does Jesus
experience God as Abba, but he teaches his disciples to pray to God as
their Father also, and enjoins upon them the practice of the rule of God
in the world. He "is the man whose joy and pleasure is in God himself."[5]
But his own experience of unshakable awareness of Abba is directed to the
full realization of the eschatological rule of God among humans. As previously explained, Jesus embodies the two truths in both vertical and horizontal dimensions. In like manner, the application of the Mahāyāna
doctrine of the embodiment of experience includes both dimensions, and
hence the understanding of Jesus as the embodiment of experience repeats

the themes of Jesus as empty, as dependently co-arisen, and as embodying the two truths.

It was because the New Testament communities came to understand themselves within the Christ meaning that they confessed Jesus as Lord. But their experience of Jesus was not a confrontational meeting with a savior figure, it was a conversion of consciousness away from clinging to self, to a deep awareness of God as Abba and the consequent commitment to transform the world into the compassionate rule of God—patterned after that of Jesus as remembered in liturgy and gospel. Their experience is modeled on and flows from that of Jesus, but it is not focused upon any actual presence of an empirical person standing in front of the believer.

It is thus that the presence of Jesus in sacrament and word continues within the present-day communities, for the resurrection faith does not involve a clinging to or confrontation with the empirical presence of Jesus, whether in his body or in our imaginations. It might be comforting to imagine oneself walking with Jesus, but that is only a metaphor and runs the risk of overshadowing the very experience of ultimate meaning that Jesus is all about, in favor of a religiously imagined hero worship. The liturgy and kerygma of the church are directed toward the realization of an Easter enlightenment that can transform our consciousness and, with that, the world we construct based upon that consciousness. It is an experience of the emptiness and dependent co-arising of all our notions and endeavors that frees one for awareness of God beyond discriminative concepts and transparently embodies the rule of compassion in the world of hard politics.

This transformation of consciousness into Abba awareness and compassion is the basis for the confession of the Spirit, who is the embodiment of transformation. In the tradition, it is the Spirit who transforms the mind of flesh and brings it to enlightenment and conversion through grace. Only in the Spirit can one say that Jesus is Lord, for the Spirit brings to awareness the immanent presence and ultimacy of God as going before and leading the mind to awakening in Christ. Such a faith affirmation cannot truly be made unless a conversion and turning around of the mind from self takes place. It is the Spirit who inspires the prophets and scripture writers, and their words are not simply illusory and discriminative, but flow directly from that awareness of Jesus as risen, of Abba as the center of Jesus' being. Transformation through the Spirit (*nirmāṇika-kāya*) to the experience of Jesus (*saṃbhoga-kāya*) as risen is based and founded upon an awareness of the ultimacy of Abba, for the Father is the embodiment of the essence (*svabhāvika-kāya*) as the foundational horizonless horizon of all conscious meaning, the fulfillment of the original orientation of the mind toward an ongoing, deepening awareness of who we are, where we come from, and where we go. The Father is, then, the ineffable content of wisdom, enun- ciated in and through Jesus and transforming our consciousness through the Spirit. The experience is unitary, for it is the one ultimate God embodied in the mind as foundation, experience, and transformation.

The Father is the support (*āśraya*) for that experience of ultimate meaning and for its transforming action. He is the original ground to which that conversion from illusory clinging turns and the immediate presence in which the mind abides. Drawing out the implications of the Mahāyāna Christology of chapter 10, focus here turns to the Father and the Spirit as the embodiment of the ineffable essence and of personal and social transformation.

ABBA, FATHER

The foundational content of Jesus' experience is Abba. The meaning of "Abba," however, has always been quite intractable to theoretical analysis. What does it mean to be directly and immediately aware of Abba? The Yogācāra analogue is the originally present objective of wisdom (*prakṛti-vyavadāna*), whose content is not amenable to verbal enunciation. It has no identifiable features that one might fasten onto and that might serve to delineate it, for it is unlimited. It is not possible to verbalize it in any way whatsoever until one has experienced it. And even then, any words chosen to describe it serve only as intimations of its contours.

What grounds are there, then, for regarding the content of the Easter experience as the ultimacy of Abba, as a personal father caring for his children? The Mahāyānists, good Buddhists as they were, never made such an affirmation, for Buddhist thought does not function within a theistic context. When the question of a creator god comes up under the name of the Almighty (*maheśvara*), it is briskly refuted, for no *dharma*, even the most supreme, can be conceived as possibly being ultimate. Did Jesus and the early Christian communities engage in images of a personal God only because they belonged to a Jewish tradition and were culturally of a theistic temper? What on earth does it mean to say that God is Abba, when he obviously fails to perform expected fatherly deeds on behalf of his children in the world? It is quite all right to say that no sparrow falls without our Father's knowledge, but he does not in any manner break its fall or save it from crushing itself on the hard surface of the earth!

The experience of the Christian community after Easter was addressed to the problem, for that community moved within the same tradition that had given rise to the anguished questioning of Agur, Job, and Qoheleth. The Christian community had witnessed the unjust execution of Jesus and well knew that God does not save from human distress. Nevertheless, in affirming Jesus as Lord, that community witnessed to its faith in the unshakable faithfulness of Abba. Despite suffering and despite death, despite the absence of any power validation in the face of human contingency, Jesus affirmed God as Abba; and his disciples, enlightened by his exaltation, reaffirmed that faith.

Yet there is no empirical evidence that they were not simply mistaken and merely projecting their subconscious desires for happiness upon a silent universe.[6] If one actually expects God to demonstrate his fatherhood in an observable manner by saving his children from suffering and dying, one might conclude, with Woody Allen, that, although God does exist, he is an underachiever.[7]

But through a Mahāyāna understanding of emptiness and dependent co-arising, the question is reformulated. No longer is the immutable being of God set off in contrast to the contingent, changing world. The dependent co-arising of being-in-the-world is coterminous and identical with emptiness and insight into ultimate meaning. The very arising of all things in interdependency is itself directly and immediately the presence of Abba. To an awakened mind, the final and ultimate cessation (*nirvāṇa*) is itself the realm of suffering (*saṃsāra*). Human death is not the negation of life, but the dependently co-arisen ending of present embodied existence. One must not expect Abba to come to the rescue of *ātman* consciousness, for such an expectancy is illusory and imagined. Abba does not come to the rescue of bodily or mental anguish. Abba simply is not a *deus ex machina*. The Old Testament skeptics were right: Yahweh does not save his people. He allowed them to be consumed in the fires of the holocaust. Why bother calling him "Abba" at all then? What kind of experience is Jesus' Abba awareness? Ineffable indeed, but unless something be said to ground and identify it within our experience, it slithers away to gibberish and dread. To wit, who is this Abba? How is he the embodiment of the ineffable essence body?

Obviously, to call God "Abba" is to use a metaphor. This metaphor may connote loving care to most, but to those whose experience with their own fathers is less than rewarding, it may communicate severity and distance. To some it implies a managerial figure presiding over an ailing world and brings up images of the old paterfamilias, in charge of things but unapproachable. As the Japanese proverb would have it, the four things to be feared are lightning, fire, earthquakes, and the old man.

Central as it is to the New Testament, and to the preceding discussion, the representation of ultimate meaning as Abba, father, is but an image (*nimitta*); the important thing is to uncover the insight (*darśana*) conveyed by its use. Haldon Willmer remarks that "even if we have an historical Jesus who revealed God in his life, it may still turn out to be no more than an idea unless the action of God in Jesus Christ is continued after the resurrection into the present. An historical memory is as much an idea as a metaphysical abstraction. Especially if an historical event is God's final or inclusive act, one cannot ignore what happens after it."[8] How is the presence of God as Abba experienced in our histories? What does the idea of Abba mean?

The answer of Scholastic theology that God is being itself, the very act of existing (*ipsum esse*), identifies God in a most inclusive way, for God is the source of the being of everything. But it is not clear just how that philosophical idea is related to, or generated from within, felt human experience. It seems clear from the Gospel record that for the early Christian community "Abba" connoted an awareness of intimacy, not a philosophical insight. It is not a matter of metaphysical theory, in which it is sufficient to relate terms in a logical, consistent fashion. All that may be necessary to theologians, but if such an awareness does not thematize our lives as experienced and actually lived, it will hardly support us through times of trial and suffering. In the face of the ultimate threat of a meaningless void, any idea of God is simply beside the point, since, having little to do with the lives we lead, it ceases to function. Who then is this Abba enunciated by Jesus?

Abba cannot be the Sunday-morning God who assures us of our goodness for being seated in a church pew, supporting our trivialization of the Christ meaning. That God is a supernatural insurance broker at the service of selfhood. The image of God as a partner in Pelagian bargains is in large measure responsible for the split in Christendom marked by the Reformation. It was this God who drove Luther back to Paul and forth to nail his ninety-five theses on the door at Wittenberg Church. Is our idea of God after all an illusion? Really not there at all?

The point of the Mahāyāna refutation of the creator deity is that any idea clung to as ultimate is an illusion, for any such idea represents a meaning constructed within the conditioned world. Thus any idea of God affirmed in a religious imagining is an idol in the mind. Such images of Jesus are idols. As the Puritans saw, statues and pictures of the divine clung to with intense devotion tend to become idols. Whatever is taken up in the imagined pattern of consciousness is illusory. How could one expect such images actually to function in the world of lived experience? Is then the Christian belief in God as Abba an illusion? Did Jesus believe in such an illusory idol?

Let us, in Harvey Cox's phrase, "turn East" once more. Not to leave Christian faith, but to seek some brotherly assistance in understanding it. The Yogācāras, besides developing a critical understanding of karmic, illusory consciousness, also took steps toward an analysis of the mind of wisdom. Using their perspective and filling it out with insights from the Christian mystic tradition, we may perhaps clarify the pattern of our questioning, if not the nature of God. In Yogācāra thought, the embodiment of the essence (*svabhāvika-kāya*) entails an awakening to an original purity that encompasses all consciousness and all things. Without a delineation of this mind of original purity and wisdom, an appeal to an Abba experience is at most dubious. Any verbalized religious idea that does not grow out of conscious experience has no identifiable ground that might render it meaningful — and that ground is not to be found in any mediated image or idea. Even objects of ultimate concern can be the ultimate concern of an illusory consciousness.

The Yogācāra masters explained that the structure of the illusory, samsaric mind is formed by the appearance of subject and object. *The Garland Arrayment* asserts: "All internal and external things, all the visible, are not apart from the mind itself. The mind of sentient beings is of two aspects, the act of grasping and the object grasped."[9] This structure of the illusory, imagined pattern of consciousness takes as normative this sense-modeled pattern of extraverted understanding, thus rendering any idea of God it might generate illusory. The objective source of any such idea is then sought in terms of that illusory consciousness with the result that its idea of God is indeed a projection of unmet needs lying deep within the psyche.

But the Yogācāra masters also speak of an original mind prior to the arising of this subject-object dichotomy. Much of the dilemma over the existence of God comes about from trying to demonstrate God's "objective existence" over against our subjective consciousness. John Wisdom's parable of the invisible gardener is here quite to the point:

> Once upon a time two explorers came upon a clearing in the jungle. In the clearing were growing many flowers and many weeds. One explorer says, "Some gardener must tend this plot." The other disagrees, "There is no gardener." So they pitch their tents and set a watch. No gardener is ever seen. "But perhaps it is an invisible gardener." So they set up a barbed-wire fence. They electrify it. They patrol with bloodhounds. (For they remember how H. G. Wells' "invisible man" could be both smelt and touched, though he could not be seen.) But no shrieks ever suggest that some intruder had ever received a shock. No movements of the wire ever betray an invisible climber. The bloodhounds never give cry. Yet the believer is not convinced. "But there is a gardener, invisible, intangible, insensible to electric shocks, a gardener who has no scent and makes no sound, a gardener who comes secretly to tend the garden which he loves." At last the skeptic despairs, "But what remains of your original assertion? Just how does what you call an invisible, intangible, eternally elusive gardener differ from an imaginary gardener or even from no gardener at all?"[10]

How could he differ indeed! How can any image of ultimate meaning as a fatherly God be anything more than imaginary? How can any object be affirmed as real, when it in fact never manifests its objective presence over against the sensing subject? Any idea of God that functions within the subject-object dichotomy by externalizing God as an object to be apprehended, as an object to be clung to in imagination, winds up by placing that God over against the subjective explorer. But, as Gregory of Nyssa says, God is not presented in any confrontational vision. As the Yogācāra masters reiterate, the pattern of subject-object is itself imagined and empty, for there is no essence to either the subject or the object. Arguments about the existence of God that are woven from an extraverted consciousness do not convince because God is not a being (*dharma*) among beings to be apprehended and affirmed. In this, the Yogācāra rejection of a theistic deity (*Īśvara*) is on the mark. But is the experience of Abba in Jesus an assertion of the existence of such a confrontational deity?

The original mind exists prior to the splitting of consciousness into subject and object. It does not become aware through apprehending an object over against a subject. It is not enmeshed in clinging to *ātman* or to *dharmas*. Jesus as the wisdom of God embodies not an idea of Abba, but a preverbal awareness of ineffable meaning thematized as Abba. God is not the supreme object of samsaric consciousness, for, in imagining ideas of this or that, that consciousness remains in the service of *ātman* consciousness, and one cannot serve two masters. A discriminated idea of God, no matter how lofty or how profound, relates to and functions as an adjunct of the subject-object pattern of *ātman* consciousness. But if God is not an object over against subjective consciousness, then the explorers' demand that God become perceptible is as illusory as the theologians' attempts to respond to that demand.

Whatever the validity of the logical argumentation for the existence of God might be, the God envisaged is a mental construct (*vijñapti*): all ideas are mental constructs (*vijñapti-mātra*). Their point of reference is not a divine essence that lies beyond and that might be defined by analyzing its content. Ideas of God indicate their reference in terms of their dependently co-arisen context and cultural milieu. This does not mean simply that ideas are inadequate to present God, but still analogically applicable. It means, rather, that the presence of God is simply not amenable to conceptual expression at all. Seeking to know about the existence of a supreme, invisible gardener who never appears in our garden is quite beside the point. It is an illusion to seek a God who is mostly absent. The exigency is to realize the pre-presence of ultimate meaning, to recognize God as already present at the base of all seeking, as the originally pure objective that impels one to question without ever adequately answering that question. Attend not to an absentee gardener, but to the garden itself in all its immediacy and empty transparency.

The death-of-God theology of a few years ago perhaps illustrates the contours of the question. Its primary intent was not to deny the factual existence of a supreme deity, but to announce that such an objective God was meaningless.[11] They proclaimed that God had died, because there was no objectively real experience of that God. An objectively real God somewhere within or transcendent to the world simply did not matter anymore.

Long ago the Yogācāra thinkers identified illusory consciousness as a pattern of clinging to objective reality over against the subjective self—even if that reality be deemed divine. Any such reality was nothing more than an idea arising conditionally within consciousness, a language-formed conception, and, if clung to as unconditioned, an illusion generated from within the pattern of mistaken, imagined thinking. When they came to thematize the mind of wisdom and awakening, however, they did treat ultimate meaning. They were not in any sense nihilists. The truth of ultimate meaning, they declared, is that which is realized personally in the abeyance of clinging to subject or object. It is this state of original simplicity that is realized in awakening and it is here that one attains direct, immediate awareness of ultimate meaning, already present and active.

The pure Dharma Realm, the realm of mystic awareness, is ultimate meaning, characterized negatively as being totally beyond language and thought. And yet, although beyond language, it can be mirrored forth in wisdom, and so the wisdom of awakening is termed a conversion of support that embodies the essence (*dharma-kāya*). Such a conversion entails the wisdom of emptiness and rejects imaginative theorizing that would identify the content of wisdom with any set of terms. The wisdom of Dharma Body is the realization of original purity.

It is perhaps here that we might be able to find a perspective from which to interpret the meaning of Jesus' Abba experience, the meaning of God as Abba. The pure Dharma Realm is presented in *The Scripture on the Buddha Land* and its commentarial *The Interpretation of the Buddha Land* through the simile of empty space. Just as empty space pervades everything and contains within it all kinds of identifiable things, without on that account being itself identifiable at all, so the pure Dharma Realm of ultimate meaning pervades all worldly and conventional knowable objects without itself being a knowable object.[12] It is the prior horizon in which all human understanding, all human activity occurs. Just as no fish swims out of water, so no understanding occurs outside some horizon, and the pure Dharma Realm is the universal horizon presupposed by the ongoing stretching forth of consciousness. It is the forever receding horizon that is the underlying dynamic of all human questioning and searching, "in which we live, and move, and have our being." The wisdom of awakening that mirrors that horizon does not function by clinging to me and mine or to subject-object polarities, for it has gained awareness of that horizon that goes before and remains after all meanings.

One does not arrive at an awareness of God by taking a logical tour of inspection of the world of our experiences. Belief in God is not an article of faith recommended to people who have previously never considered the question. Rather, the basic structure of consciousness is already directed toward ultimate meaning and rejects God-conceptions because of their failure to ground themselves in that structure. This does not mean that there are any innate ideas of God within the mind; ideas are always generated through insight into images and are constructed by conscious operations. God, however, is not found by generating ideas. Rather, in awareness of the original structuring of consciousness oriented toward ultimate meaning, one becomes aware of God as prevenient and encompassing. Atheists are seldom uneducated people, for most frequently their rejection of God springs from a radical inability to relate conceptual presentations of God, even if squarely orthodox, to felt experience. We know where the garden is, but where is the gardener? God does not come to tend our garden, but is present at the beginning of our gardening.

In the gospel the presence of the Father is revealed to children, for their lack of constructed ideas which intervene and block Abba awareness renders them docile and open to understanding that which is immediately and directly present as the encompassing horizon of all human experience. Whether mentally constructed ideas be rejected out of hand by a critical atheist or shouted from the rooftops of fundamentalist churches by unctious preachers, they remain human constructs—adequate not for representing Abba, but only for serving provisionally in worldly and conventional discourse about human understandings of ultimate meaning. *The Interpretation of the Buddha Land* explains the ultimate realm by teaching that "The pure Dharma Realm pervades the original mind of all sentient beings, since it is reality, and is not apart from them."[13]

The ultimacy of Jesus' Abba meaning is not a recommendation of some particular object for our consideration, but an identification of that which goes before and structures the mind of original purity, covered over though it may be by me-clinging and illusion. Just like a father, Abba goes before and supports the very being of his children. Not only is that ultimate horizon of Abba already present, but it is active, for "it encompasses all the phenomenal activities that universally benefit sentient beings,"[14] although it has no empirically arising activity of its own at all.

Thomas Aquinas teaches that God does not change to do this or that, but rather, "moves" in benevolent kindness to save from sin and suffering, without in any way becoming changed thereby.[15] Yet the idea of a God who comes to know and comes to will this or that seems to suggest a God who is a being like other beings, only supernatural. The Mahāyāna philosophers teach that the activity of the pure Dharma Realm in benefiting beings is like empty space encompassing all actions: although space is not purposeful and never sets about implementing any divine plan, yet it is the encompassing source for all beneficent action. "It is just like the brightness of the sun, the moon, or of lamps, which, although they do not discriminate this from that, yet, when they arise, are able to illumine all things."[16]

Just so, God makes the sun to shine and the rain to fall on sinner and saint alike, without distinction. Just so, Abba as ultimate truth is always shining in and illumining the minds of human beings. The presence of ultimate meaning at the base of human consciousness structures the quest of that consciousness and causes the arising of religious teaching; as Asaṅga explains, true teaching is always an outflow from the pure Dharma Realm. God is not a super-being who knows fragmentarily and moves occasionally into action to deliver his children. Such mighty acts of God are absent from human history, as Agur, Job, and Qoheleth knew so well, for the existence of such occasional acts would imply that ordinarily God was absent from that history.

Still, all this does not show how God can be identified as personal, as Abba, for this description is equally applicable to the *dharmadhātu* (reality realm), which can be characterized as neither personal nor impersonal. The notion of God as father has already been shown to be inappropriate in some ways, for he does not save his children from suffering and death. With Augustine and John Robinson, one may perhaps find the idea of a personal God difficult to apply, but it remains central to the Christian tradition.[17] Christians do not pray to an "it." Even rejecting the notion of an interruptive God who breaks into history to fulfill his purposes, is there not some valid ground for Jesus' recommendation that we see God as our own Father? Even should one prefer silence to a loquacious God who might answer troubling questions with divine answers, still who is it that is silent? Who is this Abba who remained silent even at the crucifixion of his Son?

God is mediated as Abba by Jesus not because we have a personal one-to-one encounter with God. We do not gently converse with God in the coolness of the evening and God does not frequent our gardens with his visible presence. Rather, Abba would seem to mean that God is present as ultimate to each more intimately than any encounter between distinct persons ever is. Augustine says that God is *interior intimo meo* (more inner than my inmost awareness), for the presence of Abba is not encountered over against and confronting the human spirit, but within and enfolding it.[18] Despite the insistence of manuals of Christian devotion, prayer is not a conversation with God. Such an understanding removes God from human affairs and necessitates the establishment of lines of communication with God's removed presence. One does not have to search the seven seas for a lost deity, but, entering quietly and consistently into the basis of one's own consciousness, plumb its depths and awaken to (his or her) presence in silence. Augustine in his *On the Trinity* says:

> God is truth. . . . Do not seek what that truth is; for at once the darkness of bodily images and the clouds of imagination crowd in and disturb that serenity which illuminated you in a sudden flash, when I said the word, truth. Behold, in that first flash by which you were seized as if by a blinding light when there is said "truth," remain if you can.[19]

One becomes aware of Abba in a flash as already present before any images or ideas. Not only is Abba intimate, forming our consciousness at the deepest levels, Abba is also a firm, unshakable ground for living. Nothing could shatter Jesus' Abba awareness, and even at the time of dying Jesus is reported to have addressed God as "Abba" and to have felt compassion for his executioners. Nothing could shatter it because Jesus did not seek to transcend his human contingency. He did not grasp after any divine status beyond the world. Had Jesus been delivered from the cross, he could scarcely have been confessed as human!

It is especially in the face of dying, of losing all constructed meanings, that the meaning of God as Abba is most crucial, for the intimacy and support of that experience go beyond me-clinging to an empty consciousness of illusion and reveal Abba not as the support and comfort for *ātman*, but as the support for a realization of meaning that conquers death by recognizing the dependently co-arisen emptiness of all self-affirmation. It is thus that one participates in the resurrection of Jesus.

The Father is then the embodiment of the original essence, the reality that forever transcends all attempts at expression. He is called "Father" and regarded as personal because this divine presence is experienced as deep and intimate, indeed more intimate than any personalist categories can express. Jesus, the voice of the Father from silence, is the human embodiment of the experience of total abandonment and commitment to the Father. For the Christian to live in Christ is to participate with Christ in embodying the Father and voicing his presence.

But that participation is not a given. It demands a radical conversion and transformation of experience, a transformation that takes place in and through the Spirit. What then is the Spirit and how does the Spirit transform our lives?

SPIRIT TRANSFORMATION

The doctrine of the Trinity serves not only to adumbrate our relationship to God through Christ, to provide us with an imageless awareness of Abba as transcendent. Trinitarian awareness also highlights the need for a personal and social transformation of human experience. In the early Christian literature, it is the Spirit who is identified as the creative activity of the transcendent God in the concrete lives of men and women. It is the Spirit who bestows baptismal grace and who is the source for conversion. It is the Spirit who moves in our hearts and makes us call out, "Abba, Father" (Rom. 8:15). Reflecting a broad Patristic understanding, Cyril, Gregory, Athanasius, and all the fathers teach that the Spirit "illumines and sanctifies" human beings. Through the Spirit "we are knit into the Godhead," and "the Spirit makes us God."[20] Paul's second Epistle to the Corinthians (3:18) describes this transformation brought about in men and women through the Spirit:

Now the Lord is the Spirit, and where the Spirit of the Lord is, there is freedom. And because there is no veil over our face, we all reflect as in a mirror the glory of the Lord; thus we are transformed (*metamorphoumetha*) into his likeness, from glory to glory; such is the influence of the Lord who is Spirit.

Not only does the Spirit bring personal renewal and dwell in the hearts of men and women,[21] but the Spirit also brings freedom and liberation. The Spirit brings about a transformation (*metamorphoumetha*) of human beings into the image of Christ: reflecting Christ's awareness of Abba and commitment to the rule of God in the world. It is this transformation that brings freedom and liberation (*eleutheria*) from *ātman* consciousness and social alienation. The trinitarian pattern of Christian living turns upon our personal realization of the Christ meaning, and entails both an awareness of the immediacy of Abba and a transformation of *ātman* consciousness into compassion and creativity in service of the rule of God in the world. Both personal consciousness and social structures are to be transformed through the Spirit.

The one unified experience of union with Christ through grace and faith meaning is the paradigmatic embodiment of Christian experience (*sambhogika-kāya*). That Christ awareness entails an experience of the silent ultimacy of Abba as the embodiment of the essence (*svabhāvika-kāya*) and the concomitant experience of transformation in the Spirit to a reengaged commitment to the rule of God (*nirmāṇika-kāya*). The Spirit is not, then, a *tertium quid*, an afterthought in Trinitarian thinking, but "consubstantial" with the experience of the essence-free Jesus as transforming consciousness through the Spirit.

The doctrine of the divinity (consubstantiality) of the Spirit did not, however, receive its final explicit formulation until the Council of Constantinople in 381, worked out in large part by applying to the Spirit the Greek ontological scheme already employed to explain the relationship between the Father and Son. But Christian awareness of the Spirit is not a fourth-century phenomenon. It is clear that, both in the scriptures and in the writings of the fathers, the Spirit is seen as the immanent presence of God converting the mind and bringing about liberation and freedom in the world from the very beginning.

What then does it mean to be transformed in the Spirit? Is it a "born-again" experience accompanied by feelings of intense devotion? What does it mean to transform society? Does the Spirit who brings liberation also provide the theological basis for movements that would enlist divine backing for political reform and revolution?

Conversion and the Ethics of the Two Truths

One can "meet" God alone through solitary prayer in the deserts of the mind. But if that "encounter" is the end of the matter, it falls short of the mark. In Mahāyāna terms the life-course of a solitary enlightened person (*pratyeka-buddha*), who wanders alone through the forest like the rhinoceros, is found wanting in compassion and hence inferior to the path of a bodhisattva, one who is committed to reengagement in the dependently co-arisen world. In Christian experience, as well, it is not enough simply to become aware of God and abide aloof in detached splendor. In mediating the silent Abba, the Christ meaning entails both personal conversion and social commitment to the rule of compassion in the world. It is aimed at a definitive transformation of inner consciousness and of social and political structures in the world. Christian faith urges commitment to practice, both personal and social. Personal practice is aimed at inner conversion and awareness of Abba. Social practice is directed toward the world and its transformation into the kingdom of God. Both involve one in concrete action in the world; both issue in ethical behavior. Personal ethics deals with one's interpersonal relationships and has been a central aspect of Christian preaching from the beginning. Social ethics deals with the patterns and structures of society and attempts to realize the rule of God's justice and compassion among peoples and nations. Often this aspect of Christian action has been overlooked in favor of "the divine right" of kings, or "legitimate" authority bestowed by God through the democratic process. Questioning authority has often been equated with questioning the authority of God, and oppressive structures and politics excused in the light of mistaken ideas of the proper place of faith in life—outside concrete living and beyond society. But Christian experience of the Spirit is embodied in this transformation of consciousness and commitment to ethical action, engaged in the concrete world of politics and society. Ethics is not a sequel to conversion or a list of recommended acts drawn up by deduction from doctrine held about God and divine will. Rather, ethical action in the world flows directly and necessarily from the basic trinitarian pattern of Christian awareness of being transformed into the image of Christ in the Spirit.

The shape of personal transformation through conversion to the Christ meaning in the Spirit is and has been treated by Christian thinkers time and again. Its contours are by and large clear, for they principally affect the individual person and his or her limited group of friends and acquaintances. Questions of course remain, and issues like abortion or homosexuality occupy center stage in present moral thinking. Personal ethics, of course, have implications for the larger society, and both Christian and Buddhist thinkers have stressed good moral living. Nāgārjuna not only wrote doctrinal expositions, such as his *Stanzas on the Middle* and *Overcoming Vain Discussions*, but also devoted his efforts to such works as *The Precious Garland*, which outlined the social implications of doctrine.[22] Despite these social implications, his focus is not on restructuring social structures, but on influencing social structures already accepted as legitimate. Ethics is here conceived as a "leaven" working through society and transforming it through justice, love, and compassion.

But what is Spirit transformation in terms of a social ethics? What concretely does commitment to the rule of God's compassion and justice mean? Does it fall within the foregoing notion of ethical commitment as a social "leaven"? These questions, raised most poignantly by the liberation theologians, are relatively new in their insistence that Christian faith must involve one in bettering and restructuring society—not in a millenarian reversal, but through concrete politics and direct action. If concrete ethical action is encompassed in the basic Christian experience of Christ as sending the Spirit and transforming our consciousnesses, how is one to address society? What is the shape of Christian social ethics?

The Mādhyamika understanding of emptiness, dependent co-arising, and the two truths issues in a social ethics that may be put to service in Christian thinking. Mahāyāna ethics does not rely on divine authority or validate its commitments in terms of any set of sacred directions. Often Christian ethical thinkers have based themselves on claims of divine authority that flow from a bifurcation of Christian thinking: first know God as supreme being and then determine God's will in concrete living. In this schema there is scant room for Spirit transformation because the "right" course of action is thought to be already clarified in an imagined pattern of God-clinging. By contrast, if we follow the Mahāyāna doctrine of the two truths, ethics function exclusively through worldly and conventional thinking, remain under the hegemony of intelligent reasoning, and become authentic only through a conversion from the imagined pattern to the other-dependent pattern, driven by the Spirit of Jesus toward reengagement. Ethical reasoning need claim no ultimate sanction or source; it remains worldly and conventional, always open to, and inevitably subject to falsification and deconstruction — not in virtue of a higher ultimate truth, but because of the openness of all intelligent reasoning. The function of reason is not to determine judgments as certainly true and above criticism, but to ascertain their conventional and temporary validity, always subject to further insights and changed conditions. Since all ideas are constructs empty of essence, and since that emptiness is not itself an essence, ideas are simply and only ideas (*vijñapti-mātra*). Dependently co-arisen thinking is simply dependently co-arisen thinking, without any possibility of "being strengthened" or "validated" by ultimate meaning, which forever remains silent to, and other from, all human endeavors.

There is then no specific Mahāyāna religious action in the world. Rather, there is a distrust of any "social gospel" as tending inevitably toward ideology, that is, idolatry. The history of Buddhism shows little direct religious engagement in the world, and Buddhism is often criticized as lacking in its commitment to social action. But this criticism, it would appear, misses the point. The presence of Mahāyāna engagement in society and worldly ethics is not to be seen in distinct movements or identifiable programs, but in an engagement that, in true Prajñāpāramitā fashion, is an engagement because it is no engagement at all.

There are examples of Buddhist liberation movements, attempts to enlist the Dharma behind specific social agendas. In Sung China the White Lotus movement took its sustenance from *The Scripture of the Lotus Blossom of the Fine Dharma*, and fueled its rebellious zeal with the messianic hope of the coming of the Buddha Maitreya.[23] The Three Stages Sect (*San-chieh-chiao*) put the Dharma to social ends by instituting an "inexhaustible treasury" of donated monies for the constant service of the poor.[24] In Japan the peasant uprisings (*ikki*) of Kamukura times against money-lenders and unfair taxation sought legitimacy in the doctrines of Pure Land and Nichiren Buddhism.[25]

But these are exceptions. Buddhist institutions for the most part, when not aloof in absorbed detachment, as Hui-yüan on Lu-shan, have supported (at times being co-opted by) the imperial states in which the found themselves and tried to affect their policies and practices. They exemplified the ethics of serving as a social "leaven" without attempting to restructure society in any sense. The usual role Buddhism played in society was not directed toward social restructuring and class liberation, but aimed at influencing rulers and emperors to nurture the people and support Buddhist monasteries and practices—much the same as the Christian role in state affairs after the public acceptance of the church under Constantine in 314 up until modern attempts to see the Gospel as entailing social restructuring and liberation. The history of Buddhist Asia does show the involvement of religion in social affairs and politics of many state monarchies, whether Indian, Chinese, Japanese, Korean, or Tibetan, all directed toward influencing the court and through the court social policy, just as was the case in the Roman Empire and medieval Europe. This does not argue for the detachment and other-worldiness of Buddhism.

Buddhism has given birth to little in the way of a "liberation theology." The function of ultimate meaning and emptiness is negative and concerned with falsifying social options that reify dependently co-arisen choices into ideological theories and party slogans. Mahāyāna presents an ethics of suspicion: even the most intense commitment to social action must be kept in dialectical tension with the dependently co-arisen concreteness of experience. But this negative thrust is not meant to excuse one from action. Rather, it urges that action be in harmony with ultimate meaning and emptiness: that it function in the real world of essence-free relationships and problems.

One can scarcely deny that there has been in Buddhism a tendency to float free from the world into the anticipated bliss of a cessation of all worldly action. The Indian Abhidharma masters taught that the world itself is an illusory construct of our defiled karma and in no need of serious consideration. When all are enlightened, it will simply disappear.[26] The Chinese master Hui-yüan confined himself within the sacred precincts of his Lu-shan monastic compound, without ever, with one unintended exception, venturing across its boundary-marking stream.[27] But in the light of the Mādhyamika understanding of the two truths, such detachment falls far of the mark. Nāgārjuna had reclaimed dependent co-arising not just as the structure of *saṃsāra* and illusion, but also as the content of emptiness. He enunciated a strong ethics of reenegagment in the concrete world of dependent co-arising and laid the foundation for compassionate and intelligent action that does not flee from the world but demands reengagement in it.

The presence of Mahāyāna action in the world is not seen in identifiable movements, but is an anonymous presence, for there is a clear disinclination to be identifiably religious in one's actions, lest that preempt intelligent decision in favor of some fixed, religious ideal. In the context of the two truths, ultimate meaning remains totally other from worldly convention and entails not only the rejection of any ultimately meaningful ideal, but also an intelligent openness to the ever-changing conditions of phenomenal being. As those conditions change—as all dependently co-arising phenomena do—then decisions and commitments must change accordingly. Mahāyāna practitioners, who are also politicians and social activists, function in the world most often without the felt need to proclaim themselves as Mahāyāna practitioners or to invoke religious authority for their own decisions.

The engagement of Mahāyāna practitioners, whether Buddhist or Christian, in social action is a nonengagement, for it functions not through a direct religious imperative to act in specific ways, but through the commitment to act with compassion as needs indicate. Having in whatever degree gained insight into emptiness, worldly convention is reaffirmed simply as worldly convention, in virtue of its own hegemony, seen as present from the beginning, and irrespective of any religious doctrinal position. If a revolution is needed, then intelligent men and women understand that a revolution must be carried out. But there is no need to attempt to legitimize that revolution by claims that God or the Buddha Maitreya is on one's side. If conciliation and diplomacy are called for, then intelligent men and women see that conciliation and diplomacy must be carried out. But not in virtue of any ultimately valid injunction to carry out conciliation and diplomacy.

We live in a secular world in which insight into emptiness entails an awareness of ultimate meaning as completely other and in which social engagement in the dependently co-arisen world is valid only as insight into worldly convention. There is no identifiable realm apart from the dependently co-arisen world that might bolster that intelligent action. There is no Mahāyāna analogue for the modern Christian "liberation theology" that would enlist ultimate meaning in the service of any, even the most needed, conventional action in the world. If God is not on the side of the poor, it does not follow that God must be on the side of the rich. But the idea of a "preferential option" for the poor runs dangerously close to imagining God as a great being among beings, the King with his heavenly hosts, with all the subsequent disappointment that that may occasion.[28] If it is argued that God is on the side of the poor, it can be equally argued that God is the source for monarchies and enjoins slaves to obey their masters. Monarchy in Israel issues from Yahweh's own prophets against the evident wishes of the people. Paul sends the escaped slave Onesimus back to his master, Philemon, without any hint of criticism against the legitimacy of slavery. In his own social context, Paul acquiesces in the givenness of his world and commits himself as surety for Onesimus. This is hardly a case of liberation theology. Religious crusades, although clearly engendered by oppressive conditions and aimed at the estabishment of justice and peace, easily turn into holy wars that feed on their own rhetoric in self-justifying sado-masochistic continuity.

This does not mean that a Mahāyāna ethics argues against the need for social reform — even revolution. It does argue that they stand in no need of any final religious authorization. It does not argue for the status quo or the entrenched symbiosis between religious institutions and oppressive regimes, although that has taken place both in the Christian West and in the Buddhist East. In a Mahāyāna Christian context, the replacement of oppressive regimes is a matter for intelligent ethical action and need have no recourse to specious religious validation. This is the intent of Paul when he preached the "theology" of the cross against the worldviews of the Corinthian factions. It is the bare fact of the cross, the unjust death of Christ, that he lifts to view, not some ideological program or social plan. The cross signified the total immersion of Jesus in the particular dependently co-arising circumstances of his time — and invites us to take up our crosses and follow, in our times and in our circumstances. It is a total commitment to the rule of justice and love, but not a supernatural plan of action. In Mādhyamika thought ultimate meaning can take no side whatsoever, for the sides in any dialectic, whether rational argumentation or political struggle, remain conventional and subject only to conventional judgments. The Spirit-filled transformation of society reflects the transformed consciousness of awakened people. It entails a turn toward ultimate meaning in silent withdrawal to Abba awareness and a reclaiming of the other-dependent structure of understanding in Spirit-inspired word and action. But, even though Spirit-inspired, those words and actions are no less dependently co-arisen. The Spirit moves the hearts of men and women to reclaim their heads, not to ignore human thinking in favor of a supposedly "already given" answer, whether scriptural or theological.

The passing of classical Western culture and the emergence of a pluralistic world of many societies and many cultures highlights the untenability of facile mixtures of religion and politics. No matter how ethical in intent or how sincerely aimed at replacing unjust societies, religious usurpations of politics or social policies tend increasingly to absolutize conventional, dependently co-arisen insight and to fabricate cultural absolutes that isolate theocratic nations and distort the very religion in whose name politics is carried out. God as politician, whether conservative, liberal, or revolutionary, can scarcely maintain validity with the passing relevance of fixed policies.

If one employs a Mādhyamika critique, all of this becomes not only unnecessary, but also destructive of reengaged ethical action in society. It is unnecessary because the world functions not through religious principles, but through intelligent decision. It is destructive of social action because it releases people from what can only be their own decisions and substitutes the illusory security of some divine remedy. It trivializes engaged social action through the opium dream of a supernatural assurance, wondrous in appearance and comforting in imagination. It obviates the need for Spirit transformation and sees as adequate the imagined projection of positions in untransformed consciousness, that is to say, in minds that identify ultimate meaning with their own personal or group bias. It not only keeps people from participating in necessary revolutions, but it also keeps them engaged in revolution when the need or the profitability of that revolution has long since disappeared. Just as religion can serve as an opiate of the people, so revolution itself, taking on quasi-religious and mythic absoluteness, dulls minds into the illusion of being a revolutionary vanguard—without any troops coming in the rear.

The Spirit-filled embodiment of transformation is, then, not limited to enunciating the content of primal experiences of Abba in personal realization, but must include both a commitment to social action and a caveat against the incursions of religion itself into areas of social and political concern. All theologies in the final point of their development must deconstruct themselves, for, in the words of Nikos Kazantzakēs, the Buddha has also come "to free people from religion,"[29]—for action in the world.

The structure of this Mahāyāna engagement in the world is articulated in the doctrine of the five factors and four wisdoms, which presents a pattern of reengagement from silent awareness to concrete action. The pure Dharma Realm (*dharmadhātu-viśuddhi*) indicates the content of ultimate wisdom, of Abba beyond all and encompassing all. Mirror wisdom (*adarśana-jñāna*) reflects all the events of human experience in their suchness and without discrimination. It is a wisdom of emptiness that enables one to realize that all ideas are dependently arisen and hence equal. The wisdom of equality (*samatā-jñāna*) engenders insight into truth in the broad spectrum of human affairs and sees all *sub specie vacuitatis*, apart from the distinctions of worldly convention. Such insight into and awareness of emptiness and the equality of all dependently co-arisen being sees all things in terms of a unified awareness of suchness, beyond any distinction between me (*ātman*) and mine (*atmya*) and in rejection of personal and group biases. Teaching and action, however, are carried out only in some particular language and in some particular deeds, and so the wisdom of discernment (*pratyavekṣana-jñāna*) expresses itself in specific teachings and thereby flows into the wisdom of duty-fulfillment (*kṛtyanuṣṭhana-jñāna*) that actually performs the tasks of compassion.[30]

The concrete forms of such transformations of consciousness and action can be filled out only in the course of historical living—by what actually happens—just as the meaning of Christ could only be filled out in the course of his living, dying, and rising. There is no universal model for all times and places. The lives of the saints will differ as cultures and conditions differ. They can be as disparate as Camilo Torres and Mother Teresa, each responding to the felt needs of their personal *Sitz im Leben*. There need be no distinction made between the revolutionary sacrifice of Torres, who left the security of the university to share the life of guerillas in the jungles of Colombia, and the humble service of Teresa, despite her lack of any attempt to reform the social structures that engender poverty and suffering. One need not shake an accusing finger at one in order to appreciate the other.

CONCLUSION

The doctrine of the Trinity reflects the pattern of Christian living that is centered on Christ. Christ is the embodiment of our experience. It is in Christ's grace that we share and it is in Christ's meaning that we live through faith and insight. That meaning draws us toward Abba as the embodiment of the silent, essence-free essence beyond any mediating image or word and not identifiable as any object in human experience. But matters do not end there. Through the embodiment of transformation in the Spirit one is converted and committed to Christian bodhisattva action in one's personal and social reengagement in the concrete world. The doctrine of the Trinity is not just an exercise in Greek metaphysics, although it does involve some of that. It is not an item of arcane lore, unintelligible to ordinary people. It is not a piece of divine knowledge. Rather, it is the shape of Christian lived experience, traditionally expressed in terms of Greek ontology but not limited to that expression. It is amenable to as many philosophical approaches as there are cultures, indeed as there are men and women. The approach recommended here as a handmaid philosophy in the service of theology is but one among many possible approaches to Christian faith and living.

Afterword

By enunciating the doctrines of the Incarnation and the Trinity, Christian theology has set itself a double problem, the facets of which are not always clearly understood. In the first place and fundamentally, it is a question not merely of the appropriate and relevant cultural language in which to express God-talk, but of the pattern of consciousness within which any theological language is interpreted. There can be found no God who effectively serves as the support or refuge for selfhood, for *sarx*, because there is no deliverance from being human and contingent, from being-unto-death, from being dependently co-arisen. Any theology that would pretend to usurp the absoluteness of God must then be rejected.

But that does not relegate the question of appropriate language to some theological dustbin, for the images and ideas projected upon the basic trinitarian experience can serve to preclude that very experience of the immediacy of Abba and transformation in the Spirit, in whom we live and have our dependently co-arisen being. By so doing, they render Jesus not the empty mirror of the divine depths, but imagine him as a savior who delivers us from being human and excuses us from becoming ethically reengaged in the world.

Without a conversion of consciousness and language, theology functions mechanically in the imagined pattern of mistaking ideas for essences. Without sensitivity to the skillful use of language to express the meaning of that conversion, theology functions only awkwardly and in detachment from concrete living, occluding that which it hopes to signify.

The present Mahāyāna-Christian hybrid interpretation of the Incarnation and the Trinity is recommended as an attempt to address both of these issues. It is derived from an examination of interiority, both mystic and samsaric, and thus its constant focus is upon the realization of conversion, the realization of a disclosure experience and awakening to the meaning of Christ. Such a focus on the immediacy of mystic experience not only leads us back to Paul and the New Testament, but opens the way to a reexamination of the mystic writings of the Christian fathers and to reclaim that mystic tradition for serious theological discourse. The Mādhyamika philosophy and the Yogācāra explication of religious meaning constitute a respectable scholarly tradition through which one may look back and reaffirm the early Christian emphasis on Christ-awareness, an awareness that has always gone beyond and threatened to break through all metaphysical theorizing. This need not entail a rejection of all Greek thinking, for within these attempts to express theoretically the meaning of Christ lies an awareness of a basic experience that is known only through unknowing in the complete darkening of all theological endeavors. But it does relativize Greek thinking. After all, Greek theology is the thinking of the Greeks and not that of most other peoples and cultures in the modern world.

In addition to opening a clear path to the reclamation of Christian mystic thinking, this Mahāyāna perspective offers a language that may be of value in expressing hitherto unnoticed depths of the meaning of Christ. Precisely because it is a different language, a different set of interlocking terms, its adoption will lead to a different set of mediated insights. It is particularly to be recommended because, although it indulges in no metaphysical thinking and attempts to construct no overall systematic or ontological theology, it still is able to enunciate the traditional understanding of Christ as the word and image of the Father and to call for commitment to Spirit-filled action to transform the world. It remains true to the faith of the Christian community, though in a different philosophical framework.

This theology questions all systems and negates any thought structure that is taken to be absolutely true. It moves at ease within a pluralist cultural perspective, for all thinking is seen as dependently co-arisen in terms of particular cultural values, languages, and ways of thinking. It takes a deconstructionist approach. But it goes beyond even that approach to draw on an ancient and well-developed tradition of religious thought. It does not leave us in the vacuum of a deconstructed metaphysics, in a junkyard of worn-out and over-used ideas. Rather, Mahāyāna Christian theology cherishes the teachings of wisdom and insight, both Buddhist and Christian. There is no need to tarry in bewilderment at the wreckage of traditional forms of theologizing, wondering what one could possibly substitute in their place. There have been and continue to be numerous attempts to think the meaning of Christ in a variety of languages and a variety of cultures. Mahāyāna theology negates only the imagined pattern of knowing, for all theologizing is an other-dependent weaving of models to express the ever-expanding horizon of meaning in Christ. All such models are grounded as conventional truth in an understanding of religious interiority, a religious interiority that is oriented proleptically toward an undefinable original awareness and that entails personal and social commitment to the compassionate rule of God in the world. Mahāyāna Christian theology takes present insight and awareness as the occasion for the constant "stretching forth" of the mind toward the presence of God as Abba, which enfolds and structures the mind of original purity, and toward the Spirit-realization of justice and peace in the concrete world.

In a word, this Mahāyāna interpretation of the meaning of Christ is an attempt to express the word of the Father from silence within one particular cultural and philosophic tradition. It is a clothing in particular words of that silence. One is not to remain in the naked awareness of Abba silence, but, clothed in the Spirit, to act ethically and intelligently in the world of dependent co-arising.

As St. Paul insists, we are to awaken to the meaning of the risen Christ:

> Wake up from your sleep,
> rise from the dead,
> and Christ will enlighten you [Eph. 4:14].

Notes

INTRODUCTION

1. Raimundo Panikkar, *The Intrareligious Dialogue*, p. 40, distinguishes an interreligious dialogue that takes place between distinct participants from an intrareligious dialogue that is "an inner dialogue with myself, an encounter in the depths of my personal religiousness, having met another religious experience on that very intimate level." Also see William Johnston, *The Mirror Mind*, p. 24n10.

2. John P. Keenan, "The Intent and Structure of Yogācāra Philosophy: Its Relevance for Modern Religious Thought," *Annual Memoirs of the Otani University Shin Buddhist Comprehensive Research Institute* 4 (1986): 41–60.

CHAPTER 1

1. See Don F. Morgan, *Wisdom in the Old Testament Traditions*, p. 139.

2. James T. Crenshaw, *Old Testament Wisdom*, pp. 39–41. Also see Crenshaw, "Method in Determining Wisdom Influence upon 'Historical' Literature," *Journal of Biblical Literature* 88 (1969): 129–42; also in *Studies in Ancient Israelite Wisdom*, pp. 418–94.

3. Crenshaw, *Old Testament Wisdom*, p. 57.

4. Ibid.

5. In his "Form Critical Problem of the Hexateuch," in *The Problem of the Hexateuch and Other Essays*, Gerhard von Rad argues that the full confession of Israel's exodus tradition includes both the five books of the Pentateuch and Joshua, which describes the settlement of the chosen people in the chosen land. Thus he prefers the term "Hexateuch" over the term "Pentateuch."

6. Gerhard von Rad, *Old Testament Theology*, vol. 1, pp. 230ff.; Crenshaw, *Gerhard von Rad*, pp. 61–62.

7. Von Rad, *Deuteronomy*, pp. 21–31. Also treated in his *Studies in Deuteronomy* and his *Das Gottesvolk im Deuteronomium*.

8. The *Jerusalem Bible* is the usual source for scriptural quotations, except where noted.

9. J. L. McKenzie, *Myths and Realities: Studies in Biblical Theology*, p. 51.

10. C. H. Dodd, *Interpretation of the Fourth Gospel*, p. 263.

11. The Elohist tradition emphasized vision experiences. See Crenshaw, *Gerhard von Rad*, p. 73.

12. McKenzie, *Myths and Realities*, p. 46.

13. Thorleif Boman, *Hebrew Thought Compared with the Greek*, pp. 69ff.

14. Oskar Grether, *Name und Wort Gottes im Alten Testament (Beihefte zur Zeitschrift für die altestamentliche Wissenschaft)*, vol. 64, pp. 59–80. Quoted in McKenzie, *Myths and Realities*, p. 44.

15. Crenshaw, *Old Testament Wisdom*, p. 202.

16. Von Rad, *Deuteronomy*, p. 23; cf. *Old Testament Theology*, vol. 1, p. 231.

17. Crenshaw, *Old Testament Wisdom*, p. 202.

18. J. L. Crenshaw, "Popular Questioning of the Justice of God in Ancient Israel," in *Studies in Ancient Israelite Wisdom*, p. 293.

19. Crenshaw, *Old Testament Wisdom*, p. 196.

20. While not attempting to offer any judgment of the prologue or epilogue of the text of Job, attention is herein focused on the verse sections as an independent unit.

21. Crenshaw, *Old Testament Wisdom*, p. 111, suggests that in the second speech from the tempest Yahweh might be interpreted as claiming that he himself is having some trouble with the problem.

22. See Crenshaw, *Old Testament Wisdom*, pp. 93–99.

23. As in Job and Qoheleth also. See Walther Zimmerli, "Concerning the Structure of Old Testament Wisdom," in *Studies in Ancient Israelite Wisdom*, p. 177.

24. Crenshaw, *Old Testament Wisdom*, p. 208; R. B. Y. Scott, *The Way of Wisdom in the Old Testament*, p. 4. For an opposing opinion that emphasizes the lack of dichotomy between wisdom thought and Yahwism, see Roland E. Murphy, "Wisdom and Yahweism," in *No Famine in the Land: Studies in Honor of John L. McKenzie*, pp. 117–27.

25. Crenshaw, *Old Testament Wisdom*, p. 209.

26. Ibid., pp. 209–10.

27. The historical source for this personification of wisdom remains unclear. It would appear that this passage from Proverbs is the first instance of such a literary usage. Crenshaw, *Old Testament Wisdom*, p. 98, thinks that this usage has a non-Israelite source, probably the Egyptian concept of Ma'at.

28. This passage is difficult to interpret. I here follow the translation and interpretation of R. B. Y. Scott, *The Way of Wisdom in the Old Testament*, pp. 166–70. Verses 7–9 of the text seem to be a prayer on riches that has been appended to the preceding verses. Thus they are omitted.

29. This information is reported in the translator's foreword to the text, written by the grandson of Sirach in 132 B.C.E.

30. This fifth verse is present in the Hebrew text, but not in the Greek. See the *Jerusalem Bible*, p. 1037, n. 1:d.

31. Scott, *The Way of Wisdom*, p. 213.

32. Ibid.

33. Crenshaw, *Old Testament Wisdom*, p. 177.

34. Ibid., p. 176.

35. W. F. Arndt and F. W. Gringrich, *A Greek-English Lexicon of the New Testament and Other Early Christian Literature*, p. 120.

36. W. Gesenius, *A Hebrew and English Lexicon of the Old Testament*, p. 210; and *The Interpreter's Dictionary of the Bible*, p. 746, under the entry "Vanity."

37. Treated later in the introduction to Western mystic thinking.

38. See Wi. 8:20, where the soul is described as entering the body. Scott, *The Way of Wisdom*, p. 220, mentions the Platonic doctrine of the preexistence of the soul.

39. Crenshaw, *Old Testament Wisdom*, p. 179.

40. F. Copelston, *A History of Philosophy*. Vol. 1: *Greece and Rome*, part 2, pp. 166–67.

41. A direct parallel to the Buddhist term *prajñā-pāramitā*, the perfection of

wisdom, which was the banner cry of the mystic movement of the early Mahāyāna Buddhists.

CHAPTER 2

1. James M. Robinson, "Logoi Sophon: On the Gattung of Q," in *Trajectories through Early Christianity*, pp. 71–113.

2. M. Jack Suggs, *Wisdom, Christology, and Law in Matthew's Gospel.*

3. Ibid., p. 28.

4. Ibid., p. 40.

5. Ibid., p. 28.

6. Ibid., pp. 13–19, 58–61.

7. Ibid., pp. 33–58.

8. Ibid., p. 57; see also chap. 4, in Suggs, where, in Mt. 11:28–30, the invitation to take up Jesus' yoke and find rest is traced back to Old Testament wisdom themes.

9. See Suggs, *Wisdom, Christology, and Law*, pp. 89–95, and Todt, *The Son of Man in the Synoptic Tradition*, pp. 250–51.

10. Suggs, *Wisdom, Christology, and Law*, p. 97.

11. Hans Conzelmann, "Paulus und die Weisheit," in *New Testament Studies*, vol. 12, pp. 213–44.

12. C. H. Dodd, *Interpretation of the Fourth Gospel*, p. 275.

13. See Raymond E. Brown, *The Gospel according to John I–XII*, pp. 21–23, for the determination of the original lines of the hymn.

14. Dodd, *Interpretation of the Fourth Gospel*, p. 282.

15. See Brown, *The Gospel according to John*, p. 13, on verse 14.

16. See Bernard Lonergan, *Method in Theology*, pp. 81–85, on contexts of meaning.

17. A. Harnack, *The Sayings of Jesus*, p. 301, cited approvingly by Suggs, *Wisdom, Christology, and Law*, p. 86.

18. In the words *kai hō ean bouletai ho hios apokalupsai*, the verb *apokalupsai* is used absolutely, with no object being specified. Suggs, *Wisdom, Christology, and Law*, p. 76, suggests that the object should be understood as "these things," rather than the traditional "him," that is, the Father. But I follow his alternate reading: "And any one to whom the Son chooses to give a revelation," since the emphasis seems to lie in the type of consciousness that can receive a wisdom revelation, and not on the content of such revelation.

19. Arndt and Gringrich, *Greek-English Lexicon of the New Testament*, p. 537.

20. For the identification of the *gattung,* see W. Wuellner, "Haggadic-Homily Genre in 1 Corinthians 1–3," *Journal of Biblical Literature* (1970): 199–204.

21. Biger A. Pearson, "Hellenistic-Jewish Wisdom Speculation and Paul," in *Aspects of Wisdom in Judaism and Early Christianity*, p. 56.

22. See Hans Conzelmann, *A Commentary on the First Epistle to the Corinthians*, "Excursus: The Parties," pp. 33–34, for the question of the difficulty in determining the nature of the factional groups.

23. Conzelmann, *A Commentary on the First Epistle to the Corinthians*, p. 38n56.

24. Ibid., p. 38.

25. Ibid., p. 47.

26. Conzelmann's translation.

27. See James M. Robinson, "The Johannine Trajectory," in *Trajectories through Early Christianity*, pp. 242–46. Cf. Brown, *The Gospel according to John*, p. 195.

28. G. Bornkamm, "Zur Interpretation des Johannes-Evangeliums 'Eine Auseinandersetzung mit Käsemanns Schrift' Jesu letzter Wille nach Johannes 17," *Geschichte und Glaube*, pp. 116–17. Translation from Robinson, "The Johannine Trajectory," p. 259.

29. E. Haenchen, *Gott und Mensch*, p. 68, cited in Robinson, "The Johannine Trajectory," p. 225. Haenchen's description of John's acceptance of the need for miracles because "man usually comes to this true faith only when a miracle opens his eyes to it" is irrelevant to those of us who have never seen a miracle.

30. Robinson, "The Johannine Trajectory," p. 246.

31. Brown, *The Gospel according to John*, pp. 116–25.

32. The term *anōthen* means both "again" and "from above." Nicodemus takes it in the former sense, while Jesus' primary meaning seems to be the latter. See Brown, *The Gospel according to John*, p. 130.

33. Joachim Jeremias, "Abba," in *The Central Message of the New Testament*, pp. 17, 20. For the fully documented version, see *Abba: Studien zur neutestamentlichen Theologie und Zeitgeschichte*.

34. For a bibliography on the subject, see Edward Schillebeeckx, *Jesus: An Experiment in Christology*, pp. 256–57.

35. Jeremias, "Abba," p. 30.

36. Ibid., p. 22.

37. Ibid., p. 17.

38. Schillebeeckx, *Jesus*, p. 262.

39. Jeremias, "Abba," p. 25.

40. Suggs, *Wisdom, Christology, and Law*, p. 76.

41. Conzelmann, *A Commentary on the First Epistle to the Corinthians*, p. 47.

42. Schillebeeckx, *Jesus*, p. 539.

43. Ibid., p. 542.

44. Ibid., p. 384.

45. Ibid., p. 395.

46. Schillebeeckx, *Christ: The Experience of Jesus as Lord*, p. 793.

47. Also see Norman Perrin, *The Resurrection according to Matthew, Mark, and Luke.*

48. Ignatius of Antioch, *Epistula ad Magnesios*, 8:2.

CHAPTER 3

1. See Bernard Lonergan, *Method in Theology*, pp. 81–85, and *The Way to Nicea: The Dialectical Development of Trinitarian Theology*, pp. 1–17, for an explanation of realms of meaning.

2. George L. Prestige, *God in Patristic Thought*, p. 236, on the involvement of the Christian thinkers, writes that they were engaged with a "genuine speculative interest to infer from the biblical data what God really is. The theological problem was for them an exercise in Christian philosophy, no less absorbing for its own sake than necessary to be undertaken in order to preserve the gospel. . . ." This seems an appropriate corrective to the overemphasis on the apologetic motives for the Greek Christian thinkers.

3. Justin, *Dialogue* 8, in Dods, Reith, and Pratten, *The Writings of Justin Martyr and Athanagoras,* in *Ante-Nicene Library,* vol. 1, p. 198. For an account of Justin's knowledge of Greek philosophy, see Erwin R. Goodenough, *The Theology of Justin Martyr,* pp. 57–77.

4. Justin, *Dialogue* 8, in *Ante-Nicene Library,* vol. 1, p. 198.

5. Bernard Lonergan in his *The Way to Nicea,* pp. 4–5, states that the desired goal of theoretical theology is the expression of dogma with the clarity and conciseness of Euclid's mathematical formulas.

6. Greek ideas were not simply transferred into Christian discourse but, rather, changed and fitted in order to accord with the understanding of Christian thinkers. Grillmeier, *Christ in Christian Tradition,* vol. 1: *From the Apostolic Age to Chalcedon (451),* p. 107, describes the process as that of "two steps forward and one step back."

7. For a complete and insightful sketch of Philo, see Louth, *The Origins of the Christian Mystical Tradition,* pp. 18–35.

8. Schillebeeckx, *Christ: The Experience of Jesus as Lord,* pp. 181–92.

9. Richard Alfred Norris, *God and World in Early Christian Theology,* pp. 99–128. See Prestige, *God in Patristic Thought,* pp. 104–6, for an account of Tertullian's acumen in the theoretical understanding of the Trinity.

10. Jaroslav Pelikan, *The Christian Tradition, a History of Doctrinal Development,* vol. 1: *The Emergence of the Catholic Tradition (100–600),* pp. 209–10.

11. Eusebius of Caesarea, *The History of the Church,* trans., G. A. Williamson, p. 216.

12. Bernard Lonergan, *Insight: A Study of Human Understanding,* pp. 226ff., on the nature of bias.

13. *Stromata,* 1:1, quoted in Edwin Hatch, *The Influence of Greek Ideas on Christianity,* pp. 130–31. Also see R. E. Lilla, *Clement of Alexandria: A Study in Christian Platonism and Gnosticism,* pp. 9–59, "Clement's Views on the Origin and Value of Greek Philosophy."

14. So Adolph von Harnack in his *Lehrbuck der Dogmengeschichte,* English trans. Neil Buchanan, *The History of Dogma.*

15. So Charles D. Gore, who writes in *The Incarnation of the Son,* p. 105, that Greek thought provided a "language fitted, as none other has been, to furnish an exact and permanent terminology for doctrinal purposes."

16. See Hatch, *The Influence of Greek Ideas,* p. 242.

17. See Prestige, *God in Patristic Thought,* pp. 37–54, on the intermingling of the meaning of the terms *agenetos* (unoriginated) and *agennetos* (unbegotten).

18. Pelikan, *The Emergence,* pp. 81–97.

19. Goodenough, *The Theology of Justin Martyr,* pp. 212ff.

20. Frederick Copleston, *A History of Philosophy,* vol. 1: *Greece and Rome,* pp. 69–73.

21. Ignatius, *Epistle to the Ephesians,* 7:2, quoted and trans. Grillmeier, *Christ in Christian Tradition,* p. 87.

22. See Richard A. Norris, *God and the World in Early Christian Theology,* chap. 1, "Greek and Hellenistic Cosmology," pp. 11–40, for a presentation of the philosophical idea of God, in light of which the foregoing Christian claims about Jesus must have appeared absurd indeed.

23. Origen, *Against Celsus,* 4:18, trans. Grillmeier, *Christ in Christian Tradition,* p. 105.

24. Goodenough, *Justin Martyr*, pp. 139–73; Grillmeier, *Christ in Christian Tradition*, pp. 108ff.

25. Grillmeier, *Christ in Christian Tradition*, pp. 138–48.

26. Athanasius, *Orations against the Arians*, 3:27, quoted in Grillmeier, *Christ in Christian Tradition*, p. 247.

27. Pelikan, *The Emergence*, p. 195.

28. William G. Rusch, *The Trinitarian Controversy*, p. 49. Denzinger and Schonmetzer, *Enchiridion Symbolum Definitionum et Declarationum de Rebus Fidei et Morum*, no. 125, p. 52.

29. Maurice Wiles, *The Making of Christian Doctrine: A Study in the Principles of Early Doctrinal Development*, pp. 33–34.

30. Maurice Wiles, "Homoousios ēmin," *Journal of Theological Studies* 16 (1965):454–61.

31. Pelikan, *The Emergence*, p. 174.

32. *Stromata*, 5:105,4, quoted in Grillmeier, *Christ in Christian Tradition*, pp. 137–38.

33. *Stromata*, 3:7,59,3, quoted in Grillmeier, *Christ in Christian Tradition*, pp. 137–38.

34. Grillmeier, *Christ in Christian Tradition*, p. 178.

35. Ibid.

36. Ibid., p. 34.

37. Ibid., p. 308.

38. Ibid., pp. 316–17.

39. Ibid., pp. 330–40.

40. Ibid., p. 345.

41. See Wiles, *The Making of Christian Doctrine*, pp. 56–59, for a discussion of the influence of liturgical practices on the doctrinal understanding of the soul of Christ.

42. Pelikan, *The Emergence*, pp. 251–52.

43. *Catechetical Homilies*, 3:5, quoted and trans. Pelikan, *The Emergence*, p. 251.

44. Grillmeier, *Christ in Christian Tradition*, p. 427.

45. Ibid., p. 477.

46. Ibid., pp. 447ff.

47. Ibid., pp. 530–39.

48. Ibid., p. 549.

49. Ibid., p. 36.

50. Pelikan, *The Emergence*, p. 229.

51. See Prestige, *God in Patristic Thought*, pp. 80ff., for a discussion on why the divinity of the Spirit was not recognized in explicit teaching. He stresses the fact that it was indeed acknowledged in the faith awareness of the church and the fathers.

52. J. N. D. Kelly, *Early Christian Doctrines*, p. 67.

53. See G. W. H. Lampe, *God as Spirit*, p. 67.

54. J. N. D. Kelly, *Early Christian Doctrines*, p. 256.

55. *Ad Seraphion*, 1:24, quoted in Pelikan, *The Emergence*, pp. 215–16; Kelly, *Early Christian Doctrines*, p. 107.

56. J. N. D. Kelly, *Early Christian Doctrines*, pp. 260–63.

57. Prestige, *God in Patristic Thought*, p. 80.

58. Kelly, J. N. D., *Early Christian Doctrines*, p. 107.

59. See Prestige, *God in Patristic Thought*, pp. 98–102, for an explanation that highlights Tertullian's deep understanding of "the economy."

60. J. N. D. Kelly, *Early Christian Doctrines*, pp. 104–8 on Irenaeus.

61. Ibid., pp. 109–10.

62. Ibid., pp. 115–23, for the distinction between dynamic monarchianism and modalistic monarchianism.

63. Reported by Epiphanius, *Against Eighty Heresies*, 62:1,4ff., quoted in Kelly, *Early Christian Doctrines*, p. 122.

64. Prestige, *God in Patristic Thought*, p. 163.

65. Ibid., p. 167.

66. Kelly, *Early Christian Doctrines*, p. 110. Also cf. Karl Rahner, *The Trinity*, whose basic thesis is the identity of the "economic" and the "immanent" Trinity.

67. Prestige, *God in Patristic Thought*, p. 188.

68. Ibid., pp. 157–60.

69. Ibid., p. 162.

70. Ibid., p. 301. Also see Rahner, *The Trinity*, pp. 42–45, 113–15, for a discussion on the problem generated by the modern connotation of self-consciousness attached to the term "person" and the question of the advisability of the continued use of the term.

71. Kelly, *Early Christian Doctrines*, p. 115.

72. Ibid., p. 110. See R. A. Markus, "Trinitarian Theology and the Economy," *Journal of Theological Studies* (1955): 89–102, for more data on the place of Hippolytus.

73. Prestige, *God in Patristic Thought*, pp. 97ff., on the nature of Tertullian's thinking on the economy.

74. *Epistles*, 214:4 and 236:6, quoted in Kelly, *Early Christian Doctrines*, p. 265.

75. *Epistles*, 38:5, and *Fourth Book against Eunomius*, 2:29, of Pseudo-Basil, quoted in Kelly, *Early Christian Doctrines*, p. 265.

76. Prestige, *God in Patristic Thought*, p. 245.

77. Ibid., pp. 243–45. The tract *De Sacrosanta Trinitate* printed at the end of Cyril's writings is the work of an unknown author not before the middle of the seventh century. See Prestige, pp. 280, 311. Large portions were included in *The Orthodox Faith* of John of Damascus.

78. Prestige, *God in Patristic Thought*, p. 291.

79. J. N. D. Kelly, *Early Christian Doctrines*, p. 274.

80. See Lonergan, *De Deo Trino*, vol. 2, pp. 201–94.

81. Thomas Aquinas, *Summa Theologiae*, pp. 146–223 (questions 27 to 43). Cf. Paul Vanier, *Theologie trinitaire chez Saint Thomas d'Aquin: Evolution du concept d'action notionelle*.

82. Prestige, *God in Patristic Thought*, p. 299.

83. Wiles, *The Making of Christian Doctrine*, p. 117.

84. Ibid., p. 174.

85. Rahner, *The Trinity*, pp. 10–15.

86. Paul Tillich, *Systematic Theology*, vol. 3, p. 291.

87. G. W. H. Lampe, "The Holy Spirit and the Person of Christ," in *Christ, Faith and History*, pp. 119–20.

CHAPTER 4

1. Pelikan, *The Emergence of the Catholic Tradition*, pp. 1–10.

2. Gregory of Nyssa, *Patrologia Graeca*, vol. 44, p. 1269c, Beatitude 6.

3. K. E. Kirk, "The Evaluation of the Doctrine of the Trinity," in *Essays on the Trinity and the Incarnation by Members of the Anglican Communion*, pp. 226–37.

4. Thomas Merton, in the foreword to William Johnston's *The Mysticism of the Cloud of Unknowing: A Modern Interpretation*, p. viii.

5. Lonergan, *Method in Theology*, p. 106.

6. Note especially the background context for the Gospel of John as explained in Schillebeeckx, *Christ: The Experience of Jesus as Lord*, pp. 307–49.

7. John Meyendorff, *Christ in Eastern Christian Thought*, pp. 118–19.

8. A. Festugière, *Contemplation et vie contemplative selon Platon*, p. 5.

9. Werner Jaeger, *Paideia* 2:65ff.; Louth, *The Origins of the Christian Mystical Tradition*, p. 2.

10. Festugière, *Contemplation et vie contemplative*, p. 217.

11. Ibid., p. 5.

12. *The Dialogues of Plato*, trans. Jowett, vol. 1, p. 456; *Phaedo*, 388:80.

13. Festugière, *Contemplation et vie contemplative*, p. 160.

14. Copleston, *A History of Philosophy: Greece and Rome*, pp. 62–63.

15. Festugière, *Contemplation et vie contemplative*, pp. 77–78.

16. Ibid., p. 215.

17. *The Dialogues of Plato*, trans. Jowett, vol. 2, pp. 341–46; *Republic*, 514^{a1}–518^{d1}.

18. See Étienne Gilson, *Being and Some Philosophers*, pp. 10–22.

19. *The Dialogues of Plato*, trans. Jowett, vol. 1, p. 454; *Phaedo*, 78.

20. Ibid., vol. 1, p. 455; *Phaedo*, 79.

21. Festugière, *Contemplation et vie contemplative*, p. 95.

22. *Nous* is a term difficult to render in translation. It is usually translated as "mind" or "intellect." Louth explains it as "more like an organ of mystical union than anything suggested by our words 'mind' or 'intellect,' " *The Origins of the Christian Mystical Tradition*, p. xvi.

23. *The Dialogues of Plato*, trans. Jowett, vol. 2, p. 361; *Republic*, 7:533d. Jowett translates "some outlandish slough."

24. Festugière, *Contemplation et vie contemplative*, pp. 128–29.

25. Ibid., p. 129, based upon *Phaedo*, 67c; trans. Jowett, vol. 1, p. 440.

26. Louth, *The Origins of the Christian Mystical Tradition*, p. 8; *The Dialogues of Plato*, trans. Jowett, vol. 1, p. 389; *Phaedo*, 67d.

27. Louth, *The Origins of the Christian Mystical Tradition*, p. 8.

28. Festugière, *Contemplation et vie contemplative*, p. 157.

29. Ibid., p. 164.

30. Ibid., p. 165.

31. Ibid., pp. 164–209, for an account of the nature of the two kinds of dialectic.

32. Ibid., p. 13.

33. *The Dialogues of Plato*, vol. 1, pp. 442–61 (*Phaedo*, 69a–84b).

34. Festugière, *Contemplation et vie contemplative*, pp. 260–62, 343–46.

35. Ibid., pp. 226–27.

36. See Festugière, *Contemplation et vie contemplative*, p. 227n, where he explains the similarity of this with the apophatic thinking of the Neoplatonists and of Pseudo-Dionysius. Festugière interprets Plato in the light of these Neoplatonists and argues for the correctness of their interpretations.

37. See Louth, *The Origins of the Christian Mystical Tradition*, chaps. 2–3, for accounts of Plotinus and the Jewish Platonist thought of Philo.

38. Festugière, *Contemplation et vie contemplative*, p. 5.

39. Meyendorff, *Christ in Eastern Christian Thought*, p. 144.

40. See Erwin R. Goodenough, *The Theology of Justin Martyr*, pp. 66–71.

41. Meyendorff, *Christ in Eastern Christian Thought*, chap. 3, pp. 47–68, for the condemnation of Origenism.

42. Louth, *The Origins of the Christian Mystical Tradition*, p. 76.

43. Anders Nygren, *Eros and Agape*, p. 230n.

44. So Karl Barth, *Church Dogmatics*, III.1, pp. 191ff.; Emil Brunner, *Man in Revolt: A Christian Anthropology*, p. 449; and A. Nygren, *Eros and Agape*, p. 230.

45. Vladimir Lossky, *In the Image and Likeness of God*, p. 129.

46. Louth, *The Origins of the Christian Mystical Tradition*, p. 79.

47. Athanasius, *Contra Gentes*, 34, quoted in Louth, *The Origins of the Christian Mystical Tradition*, p. 79.

48. Maurice Wiles, *Christian Fathers*, p. 84.

49. Jaroslav Pelikan, *The Light of the World: A Basic Image in Early Christian Thought*, pp. 55–57.

50. Louth, *The Origins of the Christian Mystical Tradition*, p. 80.

51. Meyendorff, *Christ in Eastern Christian Thought*, p. 114.

52. Ibid.

53. Cyril of Alexandria, *Commentary on John*, 1:9, quoted in Meyendorff, *Christ in Eastern Christian Thought*, p. 115.

54. Cyril, *In Rom*, in *Patrologia Graeca*, vol. 74, p. 789a–b, quoted in Meyendorff, *Christ in Eastern Christian Thought*, pp. 116–17.

55. Pelikan, *The Emergence*, p. 285.

56. Wiles, *Christian Fathers*, p. 84.

57. Athanasius, *De Incarnatione*, 20; *Patrologia Graeca*, vol. 25, p. 132b; quoted in Meyendorff, *Christ in Eastern Christian Thought*, pp. 117–18.

58. Festugière, *Contemplation et vie contemplative*, p. 61.

59. See Wiles, "Does Christology Rest on a Mistake?" in *Christ, Faith and History*, pp. 3–12, for a critique of the doctrines of creation, fall, and redemption as they influenced the evolution of Christology.

60. Wiles, *Christian Fathers*, p. 95.

61. Ibid., pp. 78, 94.

62. Festugière, *Contemplation et vie contemplative*, pp. 220ff., 247–49.

63. Louth, *The Origins of the Christian Mystical Tradition*, pp. xv–xvi.

64. Lonergan, *Insight*, pp. 251–62; "Cognitional Structure," *Continuum* 2, no. 3 (1964): 530–42.

65. William James, *The Varieties of Religious Experience*, p. 367.

66. Jaroslav Pelikan, *The Christian Tradition: A History of the Development of Doctrine*, vol. 2: *The Spirit of Eastern Christendom (600–1700)*, pp. 30–31.

67. This theme will be treated in chap. 5, below. Cf. the account of Jacques Maritain, *The Degrees of Knowledge*, pp. 236ff., and chap. 7, pp. 310–87, for the development of apophatic theology in St. John of the Cross.

68. Schillebeeckx, *Christ*, pp. 31–34.

69. In his *Mysticism: Sacred and Profane*, R. C. Zaehner presents a typology of mystic experiences. For a concise study of Zaehner's thought, see William Lloyd Newell, *Struggle and Submission: R. C. Zaehner on Mysticism*. While the competitive thrust of Zaehner can perhaps be understood in light of his argumentation with Huxley's *philosophia perennis* version of Vedanta, Zaehner's interpretation of Buddhist texts is mistaken at almost every point.

70. Lonergan, *Method in Theology*, p. 106.

71. Ibid., p. 29.

72. Ibid., p. 77.

73. Ibid., p. 76.

74. Ibid., p. 273.

75. *Pseudo-Macarie, Oeuvres spirituelles*, vol. 1: *Homilies propes a la collection III, introduction, traduction, et notes (avec le texte Grec)*, trans., Vincent Desprez, p. 189.

76. Louth, *The Origins of the Christian Mystical Tradition*, p. 74.

77. The placing of the Song of Songs within the broad context of the wisdom literature of the Old Testament has been a subject of varied and differing opinions. It is clearly of a different genre from the wisdom texts treated in chap. 1, above, and thus was not mentioned there. But, because it was attributed to Solomon, the model of Israelite wisdom, it was treated by both Jewish and Christian thinkers together with that wisdom literature. For an account, see Marvin H. Pope, *Song of Songs: A New Translation with Introduction and Commentary*, pp. 17–229. Its intense imagery is quite clearly sexual, and attempts to understand just why such a work was included among the scriptures seem to have been the chief factor in the development of allegorizing interpretations of the poem to represent the love between Yahweh and Israel, or between God and the church. Following the lead of the rabbis, the Christian fathers also insisted upon this allegorization.

78. The title of this work is "The Words of Qoheleth, Son of David, King in Jerusalem." The term "Qoheleth" most likely refers to the function of one who speaks in the assembly (*qahal*, Greek: *ekklesia*), thus resulting in the Greek and Latin form, "Ecclesiastes." See the introduction in *The Jerusalem Bible*, pp. 978–79.

79. *Origen: An Exhortation to Martyrdom, Prayer, First Principles: Book IV, Prologue to the Commentary on the Song of Songs, Homily XXVII on Numbers*, trans. and introduction by Rowan A. Greer, p. 232.

80. Karl Rahner, "Le début d'une doctrine des cinq sens spirituelles chez Origène," *Revue d'ascétique et de mystique* (1932), p. 132.

81. See *Pseudo-Macarie*, Desprez, p. 77.

82. *Evagrius Ponticus: The Pratikos, Chapters on Prayer*, trans. with introduction and notes by John Eudes Bamberger, p. 63n52.

83. *Evagrius*, Bamberger, p. 49.

84. Rahner, "Le début," p. 132.

85. *Origen*, Greer, p. 234.

86. Ibid.

87. Ibid., p. 99.

88. Pelikan, *The Emergence*, p. 48.

89. J. N. D. Kelly, *Early Christian Doctrines*, p. 180.

90. Translation from *On First Principles*, 1:8,1, given in Kelly, *Early Christian Doctrines*, pp. 180–81.

91. *Origen*, Greer, p. 216.

92. Ibid., pp. 214–15.

93. Ibid., p. 76.

94. Ibid., pp. 203–4.

95. Ibid., p. 25.

96. *Evagrius*, Bamberger, p. xxv.

97. Antoine Guillaumont, *"Kephālaia Gnostica" d'Evagre le Pontique et l'histoire de l'Origénisme chez les Grecs et chez les Syriens*, p. 158.

98. *Evagrius*, Bamberger, p. lxxviii.

99. Ibid., p. 34.

100. *Pseudo-Macarie*, Desprez, pp. 37–46.

101. Ibid., p. 38.

102. Werner Jaeger, *Two Rediscovered Works of Ancient Christian Literature: Gregory of Nyssa and Macarius*, p. 229.

103. *Pseudo-Macarie*, Desprez, p. 280.

104. Ibid., p. 305.

105. Ibid., p. 303.

106. Ibid., p. 75.

107. Ibid., p. 77.

108. Ibid., p. 147.

109. *Origen*, Greer, p. 234.

110. *Pseudo-Macarie*, Desprez, p. 105.

111. Quoted from A. J. Mason, *Macarius: Fifty Spiritual Homilies*, in Louth, *The Origins of the Christian Mystical Tradition*, p. 122.

112. Mason's text quoted in Louth, *The Origins of the Christian Mystical Tradition*, p. 123.

113. Meyendorff, *Christ in Eastern Christian Thought*, p. 60.

114. *Origen*, Greer, p. 204.

115. *Evagrius*, Bamberger, p. 33.

116. Ibid., p. 64.

117. Ibid., p. 56.

118. Ibid., p. 66.

119. *Pseudo-Macarie*, Desprez, p. 187.

120. See Meyendorff, *Christ in Eastern Christian Thought*, p. 93.

121. A. Guillaumont, *Les Six Centuries des "Kephālaia Gnostica" d'Evagre le Pontique. Édition critique de la version syriaque commune et édition d'une nouvelle version syriaque, intègrale, avec une double traduction française*, p. 199. Also cf. Guillaumont, *Les "Kephālaia Gnostica" d'Evagre le Pontique et l'histoire de l'Origénisme chez les Grecs et chez les Syriens*, pp. 49–50.

122. *Evagrius*, Bamberger, p. 48.

123. *Pseudo-Macarie*, Desprez, p. 185.

CHAPTER 5

1. Jean Daniélou, *Platonisme et théologie mystique: Doctrine spirituelle de Saint Gregoire de Nysse*, pp. 6–7.

2. Ibid., p. 10.

3. *Patrologia Graeca*, vol. 44, p. 758b.

4. Ibid., p. 722a; Daniélou, *Platonisme et théologie mystique*, p. 18, for a French translation.

5. Ibid., p. 1000c; Daniélou, *Platonisme et théologie mystique*, p. 18. See Herbert Musurillo, *From Glory to Glory: Texts from Gregory of Nyssa's Mystical Writings*, selected and with an introduction by Jean Daniélou, p. 247, for an English translation.

6. Gregory of Nyssa, "Homily on the Beatitudes," *Patrologia Graeca*, vol. 44, p. 1125c.

7. *Patrologia Graeca*, vol. 44, p. 136c–d.

8. Ibid., p. 137a–b; Daniélou, *Platonisme et théologie mystique*, p. 49.

9. Ibid., p. 137b–c.

10. Ibid., p. 89c; Daniélou, *Platonisme et théologie mystique*, p. 43.

11. Ibid., pp. 949c–952a; Musurillo, *From Glory to Glory*, pp. 219–20.

12. Daniélou, *Platonisme et théologie mystique*, pp. 38–39.

13. *Patrologia Graeca*, vol. 46, p. 81b; Daniélou, *Platonisme et théologie mystique*, p. 39.

14. Ibid., p. 93c; Daniélou, *Platonisme et théologie mystique*, p. 39.

15. See Daniélou, *Platonisme et théologie mystique*, p. 46.

16. Schaff and Wace, *A Select Library of Nicene and Post-Nicene Fathers of the Christian Church*, vol. 6, p. 483a; Daniélou, *Platonisme et théologie mystique*, p. 71.

17. See Daniélou, *Platonisme et théologie mystique*, pp. 71–83, for a discussion of the passions.

18. *Patrologia Graeca*, vol. 46, p. 57b; Schaff, *Nicene and Post-Nicene Fathers*, p. 441a.

19. *Patrologia Graeca*, vol. 44, p. 428c; Gregory of Nyssa, *The Life of Moses,* trans., introduction, and notes by Abraham J. Malherbe and Everett Ferguson, p. 135.

20. For a discussion of the two types of *apatheia* in Gregory, the control of the passions during life and their final elimination after death, see Daniélou, *Platonisme et théologie mystique*, pp. 92–103.

21. *Patrologia Graeca*, vol. 44, p. 769d.

22. Cf. Daniélou, *Platonisme et théologie mystique*, pp. 119–20.

23. *Patrologia Graeca*, vol. 44, p. 100d; Musurillo, *From Glory to Glory*, p. 247.

24. See Gregory, "On Virginity," *Patrologia Graeca*, vol. 46, p. 376b–c; Daniélou, *Platonisme et théologie mystique*, p. 120.

25. *Patrologia Graeca*, vol. 44, p. 737c; Daniélou, *Platonisme et théologie mystique*, p. 123.

26. Ibid., p. 445b; Daniélou, *Platonisme et théologie mystique*, p. 123.

27. Ibid., p. 736b–c; Daniélou, *Platonisme et théologie mystique*, p. 124.

28. Ibid., p. 996a–b; Daniélou, *Platonisme et théologie mystique*, pp. 126–27; Musurillo, *From Glory to Glory*, p. 243.

29. On the original image and the garments of skin, see Daniélou, *Platonisme et théologie mystique*, pp. 48–62.

30. *Patrologia Graeca*, vol. 44, p. 633a–b; Daniélou, *Platonisme et théologie mystique*, p. 128.

31. Daniélou, *Platonisme et théologie mystique*, p. 128.

32. *Patrologia Graeca*, vol. 44, p. 633c; Daniélou, *Platonisme et théologie mystique*, p. 128.

33. Ibid., p. 1001b; Daniélou, *Platonisme et théologie mystique*, p. 177; Musurillo, *From Glory to Glory*, p. 248.

34. Ibid., p. 453b; Daniélou, *Platonisme et théologie mystique*, p. 185.

35. Daniélou, *Platonisme et théologie mystique*, p. 185.

36. *Patrologia Graeca*, vol. 44, p. 345d; Gregory, *The Life of Moses*, p. 70.

37. Ibid., p. 345d; Gregory, *The Life of Moses*, p. 70; Daniélou, *Platonisme et théologie mystique*, p. 186.

38. Ibid., p. 504b; Daniélou, *Platonisme et théologie mystique*, p. 190.

39. Ibid., p. 377c; Gregory, *The Life of Moses*, p. 95; Daniélou, *Platonisme et théologie mystique*, p. 190.

40. Ibid., pp. 376c–377a; Gregory, *The Life of Moses*, pp. 94–95; Daniélou, *Platonisme et théologie mystique*, p. 193.

41. Ibid., p. 1000d; Musurillo, *From Glory to Glory*, p. 247; Daniélou, *Platonisme et théologie mystique*, p. 193.

42. Ibid., p. 893a; Musurillo, *From Glory to Glory*, p. 201.

43. Ibid., p. 1001b–c; Musurillo, *From Glory to Glory*, p. 248; Daniélou, *Platonisme et théologie mystique*, pp. 195–96.

44. Daniélou, *Platonisme et théologie mystique*, p. 21.

45. See Louth, *The Origins of the Christian Mystical Tradition*, p. 114.

46. *Patrologia Graeca*, vol. 46, p. 97b; Daniélou, *Platonisme et théologie mystique*, p. 204.

47. *Patrologia Graeca*, vol. 44, p. 1269c; Daniélou, *Platonisme et théologie mystique*, p. 209.

48. See Daniélou, *Platonisme et théologie mystique*, p. 9, for his criticism of the work of P. Arnou and P. Festugière, which implies that Gregory substituted Greek Platonism for Christian faith.

49. A reference to baptism, for which see Daniélou, *Platonisme et théologie mystique*, pp. 23–35.

50. Here, as throughout the Greek fathers, the influence of Platonic themes and terms is apparent. The intent of Daniélou's *Platonisme et théologie mystique* is to refute the thesis that by so adopting Platonic terms, the Greek fathers have distorted the gospel message.

51. *Patrologia Graeca*, vol. 46, p. 1272a–c; Daniélou, *Platonisme et théologie mystique*, p. 211.

52. Ibid., p. 89c; Daniélou, *Platonisme et théologie mystique*, p. 212.

53. *Patrologia Graeca*, vol. 44, p. 821a–b; Daniélou, *Platonisme et théologie mystique*, p. 221.

54. See Daniélou, *Platonisme et théologie mystique*, p. 252.

55. *Patrologia Graeca*, vol. 46, p. 324b; Daniélou, *Platonisme et théologie mystique*, p. 254.

56. Ibid., p. 373a; Daniélou, *Platonisme et théologie mystique*, p. 254.

57. *Patrologia Graeca*, vol. 44, p. 828b; Musurillo, *From Glory to Glory*, pp. 167–68; Daniélou, *Platonisme et théologie mystique*, p. 255.

58. Ibid., p. 829a; Musurillo, *From Glory to Glory*, p. 167.

59. Ibid., pp. 1245d–1248b; Daniélou, *Platonisme et théologie mystique*, p. 257.

60. On ecstasy, see Daniélou, *Platonisme et théologie mystique*, p. 261.

61. *Patrologia Graeca*, vol. 44, p. 332b–c; Gregory, *The Life of Moses*, p. 59; Daniélou, *Platonisme et théologie mystique*, p. 36.

62. *Patrologia Graeca*, vol. 46, p. 361a–b; Schaff, *Nicene and Post-Nicene Fathers*, pp. 354–55; Daniélou, *Platonisme et théologie mystique*, p. 265.

63. Daniélou, *Platonisme et théologie mystique*, p. 266.

64. *Patrologia Graeca*, vol. 45, p. 940a–c; Musurillo, *From Glory to Glory*, p. 119; Daniélou, *Platonisme et théologie mystique*, p. 268.

65. Musurillo, *From Glory to Glory*, p. 291n16.

66. *Patrologia Graeca*, vol. 44, p. 873a–b; Daniélou, *Platonisme et théologie mystique*, p. 270.

67. See Daniélou, *Platonisme et théologie mystique*, pp. 271–72, for the relationship between the Eucharist and mystic ecstasy. Daniélou frequently brings out in clear and penetrating terms Gregory's deep understanding of the sacramental dimensions of mystic awareness, themes not highlighted here simply because of a diverse agenda.

68. *Patrologia Graeca*, vol. 44, p. 989c; Daniélou, *Platonisme et théologie mystique*, p. 271; Musurillo, *From Glory to Glory*, p. 240.

69. Ibid., p. 989d; Musurillo, *From Glory to Glory*, p. 239; Daniélou, *Platonisme et théologie mystique*, p. 272.

70. Daniélou, *Platonisme et théologie mystique*, pp. 291–307; Musurillo, *From Glory to Glory*, pp. 56–71 in Daniélou's introduction.

71. Cf. Bernard Lonergan, "Metaphysics as Horizon," *Current* 5 (1964): 307–18, for a parallel notion of the expanding fulfillment of the philosophic desire to know.

72. *Patrologia Graeca*, vol. 46, p. 888d; Musurillo, *From Glory to Glory*, p. 50.

73. *Patrologia Graeca*, vol. 44, p. 628c–d; Gregory, *The Life of Moses*, p. 217; Musurillo, *From Glory to Glory*, p. 51.

74. *Patrologia Graeca*, vol. 46, p. 285b–c; Musurillo, *From Glory to Glory*, pp. 51–52, 83–84.

75. *Patrologia Graeca*, vol. 45, p. 940d; Musurillo, *From Glory to Glory*, pp. 59, 120.

76. See *Patrologia Graeca*, vol. 44, p. 876b; Musurillo, *From Glory to Glory*, pp. 68, 190.

77. Ibid., pp. 729d–732a; Musurillo, *From Glory to Glory*, pp. 42, 127–28.

78. Ibid., p. 1264c; Musurillo, *From Glory to Glory*, pp. 42–43.

79. Ibid., p. 404a–d; Gregory, *The Life of Moses*, p. 115; Musurillo, *From Glory to Glory*, p. 55.

80. Ibid., p. 377a; Gregory, *The Life of Moses*, p. 95.

81. It should be remembered that when Dionysius wrote, there was little felt need to refute Greek philosophy, for its influence had already been eclipsed. A. A. Vasiliev writes that the Greek "academy had already outlived its purpose. It was no longer of great import in a Christian empire" (*History of the Byzantine Empire*, vol. 2, p. 187). Jaroslav Pelikan notes that "the closing of the Athenian academy was more the act of a coroner than an executioner," and that "teachers of philosophy then were regarded as both unwanted and harmless" (*Emergence*, p. 41). On the history of thought on the authenticity of the Dionysian corpus, see Ronard F. Hathaway, *Hierarchy and the Definition of Order in the Letters of Pseudo-Dionysius: A Study in the Form and Meaning of the Pseudo-Dionysian Writings*, introduction. On the opinions about the place of Dionysius in Christian tradition, see

H. Koch, "Die Lehre vom Bösen nach Pseudo-Dionysius Aeropagita," *Philologus* (1895): 438–54; and "Der Pseudepigraphische Character der Dionysischen Schriften," *Theologische Quartalschrift* 77 (1898): 353–420; J. Stigmayr, "Der Neuplatoniker Proklus als Vorlage der sogen. Dionysius Aeropagita in der Lehre vom Ubel," *Historisches Jarhbuch im Auftrag der Görresgesellschaft* 16 (1895): 253–73, 721–48; J. Vanneste, *Le mystique de Dieu: Essai sur la structure rationelle de la doctrine mystique de Pseudo-Denys Aeropagite* (Paris, 1959); and L. H. Grondys, "La terminologie métalogique dans la théologie Dionysienne," *Nederlands Theologisch Tijdschrift* 14ᵉ Jaargang, Afl. 6 (1960): 420–30.

82. Hathaway, *Hierarchy and the Definition of Order*, p. 136.

83. Ibid., pp. 136–37.

84. Ibid., p. xvii.

85. Copleston, *History of Philosophy*, vol. 1: *Greece and Rome*, p. 222.

86. Ibid., p. 223.

87. *Patrologia Graeca*, vol. 3, p. 640d; see Meyendorff, *Christ in Eastern Christian Thought*, p. 96.

88. Ibid., p. 165.

89. Ibid., p. 713a.

90. Quoted in Hathaway, *Hierarchy and the Definition of Order*, p. 54, from Proclus, *Elements of Theology*, p. 106.

91. *Patrologia Graeca*, vol. 3, p. 593d.

92. Ibid., p. 1000c–d.

93. Ibid., p. 998a–b.

94. *Patrologia Graeca*, vol. 4, p. 186; see U. von Balthasar, "Das Scholienwerk des Johannes von Skythopolis," *Scholastik* 15 (1940): 31–32, for a discussion of the authorship of this scholia.

95. *Patrologia Graeca*, vol. 3, p. 998a.

96. *Patrologia Graeca*, vol. 4, p. 416c.

97. Aptly translated as *cogitationis vacuitatem* by Petrus Lansselius in *Patrologia Graeca*, vol. 4, p. 418a.

98. *Patrologia Graeca*, vol. 3, p. 998b.

99. *Patrologia Graeca*, vol. 4, p. 418a.

100. Ibid., p. 418b.

101. *Patrologia Graeca*, vol. 3, pp. 586b–87a.

102. Ibid., p. 588a.

103. Ibid., p. 588b.

104. *Tēs thearchikēs agathotētos* is translated by Cordier as *Dei bonitatis*.

105. *Patrologia Graeca*, vol. 3, p. 588b.

106. *Patrologia Graeca*, vol. 4, p. 189c–d.

107. *Patrologia Graeca*, vol. 3, p. 588c.

108. Ibid., p. 588c.

109. Ibid., p. 590b.

110. Hathaway, *Hierarchy and the Definition of Order*, pp. 61–76, describes the hierarchic design of the *Letters*. They are not occasional letters addressed to friends on sundry occasions, but contain an identifiable progression of thought.

111. Ibid., p. 82.

112. *Patrologia Graeca*, vol. 3, p. 1003a; Hathaway, *Hierarchy and the Definition of Order*, p. 107.

113. Ibid., p. 1105d; Hathaway, *Hierarchy and the Definition of Order*, p. 111, and again on p. 155.

114. Hathaway, *Hierarchy and the Definition of Order*, p. 154.

115. *Patrologia Graeca*, vol. 3, p. 1108b; Hathaway, *Hierarchy and the Definition of Order*, p. 155.

116. René Roques, *L'univers Dionysien, structure hiérarchique du monde selon le Pseudo-Denys*, p. 313.

117. See Meyendorff, *Christ in Eastern Christian Thought*, p. 99.

118. Roques, *L'univers Dionysien*, p. 305.

119. *Patrologia Graeca*, vol. 3, p. 1033.

120. Ibid., p. 648a.

121. *Patrologia Graeca*, vol. 4, p. 416c. p. 592a.

122. Ibid., p. 416c.

123. Hathaway, *Hierarchy and the Definition of Order*, p. 134. See Pelikan, *The Spirit of Eastern Christendom*, pp. 65–66, on the last line, which figured in the monothelite controversy.

124. *Patrologia Graeca*, vol. 3, pp. 477c–480a.

125. W. Inge, *The Philosophy of Plotinus*, vol. 2, p. 112.

126. Christian Baur, *Christliche Lehre von der Dreieinigkeit und Menschwerdung Gottes*, vol. 2, pp. 207–51.

127. Étienne Vacherot, *Histoire critique de l'École d'Alexandrie*, p. 34.

128. Thomas Aquinas, *Summa Theologiae*, I, q. 13, a. 11.

129. Ibid., *In. Metaphysica*, lib. 5:1. See Gilson, *The Spirit of Medieval Philosophy*, p. 86.

130. Ibid., *Summa Theologiae*, I, q. 44, a. 1.

131. Gilson, *The Philosophy of St. Thomas Aquinas*, p. 105.

132. See *Summa Theologiae*, I, q. 13, where Dionysius figures as the counterfoil in six of the twelve articles.

133. Gilson, *Elements of Christian Philosophy*, p. 142.

134. Ibid., p. 140.

135. *De Potentia* q. 7, a. 5, quoted in Gilson, *Elements*, p. 140.

136. Lonergan, *Method in Theology*, pp. 81–85. Lonergan's *Insight: A Study of Human Understanding* as well as other works such as Emerich Coreth's *Metaphysics* (trans. Donceel) attempt a critical, transcendental analysis of understanding. The following Yogācāra attempt focuses more narrowly upon the structure of religious interiority and tries to explicate its inner structure. They are not, I think, rival systems, but their emphasis clearly differs.

CHAPTER 6

1. The date accepted by Étienne Lamotte, *Histoire du Bouddhisme Indien: Des origines a l'ere Śaka*, p. 15.

2. See Mascaro, *The Upanishads*, p. 117.

3. See Noriaki Hakamaya, "Kūshō rikai no mondaiten" [The Point in Understanding Emptiness], *Riso* 610 (1984): 50–64.

4. Lamotte, *Histoire*, pp. 38–43.

5. The *Nikāyas* are the earliest extant texts preserved in the Pali translations. The *Āgamas* are parallel Chinese translations. The unraveling of the literary layers

contained in these texts and the questions about their interrelationships remain a task for the future. Little literary criticism, such as has been used in understanding the Christian scriptures in the West, has been applied to these early Buddhist scriptures, which outnumber their Christian analogues by increments of ten.

6. *Mahānidadopāyasūtra*; Chinese *Āgama*, *Ta-yüan-fang-p'ien ching*, in Chalmers, *Further Dialogues of the Buddha*, pp. 305–6. See p. 342 for a parallel account of Buddha refusing to speculate with the Wandered Vacchagotta.

7. See Yuichi Kajiyama, "Bukkyō ni okeru kotoba to chinmoku" [Speech and Silence in Buddhism], in *Shukyō taiken to kotoba: Bukkyō to kirisutokyō no taiwa* [Religious Experience and Language: Buddhist Christian Dialogue], pp. 21–22. Also see *Digha-Nikāya*, ii.30; ii.56; *Milinda's Questions*, trans. I. B. Horner, p. 68.

8. *Mahāsīhanādasūtta*, as in Chalmers, *Dialogues*, pp. 52–53; see I. B. Horner, trans., *Middle Length Sayings*, 1, pp. 95–96.

9. See F. L. Woodward, *The Book of Kindred Sayings*, 5, p. 354.

10. Takeshi Sakurabe, *Kusharon no kenkyū* [A Study of Abhidharma], p. 15.

11. Taigen Kimura in his *Abhidharmaśāstra no kenkyū* (1922) first examined the historical development of Abhidharma thinking. See especially pp. 32–58.

12. Sakurabe, *Kusharon*, p. 16.

13. Nyanatiloka, *Guide through the Abhidhammapitmaka*, p. 1.

14. See Louis de la Vallée Poussin, *L'Abhidharmakośa*, introduction, p. vii. Also Leo M. Pruden's "The Abhidharma: The Origins, Growth and Development of a Literary Tradition," in *Abhidharmakośabhāṣyam* (English translation of Louis de la Vallée Poussin), pp. xxxviii-xl.

15. T. (*Taisho Shinshū Daizokyo* — the Chinese Buddhist Canon) 24, p. 408b.

16. Vasubandhu is one of the principal figures in the school of Yogācāra, to which, it is reported, he was converted by his brother Asaṅga. Erich Frauwallner in his *On the Date of the Master of the Law Vasubandhu*, argues that the works attributed to Vasubandhu are so diverse and their dating so different that there must have been two different Vasubandhus. Noel Péri, "A propos de la date de Vasubandhu," *Bulletin de l'École francaise d'Extreme-Orient*, 9 (1911), argues for the traditional recognition of a single Vasubandhu, who changed his thinking from the time when he wrote the *Abhidharmakośabhāṣya* to his later period of Yogācāra thinking.

17. De la Vallée Poussin, *L'Abhidharmakośa*, 1, 3; Pruden, p. 56.

18. Ibid., 6, 139.

19. Akira Hirakawa, *Index to the Abhidharmakośa*, pp. xii-xx.

20. Nyanatiloka, *Guide*, p. 9.

21. *Attasālinī* 3:488; quoted in Herbert Guenther, *Philosophy and Psychology in the Abhidharma*, p. 2.

22. See Lamotte, *Histoire*, pp. 444–45, 667–705, 756–59.

23. Nyanatiloka, *Guide*, p. xiv.

24. Richard Magliola in his *Derrida on the Mend* interprets the philosophy of Jacques Derrida as performing the same function vis-à-vis Western metaphysics as did Nāgārjuna vis-à-vis Abhidharma metaphysics. However, in contrast to Derrida, the central place of Nāgārjuna in Mahāyāna Buddhist thought was recognized by all Mahāyāna thinkers.

25. See Har Dayal, *The Bodhisattva Ideal in Buddhist Sanskrit Literature*, pp. 18–19.

26. Mervyn Sprung, *Lucid Exposition of the Middle Way: The Essential Chapters from the Prasannapadā of Chandrakīrti*, p. 1.

27. Conze, *The Prajñāpāramitā Literature*, p. 6.

28. Edward Conze, trans., *The Large Sutra on Perfect Wisdom, with the Divisions of the Abhisamaya-alankāra*, p. 58. According to Conze, one of the foremost authorities on the Prajñāpāramitā texts, the basic text was *The Perfection of Wisdom in Eight Thousand Verses*, which was then expanded into the larger texts of ten, fifteen, and eighteen thousand verses. The differences in these larger texts consists principally in the number of repetitions and thus the total length of the text. *The Large Sutra* refers to Conze's combined translation of the eight-, fifteen-, and eighteen-thousand-verse texts.

29. See Frederick Streng, *Emptiness: A Study in Religious Meaning*, pp. 139–152.

30. T. 30, p. 1b.

31. T. 30, p. 34b. *Nāgārjuna: Mūlamadhyamakakārikāḥ*, de Jong ed., p. 43; chap. 27, stanza 30.

32. Conze, *The Prajñāpāramitā Literature*, p. 7.

33. Conze, *Buddhist Wisdom Books: The Diamond Sutra*, p. 85.

34. Conze, *Buddhist Texts through the Ages*, p. 7.

35. Conze, *The Large Sutra*, p. 101.

36. Conze, *Buddhist Wisdom Books*, pp. 77–78, 85.

37. Ibid., p. 61.

38. Sprung, *Lucid Exposition of the Middle Way*, p. 262.

39. T. 30, p. 36b. *Nāgārjuna: Mūlamadhyamakakārikāḥ*, de Jong ed., p. 40; chap. 25, stanza 24. See Sprung, *Lucid Exposition of the Middle Way*, p. 217.

40. Conze, *The Accumulation of Precious Qualities (Ratnaguṇasamuccaya-gāthā)*, p. 260.

41. Conze, *The Large Sutra*, p. 57.

42. Conze, *Buddhist Wisdom Books*, p. 65.

43. Sprung, *Lucid Exposition of the Middle Way*, p. 33.

44. The following treatment of Mādhyamika philosophy is drawn from Gadjin Nagao's "Chūkan tetsugaku no konponteki tachiba," in his *Chūkan to yuishiki*, pp. 3–144. English translation by John Keenan, *The Foundational Standpoint of Mādhyamika Philosophy*.

45. T. 30, p. 18c: *Nāgārjuna: Mūlamadhyamakakārikāḥ*, de Jong ed., p. 18; chap. 13, stanzas 7–8.

46. Jacques May, *Chandrakīrti: Prasannapadā Madhyamikavṛtti. Douze chapitres traduits du Sanskrit et du Tib'tain, accompagn's d'une introduction, de notes et d'une 'dition critique de la version Tib'taine*, pp. 223–24. For a different translation, see Sprung, *Lucid Exposition of the Middle Way*, pp. 172–73.

47. May, *Chandrakīrti*, pp. 223–24.

48. See Theodore Stcherbatsky, *The Concept of Buddhist Nirvana*, index, p. 38.

49. Quoted in Susumu Yamaguchi, *Bukkyō ni okeru yu to mu to no tairon* [The Dispute over Being and Non-Being in Buddhism], p. 20n3.

50. In the West the medieval Scholastics defined the properties (one, truth, goodness, beauty) that belong to being-as-being as the transcendentals. They were called *transcendentia* because these properties transcend all genera and categories and are predicable of being in its bare fact of existing. The terms "being," "one," "truth," "good," and "beauty" are convertible because each adds nothing to the

other; differing only in approach. A being is one (or good, etc.) inasmuch as it exists, and it exists inasmuch as it is one. See Étienne Gilson, *The Elements of Christian Philosophy*, pp. 145, 308n19. In adopting the term "convertible" for Mādhyamika, the intent is to stress that the notions of emptiness and dependent co-arising refer co-terminously to the same experienced world. In contrast to the Scholastic usage, in which priority is always on the being of that which is one, true, good, and beautiful, in Mādhyamika there is no adherence to any philosophy of being. Emptiness and dependent co-arising both transcend all genera and categories and indicate the world of experience, just as it is.

51. T. 30, p. 1b; Inada, *Nāgārjuna: Mūlamadhyamakakārikāḥ*, p. 38.

52. *Vigrahavyāvartanī*, stanza 71.

53. *Yuktiṣaṣṭikā*, stanza 1; See Lindtner, *Master of Wisdom*, pp. 72–73.

54. T. 30, p. 33b; *Nāgārjuna: Mūlamadhyamakakārikāḥ*, de Jong ed., p. 35; chap. 24, stanza 18, which states: "yaḥ pratītyasamutpādaḥ śūnyatāṃ tāṃ pracakaṣmahe/ sā prajñaptir upādāya pratipat saiva madhyamā/"

55. Sprung, *Lucid Exposition of the Middle Way*, p. 17. Also see Sprung, "Non-Cognitive Language in Mādhyamika Buddhism," *Buddhist Thought and Asian Civilization*, pp. 241–53.

56. See Magliola, *Derrida on the Mend*, for a discussion of philosophies that attempt to center their thinking on essential being.

57. T. 30, p. 33b; *Nāgārjuna: Mūlamadhyamakakārikāḥ*, de Jong ed., p. 35; chap. 24, stanza 19.

58. See Nagao, *Chūkan to yuishiki*, p. 23.

59. T. 30, p. 32c; *Nāgārjuna: Mūlamadhyamakakārikāḥ*, de Jong ed., pp. 34–35; chap. 24, stanzas 8–10.

60. *Vigrahavyāvartanī*, stanza 1.

61. Thomas Aquinas states: "The meaning of a negation is always founded in an affirmation, as appears from the fact that every negative proposition is proved by an affirmative one" (Gilson, *Elements of Christian Philosophy*, p. 140).

62. *Vigrahavyāvartanī*, stanza 23.

63. Ibid., stanza 29.

64. Sprung, *Lucid Exposition of the Middle Way*, p. 6.

65. Ibid., p. 38.

66. Ibid., p. 10.

67. Ibid., p. 14.

68. Ibid., p. 177.

69. Jikidō Takasaki, *A Study of the Ratnagotravibhāga (Uttaratantra), Being a Treatise on the Tathāgatagarbha Theory of Mahāyāna Buddhism*, pp. 305–6.

70. Ibid., p. 305.

71. *Nāgārjuna: Mūlamadhyamakakārikāḥ*, de Jong ed., p. 11; chap. 7, stanza 34.

72. See Takasaki, *Nyoraizō shisō no keisei* [The Formation of Tathāgatagarbha Thinking], pp. 76–77, on the understanding of *sat-tva*.

73. *Anūnatvapūrṇatvanirdeśa*; T. 16, p. 467b.

74. Takasaki, *A Study of the Ratnagotravibhāga*, p. 167n28.

75. See Takasaki, "Hōshin no ichigenron: Noraizō shisō no hō kannen" [The Monism of Dharmakāya as It Relates to Tathāgatagarbha Thinking], in *Hirawakawa Akira hakase kanreki kinen ronshū: Bukkyō ni okeru hō no kenkyū* [Studies in Honor of Doctor Akira Hirakawa on Dharma in Buddhism].

76. Alex and Hideko Wayman, *The Lion's Roar of Queen Śrīmālā*, p. 99; T. 12, p. 221c.

77. Gadjin Nagao, " 'What Remains' in Sūnyatā: A Yogācāra Interpretation of Emptiness," in *Mahāyāna Buddhist Meditation: Theory and Practice*, ed. Minoru Kiyota, p. 776.

78. Wayman and Wayman, *Lion's Roar of Queen Śrīmālā*, p. 106–7.

79. Takasaki, *A Study of the Ratnagotravibhāga*, p. 296.

80. The *Mahāyānasūtrālaṃkāra* is traditionally attributed to Maitreya, the semilegendary founder of Yogācāra, and this attribution is upheld by such scholars as Hakuju Ui, "On the Authorship of the Mahāyānasūtra-alaṃkāra," in *Zeitschrift für Indologie und Iranistik*, 6 (1928):215–25. However, Susumu Yamaguchi, Giuseppe Tucci, and Paul Demiéville deny that Maitreya was a historical person and the actual author of this text. See "La Yogācārabhūmi de Saṅgharakṣa," *Bulletin de l'École française d'Extreme-Orient* 44 (1954) 381n4.

81. *Mahāyānasūtra-alaṃkāra, Exposé de la Doctrine du Grand Véhicle*, ed. and trans. Sylvain Lévi, 1, p. 88. Hakuju Ui, *Daijōshōgonkyō kenkyū*, p. 284.

82. *Mahāyānasūtrālaṃkāra*; Lévi ed., vol. 1, p. 40; Ui, p. 153.

83. Ibid., p. 40; Ui, p. 153.

84. Ibid., p. 58; Ui, p. 204.

85. Ibid., p. 58; Ui, pp. 202–203.

86. Ibid., p. 58; Ui, p. 203.

87. Takasaki, *A Study of the Ratnagotravibhāga*, pp. 58–60. Also see John Keenan, "Original Purity and the Focus of Early Yogācāra," *Journal of the International Association of Buddhist Studies* 5, no. 1 (1982): 7–18.

CHAPTER 7

1. *Triśatikāyāḥ–prajñāpāramitāsaptaiḥ*. Text and English translation in Giuseppe Tucci, *Minor Buddhist Texts*, vol. 1, pp. 1–128.

2. *Madhyamaka - śāstrārthānugata - mahāprajñāpāramitā - sūtrādiparivarta - dharmaparyāya-praveśa*. Extant only in Chinese translation, T. 30, pp. 39–50.

3. *Āryabhagavatī-prajñāpāramitā-vajracchedikakāyāḥ saptapadārthāṭīkā*. Extant only in Chinese translations by I-ching (T. 25, pp. 875–84) and by Bodhiruci (T. 25, pp. 781–97). Also given in Tucci, *Minor Buddhist Texts*, vol. 1, pp. 129–92.

4. *Mūlamadhyamaka-saṃdhinirmocana-vyākhyāna*. T. 30, pp. 136–58.

5. *Śataśāstravaipulyaṭīkā*. Extant only in Chinese, T. 30, pp. 187–250.

6. See Kenneth Inada, *Guide to Buddhist Philosophy*, pp. 18–20. Note particularly the excellent articles by Alan Sponberg in the bibliography.

7. For example, Mervyn Sprung's *Lucid Exposition of the Middle Way* and Frederick Streng's *Emptiness: A Study in Religious Meaning*, and Kenneth Inada's *Nāgārjuna: A Translation of His Mūlamadhyamakakārikā*.

8. *Saṃdhinirmocana-sūtra: L'Explication des Mystères*, trans. Étienne Lamotte. My English translation soon to appear in the Bukkyo Dendo Kyokai series.

9. There is no extant biography of Asaṅga, but information on him is contained in the account of his brother Vasubandhu's life. See J. Takakusu, "The Life of Vasubandhu by Paramārtha," *Journal of the Royal Asiatic Society* (1935): 33–53.

10. *Mahāyānasūtra-alaṃkāra, Exposé de la Doctrine du Grand Véhicle*, ed. and trans. Sylvain Lévi, 2 vols. *Daijōshōgonkyō kenkyū*, trans. Hakuju Ui.

11. *Madhyāntavibhāgabhāṣya, A Buddhist Philosophical Treatise Edited for the First Time from a Sanskrit Text,* ed. Gadjin Nagao. An earlier and less accurate translation is Theodore Stcherbatsky's *Madhyāntavibhāga, Discourse on Discrimination between Middle and Extremes.*

12. T. 30, pp. 279–883. One chapter is translated into English by Janice Dean Willis, *On Knowing Reality: The Tattvārtha Chapter of Asaṅga's Bodhisattvabhūmi.* The Sanskrit of the Bodhisattvabhūmi section is edited by Nalinaksha Dutt, *Bodhisattvabhūmi (Being the XVth Section of Asaṅgapāda's Yogācārabhūmi).*

13. On the question of authorship, see Hakuju Ui's affirmative judgment, "On the Authorship of the Mahāyānasūtra-alamkāra," *Zeitschrift für Indologie und Iranistik* 6 (1928):215–25, and his "Maitreya as an Historical Person," *Indian Studies in Honor of Charles Rockwell Lanman,* pp. 95–102. Susumu Yamaguchi, Giuseppe Tucci, and Paul Demiéville all deny that Maitreya was a historical person and the actual author of this text. See Demiéville, "La Yogācārabhūmi de Saṅgharakṣa," *Bulletin de l'École française d'Extreme-Orient* 44 (1954): 381n4.

14. *La Somme du Grand Véhicle d'Asaṅga (Mahāyānasaṃgraha), Traduction et Commentaire,* trans. Étienne Lamotte. All four extant Chinese vesions and the Tibetan are included in *Kanyaku shihon taishō Shodaijōron,* Gessho Sasaki, Tokyo, 1977.

15. De la Vallée Poussin, *L'Abhidharmakośa.*

16. *Vijñaptimātratāsiddhi, La Siddhi de Hiuan-Tsang,* trans., De la Vallée Poussin; *Ch'eng Wei-shih Lun, Doctrine of Mere Consciousness,* trans., Wei Tat.

17. *Mahāyānasaṃgrahabhāṣya,* extant in three Chinese translations (by Paramārtha: T. 31, pp. 152–270; Dharmagupta: T. 30, pp. 271–320; and Hsüan-tsang: T, 30. pp. 321–79), and one Tibetan: *Theg pa chen po bsdus pa,* P. 5549, trans. Ye shes sde.

18. *Mahāyānasaṃgrahopanibandhana,* extant only in Chinese and Tibetan. The Chinese is by Hsüan-tsang (T. 30, pp. 380–450) and the Tibetan, P. 5552.

19. *Sūtrālamkāraṭīkā,* extant only in Tibetan, P. (Peking ed., Tibetan canon) 5531.

20. *Madhyāntavibhāgaṭīkā.* Sanskrit text in *Sthiramati: Madhyānta-vibhāgaṭīkā, Exposition systématique du Yogācāravijñaptivāda,* introduction by Susumu Yamaguchi. Yamaguchi also provides a Japanese translation, *Anne ajiyaru zō chuhen-funbetsuron shakusho.*

21. See n. 15 above.

22. See Shunkyo Katsumata, *Bukkyō ni okeru shinishikisetsu no kenkyū,* pp. 191–294, on the comparison of Dharmapāla's thought in the *Ch'eng Wei-shih lun* with Sthiramati's *Trimśikāvijñaptibhāṣya.*

23. *Śataśāstravaipulyaṭīkā,* T. 30, pp. 187–249.

24. On Paramārtha's biography, see Diana Y. Paul, *Philosophy of Mind in Sixth-Century China: Paramārtha's "Evolution of Consciousness,"* pp. 11–37.

25. See Kyōyu Nishio, *The Buddhabhūmisūtra and the Buddhabhūmivyākhyāna,* and *Buchikyōron no kenkyū.* On Bandhuprabha's text, see John Keenan, *A Study of the Buddhabhūmyupadeśa: The Doctrinal Development of the Notion of Wisdom in Yogācāra Thought.*

26. *Mahāyānasaṃgraha,* Lamotte ed., 2.32 (the chapter and section numbers also apply to Gadjin Nagao's *Shōdaijōron: Wayaku to chūkai).*

27. Nagao, *Madhyāntavibhāgabhāṣya,* p. 21. For a Japanese translation, see Nagao, *Daijō butten 15 Seishin ronshū,* p. 228. The texts of the two Chinese and the

single Tibetan translations are found in Yamaguchi, *Kanzō taishō Benchūheron*, pp. 10–11.

28. *Saṃdhinirmocana*, Lamotte ed., pp. 58, 186–87: "The container consciousness is profound and subtle. It is like a violent stream, proceeding together with all the seeds [of past experiences]. Fearing that the immature would imagine it to be a self, I have not revealed it to them."

29. *Saṃdhinirmocana*, Lamotte ed., p. 185: "The seed consciousness matures, becomes active, unifies, grows, and reaches its development because it makes its own two things: the physical body with its sense organs and a proclivity toward the fabrication of names and images in discriminative language."

30. *Mahāyānasaṃgraha*, Lamotte ed., 1.7.

31. Passage taken from the demonstrations of the existence of the container consciousness, which appear in the Viniścayasaṃgrahaṇī section of the *Yogācārabhūmi* (T. 30, p. 579a) and are repeated in Asaṅga's *Abhidharmasamuccaya* (T. 31, p. 701b) and *Śāsanodbhāvana* (T. 31, p. 565b). I here follow a comparative Japanese translation of Noriaki Hakamaya, "Ālaya shiki sonzai no hachi ronshō ni kansuru shobunken" [Source Materials on the Eight demonstrations of the Ālaya Consciousness], *Komazawa daigaku bukkyō gakubu kenkyū kiyō*, 36, p. 19.

32. *Mahāyānasaṃgraha*, Lamotte ed., 1.17: "The container consciousness and defiled states of mind are simultaneously causes one of the other." See also 1.27.

33. See the discussion of whether images are present in awakened wisdom, in Bandhuprabha's *Buddhabhūmyupadeśa* (T. 26, p. 303b-c); Keenan, pp. 577–84.

34. *Mahāyānasaṃgraha*, Lamotte ed., 2.32.2.

35. *rgyu mtshan lta ba dang bcas pa las// de dag mtshan nyid gsum shes bya ba/ zhes ji skad gsungs pa lta bya'o//* In place of the italicized words, which identify the entire passage as an instrumental ablative, all Chinese translations simply have "because of this" (*yü shih*), which is not quite so explicit.

36. *Mahāyānasaṃgrahabhāṣya*, Lamotte ed., 2.29. The few remaining fragments of the *Mahāyānābhidharma* are collected and examined in Reimon Yūki, *Shinishikiron yori mitaru yuishiki shisōshi*, pp. 240–50.

37. *Mahāyānasaṃgraha*, Lamotte ed., 2.2.

38. *Madhyāntavibhāga*, Nagao ed., p. 17. For a comparison of the various texts and a Japanese translation and exegesis, see Yeh A-yüeh, *Yuishiki shisō no kenkyū*, appendix, p. 1.

39. *Madhyāntavibhāgaṭīkā*, Yamaguchi ed., p. 13.

40. *Mahāyānasaṃgraha*, Lamotte ed., 2.3.

41. *Mahāyānasaṃgrahabhāṣya*, n. 3 to section 2.3.

42. *Madhyāntavibhāgabhāṣya*, Nagao ed., p. 18.

43. *Mahāyānasaṃgraha*, Lamotte ed., 2.4.

44. See Nagao, "Tenkan no ronri," in *Chūkan to yuishiki*, p. 244.

45. *Mahāyānasaṃgraha*, Lamotte ed., 2.17. See Nagao, "I-mon (paryāya) to iu kotoba," in *Chūkan to yuishiki*, pp. 406–13.

46. *Mahāyānasaṃgraha*, Lamotte ed., 10.3.

47. *Vijñaptimātratāsiddhi*, De la Vallée Poussin ed., pp. 133–34; Ch'eng Wei-shih lun, Wei Tat, p. 143.

48. *Śataśāstravaipulyaṭīkā*, T. 30, p. 248a.

49. The present discussion is limited to the structural patterns of consciousness and scant attention is directed to just how one implements practices to bring about such a conversion. Of course, this is a central issue for the Yogācāra masters and

is treated at length in their presentations of the path. See Alan Sponberg, "Dynamic Liberation in Yogācāra Buddhism," *Journal of the International Association of Buddhist Studies* 2, no. 1 (1979): 44–64.

50. *Saṃdhinirmocana*, Lamotte ed., 7.3

51. *Mahāyānasaṃgrahopanibandhana* in *Mahāyānasaṃgraha*, Lamotte ed., 32.3n.3.

52. *Saṃdhinirmocana*, Lamotte ed., 7.30.

53. Jikidō Takasaki, *A Study of the Ratnagotravibhāga*, p. 59.

54. *Boddhisattvabhūmi*, Dutt ed., p. 25; Willis, *On Knowing Reality*, p. 149.

55. *Madhyāntavibhāgabhāṣya*, Nagao ed., p. 72.

56. *Saṃdhinirmocana*, Lamotte ed., 8.7.

57. "de la chos gang yang chos gang la 'ang rtog par mi byed mod"—a clear denial that understanding functions by a mental "looking."

58. *Saṃdhinirmocana*, Lamotte ed., 8.7, response.

59. *Mahāyānasaṃgrahopanibandhana*, in *Mahāyānasaṃgraha*, Lamotte ed., 3.1n; T. 31, p. 413b.

60. *Mahāyānasaṃgraha*, Lamotte ed., 2.22.10.

CHAPTER 8

1. *Vajracchedika*, Conze, *Buddhist Wisdom Books*, pp. 47–48.

2. *Triśatikāyāḥ-prajñāpāramitāsaptaiḥ*, Tucci ed., 1.70, verse 34.

3. *Vajracchedika*, Conze, *Buddhist Wisdom Books*, p. 46, verse 10b.

4. *Triśatikāyāḥ*, Tucci ed., p. 1.63, verse 20.

5. *Madhyāntavibhāgabhāṣya*, Nagao ed., p. 41.

6. Monier Williams, *Sanskrit Dictionary*, p. 90. See Nagao, *Shōdaijōron: Wayaku to chūkai*, p. 281n3. A similar usage of the term *artha* as objective is found in Haribhadra: "[The bodhisattva's] own objective (*svako'rthaḥ*) is twofold: the attainment of the beneficial and the abandonment of the unbeneficial," in *Aṣṭasāhaśrika Prajñāpāramitā with Haribhadra's Commentary called Āloka*, Vaidya ed., p. 273. See Baghi's "Glossary and Critical Notes," p. 574. Similarly I.B. Horner in *Milinda's Questions*," 1.26, translates *paramattha* as "the highest goal."

7. *Madhyāntavibhāgaṭīkā, Exposition systématique du Yogācāra-vijñaptivāda*, Sylvain Lévi ed., p. 125. For a Japanese translation, see Yamaguchi, *Anne ajiyaru zō chuhen funbetsuron shakusho*, p. 197.

8. *Madhyāntavibhāgabhāṣya*, Nagao ed., p. 41.

9. *Madhyāntavibhāgaṭīkā*, Lévi ed., p. 123. Yamaguchi trans., p. 195.

10. Nagao, "Chūkan tetsugaku no konponteki tachiba," in *Chūkan to yuishiki*, p. 42. English translation "The Foundational Standpoint of Madhyamika Philosophy," John Keenan, trans.

11. *Mahāyānasaṃgraha*, Lamotte ed., 2.26.2.

12. See Shinjō Suguro, "Joyuishikiron ni okeru gohō setsu no tokushoku" [The Specific Character of Dharmapāla's Teaching in the Ch'eng Wei-shih lun], in *Yūki kyōju shōju kinen bukkyō shisōshi ronshū* [Essays on the History of Buddhist Thought in Honor of Professor Reimon Yūki].

13. *Śataśāstravaipulyaṭīkā*, T. 30, p. 243a.

14. Ibid., T. 30, p. 247a.

15. *Buddhabhūmyupadeśa*, T. 26, pp. 302c–303a; Keenan, p. 565.

16. Nagao, "Chūkan tetsugaku," *Chūkan to yuishiki*," p. 39.

17. See N. Hakamaya, "The Realm of Enlightenment in Vijñaptimātratā: The Formulation of the 'Four Kinds of Pure Dharmas,'" *Journal of the International Association of Buddhist Studies*, 3, no. 2 (1980):21–22, 35–36.

18. *Mahāyānasaṃgraha*, Lamotte ed., 2.26.3.

19. See *Aṣṭadaśasāhasrikā-prajñāpāramitā*, Vaidya ed., pp. 2.10–3.2; Conze, *The Perfection of Wisdom in Eight Thousand Lines*, p. 83.

20. Monier Williams, *Sanskrit Dictionary*, p. 153b, gives the root of *ālambana* as *ālamb*, "to hang down, support, bring near, depend." It means here that which depends on verbal doctrine, i.e., its import, referent, intention.

21. *Mahāyānasaṃgrahabhāṣya*, Lamotte ed., note to 2.26.3; T. 31, p. 406b.

22. See *Mahāyānasaṃgraha*, Lamotte ed., 3.1, where it is explained that, in order to realize purification, the container consciousness must be countered by the permeations of doctrine that flow from the Dharma Realm.

23. *Mahāyānasaṃgraha*, Lamotte ed., 1.1.

24. The question is just what is meant by "the beginningless realm." Asaṅga, Vasubandhu, and Dharmapāla (in his *Ch'eng Wei-shih lun*, De la Vallée Poussin ed., p. 169), interpret it to refer to the container consciousness, while the *Ratnagotravibhāga* and Paramārtha's translation of Vasubandhu's *Mahāyānasaṃgrahabhāṣya* interpret it as referring to the *tathāgatagarbha*.

25. *Mahāyānasaṃgrahopanibandhana*, Lamotte ed., 1.1n; T. 31, p. 383a.

26. *Karuṇāpuṇḍarika, edited with introduction and notes*, Isshi Yamada.

27. See *Karuṇāpuṇḍarika*, p. 163, and Gadjin Nagao, "On the Theory of Buddha-Body," *Eastern Buddhist* 6 (May 1973):1. On the development from the two-body to the three-body doctrine, see Nagao, "Kongohannyakyō ni okeru Muchaku no shakuge" [Asaṅga's Commentary on the Diamond Sūtra], *Chūkan to yuishiki*, pp. 569–74.

28. *Mahāyānasaṃgraha*, Lamotte ed., 10.1.

29. *Mahāyānasūtra-alaṃkāra*, Lévi ed., p. 189.

30. *Mahāyānasutrālaṃkāraṭīkā*, D. 4029, p. 174a[67].

31. *Mahāyānasaṃgraha*, Lamotte ed., 10.3.1.

32. Ibid., 10.4.

33. *Buddhabhūmisūtra*, T. 16, pp. 720–23. See John P. Keenan, "Pure Land Systematics in India: The Buddhabhūmisūtra and the Trikāya Doctrine," *The Pacific World*, N.S.3 (Fall 1987): 29–35.

34. *Mahāyānasaṃgraha*, Lamotte ed., 10.5.5.

35. Ibid., 2.26.3.a.

36. *Mahāyānasaṃgrahopanibandhana*, in *Mahāyānasaṃgraha*, Lamotte ed., 10.5.5n.

37. See Bandhuprabha's discussion, *Buddhabhūmyupadeśa*, Keenan, pp. 850–56; T. 26, p. 326a.

CHAPTER 9

1. See Edward Conze's comparison of Mahāyāna Buddhism with Greek Sophism in his article "Buddhist Philosophy and Its European Parallels." In the light of Christian attempts at deconstructing the metaphysical basis of theology, perhaps one could reexamine the gospel in the "light" of the skeptics and their insistence on philosophical suspicion.

2. For example, see W. T Stace, *Mysticism and Philosophy*, pp. 31–38.

3. "Heller, History of Religions as a Preparation for the Co-operation of Religions," in *The History of Religion: Studies in Phenomenology*, pp. 142–53.

4. See the discussion on "nothingness" in Hasidism and Buddhism by Steven T. Katz, "Language, Epistemology, and Mysticism," in *Mysticism and Philosophical Analysis*, pp. 51–55.

5. Lao Tzu, *Tao Te Ching*, 41; D.C. Lau, trans. p. 117.

6. The thesis of his *Mysticism: Sacred and Profane*.

7. Katz, "Language, Epistemology, and Mysticism," p. 26.

8. Ibid., p. 27.

9. Ibid., p. 33.

10. Ibid., p. 52.

11. *The Encyclopedia of Religion*, ed. Mircea Eliade, vol. 12, p. 330.

12. Katz, "Language, Epistemology, and Mysticism," p. 54.

13. Note the similarity with Tathāgatagarbha thought.

14. See Keenan, *A Study of the Buddhabhūmyupadeśa: The Doctrinal Development of the Notion of Wisdom in Yogācāra Thought*, pp. 273–303.

15. *Bankei Zen: Translations from the Record of Bankei*, by Peter Haskel, pp. 4, 79, 117.

16. Lonergan, *Method in Theology*, pp. 76–77, emphasizes the passage from the immediacy of the nursery to a gradually richer participation in the world of mediated meaning.

17. The two mandalas of the thunderbolt and the womb present an image of awakening as integration or union. See Minoru Kiyota, *Shingon Buddhism: Theory and Practice*, pp. 81–104.

18. Smart, "Understanding Religious Experience," in *Mysticism and Philosophical Analysis*, p. 15.

19. Katz, "Language, Epistemology, and Mysticism," p. 62. George Lindbeck's *The Nature of Doctrine: Religion and Theology in a Postliberal Age* presents an engaging and thoughtful argument for this position (see pp. 30–42). But he too fails to offer an argument why interpretation must be constitutive of experience. He seems content to refute the idea of a common core, as if that were sufficient to demonstrate the point. Lindbeck states that it "is a complex thesis, and its full discussion lies beyond the scope of this essay" (p. 37).

20. Lonergan, *Method in Theology*, p. 106.

21. Katz, "Language, Epistemology, and Mysticism," p. 22.

22. *The Complete Works of Chuang Tzu*, trans. Burton Watson, pp. 57–58: "May I ask what the fasting of the mind is? . . . Make your will one! Don't listen with your ears, listen with your mind. No, don't listen with your mind, listen with your spirit. Listening stops with the ears, the mind stops with recognition, but spirit is empty and waits on all things. The Way gathers in emptiness alone. Emptiness is the fasting of the mind."

23. Lonergan, *Method in Theology*, pp. 236–37.

24. Nagao, "Bukkyōteki shutaisei ni tsuite," in *Chūkan to yuishiki*, pp. 333–40. English translation, "Buddhist Subjectivity" in *Religious Studies in Japan*, pp. 257–62.

25. *The Bhagavad-Gita: Krishna's Counsel in Time of War*, trans. Barbara Stoler Miller, pp. 29–47.

26. De la Vallée Poussin, *La Siddhi de Huien-Tsang*, p. 30; Wei Tat, *Mere Consciousness*, p. 39.

27. See Louth, *The Origins of the Christian Mystical Tradition*, pp. 75–77, on the central importance of the doctrine of *creation ex nihilo*.

28. Maximus in Pelikan, *The Spirit of Eastern Christendom*, p. 32.

29. Ibid., pp. 32–33.

30. Ibid., p. 33.

31. Lonergan, *Method in Theology*, p. 342.

32. Lamotte, *La Somme*, p. 121.

33. See Hans Waldenfels, *Absolute Nothingness: Foundations for a Buddhist-Christian Dialogue*, esp. pp. 138–54.

34. Smart, "Understanding Religious Experience," pp. 17–18.

35. Gregory's notion of "the unsubstantial" presents the closest doctrinal parallel to Mahāyāna emptiness, not, as is often assumed, the kenosis theology based on Philippians 2:5–8, which says that Christ willingly left his divine state by emptying himself. Mahāyāna emptiness admits of no state from which one may be emptied.

36. Gilson, *Christian Philosophy in the Middle Ages*, p. 398.

37. Smart, *The Yogi and the Devotee*, p. 40.

38. There is a significant body of literature on Buddhist-Christian dialogue and there are some theologians, such as Hans Waldenfels, who do accept the notions of emptiness. In Waldenfels' case, emptiness is mediated through the Kyoto school philosophy of Keiji Nishitani (*Religion and Nothingness*). Also to be noted are the deconstruction theologians. Joseph S. O'Leary in his *Questioning Back: The Overcoming of Metaphysics in Christian Tradition*, and Mark C. Taylor, *Erring: A Post-Modern A/Theology*, are attempting a deconstruction of Christian "metaphysical" thinking that has strong similarities with Nāgārjuna's deconstruction of Abhidharma "metaphysics." These modern thinkers draw from the philosophy of Jacques Derrida, which itself is parallel to the thinking of Nāgārjuna. Also see Robert Magliola, *Derrida on the Mend*, part 3, esp. pp. 91–97.

39. In Pelikan, *The Emergence of the Catholic Tradition*, p. 229.

40. In Pelikan, *The Spirit of Eastern Christendom*, p. 17.

41. Ibid., p. 35.

42. Vasubandhu, *Wei Shih Er Shih Lun or the Treatise of Twenty Stanzas on Representation-Only*, trans., Clarence H. Hamilton, New Haven, 1938, p. 21.

43. De la Vallée Poussin, *La Siddhi de Huien-Tsang*, pp. 428–29; Wei Tat, *Mere Consciousness*, p. 521.

44. Cf. Lonergan, *Method in Theology*, pp. 263–64.

45. Keenan, *Buddhabhūmyupadeśa*, p. 722n.499.

46. Ibid., p. 723.

47. Ibid., p. 739.

48. Ibid., p. 742.

49. Lonergan, *Insight*, pp. 271–78.

50. *Saṃdhinirmocana*, Lamotte ed., pp. 262–65; T. 6, p. 709b.

51. Hajime Nakamura, *Religions and Philosophies of India: A Survey with Bibliographical Notes, the Fourth Chapter: Orthodox Philosophical Systems*, pp. vi–35.

52. Ibid.

53. See Masaaki Hattori, *Dignāga on Perception, Being the Pratyakṣapariccheda of Dignāga's Pramāṇsamuccaya*, for the best treatment in English to date on Dignāga's epistemological thinking.

54. See Lonergan, "Metaphysics as Horizon."
55. Such differences were realized by Nagao, *Chūkan to yuishiki*, pp. 276–77.
56. Karl Rahner, *The Trinity*, pp. 99–103.
57. *The Platform Sutra of the Sixth Patriarch*, trans. Philip Yampolsky, p. 141.
58. Lonergan, *Method in Theology*, p. 285.
59. Ibid., pp. 285–93.
60. See Lonergan, *Method in Theology*, pp. 125–44, for his treatment of dialectics and foundations.
61. Ibid., pp. 267–93. One of the achievements of Bernard Lonergan was to reinterpret foundations as concerned with conversion rather than with a truncated apologetics.
62. Concrete questions of just how to bring about such a conversion are treated in the literature of practice (*mārga*) and, although central to Buddhist teaching, are beyond the purview of the present endeavor.
63. *Mahāyānasūtrālaṃkāra*, Lévi ed., p. 96.
64. *La Somme*, Lamotte ed., p. 268; T. 31, p. 294b.
65. *Mahāyānasūtrālaṃkāra*, Lévi ed., p. 44. These stanzas are also included in the *Buddhabhūmyupadeśa*, Keenan, pp. 803–4.
66. Sthiramati, *Sūtrālaṃkāravṛttibhāṣya*, Derge ed., no. 4034, Mi, 113^b-7 to 134^a-7; Asvabhāva, *Mahāyānasūtrālaṃkāraṭīkā*, Derge ed., no. 4029, Bi, 72^b-3 to 73^a-1.
67. Ibid., Derge ed., no. 4029, Bi, 72^b-5.
68. Ibid., Derge ed., no. 4034, Mi, 134^a-3.
69. Ibid., Derge ed., no. 4034, Mi, 134^a-7.
70. *Abhidharmasamuccayaśāstra*, Derge ed., no. 4049, Ri, 99^b-5 to 100^a-7. *Le Compendium de la Super Doctrine*, trans. Walpola Rahula, p. 127. For a treatment of these three conversions, see Noriaki Hakamaya, "Sanshu tenne kō" [An Examination of the Threefold Conversion], *Journal of Indian and Buddhist Studies* 11 (November 1976):46–76.
71. T. 31:742c. Derge ed., no. 4053, Li, 67^b-4 to 67^b-8.
72. Derge ed., no. 4022, Phi, 47^b-3.

CHAPTER 10

1. Schillebeeckx, *Jesus*, pp. 600–601.
2. Ibid., p. 307.
3. Ibid., p. 304.
4. Albert Schweitzer, *The Quest of the Historical Jesus*, pp. 398–403.
5. *Mahāyānasūtrālaṃkāra*, Lévi ed., vol. 1, p. 38.
6. Schillebeeckx, *Jesus*, p. 384.
7. Ibid., p. 213 and p. 637.
8. Ibid., pp. 390–91.
9. Thus I do not agree with G. W. H. Lampe that the Christian pattern of experience is of the same God as Spirit that was in Jesus. See his *God as Spirit* (Oxford, 1977) and "The Holy Spirit and the Person of Christ," in *Christ, Faith and History* (Cambridge, 1972), pp. 111–30.
10. John Robinson, "Need Jesus Have Been Perfect?" in *Christ, Faith and History*, pp. 48–50.
11. On the understanding of eschatology as a single definitive revelation, not

a future event, see Gregory Dix, *The Shape of the Liturgy*, pp. 256–59.

12. Schillebeeckx, *Jesus*, p. 362.

13. Dix, *The Shape*, pp. 303–96.

14. Christian Duquoc, *Christologie*, vol. 2, *Le Messie*, pp. 350–51, quoted in Schillebeeckx, *Jesus*, p. 601–02.

15. Schillebeeckx, *Jesus*, p. 638.

16. Dix, *The Shape*, p. 390.

17. A central part of Schweitzer's "quest" was to place Jesus in his times, not in the modern dress of theologically reconstructed lives of a nineteenth-century Jesus. A Mahāyāna Christology argues not only that Jesus did live in his times, but also that the dependently co-arisen context of the Gospels and the liturgy constitute his identity.

18. Pelikan, *The Emergence of the Catholic Tradition*, p. 161.

19. *Epistola ad Magnesios*, 8:2, in *Enchiridion Patristicum*, M. J. Rouet de Journel, no. 45.

20. Irenaeus, *Adversos Haereses*, 4:6; quoted in Kelly, *Early Christian Doctrines*, p. 107.

21. See Kelly, *Early Christian Doctrines*, pp. 104–8.

22. Schillebeeckx, *Jesus*, p. 358.

23. Ibid., *Jesus*, p. 358.

24. In Lampe, *God as Spirit*.

25. *La Somme*, Lamotte ed., 2:26.3.

26. The problem is incisively portrayed in Van A. Harvey, *The Historian and the Believer: The Morality of Historical Knowledge and Christian Belief* (New York, 1966).

27. M. F. Wiles, "Does Christology Rest on a Mistake?" in *Christ, Faith and History*, pp. 8–9.

28. John A. T. Robinson, "A Reply to Mr. Sykes," in *Christ, Faith and History*, p. 74.

29. Käsemann, *The Testament of Jesus*, pp. 25ff.

30. Schillebeeckx, *Jesus*, pp. 424–28.

31. Toynbee, *Christianity among the Religions of the World*, pp. 95ff.

CHAPTER 11

1. Kelly, *Early Christian Doctrines*, p. 95.

2. Irenaeus, *Adversos Haereses*, 4:6,6, quoted in Kelly, *Early Christian Doctrines*, p. 107.

3. The use of the term *svabhāva*, own-being or essence, was refuted by the Prajñāpāramitā and Mādhyamika thinkers as implying an essentialist, conceptualist illusion. But the Yogācāra reformulation of Abhidharma theory in light of the three patterns of consciousness freely employs this term as indicating the definition of a thing, here the ineffable content of mystic awakening. It may perhaps be better translated here as "foundation."

4. T. 26, p. 325; *Buddhabhūmyupadeśa*, Keenan, p. 867.

5. Schillebeeckx, *Jesus*, p. 142.

6. In his *Future of an Illusion* this is precisely what Sigmund Freud argues.

7. In Woody Allen's movie, *Love and Death*.

8. C. F. D. Moule, *The Origin of Christology* (New York, 1977), p. 167.

9. T. 16, p. 735a.

10. John Wisdom, *Proceedings of the Aristotelian Society*, 1944–45, reprinted as chap. 10 of *Logic and Language*, vol. 1, and in *Philosophy and Psycho-Analysis*. Quoted here from Anthony Flew, "Theology and Falsification," in *The Existence of God*, ed. John Hick (1964), p. 225.

11. See the treatment of the thought of William Hamilton, Thomas Altizer, Paul van Buren, and Richard L. Rubenstein, in Langdon Gilkey, *Naming the Whirlwind: The Renewal of God Language*, pp. 107–45.

12. *Buddhabhūmyupadeśa*, Keenan, pp. 594ff.

13. T. 26, p. 721a; *Buddhabhūmyupadeśa*, Keenan, pp. 601–2.

14. T. 26, p. 721a; *Buddhabhūmyupadeśa*, Keenan, p. 610.

15. Thomas Aquinas, *Summa Theologiae*, I, q. 9, and I, q. 19.

16. T. 26, p. 306a; *Buddhabhūnyupadeśa*, Keenan, p. 614.

17. See Kelly, *Early Christian Doctrines*, p. 274 and John A. T. Robinson, *Honest to God* (London, 1963), pp. 48–51.

18. Quoted from Augustine's *Confessions*, in Louth, *The Origins of the Christian Mystical Tradition*, p. 40: "tu autem eras interior intimo meo et superior summo meo."

19. Augustine, *De Trinitate*, 8:2,3; quoted in Louth, *Origins of the Christian Mystical Tradition*, p. 148.

20. Pelikan, *The Emergence*, pp. 215–16.

21. The classic treatment is found in Edward Leen's *The Holy Ghost*.

22. Nāgārjuna in his *Precious Garland* not only offers copious advice on ethical living, but also insists that the royal policy must reflect righteousness and support for the Dharma. See *The Precious Garland and the Song of the Four Mindfulnesses*, trans., Jeffrey Hopkins and Lati Rimpoche, pp. 62–77.

23. Ch'en, *Buddhism in China*, pp. 429–33.

24. Ibid., pp. 297–300. The only full study in English on the Three Stages sect is James Hubbard, "Salvation in the Final Period of the Dharma: The Inexhaustible Storehouse of the San-chieh-chiao," unpublished Ph.D. dissertation, University of Wisconsin–Madison, 1986.

25. Daigan and Alicia Matsunaga, *Foundations of Japanese Buddhism*, vol. 2, pp. 8–9.

26. See Paul Griffiths' article on "Karma," *Religious Studies* 18 (1982), p. 277–91.

27. Whalen Lai, draft manuscript "The Spirit of Chinese Buddhism."

28. See Leonardo Boff and Clodovis Boff, *Introducting Liberation Theology*, p. 44.

29. *Report to Greco*, pp. 349–52.

30. *Buddhabhūmyupadeśa*, Keenan, pp. 645–781.

Bibliography

WESTERN WORKS

Primary Sources

Aquinas, Thomas. *Summa Theologiae*. Rome: Marietti, 1952.

Eusebius of Caesarea. *The History of the Church*. New York: New York University Press, 1966.

Evagrius. *Evagrius Ponticus: The Pratikos, Chapters on Prayer*. Trans. with an introduction and notes, by John Eudes Bamberger. Spencer: Cistercian Publications, 1970.

————. *Les "Kephālaia Gnostica" d'Evagre le Pontique et l'histoire de l'origénisme chez les greis et chez les syriens*, Paris: Poticus, 1962.

————. *Les Six Centuries des "Kephālaia Gnostica" d'Evagre le Pontique. Édition critique de la version syriaque commune et édition d'une nouvelle version syriaque, intègrate, avec une double traduction française*, by Antoine Guillaumont. Paris: Ponticus, 1958.

Gregory of Nyssa. *Against Eunomius*. In *Patrologia Graeca*, ed. J. P. Minge. Paris, 1857–66; vol. 45, pp. 237–1121.

————. *Commentary on the Beatitudes*. In *Patrologia Graeca*, ed. J. P. Minge. Paris, 1857–66, vol. 44, pp. 1193–1301. English translation by Hilda C. Graef, *Gregory of Nyssa: The Lord's Prayer. The Beatitudes*. Philadelphia: Westminster Press, 1954.

————. *Commentary on Ecclesiastes*. In *Patrologia Graeca*, ed. J. P. Minge. Paris, 1857–66; vol. 44.

————. *Commentary on the Psalms*. In *Patrologia Graeca*, ed. J. P. Minge. Paris, 1857–66; vol. 44.

————. *Commentary on the Song of Songs*. In *Patrologia Graeca*, ed. J. P. Minge. Paris, 1857–66; vol. 44, pp. 756–1120.

————. *Dialogue with Macrina on the Soul and the Resurrection*. In *Patrologia Graeca*, ed. J. P. Minge. Paris, 1857–66; vol. 46, pp. 12–160.

————. *From Glory to Glory: Texts from Gregory of Nyssa's Mystical Writings*. Trans. Herbert Musurillo. Crestwood: St. Vladimir's Press, 1979.

————. *Funeral Oration for Placilla*. In *Patrologia Graeca*, ed. J. P. Minge. Paris, 1857–66; vol. 46.

————. *The Great Catechism*. In *Patrologia Graeca*, ed. J. P. Minge. Paris, 1857–66, vol. 45. English translation in *A Select Library of Nicene and Post-Nicene Fathers of the Christian Church*, vol. 5. Trans. P. Schaff and Wace. Oxford and New York, 1893.

————. *The Life of Moses*. In *Patrologia Graeca*, ed. J. P. Minge. Paris, 1857–66; vol. 44, pp. 297–430. *The Life of Moses*, English trans. Abraham J. Malherbe and Everett Ferguson. New York: Paulist Press, 1978.

————. *On Perfection*. In *Patrologia Graeca*, ed. J. P. Minge. Paris, 1857–66; vol. 46.

————. *On Virginity*. *Patrologia Graeca*, ed. J. P. Minge. Paris, 1857–66; vol. 46.

Irenaeus. *Epistola ad Magnesios*. Passages in M. J. Rouet de Journel, *Enchiridion Patristicum*. Barcelona: Herder, 1959, pp. 13–23.

The Jerusalem Bible. Garden City, N.Y.: Doubleday, 1970.

Justin Martyr. *The Writings of Justin Martyr and Athanagoras*. Trans. Dods, Reith, and Pratten. In *Ante-Nicene Library*. Edinburgh: Clark, 1879.

Macarius. *Two Rediscovered Works of Ancient Christian Literature: Gregory of Nyssa and Macarius*, Werner Jaeger. Leiden: Brill, 1954.

————. *Macarius: Fifty Spiritual Homilies*. Trans. A. J. Mason. London, 1921.

————. *Pseudo-Macarie, Oeuvres spirituelles 1: Homilies propes a la collection III, introduction, et notes (avec le texts Grec)*. Trans. Vincent Desprez. Paris, 1980.

Maximus Confessor. *Scolia on the Divine Names*. In *Patrologia Graeca*, ed. J. P. Minge. Paris, 1857–66; vol. 4, pp. 185–414.

————. *Scolia on the Mystical Theology*. In *Patrologia Graeca*, ed. J. P. Minge. Paris, 1857–66; vol. 4, pp. 415–52.

Origen. *Origen: An Exhortation to Martyrdom, Prayer, First Principles, Book IV: Prologue to the Commentary on the Song of Songs, Homily XXVII on Numbers*. Trans. Rowan A. Greer. New York: Paulist Press, 1979.

Plato. *The Dialogues of Plato*. Trans. Benjamin Jowett. Oxford: Clarendon Press, 1924.

Pseudo-Dionysius. *The Divine Names*. In *Patrologia Graeca*, ed. J. P. Minge. Paris, 1857–66; vol. 3, pp. 585–996.

————. *Ecclesiastical Hierarchy*. *Patrologia Graeca*, ed. J. P. Minge. Paris, 1857–66; vol. 3.

————. *The Heavenly Hierarchy*. In *Patrologia Graeca*, ed. J. P. Minge. Paris, 1857–66; vol. 3.

————. *Letters*. In *Hierarchy and the Definition of Order in the Letters of Pseudo-Dionysius: A Study in the Form and Meaning of the Pseudo-Dionysian Writings*. Trans. Ronald F. Hathaway. The Hague: Nijhoff, 1969.

————. *Mystical Theology*. In *Patrologia Graeca*, ed. J. P. Minge. Paris, 1857–66; vol. 3, pp. 997–1064.

Pseudo-Macarius, *see* Macarius.

Solomon. *Song of Songs: A New Translation with Introduction and Commentary*. Trans. Marvin H. Pope. Garden City, N.Y.: Doubleday, 1977.

Secondary Sources

Arndt, W. F., and Gringrich, F. W. *A Greek-English Lexicon of the New Testament and Other Early Christian Literature*. Chicago: University of Chicago Press, 1979.

Barth, Karl. *Church Dogmatics*. Edinburgh: Clark, 1958.

Baur, Ferdinand Christian, *Christliche Lehre von der Dreieinigkeit und Menschwerdung Gottes*. 1842.

Boff, Leonardo and Clodovis. *Introducing Liberation Theology*. Maryknoll, N.Y.: Orbis Books, 1987.

Boman, Thorleif. *Hebrew Thought Compared with the Greek.* London: SCM Press, 1960.

Bornkamm, G. "Zur Interpretation des Johannes-Evangeliums 'Eine Auseinandersetzung mit Käsemanns Schrift' Jesu letzter Wille nach Johannes 17." In *Geschichte und Glaube.* Munich, 1968.

Brown, R. E. *The Gospel according to John I–XII.* Garden City, N.Y.: Doubleday, 1966.

Brunner, Emil. *Man in Revolt: A Christian Anthropology.* Philadelphia: Westminster Press, 1939.

Buchanan, Neil. *The History of Dogma.* New York: Russel & Russel, 1971.

Buttrick, George, A., ed. *The Interpreter's Dictionary of the Bible.* Nashville: Abingdon Press, 1962.

Conzelmann, Hans. *A Commentary on the First Epistle to the Corinthians.* Philadelphia: Fortress Press, 1975.

———. *New Testament Studies.* Manchester, Eng.: Manchester University Press, 1967.

———. "Paulus und die Weisheit." *New Testament Studies* 12 (1968), pp. 213–44.

Copleston, F. *A History of Philosophy.* Vol. 1: *Greece and Rome.* New York: Newman Press, 1946.

Crenshaw, James L. *Gerhard von Rad.* Waco, Tex.: Word Books, 1978.

———. "Method in Determining Wisdom Influence upon 'Historical' Literature." *Journal of Biblical Literature* 88 (1969): 129–42.

———. "Popular Questioning of the Justice of God in Ancient Israel." *Studies in Ancient Israelite Wisdom,* ed. James Crenshaw. New York: Ktav Press, 1976.

———. *Old Testament Wisdom.* Atlanta: John Knox Press, 1981.

———, ed. *Studies in Ancient Israelite Wisdom.* New York: Ktav Press, 1976.

Daniélou, Jean. *Platonisme et théologie mystique: Doctrine spirituelle de Saint Gregorie de Nysse.* Paris: Aubier, Éditions Montaigne, 1944.

Denzinger, H., and Schonmetzer, A. *Enchiridion Symbolum Definitionum et Declarationum de Rebus Fidei et Morum.* Barcelona: Herder, 1963.

Dix, Dom Gregory. *The Shape of the Liturgy.* London: Black, 1945; reprint, New York & San Francisco: Harper & Row, 1982.

Dodd, C. H. *The Interpretation of the Fourth Gospel.* Cambridge, Eng.: Cambridge University Press, 1953.

Duquoc, Christian. *Christologie.* Vol. 2: *Le Messie.* Paris, 1972.

Festugière, A. *Contemplation et vie contemplative selon Platon.* Paris: J. Vrin, 1950.

Flanagan, J. W. *No Famine in the Land: Studies in Honor of John L. McKenzie.* Claremont: Scholars Press, 1975.

Flew, Anthony. "Theology and Falsification." *The Existence of God,* ed. John Hick, pp. 224–27. New York: Macmillan, 1964.

Freud, Sigmund. *The Future of an Illusion.* Garden City, N.Y.: Doubleday, 1957.

Gesenius, W. *A Hebrew and English Lexicon of the Old Testament.* Boston: Crocker & Brewster, 1861.

Gilkey, Langdon. *Naming the Whirlwind: The Renewal of God Language.* New York: Seabury Press, 1976.

Gilson, Étienne. *The Spirit of Medieval Philosophy.* New York: Scribners, 1936.

———. *The Philosophy of St. Thomas Aquinas.* St. Louis, Mo.: B. Herder, 1937.

———. *Being and Some Philosophers.* Toronto: Pontifical Institute of Medieval Studies, 1952.

————. *History of Christian Philosophy in the Middle Ages.* New York: Random House, 1955.

————. *Elements of Christian Philosophy.* Garden City, N.Y.: Doubleday, 1960.

Goodenough, Edwin R. *The Theology of Justin Martyr.* Jena, 1923.

Gore, Charles D. *The Incarnation of the Son of God.* Oxford, 1891.

Grether, Oskar. *Name und Wort Gottes im Alten Testament (Beihefte zur Zeitschrift für die Altestamentliche Wissenschaft).* Giessen: A. Töpelmann, 1934.

Grillmeier, A. *Christ in Christian Tradition.* Vol. 1: *From the Apostolic Age to Chalcedon (451).* Atlanta: John Knox Press, 1965.

Grondys, L. H. "La terminologie métalogique dans la théologie Dionysienne." *Netherlands Theologisch Tijdschrift 14ᵉ,* Jaargang, Afl. 6 (1960): 420–30.

Haenchen, E. *Gott und Mensch.* Tübingen: Mohr, 1965.

Harnack, Adolph von. *The Sayings of Jesus.* London: Williams & Norgate; New York: G. P. Putnam, 1908.

————. *Lehrbuck der Dogmengeschichte.* Tübingen: Mohr, 1931.

Harvey, Van A. *The Historian and the Believer: The Morality of Historical Knowledge and Christian Belief.* New York: Macmillan, 1966.

Hatch, Edwin. *The Influence of Greek Ideas on Christianity.* New York: Harper & Row, 1957.

Inge, W. *The Philosophy of Plotinus.* Chicago: Greenwood, 1958.

Jaeger, Werner. *Paideia: The Ideals of Greek Culture.* 3 vols. New York: 1945.

————. *Two Rediscovered Works of Ancient Christian Literature: Gregory of Nyssa and Macarius.* Leiden: Brill, 1954.

James, William. *The Varieties of Religious Experience.* New York: Modern Library, 1960.

Jeremias, Joachim. *The Central Message of the New Testament.* Philadelphia: Fortress Press, 1981.

Johnston, William. *The Mysticism of the Cloud of Unknowing: A Modern Interpretation.* New York: Desclée, 1967.

————. *The Mirror Mind.* New York & San Francisco: Harper & Row, 1981.

Käsemann, E. *The Testament of Jesus according to John 17.* Philadelphia: Fortress Press, 1968.

Katz, Steven T. "Language, Epistemology, and Mysticism." *Mysticism and Philosophical Analysis,* ed. Steven T. Katz. London: Sheldon, 1976.

Kazantzakēs, Nikos. *Report to Greco.* New York: Simon & Schuster, 1965.

Kelly, J. N. D. *Early Christian Doctrines.* New York & San Francisco: Harper & Row, 1978.

Kirk, K. E., "The Evaluation of the Doctrine of the Trinity." *Essays on the Trinity and the Incarnation by Members of the Anglican Communion,* pp. 226–37. New York: Green, 1928.

Koch, H. "Die Lehre vom Bösen nach Pseudo-Dionysius Aeropagita." *Philologus* (1895), pp. 438–54.

————. "Der Pseudepigraphische Character der Dionysischen Schriften." *Theologische Quartalscrift* 77 (1898): 353–420.

Lampe, G. W. H., "The Holy Spirit and the Person of Christ." *Christ, Faith, and History,* ed., Sykes, pp. 111–30.

————. *God as Spirit.* Oxford: Clarendon Press, 1977.

Leen, Edward. *The Holy Ghost.* New York: Sheed & Ward, 1953.

Lilla, R. E. *Clement of Alexandria: A Study in Christian Platonism and Gnosticism.* London: Oxford University Press, 1971.

Lindbeck, George A. *The Nature of Doctrine: Religion and Theology in a Postliberal Age.* Philadelphia: Westminster Press, 1984.

Lonergan, Bernard F. "Cognitional Structure." *Continuum* 2, no. 3 (1964): 530–42.

———. *De Deo Trino.* Rome: Apud Aedes Universitatis Gregorianae, 1964.

———. *Insight: A Study of Human Understanding.* New York: Philosophical Library, 1971.

———, "Metaphysics as Horizon." *Gregorianum* 44 (1963): 6–23.

———. *Method in Theology.* New York: Herder & Herder, 1972.

———. *The Way to Nicea: The Dialectical Development of Trinitarian Theology.* Philadelphia: Westminster Press, 1976.

Lossky, Vladimir. *In the Image and Likeness of God.* Crestwood: St. Vladimir's Press, 1974.

Louth, Andrew. *The Origins of the Christian Mystical Tradition.* New York: Oxford University Press, 1981.

Magliola, Richard. *Derrida on the Mend.* West Lafayette, Ind.: Purdue University Press, 1984.

Maritain, Jacques. *The Degrees of Knowledge.* New York: Scribners, 1959.

Markus, R. A. "Trinitarian Theology and the Economy." *Journal of Theological Studies* 6 (1955): 89–102.

McKenzie, John L. *Myths and Realities: Studies in Biblical Theology.* Milwaukee: Bruce, 1963.

Meyendorff, John. *Christ in Eastern Christian Thought.* Crestwood: St. Valdimir's Press, 1975.

Morgan, Don F. *Wisdom in the Old Testament Traditions.* Atlanta: John Knox Press, 1981.

Moule, C. F. D. *The Origin of Christology.* Cambridge, Eng.: Cambridge University Press, 1977.

Newell, William Lloyd. *Struggle and Submission: R. C. Zaehner on Mysticism.* Washington, D.C.: University Press of America, 1981.

Norris, Richard Alfred. *God and World in Early Christian Theology.* London: Black, 1966.

Nygren, Anders. *Eros and Agape.* Philadelphia: Harper & Row, 1953.

O'Leary, Joseph. *Questioning Back: The Overcoming of Metaphysics in Christian Tradition.* Minneapolis: Winston, 1985.

Panikkar, Raimundo. "The Category of Growth in Comparative Religion: A Critical Self-Examination." *The Intrareligious Dialogue.* New York: Paulist Press, 1978.

Pearson, Biger A. "Hellenistic-Jewish Wisdom Speculation and Paul." *Aspects of Wisdom in Judaism and Early Christianity.* Notre Dame: University of Notre Dame Press, 1975.

Pelikan, Jaroslav. *The Light of the World: A Basic Image in Early Christian Thought.* New York: Harper & Row, 1962.

———. *The Christian Tradition, a History of Doctrinal Development.* Vol. 1: *The Emergence of the Catholic Tradition.* Chicago: University of Chicago Press, 1971.

———. *The Christian Tradition, a History of Doctrinal Development.* Vol. 2: *The Spirit of Eastern Christendom (600–1700).* Chicago: University of Chicago Press, 1974.

Perrin, Norman. *The Resurrection according to Matthew, Mark, and Luke.* Philadelphia, Fortress Press, 1977.

Prestige, George L. *God in Patristic Thought.* Toronto: W. Heinemann, 1936.

Rad, Gerhard von. *Das Gottesvolk im Deuteronomium.* Stuggart: W. Kohlhammer, 1929.

————. *Studies in Deuteronomy.* London: SCM Press, 1953.

————. *Old Testament Theology.* New York: Harper & Row, 1965.

————. *The Problem of the Hexateuch and Other Essays.* Edinburgh & London: Oliver & Boyd, 1966.

Rahner, Karl. "Le début d'une doctrine des cinq sens spirituelles chez Origène." *Revue d'ascétique et de mystique* 13 (1932): 113–45. English translation in *Theological Investigations,* vol. 16, pp. 81–103. London: Darton, Longman, & Todd.

————. *The Trinity.* New York: Herder & Herder, 1970.

Robinson, James M. "Logoi Sophon: On the Gattung of Q." *Trajectories through Early Christianity.* Philadelphia: Fortress Press, 1971.

Robinson, John A. T. *Honest to God.* London: SCM Press, 1963.

————. "Need Jesus Have Been Perfect?" *Christ, Faith, and History,* ed. Sykes; pp. 39–52.

————. "A Reply to Mr. Sykes." *Christ, Faith, and History,* ed. Sykes; pp. 73–78.

Roques, René, *L'Univers Dionysien: Structure hiérarchique du monde selon le Pseudo-Denys.* Paris: Aubier, 1954.

Rusch, William, G. *The Trinitarian Controversy.* Philadelphia: Fortress Press, 1980.

Schillebeeckx, Edward. *Jesus: An Experiment in Christology.* New York: Seabury Press, 1978.

————. *Christ: The Experience of Jesus as Lord.* New York: Seabury Press, 1980.

Schweitzer, Albert. *The Quest of the Historical Jesus.* London: Black; New York: Macmillan, 1910.

Scott, R. B. Y. *The Way of Wisdom in the Old Testament.* New York: Macmillan, 1972.

Smart, Ninian. *The Yogi and the Devotee.* London: Allen & Unwin, 1968.

————. "Understanding Religious Experience." *Mysticism and Philosophical Analysis,* ed. Steven T. Katz. London: Sheldon, 1978.

Stace, W. T. *Mysticism and Philosophy.* London: Macmillan, 1960.

Stigmayr, J. "Der Neuplatoniker Proklus als Vorlage der sogen: Dionysius Aeropagita in der Lehre vom Ubel." *Historisches Jarhbuch im Auftrag der Görresgesellschaft* 16 (1895): 253–73, 721–48.

Suggs, M. Jack. *Wisdom, Christology, and Law in Matthew's Gospel.* Cambridge, Mass.: Harvard University Press, 1970.

Sykes, S. W., ed. *Christ, Faith, and History: Cambridge Studies in Christology.* London: Cambridge University Press, 1972.

Taylor, Mark C. *Erring: A Post-Modern A/Theology.* Chicago: University of Chicago Press, 1985.

Tracy, David. *The Achievement of Bernard Lonergan.* New York: Herder & Herder, 1970.

Tillich, Paul. *Systematic Theology.* 3 vols. Chicago: University of Chicago Press, 1967.

Tödt, H. E. *The Son of Man in the Synoptic Tradition.* London: SCM Press, 1965.

Toynbee, Arnold. *Christianity among the Religions of the World.* New York: Scribners, 1957.

Vacherot, Étienne. *Histoire critique de l'École d'Alexandrie.* Paris: Coronet Books, 1851.

Vanier, Paul. *Theologie trinitaire chez Saint Thomas d'Aquin: Evolution du concept d'action notionelle.* Paris: J. Vrin, 1953.

Vanneste, J. *Le mystique de Dieu: Essai sur la structure rationelle de la doctrine mystique de Pseudo-Denys Aeropagite.* Bruges: Desclée de Bouwer, 1959.

Vasiliev, A. A. *History of the Byzantine Empire.* 2 vols., reprint, Madison: University of Wisconsin Press, 1958.

von Balthasar, U. "Das Scholienwerk des Johannes von Skythopolis." *Scholastik* 15 (1940): 16–39.

Waldenfels, Hans. *Absolute Nothingness: Foundations for a Buddhist-Christian Dialogue.* New York: Paulist Press, 1976.

Wiles, Maurice. "Homoousios ēmin." *Journal of Theological Studies* 16 (1965): 454–61.

———. "Does Christology Rest on a Mistake?" *Christ, Faith, and History,* ed. Sykes; pp. 3–12.

———. *The Making of Christian Doctrine: A Study in the Principles of Early Doctrinal Development.* London: Cambridge University Press, 1967.

———. *Christian Fathers.* New York: Oxford University Press, 1982.

Wisdom, John. "Gods." *Proceedings of the Aristotelian Society,* 1944–1945; reprinted as chap. 10 of *Logic and Language,* London: Blackwell, 1951, and in *Philosophy and Psycho-Analysis,* London: Blackwell, 1953.

Wuellner, W. "Haggadic-Homily Genre in 1 Corinthians 1–3." *Journal of Biblical Literature* (1970): 199–204.

Zaehner, R. C. *Mysticism: Sacred and Profane.* Oxford: Clarendon Press, 1957.

Zimmerli, Walther. "Concerning the Structure of Old Testament Wisdom." *Studies in Ancient Israelite Wisdom,* ed. James Crenshaw; pp. 175–207.

EASTERN WORKS

Primary Sources

SCRIPTURES (SŪTRA) AND CLASSICS

Bhagavad-Gita: Krishna's Counsel in Time of War. Trans. Barbara Stoler Miller. New York: Bantam Books, 1986.

Book of Kindred Sayings [Saṃyutta-nikāya]. 5 vols. Trans. Rhys-Davids and F. L. Woodward. London: Pali Text Society, 1917–30.

Dialogues of the Buddha [Digha-nikāya]. 3 vols. Trans. T. W. Rhys-Davids and C. A. F. Rhys-Davids. In series Sacred Books of the Buddhists, vols. 2–4. London: Pali Text Society, 1899–1921.

The Diamond Sutra. In *Buddhist Wisdom Books.* Trans. Edward Conze. London: Allen & Unwin, 1958.

Greater Discourse on the Lion's Roar. In Chalmers, *Further Dialogues of the Buddha.* London: Oxford Universeity Press, 1926–27. Also in *Middle Length Sayings.*

The Heart Sutra. In *Buddhist Wisdom Books.* Trans. Edward Conze. London: Allen & Unwin, 1958. Also in *Buddhist Texts through the Ages.* New York: Philosophical Library, 1954.

The Large Sutra on Perfect Wisdom, with the Divisions of the Abhisamayālaṅkāra. Trans. Edward Conze. Berkeley: University of California Press, 1975.

The Lion's Roar of Queen Śrīmālā [Śrīmālādevīsiṃhanādasūtra]. Trans. Alex and

Hideko Wayman. New York: Columbia University Press, 1974.

The Lotus Blossom of Compassion [Karuṇāpuṇḍarika]. 2 vols. Sanskrit text with English summary by Isshi Yamada. London: University of London, 1968.

Middle Length Sayings [Majjhima-nikāya]. 3 vols. Trans. I. B. Horner. London: Pali Text Society, 1954–59.

The Perfection of Wisdom in Eight Thousand Lines. Trans. Edward Conze. San Francisco: Four Seasons, 1973.

The Platform Sutra of the Sixth Patriarch: The Text of the Tun-Huang Manuscript. Trans. with notes, Philip B. Yampolsky. New York: Columbia University Press, 1967.

The Scripture on Neither Increase nor Decrease [Anūnatvāpūrṇatvanirdeśasūtra]. Extant in Chinese only, T. 668.

The Scripture on the Buddha Land [Buddhabhūmisūtra]. (1) Critical edition of Tibetan and Chinese texts in Kyōyu Nishio, *The Buddhabhūmisūtra and the Buddhabhūmivyākhyāna.* Nagoya, 1939. (2) English translation in *The Interpretation of the Buddha Land.* Trans. John P. Keenan (forthcoming in Bukkyō Dendō Kyōkai series).

The Scripture on the Explication of Underlying Meaning [Saṃdhinirmocanasūtra]. (1) *Saṃdhinirmocana-sūtra: L'Explication des Mystères.* French trans. Étienne Lamotte. Paris: Maisonneuve, 1935. (2) *Scripture on the Explication of Underlying Meaning.* English trans. John P. Keenan (forthcoming in Bukkyō Dendō Kyōkai series).

Verses on the Accumulation of Precious Qualities [Ratnaguṇasamuccayagāthā]. Trans. Edward Conze. New Delhi: International Academy of Indian Culture, 1962.

CLASSICAL COMMENTARIES AND TRACTS (SĀSTRA)

Asaṅga. *The Bodhisattva Stages [*In the *Yogācarabhūmiśāstra].* T. 1579. (1) *Bodhisattvabhūmi (Being the XVth Section of Asaṅgapāda's Yogācārabhūmi.* Sanskrit text edited by Nalinaksha Dutt. Patna: K. J. Jayaswal Research Institute, 1966. (2) *On Knowing Reality: The Tattvārtha Chapter of Asaṅga's Bodhisattvabhūmi.* Trans. and examined by Janice Dean Willis. New York: Columbia University Press, 1979.

———. *The Compendium of Abhidharma [Abhidharmasamuccaya].* T. 1605. (1) *La Compendium de la Super-doctrine: Philosophie (Abhidharmasamuccaya).* French trans. of the Chinese text by Walpola Rahula. Paris: École français d'Extreme-Orient, 1971. (2) *Abhidharmasamuccaya of Asaṅga.* Sanskrit edition by Pralhad Pradhan. Śāntinoketan: Visva-Bharati, 1950.

———. *An Exposition of the Doctrine of the Introductory Teaching of the Prajñāpāramitā according to the Interpretation of the Mādhyamika Treatise [of Nāgārjuna] [Madhyamakaśāstrārthānugatamahāprajñāpāramitāsūtrādiparivartadharma - paryāyapraveśa].* Extant in Chinese only. T. 1565.

———. *Instructions for Students [Śāsanodbhāvana].* Extant in Chinese only. T. 1603.

———. *Seventy Stanzas on the Perfection of Wisdom in Three Hundred Stanzas [Triśatikāyaḥ–prajñāpāramitāsaptaiḥ].* Text and English trans. Giuseppe Tucci, in *Minor Buddhist Texts,* pp. 1–128. Rome, 1956; reprint, Delhi: Motilal Barnarsidass, 1986.

———. *The Summary of the Great Vehicle [Mahāyānasaṃgraha].* T. 1592, 1593, 1594. (1) *La Somme du Grand Véhicle d'Asaṅga (Mahāyānasaṃgraha). Traduction et*

Commentaire. Trans. Étienne Lamotte. Louvain: Institut Orientaliste, 1973. (2) *The Summary of the Great Vehicle.* Trans. John P. Keenan (forthcoming in Bukkyō Dendō Kyōkai series). (3) *Kanyaku shihon taishō Shodaijōron* [The Four Chinese Translations of the Mahāyānasaṃgraha in Parallel Columns]. Ed., Gessho Sasaki. Tokyo: Ringawa, 1977. (4) *Shōdaijōron: Wayaku to chūkai* [The Mahāyānasaṃgraha: Japanese Translation and Notes]. 2 vols. The now standard work on this text by Gadjin Nagao. Tokyo: Kodansha, 1982, 1987.

Asvabhāva. *Exposition of the Summary of the Great Vehicle [Mahāyānasaṃgrahopanibandhana].* T. 1598; P. 5552. (1) *The Realm of Awakening: Chapter Ten of Asaṅga's Mahāyānasaṃgraha.* English trans. Noriaki Hakamaya, John P. Keenan, Paul Griffiths, and Paul Swanson. Contains an English translation of the Asvabhāva exposition for chap. 10 (forthcoming from Oxford University Press).

Bandhuprabha. *The Interpretation of the Buddha Land [Buddhabhūmyupadeśa].* T. 1530. English trans. of the Chinese text, in John P. Keenan, "A Study of the Buddhabhūmyupadeśa: The Doctrinal Development of the Notion of Wisdom in Yogācāra Thought." Ph.D. dissertation, University of Wisconsin, Madison, 1980.

Bankei. *Bankei Zen: Translations from the Record of Bankei.* Trans. Peter Haskel. New York: Grove Press, 1984.

Candrakīrti. *Lucid Exposition of the Middle Way: The Essential Chapters from the Prasannapadā of Candrakīrti.* Trans. Mervyn Sprung. Boulder, Colo.: Prajna Press, 1979.

———. *Prasannapadā Madhyamikavṛtti.* Douze chapitres traduits du sanskrit et du tibetain, accompagnes d'une introduction, de notes et d'une edition critique de la version tibetain. Trans. Jacques May. Paris: Adrien-Maisonneuve, 1959.

Chuang-tzu. *The Complete Works of Chuang Tzu.* Trans. Burton Watson. New York: Columbia University Press, 1968.

Dharmapāla. *An Extensive Sub-Commentary on [Āryadeva's] Hundred Stanzas [Śataśāstravaipulyaṭīkā].* Extant in Chinese only. T. 1571.

——— and others. *Commentary on the Thirty Stanzas on the Establishment of Conscious Construction-Only [Ch'eng Wei-shih lun].* T. 1585. (1) *Vijñaptimātratāsiddhi: La Siddhi de Huien-Tsang.* Trans. Louis de la Vallée Poussin. Paris: P. Guethner, 1928–48. (2) *Ch'eng Wei-shih Lun: Doctrine of Mere Consciousness.* English trans. Wei Tat. Hong Kong: Ch'eng Wei-shih Publishing Committee, 1973.

Digñāga, *Digñāga on Perception, Being the Pratyakṣapariccheda of Dignāga's Pramāṇasamuccaya.* Trans. Masaaki Hattori. Cambridge, Mass.: Harvard University Press, 1968.

Haribhadra. *Aṣṭasāhasrika Prajñāpāramitā with Haribhadra's Commentary called Āloka.* Ed. P. L. Vaidya. Darbhanga, 1960.

Lao-tzu. *Lao Tzu: Tao Te Ching.* Trans. D. C. Lau. Harmondsworth, Eng.: Penguin Books, 1963.

Maitreya. *Analysis of the Middle and Extremes [Madhyāntavibhāga].* T. 1601. See under Vasubandhu, *Commentary on the Analysis of the Middle and Extremes.*

———. *The Ornament of the Scriptures of the Great Vehicle.* (1) *Mahāyānasūtrālaṃkāra, Exposé de la Doctrine du Grand Véhicle.* Ed. and French trans. Sylvain Lévi. Paris: H. Champion, 1907–10. (2) *Daijōshōgonkyō kenkyū* [A Study of the Mahāyānasūtrālamkāra]. Japanese trans. Hakuju Ui. Tokyo: Iwanami Shōten, 1961.

Nāgārjuna. *Sixty-Verse Treatise on Logic [Yuktiṣaṣṭikā].* In Lindtner, *Master of Wisdom,* pp. 72–93. Oakland: Dharma Press, 1986.

———. *Stanzas on the Middle. [Madhyamikakārikāḥ].* (1) *Mūlamadhyamakakārikāḥ.* Sanskrit text ed. J. W. de Jong. Madras: Adyar Library and Research Center, 1977. (2) *Nāgārjuna: A Translation of His Mūlamadhyamakakārikā.* Trans. Kenneth Inada. Tokyo: Hokuseido, 1970. (3) *Nāgārjuna: The Philosophy of the Middle Way.* Trans. David J. Kalupahana. Albany: State University of New York, 1986.

———. *Overcoming Vain Discussions [Vigrahavyāvartanī].* (1) Sanskrit text and English trans. in *The Dialectical Method of Nāgārjuna: Vigrahavyāvartanī.* Text critically ed. E. H. Johnston and Arnold Kunst. Trans. Kamaleswar Bhattacharya. Delhi: Motilal Barnarsidass, 1978. (2) French trans. "Pour écarter les vaines discussions," by Susumu Yamaguchi. *Journal Asiatique,* (July–September 1929): 1–86. (3) English trans. Giuseppe Tucci, in *Pre-Diṅnaga Buddhist Texts on Logic from Chinese Sources,* pp. 1–77. Baroda, 1929. (4) Sanskrit and Tibetan texts in Lindtner, *Master of Wisdom,* pp. 207–29.

Paramārtha, *The Evolution of Consciousness [Chuan shih lun].* T. 1587. English trans. and study of the development of the thought of Paramārtha in Diana S. Paul, *Philosophy of Mind in Sixth-Century China.* Stanford: Stanford University Press, 1984.

Saramati. *Participation in the Jeweled Lineage.* English trans. in Jikidō Takasaki, *A Study of the Ratnagotravibhāga (Uttaratantra), Being a Treatise on the Tathāgatagarbha Theory of Mahāyāna Buddhism.* Rome: Instituto Italiano per il Medio ed Estremo Oriente, 1966.

Śīlabhadra. *Interpretation of the Buddha Land [Buddhabhūmivyākhyāna].* Text and Japanese trans. Kyōyu Nishio, in *The Buddhabhūmisūtra and the Buddhabhūmivyākhyāna,* Nagoya, 1939, and *Buchikyōron no kenkyū* [A Study of the Interpretation of the Buddha Land], Nagoya, 1940.

Sthiramati. *Commentary on the Ornament of the Scriptures of the Great Vehicle [Sūtrālamkāraṭīkā].* Extant in Tibetan only. P. 5531.

———. *Exposition on the Underlying Meaning of the Mādhyamika (Stanzas of Nāgārjuna) [Mūlamadhyamakasaṃdhinirmocanavyākhyāna].* Extant in Chinese only. T. 1567.

———. *Sub-Commentary on the Analysis of the Middle and Extremes. [Madhyāntavibhāgaṭīkā].* (1) *Sthiramati: Madhyāntavibhāgaṭīkā, Exposition systématique du Yogācāravijñaptivāda.* Sanskrit text ed. Sylvain Lévi and French introduction Susumu Yamaguchi. Nagoya: Hajinkaku, 1934, reprint, Tokyo: Suzuki Research Foundation, 1966. (2) *Anne ajiyaru zō chuhen-funbetsuron shakusho* [Sub-Commentary on the Analysis of the Middle and Extremes by Acārya Sthiramati]. Japanese trans. Susumu Yamaguchi. Nagoya: Hajinkaku; reprint, Tokyo: Suzuki Research Foundation, 1965.

Vasubandhu. *A Commentary in Seven Topics on the Noble Bhagavat's Diamond-Cutter Perfection of Wisdom [Āryabhagavatīprajñāpāramitāvajracchedikakāyaḥ saptapadārthāṭīkā].* Extant in two Chinese translations only, T. 1511 and 1512. Synopsis in Giuseppe Tucci, *Minor Buddhist Texts,* pp. 129–71.

———. *Commentary on the Abhidharma Treasury, L'Abhidharmakośa de Vasubandhu.* Trans. Louis de la Vallée Poussin. 6 vols. Paris: Paul Geuthner, 1923–25. English trans. of de la Vallée Poussin in *Abhidharmakośabhāṣyam.* Trans. Leo M. Pruden. Berkeley, Calif.: Asian Humanities Press, 1988–89.

———. *Commentary on the Analysis of the Middle and Extremes [Madhyā-ntavibhāgaṭīkā].* (1) *Madhyāntavibhāgabhāṣya: A Buddhist Philosophical Treatise Edited for the First Time from a Sanskrit Manuscript.* Ed. Gadjin Nagao. Tokyo: Suzuki Research Foundation, 1964. (2) *Kanzō taishō Benchūheron* [A Comparative Presentation of the Chinese Translations of the *Madhyāntavibhāgabhāṣya*]. Comparison of the Chinese of Hsüan-tsang and Paramārtha, together with the Tibetan trans., by Susumu Yamaguchi. Tokyo: Suzuki Research Foundation, 1966.

———. *Commentary on the Summary of the Great Vehicle.* Extant in three Chinese trans. by Paramārtha, Dharmagupta, and Hsüan-tsang, respectively, T. 1595, 1596, and 1597, and one Tibetan trans., P. 5549, by Ye shes de. (1) *The Realm of Awakening: Chapter Ten of Asaṅga's Mahāyāna- saṃgraha.* English trans. Noriaki Hakamaya, John P. Keenan, Paul Griffiths, and Paul Swanson. Contains an English trans. of Vasubandhu's commentary for chap. 10. (Oxford University Press, 1989).

———. *Wei Shih Er Shih Lun or the Treatise of Twenty Stanzas on Representation-Only.* Trans. Clarence H. Hamilton. New Haven: American Oriental Society, 1938.

Secondary Sources

Chang, Garma C. C. *The Buddhist Teaching of Totality: The Philosophy of Hwa Yen Buddhism.* University Park, Pa.: Penn State University Press, 1971.

Conze, Edward. "Buddhist Philosophy and Its European Parallels." *Philosophy East and West.* 13, no. 1 (April 1963): 9–23.

———. *The Prajñāpāramitā Literature.* The Hague: Mouton, 1960; reprint, Tokyo: Reiyukai, 1978.

Ch'en, Kenneth. *Buddhism in China: A Historical Survey.* Princeton: Princeton University Press, 1964

Dayal, Har. *The Bodhisattva Ideal in Buddhist Sanskrit Literature.* London: Kegan Paul, 1932.

Demiéville, Paul. "La Yogācārabhūmi de Saṅgharakṣa." *Bulletin de l'École française d'Extrême-Orient* 44 (1954).

Frauwallner, Erich. *On the Date of the Master of the Law Vasubandhu.* Rome, 1951.

Griffiths, Paul. "Karma," *Religious Studies* 18 (1982): 277–91.

Guenther, Herbert. *Philosophy and Psychology in the Abhidharma*, Lucknow: Buddha Vihara, 1959.

Hakamaya, Noriaki. "Ālaya-shiki sonzai no hachi ronshō ni kansuru shobunken" [Source Materials on the Eight Demonstrations of the Ālaya Consciousness]. *Komazawa daigaku bukkyō gakubu kenkyū kiyō* [Research Memoirs of the Department of Buddhology of Komazawa University] 36 (1978): 1–27.

———. "Kūshō rikai no mondaiten" [The Point in Understanding Emptiness]. *Riso* 610 (1984): 50–64.

———. "The Realm of Enlightenment in Vijñaptimātratā: The Formation of the 'Four Kinds of Pure Dharmas,'" *Journal of the International Association of Buddhist Studies* 3, no. 2 (1980): 21–41.

Hirakawa, Akira. *Index to the Abhidharmakośa.* Tokyo: Daizo Shuppan, 1973.

Hubbard, James. "Salvation in the Final Period of the Dharma: The Inexhaustible

Storehouse of the San-chieh-chiao," unpublished Ph.D. dissertation, University of Wisconsin-Madison, 1986.

Inada, Kenneth. *Guide to Buddhist Philosophy*. Boston: G. K. Hall, 1985.

Kajiyama, Yuichi. "Bukkyō ni okeru kotoba to chinmoku" [Speech and Silence in Buddhism]. *Shukyō taiken to kotoba: Bukkyō to kirisutokyō no taiwa* [Religious Experience and Language: A Dialogue between Buddhism and Christianity]. Tokyo: Kinokuniya, 1978.

Katsumata, Shunkyo. *Bukkyō ni okeru shinishikisetsu no kenkyū* [A Study of the Citta-Vijñānai Thought in Buddhism]. Tokyo: Sankibo, 1974.

Keenan, John P. "The Intent and Structure of Yogācāra Philosophy: Its Relevance for Modern Religious Thought," *Annual Memoirs of the Otani University Shin Buddhist Comprehensive Research Institute* 4 (1986): 41–60.

———. "Original Purity and the Focus of Early Yogācāra." *Journal of the International Association of Buddhist Studies* 5, no. 1 (1982): 7–18.

Kimura, Taigen. *Abhidharmaśāstra no kenkyū* [A Study of the Abhidharmaśāstra]. Tokyo, 1922.

Kiyota, Minoru. *Shingon Buddhism: Theory and Practice*. Los Angeles and Tokyo: Buddhist Books International, 1978.

Knitter, Paul. *No Other Name? A Critical Survey of Christian Attitudes toward the World Religions*. Maryknoll, N.Y.: Orbis Books, 1985.

Lamotte, Étienne. *Histoire du Bouddhisme Indien: Des Origines a l'ere Śaka*, Louvain-La-Neuve: Institut Orientaliste, 1976.

Lindtner, Christian. *Master of Wisdom: Writings of the Buddhist Master Nāgārjuna*. Oakland, Calif.: Dharma Press, 1986.

Mascaro, Juan. *The Upanishads: Translations from the Sanskrit with an Introduction*. New York: Penguin Books, 1985.

Matsunaga, Daigan and Alice. *Foundations of Japanese Buddhism*. San Francisco: Buddhist Books International, 1974.

Nagao, Gadjin. "Asaṅga's Commentary on the Diamond Sūtra" *[Kongohannyakyō ni okeru muchaku no shakuge]*. In *Chūkan to yuishiki [Mādhyamika and Vijñaptimātratā]*, pp. 569–74. Tokyo: Iwanami, 1978.

———. "Buddhist Subjectivity." *Chūkan to yuishiki*, pp. 333–40. English trans. in *Religious Studies in Japan*, ed. Japanese Association for Religious Studies and the Japanese Organizing Committee of the Ninth International Congress for the History of Religions. Tokyo: Maruzen, 1959.

———. "The Foundational Standpoint of Mādhyamika Philosophy" *[Chūkan tetsugaku no konponteki tachiba]*. In *Chūkan to yuishiki*, pp. 3–144. English trans. John P. Keenan (forthcoming from SUNY in the Nanzan Studies in Religion and Culture).

———. "The Logic of the Evolution [of Consciousness]" *[Tenkan no ronri]*. In *Chūkan to yuishiki*, pp. 237–65.

———. "On the Term paryāya" *[I-mon (paryāya) to iu kotoba]*. In *Chūkan to yuishiki*, pp. 406–13.

———. "On the Theory of Buddha-Body." *Eastern Buddhist* 6 (May 1973): 25–53. *Chūkan to yuishiki*, pp. 266–92.

———. " 'What Remains' in Śūnyatā: A Yogācāra Interpretation of Emptiness." *Mahāyāna Buddhist Meditation: Theory and Practice*. Ed. Minoru Kiyota. Honolulu: University of Hawaii Press, 1978.

Nakamura, Hajime. *Religions and Philosophies of India: A Survey with Bibliographical*

Notes. The Fourth Chapter: Orthodox Philosophical Systems. Tokyo: Kokuseido Press, 1973.

Nishitani, Keiji. *Religion and Nothingness.* Trans. with introduction by Jan Van Bragt. Berkeley: University of California Press, 1982.

Nyanatiloka, Mahāthera. *Guide through the Abhidhammapiṭaka, Being a Synopsis of the Philosophical Collection Belonging to the Buddhist Pali Canon, followed by an Essay on the Paṭiccasamuppāda.* Colombo, Sri Lanka: Bauddha Sahitya Sabha, 1957.

Peri, Noel. "A propos de la date de Vasubandhu." *Bulletin de l'École française d'Extreme-Orient* 9 (1911).

Sakurabe, Takeshi. *Kusharon no kenkyū* [A Study of Abhidharma]. Kyoto: Hōzōkan, 1969.

Sponberg, Alan. "Dynamic Liberation in Yogācāra Buddhism." *Journal of the International Association of Buddhist Studies* 2, no. 1 (1979): 44–64.

————. "The Trisvabhāva Doctrine in India and China: A Study of Three Exegetical Models." *Ryūkoku daigaku bukkyō bunka kenkyūjo kiyō* 21 (1983): 97–119.

Sprung, Mervyn. "Non-Cognitive Language in Mādhyamika Buddhism." *Buddhist Thought and Asian Civilization*, Oakland, Calif.: Dharma Press, pp. 241–53.

Stcherbatsky, Theodore. *The Concept of Buddhist Nirvāṇa.* Leningrad, 1927; reprint, Delhi: Motilal Banarsidass, 1977.

Streng, Frederick. *Emptiness: A Study in Religious Meaning*, Nashville: Abingdon Press, 1967.

Suguro, Shinjō. "Joyuishikiron ni okeru gohō setsu no tokushoku" [The Specific Character of Dharmapāla's Teaching in the Ch'eng Wei-shih lun]. In *Yūki kyōju shōju kinen bukkyō shisōshi ronshū* [Essays on the History of Buddhist Thought in Honor of Professor Reimon Yūki]. Tokyo, 1964.

Takakusu, J. "The Life of Vasubandhu by Paramārtha." *Journal of the Royal Asiatic Society* (1935), pp. 33–53.

Takasaki, Jikidō. "Hōshin no ichigenron: Noraizō shisō no hō kannen" [The Monism of Dharmakāya as It Relates to Tathāgatagarbha Thought]. In *Hirakawa akira hakase kanreki kinen ronshū: Bukkyō ni okeru hō no kenkyū* [Studies in Honor of Doctor Akira Hirakawa on Dharma in Buddhism]. Tokyo: Shunjūsha, 1975–76.

————. *Nyoraizō shisō no keisei* [The Formation of Tathāgatagarbha Thought]. Tokyo: Shunjūsha, 1974.

Ui, Hakuju. "Maitreya as an Historical Person." In *Indian Studies in Honor of Charles Rockwell Lanman.* Cambridge, Mass.: Harvard University Press, 1929.

————. "On the Authorship of the Mahāyānasūtra-alaṃkāra." *Zeitschrift für Indologie und Iranistik* 6 (1928): 215–25.

Yamaguchi, Susumu. *Bukkyō ni okeru yu to mu to no tairon* [The Dispute over Being and Non-Being in Buddhism]. Tokyo: Sankibo, 1941; reprint, 1975.

Yeh, A-yüeh. *Yuishiki shisō no kenkyū* [A Study of Vijñaptimātra Thought]. Tokyo: Kokusho, 1975.

Yuki, Reimon. *Shinishikiron yori mitaru yuishiki shisōshi* [The History of Vijñaptimātra Thought Seen from the Discussion on Consciousness]. Tokyo, 1935.

Index